Fantastic Adventures
in the Comics

ALSO BY WILLIAM SCHOELL
AND FROM MCFARLAND

Al Pacino: In Films and on Stage, 2d ed. (2016)
Creature Features: Nature Turned Nasty in the Movies (2008; paperback 2014)
The Horror Comics: Fiends, Freaks and Fantastic Creatures, 1940s–1980s (2014)
The Opera of the Twentieth Century: A Passionate Art in Transition (2006)

Fantastic Adventures in the Comics

Rockets, Genies, and Bug-Eyed Monsters, 1940s–1980s

WILLIAM SCHOELL

McFarland & Company, Inc., Publishers
Jefferson, North Carolina

LIBRARY OF CONGRESS CATALOGING-IN-PUBLICATION DATA

Names: Schoell, William author
Title: Fantastic adventures in the comics : rockets, genies, and bug-eyed monsters, 1940s–1980s / William Schoell.
Description: Jefferson, North Carolina : McFarland & Company, Inc., Publishers, 2026. | Includes bibliographical references and index.
Identifiers: LCCN 2025035338 | ISBN 9781476694757 paperback ∞
ISBN 9781476655321 ebook
Subjects: LCSH: Science fiction comic books, strips, etc.—United States—History and criticism | Fantasy comic books, strips, etc.—United States—History and criticism | Comic books, strips, etc.—20th century—History and criticism | BISAC: LITERARY CRITICISM / Comics & Graphic Novels | LCGFT: Comics criticism
Classification: LCC PN6725 .S375 2025 | DDC 741.5/973—dc23/eng/20250819
LC record available at https://lccn.loc.gov/2025035338

ISBN (print) 978-1-4766-9475-7
ISBN (ebook) 978-1-4766-5532-1

© 2026 William Schoell. All rights reserved

No part of this book may be reproduced or transmitted in any form or by any means, electronic or mechanical, including photocopying or recording, or by any information storage and retrieval system, without permission in writing from the publisher.

Front cover illustration by Wally Wood and Joe Orlando from *Strange Worlds*, Number 6, 1952 (Avon Comics)

Printed in the United States of America

McFarland & Company, Inc., Publishers
Box 611, Jefferson, North Carolina 28640
www.mcfarlandpub.com

Acknowledgments

All photographs of comic books in this book come from the author's private collection. They are reproduced here under the professional practice of fair use for the purposes of historical and critical discussion. All characters and images remain the property of their respective copyright holders.

Some of the material in this book concerning Charlton's Silver Age comics and comic book movie-TV adaptations was originally published in the magazine *bare•bones*. My thanks to editors Peter Enfantino and John Scoleri for permission to reprint it here. My thanks as well to the team at McFarland.

Table of Contents

Acknowledgments v

Preface 1

Part One—The Golden Age 5
1. Ace; ACG; Ajax-Farrell; Atlas 7
2. Avon 29
3. Charlton 38
4. DC; Dell 46
5. EC; Fawcett 58
6. Fiction House; Fox 73
7. Key–Stanley Morse; Magazine Enterprises; Prize; Standard; Star 81
8. Youthful; Ziff-Davis 92

Part Two—The Silver Age 107
9. American Comics Group (ACG) 109
10. Charlton 127
11. Classics Illustrated; DC 149
12. Dell; Fago 183
13. Gold Key; Harvey 196
14. Marvel 212

Part Three—The Bronze Age 225
15. Charlton; DC 227
16. Gold Key; Marvel 245

Bibliography 255
Index 257

Preface

Science fiction and fantasy, in a variety of forms and often combined, have long been a staple of the comic book industry. For our purposes, fantasy refers to stories that are simply too fantastic to ever be credible or realistic (there is no hard science in them, for instance), while science fiction *should* refer to tales within the realm of the possible but rarely do. We think of stories with spacemen firing ray guns at aliens with big heads and bug eyes as science fiction, but if the spacemen fly from Earth to the moon in only a couple of hours, we're purely in the land of fantasy. It is *that* kind of fantasy that is discussed in this book, not the stuff of Tolkien or his imitators.

Amazing Stories, the very first science fiction prose magazine, appeared in 1926. At first it reprinted old stories by such authors as Jules Verne, but when there was a demand for all-new material, editor Hugo Gernsback complied. Before long, there were a plethora of newsstand sci-fi mags, their cover art greatly influencing the artwork in the comic strips that were to follow. In 1928, *Amazing Stories* ran a story by Philip Nowland called "Armageddon 2419." The hero, 20th-century pilot Anthony Rogers, falls into suspended animation and wakes up in the war-torn 25th century. This was the progenitor of the wildly popular comic strip *Buck Rogers*, which debuted in 1929. It wasn't long before there were numerous *Buck Rogers* imitations, all featuring heroic figures in tales of astounding sci-fi and outlandish fantasy. Of these, the most successful was *Flash Gordon*.

In 1934, some of the comic strips, including the sci-fi adventure strips, were collected in a brand-new comic *book* called *Famous Funnies*, the first of its kind. Again, there was soon a demand for new material. As the comic book industry exploded throughout the '30s, new titles—and new heroes—emerged. The first was Don Drake of *New Fun* comics, the second comic book series to appear and the first to feature all-new material. Drake was followed by an array of futuristic adventurers such as Dan Hastings of *Star*, Mark Swift of *Slam Bang*, Skyrocket Steele of *Amazing Mystery Funnies*, Space Detective Lance Lewis of *Startling*, and a great many others. Most of these often deservedly forgotten strips do not fit into the focus of this book—they appeared in anthology books where they shared space with private eyes and superheroes.

The first comic to feature science fiction material and nothing else was 1940's *Planet*, from Fiction House. This comic was an outgrowth of the *Planet Stories* pulp

Planet was the first comic book to feature nothing but science fiction stories.

magazine. EC Comics, famous for their horror stories, also published science fiction and fantasy comics. These comics featured stories that weren't the typical space operas with square-jawed heroes (with scantily clad "babes" at their sides) squaring off against bug-eyed monsters, but offered more bite and sophistication. Meanwhile, such writers as Edmond Hamilton, who is credited with coming up with many innovative ideas in his prose stories, moved over to comic books and became quite prolific.

In order not to write a book of unwieldy length, I have had to eliminate some material. At the outset, I decided not to include most heroic figures (the aforementioned comic strip and comic book anthology space adventurers such as DC's Adam Strange character of *Mystery in Space*), because Strange and others like him are practically superheroes; Strange interacted on many occasions with the Justice League and was almost a member of that group. *Blackhawk, Rip Hunter, Time Master*, and *Sea Devils* had adventures that could be considered science fiction, but they were also very similar to superheroes, whether they had extra-special powers or not. People with superpowers had series in such comics as *Strange Adventures* and *Tales of the Unexpected*, but with some exceptions they are mentioned only in passing. As for legitimate superheroes, whether they are seen as creatures of science fiction or of fantasy, they have no place in this book.

In this volume, I also do not discuss sword-and-sorcery heroes such as Conan the Barbarian, who had a long-lasting Marvel comic, as this is a kind of fantasy that is virtually its own genre. Similarly, such figures as Tarzan, John Carter of Mars, and other Edgar Rice Burroughs characters and imitations, as well as other jungle action figures, don't quite fit into this book's scope, as they too could be considered a separate genre. I do cover the *Star Trek* comic books, but I have excluded *Star Wars* comics, as they, too, are practically a genre unto themselves.

There are occasional exceptions. I included certain heroic figures who are not well-known today but whose stories and adventures are worthy of discussion and rediscovery, especially those who originally appeared way back in the Golden Age, as well as those who influenced what came later. The comic stories covered in this book, both fantasy and science fiction or a combination of both, concern: astronauts who land on uncharted worlds or in undiscovered universes; people who inadvertently or deliberately save the Earth and become unsung heroes; animals or people who grow to giant size; microscopic worlds and their inhabitants, as well as visitors who shrink into sub-atomic worlds; aliens determined to conquer the Earth by fair means or foul; greedy people who are undone by schemes that ultimately make life worse for them instead of better; genies, mummies, wizards, and sorcerers out of time who plague modern-day humankind; poor schnooks who hope for a brighter day and a better life and sometimes achieve it, sometimes not; and others who find themselves in utterly fantastic and unbelievable situations. Science fiction stories in comic books are about evenly divided between those who present a positive view of the future (despite criminals and the like still operating) and a negative view complete with apocalyptic visions, end-of-the-world scenarios, and predictions of mankind being enslaved by outer space conquerors.

Let me make it clear that this book concentrates on the comics themselves and not on sociopolitical, pseudo-intellectual or psychosexual *distortions* of them. I am perfectly willing to discuss subtext even when such subtext is not intended by the creators, but I will not impose suspect, pretentious or ill-advised—and wrong-headed—"meanings" on this material when it is not warranted. I realize that this may cause some to label this tome as "superficial," but I hope most readers will see this book on its own terms as an in-depth historical and critical examination. The very few books previously published on this subject tend not to offer critical notes on the material in question.

My goal in this book—and in all books I have written on comics—is to introduce the reader to series and stories that they may not be familiar with, and to highlight the most notable tales, writers and artists. I have listed the credits for these stories whenever possible—it is generally easier to discern an artist's style than a writer's—but often the names of the scripters have been lost to history. The names of the writers and artists, including both penciler and inker when available, are in parentheses after the name of the story.

This book is also intended as a companion to my McFarland title *The Horror Comics: Fiends, Freaks and Fantastic Creatures, 1940s–1980s*. As in that book, the material here is divided into sections covering the Golden Age (pre–1956), Silver Age (1956–69) and Bronze Age (1970—approximately 1983). Within these sections, there are chapters devoted to different publishers in alphabetical order.

Science fiction and fantasy comics are often infantile, derivative, and poorly drawn, but they can also be exciting, original, imaginative, and quite beautiful to look at. This book will examine both colorful ends of the spectrum.

Part One
The Golden Age

1

Ace; ACG; Ajax-Farrell; Atlas

Ace

Space Action

Space Action debuted in 1952 and ran for three issues. It ran short stories in which Earth was endangered, usually by the machinations of an evil man, a dictator or an alien. The stories are acceptable if bland. However, the second issue features an exciting tale, drawn by Lou Cameron, wherein an expedition to an unexplored planet is menaced by a variety of large and voracious carnivorous plants. Although some of the astronauts manage to escape, the plant world sends spores to Earth, endangering the entire population. Leading scientists send out chemicals that destroy not only the alien plants but also all plant life on our planet. Fortunately, Earth's vegetation begins to reassert itself even as the plant world with its hungry, evil flora is sent hurtling into the sun and destruction. In *SA* 3, the best story deals with an evil man who gains control of a mass of living biological meteorites, using their fiery forms to wipe out whole planets. A brave Earthman disguises himself as one of these creatures so that he can join their swarm and eventually uncover the person directing their murderous actions. Bill Molno did the art.

The cover of *Space Action* 2 depicts a space explorer whose goggles reveal the reflection of an alien creature holding a pretty blond woman. In *The Horror! The Horror! Comic Books the Government Didn't Want You to Read!* author Jim Trombetta somehow gleaned the following from this cover:

> Lesbian scenes in fifties horror comics can be equally sadistic and discomfiting. *Space Action* 2 presents us with a space-exploring "lipstick lesbian." Her phallic gun evidently has no effect on the female monster that confronts her. Reflected in her goggles, it's a large-breasted but tactilely [sic] repulsive entity, a hideous parody of a mother, that has already taken possession of her partner.

The only problem is that *there is no story* with a female space explorer, gay or straight, in the comic itself. The spaceman on the cover does indeed have red lips, but this doesn't mean he's wearing lipstick or that he's actually female; it's just as likely that the colorist overdid it with the lip color (although one could point out that the hand seems a bit feminine). There is certainly nothing to indicate that the space

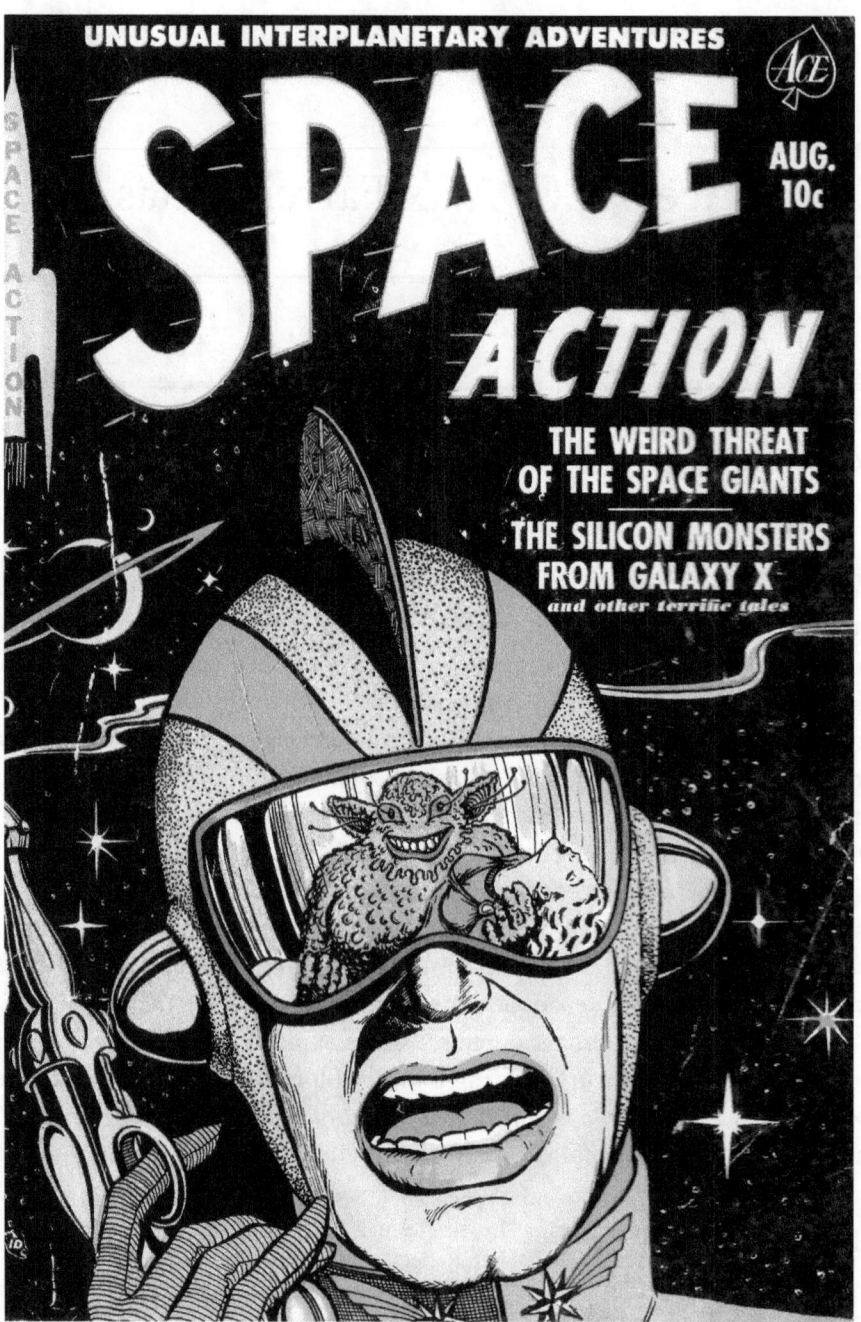

Ace's *Space Action* was a short-lived science fiction comic.

explorer is a lesbian or that the woman held in the arms of the monster is her partner! Of course, people are free to read anything they want into an illustration, but there's no reason to think the artist for this particular cover was thinking in homoerotic terms—it's just another cover. There are aliens inside the comic who somewhat resemble the creature on the cover, but they all appear to be male.

Space Action #3 features "living biological meteorites."

Atomic War!

Ace's *Atomic War!* debuted in 1952, the cover of 1 showing Manhattan skyscrapers, the Empire State Building included, being blown apart by an atomic blast. "Only a Strong America Can Prevent *Atomic War!*" blasted the logo on the cover. Inside, the story begins in 1960 with America and Russia agreeing on a lasting peace, only for Russia to attack the U.S. and other countries a few hours later. A-bombs are dropped on New York, Chicago and Detroit, but the bomb that nearly lands on

Washington, D.C., is exploded in midair by a flier who sacrifices his life to save the city. Scenes detailing the destruction of New York take up several pages, complete with tidal waves, collapsing subways, bridges and tunnels, and other scenes of devastation. There are also related stories about Russia attacking West Berlin, and a saboteur planting bombs on American planes at a base in Greenland.

In the exciting second issue, an American bomber makes it all the way to Moscow, where it wipes out the city with a hydrogen bomb a hundred times more powerful than the A-bomb. The Russians launch guided missiles at London in *AW* 3 and there is an all-out battle in the Arctic in *AW* 4, the final issue. Despite its interesting premise and concepts, such as a huge underground city from which the Russians fire missiles, *Atomic War!* basically became a prosaic, if well-done, war series with stories of mostly aerial combat in strategic areas. Ace apparently liked the idea so much that they tried again in 1953 with *World War III* ("The War That Will Never Happen If America Remains Strong and Alert"), which has the same premise; this time the Russian bombers start with Washington, D.C., before going on to New York and other cities. A guided missile sent by U.S. forces strikes the Kremlin. The second issue reads like leftovers from *Atomic War!* And then *World War III* was canceled.

Artists for both series included Ken Rice, Lou Cameron, Chic Stone, and Bill Molno. *World War III* scripts have been attributed to Robert Turner.

ACG (American Comics Group)

Commander Battle and the Atomic Sub

Commander Battle and the Atomic Sub (1954) was ACG's entry in the sci-fi sweepstakes. The first issue was printed in the "TruVision" process (a supposed 3D effect that didn't require special glasses) that was briefly employed for *Adventures into the Unknown*. Commander Bill Battle, who has been investigating flying saucers and saw a friend kidnapped by one, is chosen by President Eisenhower to helm a new atomic submarine alongside "Doc," a master physicist; "Champ," a heavyweight champion; and Tony, a great escape artist. In the first issue, they discover that ugly aliens from Mercury have built an undersea base around the remains of Atlantis and plan to wage war upon Earth. The intrepid foursome are captured by the Mercurians and nearly crushed to death in their execution chamber, escape, get past a monstrous dragon from Mercury, and blow the alien base to smithereens.

In the second issue, the "Atomic Commandos," as they are now called (the sub itself was never given a name), fight giants who live in the center of the Earth and want the surface world to destroy all atomic weapons. During the battle, the sub

ACG's *Commander Battle* lasted only seven issues.

encounters a gargantuan octopus. The commandos don't try reasoning with the giants or attempting to understand their hatred of atomic weapons, they just wipe out the entire race. (Admittedly, the giants did intend to plunge the Earth into a fiery maelstrom!) After using the sub to drill their way into the Earth, in the next issue the commandos manage to convert the sub into a spaceship. Landing on the moon, they get embroiled in a war between Russians firing bombs at the U.S. and a race of moon men who think that all Earthlings are as bad as the Russians. The third issue introduces little Jonnie, a quiz kid and scientific genius who stows away on the flight to the moon. Proving his mettle by rescuing the fellows more than once, he is made a junior member of the team. A gigantic moon snake slithers after our heroes but they manage to keep away from its fangs.

In the fourth issue, the commandos are instructed to protect a scientist whose formula could dry up swamplands and turn them into fertile regions. The Russians steal the formula and plan to use it to turn America's farmlands into deserts. There are also a host of man-eating vampire trees. The commandos save the day but at the cost of Tony's life. The fifth issue has the commandos stopping the Red Chinese from destroying the U.S. with missiles from an Arctic base, using the drill from *CB* 2 to cut through the ice from below. They encounter toothy giant devil fish along the way. A civilization hidden under Antarctic ice launches attacks on the world with globular flying ships but are defeated when the commandos use their own sub as an atomic missile and drop it on top of their power source (*CB* 6). In the seventh and final issue, the boys masquerade as Russian generals to stop a Communist plot to use flying saucers armed with bombs as missiles against America.

The scripts are by Richard Hughes, with art by Sheldon Moldoff, Ed Good, and Ken Landau.

Adventures into the Unknown

Adventures into the Unknown is best-known as the very first horror comic book. Along with the horrific material, however, *Adventures into the Unknown* also had its share of weird whimsical tales. "The Boy Who Could Fly" in *Adventures* 9, drawn by Bob Jenney, is a strange piece in which young Bobby is able to fly whenever he sees the spirit of his father, a pilot killed during the war. No one can see Bobby as he floats about saving the lives of numerous pets and people, even preventing a train crash. He is dubbed "the saving spirit." Razzed by his classmates during a field trip, Bobby brags about his ability, but no one believes him. When one of the other boys falls from a cliff, Bobby decides to fly after him even though his father's guiding spirit isn't there. He saves the other boy, but at the cost of his own life. At the last moment, his father appears to take him off with him into the Great Beyond. His father explains that, at first, the gift of flight was a good thing, "but now it can only mean pain and danger." While this may not have been the writer's intention, it almost seems as if the father lets his own son die as a bizarre way of protecting him.

In *Adventures into the Unknown* 13, there is an even odder father-son narrative. In "Beware the Jabberwock!" drawn by Ogden Whitney, Bruce Godwin is amazed to learn that his two precocious boys have figured out that author and mathematician Lewis Carroll discovered a strange world inside a mirror dimension; Carroll not only wrote about it in his poem "Jabberwock"—he gave instructions in the poem as to how to construct a "brillig" that will allow entrance to the dimension. Godwin and his psychiatrist, Dr. Bancroft, follow the boys into this weird world, where Bruce is killed. Following the instructions in the poem, the boys defeat the dragon-like Jabberwock with special swords, and Bancroft decides to *leave them there* (with their father's dead body!) as he feels they were never part of the real world anyway. Both will be happy and safe as long as they have their swords!

Adventures into the Unknown ran its first science fiction story, "Menace from Mars," drawn by Charles Sultan, in its thirteenth issue. Private eye Larry Garner, hired by a World Peace organization, investigates claims that a cult is brainwashing people into thinking a massive and destructive world war is the only thing that will save civilization. Garner learns that the cultists are actually red-hued, tentacled Martians in disguise, and they already have spies in key governmental positions. The Martians need a certain element which is abundant on Earth but has been depleted on Mars. When Larry discovers that this element is simple iodine, it seems as if the invasion is unnecessary and will be called off. But the power-mad king of Mars wants to kill anyone who knows the truth and might stymie his original plans of conquest. A Martian emissary (who knows the truth and planned to call off the invasion) is killed along with the king, leaving Larry to wonder how he will ever convince anyone of the truth; the Martians still on Earth have no idea that their actions are no longer required. The same issue has a cover showing a gigantic dinosaur attacking a skyscraper, possibly the Empire State Building, but there is no corresponding story inside the comic. The sixteenth issue explores another familiar sci-fi trope: A scientist and his girlfriend travel to the future through a time machine.

On occasion *Adventures into the Unknown* ran semi-humorous stories such as the charming "When Time Turned Back" in the 23rd issue. Samuel Coulter has just turned 70 and plans to commit suicide due to what he sees as a wasted life. He has run through his grandfather's inheritance and let his old mansion fall into ruin. His grandfather's spirit prevents him from killing himself, and directs him to set back the old clock an hour for daylight saving time. But the clock continues to run backward, and as it does so, Coulter finds himself becoming younger and younger. His doctors (and everyone else in town) notice the change in Coulter, and many run to him to learn his secret. He charges people money to hang out in his living room, where the strange spell of the clock makes everybody younger. But this comes at a price: The newly invigorated townspeople discover that other people don't know who they are due to their drastic change in age and appearance. The 80-year-old bank president—now looking like a man of 30—is turned away at the door! Meanwhile, Coulter himself is turning into a child. He manages to stop the clock, reversing its effects, and uses the money he collected to open the Second Chance senior citizen center, where "old folks can forget their worries and be happy." And everything is free!

Ajax-Farrell

Rocketman is a 1952 one-shot. Rocketman flies his ship on various assignments. In one adventure, he stops a horde of pirates near Mercury who waylay ships and demand ransom. In another, he contends with Morona, the idiot king of Pluto, who kidnaps scientists so he can use their brain power. Crudely drawn and poorly written, it almost comes off like a parody. The stories were lifted from *Captain Flight* and *Planet*.

Atlas

In the Golden Age, many of the comic series published by Atlas (aka Timely Publications) featured stories in the horror and mystery genres. Some of their titles switched over to horror from sci-fi when the gruesome terror tale rose in popularity, then switched back when the public outcry against these comics started getting a little too loud for comfort.

Journey into Mystery

Journey into Mystery had done away with horror stories by 1955. In *JIM* 25, there is a whimsical piece entitled "Foster's Fate," written by Carl Wessler and drawn by Ann Brewster. In London during World War II, soldier Steve wants his pal Wally Foster to come home with him to meet his sister Barbara. But Wally is smitten with Joyce, a woman he spent a couple of hours with during an air raid, and spends the evening with her and her family. Wally and Joyce are convinced they are in love, and Wally goes off to the European conflict determined to return to her. During the war, he keeps running into women—French, German, and other nationalities—who are exact lookalikes of Joyce, along with her parents. But at war's end when he looks up each of these ladies, there is no record of them or their families—and that also turns out to be true for Joyce and her parents. So in perplexed defeat, he goes home with Steve to meet Barbara and her parents, who of course are exact duplicates of Joyce and her folks. Another tale in this issue, "The Little Man" (Ayers-Bache), employs the popular theme of the nobody who saves the day and doesn't even realize it: The protagonist literally trips up and thereby alters the plans of two men who had intended to plant a bomb at the United Nations.

In *Journey into Mystery* 26, "The Plane to Nowhere" (Carl Wessler-Mort

Lawrence) purports to be a parallel world story but muffs it. Arthur gets into a fight with his wife Ruth, runs to the airport and takes the first available flight, just wanting to get away. The plane is empty and he falls asleep; the plane lands at the same airport two hours later. He insists on a refund because the plane had apparently turned back, but the clerk claims he never sold him a ticket. Back home, he finds Ruth, but he also finds *another* Arthur. And his dog, Rags, doesn't recognize him. Arthur grabs the dog's collar and tears it off as the animal attacks him. Arthur goes back to the airport, gets on the same plane, and finally winds up back in his own home and with his real wife. But he finds the alternate Rag's collar in his hand, and his own dog's collar is missing. This last part makes little sense if he indeed traveled to a parallel dimension.

Journey into Mystery 27 has an especially mediocre crop of stories: the old stopwatch-that-actually-stops-time chestnut; a plain woman transformed by the actual spirit of St. Valentine's; a broken-hearted astronaut turned down by the woman he loves but who finds another beauty in the form of a Martian princess, etc. Slightly better is the John Severin tale of an artist who can only do copies of an Old Master's paintings: When he attempts to do his own work, he can only mimic the dead genius' style. The famous painter does him a favor by signing the artist's work from the grave.

Journey into Mystery 28 presents one interesting story, "The Last Chance" (Paul Reinman). To prevent war, King Roland realizes that he must marry Alicia, the homely daughter of King Gort, but he just can't bring himself to do it. Sorcerer's apprentice Woltan offers his services, but is consistently rebuffed. A love potion is given to Roland, but although he does fall in love with Alicia, he still can't abide the thought of an ugly bride. Cosmeticians come to work their magic, but the poor princess only looks like a clown. In desperation, Roland allows Woltan to effect a transformation, and his magic turns Alicia into a beauty. But by now King Gort has already begun to wage war on Roland's country, and Alicia is nowhere to be found: She and Woltan ran off to get married!

"Someone Is in My Room" (Bob Brown) in *Journey into Mystery* 29 presents an interesting puzzle: George Johnson discovers an extra bed in his bedroom and can tell that someone has slept in it. The super has no idea how the bed got there. George tries to stay awake nights but he can never catch the intruder. He throws the extra bed in an abandoned lot but it winds up back in his apartment the next day. He sleeps in *this* bed and the other one, his own bed, is slept in during the night. He asks the super to check on him during the evening; the super sees only George sleeping in the single bed in his room. This is certainly an intriguing situation but the denouement—it was George's spirit, temporarily separated from his body, that slept in the other bed—is criminally disappointing.

Astonishing

The editors of *Astonishing* guaranteed "This is one of the most astonishing stories you have ever read" on the splash page of every story. In issue 47's "The Fat

Man," drawn by Larry Woromay, a reporter tries to find out why a fellow who weighs around 250 pounds goes into a panic when he loses a pound or two and immediately gobbles a lot of fattening foods until he again reaches his desired weight. The reporter goes so far as to pose as the fat man's doctor to keep him from devouring unhealthy foods. In desperation, the portly fellow tells the reporter that he comes from Saturn, where the gravitational pull is different and he *has* to stay hefty. "Now will you let me gain back the pounds I need?" he asks as he begins to float up up upward into the air.

Issue 48's "One of Our Ships Is Missing" (Carl Wessler and Bill Everett) has an intriguing premise with a woeful conclusion. In different countries around the world, various large items—such as an ocean liner, an entire train, and an airplane—disappear and then reappear sometime later. A little boy's bicycle goes missing but it is not returned. The explanation is that the larger items were gifts for an alien boy who preferred to keep the bicycle but didn't want the others. It begs the question: What would a child, even an alien child, want with an ocean liner in the first place?

Astonishing 48's "The Man Behind the Mask," drawn by John Forte, is a charming piece in which a man in a weird mask goes about doing good deeds for the needy, such as delivering food baskets to a hungry family, money to a mother whose child needs a doctor, etc. This man, a prosperous miller who wants no one to know his true identity, becomes known as the Good Fairy. Even after the miller falls on hard times, he continues to give the less fortunate the last bits of his food and cash. As he lies on his bed near death, a group of people—those he helped in the past—shows up with food and warm clothing. He can't understand how his identity was exposed, but then discovers—in the only element of the story that is fantastic—that the mask he wore as a disguise has been mysteriously altered so that it now shows his true face.

Most of the *Astonishing* stories did little more than present a premise and come up with an unimaginative ending. A couple buys a house with a flooded basement, to the puzzlement of the owners—but the buyers turn out to be a mermaid and merman. A gigantic creature pursued by hunters is a prehistoric mammoth that has escaped from an interplanetary zoo ship. At least "Build Me a Machine" (Carl Wessler and Steve Ditko) in issue 53 has a novel take on time travel: A dictator, on the verge of losing a war along with everything he owns, forces a scientist to build him a time machine to take him 50 years into the past, before the atomic age. He plans carefully, bringing gold and blueprints for atomic weapons which he will use to take over the world of the past. But as he travels into the past, everything regresses—the gold turns to ore, blueprints to wood chips—and the dictator into a squealing baby.

Similarly, "The Secret Beyond Belief," with art by George Woodbridge, in issue 63 has a twist on the immortality theme: John, a scientist, is assigned to go over the notes of scientist Calvin Bart, who has been killed in an accident. John discovers that Bart was actually a famous scientist who disappeared years ago and that he was 140 years old at the time of his death. Bart's notes reveal that he was one of several scientists who underwent a rejuvenation process, and that most of them are now in an enclave in South America working on various important projects. Traveling to the enclave, John learns the depressing truth: These geniuses have accomplished *nothing* over the decades. Knowing that they will live forever (barring accidents) has stripped them of any urgency to actually complete a task. "Don't you see what rejuvenation has brought? Stagnation!" the rejuvenator machine's creator tells John. "A man who has but one lifetime works hard to make that lifetime count. But a man who has *many* lifetimes, loses his objective, his direction…" (The story may have been influenced by "The Men Who Lived Forever," featured in the first issue of DC's *Mystery in Space*.)

Astonishing 58's "The Endless Journey" (Carl Wessler-Ed Winiarski) presents a new take on teleportation: A convict swallows a compound that allows him to merely *think* himself to any place he wants to go—New York, Paris, China. But each time, he is pulled away to an empty void after only a few moments; he doesn't even have time to finish a meal. He begs the compound's creator to help him but there's nothing the latter can do; the convict will bounce from place to place for five years, the length of his sentence. One has to wonder, if he never has time to finish a meal, will he starve to death before the five years are up?

Some *Astonishing* stories seem positively improvisational, such as "Trapped in the Tunnel" in 53 (Forte). Biff Corbin, a sandhog working on tunnels under the river, is constantly ribbed by his co-workers because he can't get a girlfriend. He tears a photo out of a magazine and brings it to work, but nobody believes that Biff knows her. Later, when Biff and the others are trapped in the tunnel with no hope of rescue, the elevator cage suddenly descends from above, and who should be inside it but Biff's beautiful girlfriend! Biff and the others get in the cage and narrowly avoid death. On the surface, reporters wonder how anyone could have gotten into the elevator when it was stuck in the middle of the shaft, and also wonder what became of Biff's girlfriend, who's disappeared. Biff shows them the picture, and one reporter tells him that the woman, Janet Marlowe, died five years ago in Hollywood. "Did she?" asks Biff, with a smile on his lips and a lipstick print on his cheek. Yes, we can surmise that Ms. Marlowe's ghost, touched by Biff's situation, came down to save his life, but the story still makes so little sense that it's almost as if the *artist* made it up as he went along.

"The Strange Power of Mr. Dunn" (John Romita) in *Astonishing* 57 is of note if only because it forecasts the superhero boom. A scientist-turned-hobo uses a formula to grow to about 12 feet tall. He doesn't don a costume and battle villains, however, but merely becomes a sideshow attraction. In his off-hours, he works to find an antidote so he can return to his normal size. "It Comes Out at Night" (*Astonishing* 62), drawn by Richard Doxsee, seems influenced by Superman in its tale of a young boy who can levitate towards the stars. His parents—farmers reminiscent of Ma and Pa Kent—found him when he was a toddler. He grows up to become an astronomer and is fascinated by one particular world that turns out, of course, to be his birthplace. He was sent to Earth so that the inhabitants of the two planets could eventually become allies.

"The Girl in the Glass" in *Astonishing* 59, drawn by Jay Scott Pike, plays around with the notions of mermaids and Atlantis. A diver sees a city in a dome at the bottom of the ocean and is infatuated by a gorgeous blonde inside. When he returns and encounters the woman *outside* the dome, she is about eight feet tall, has gills and a tail, and her mouth is full of jagged teeth—the better to eat him with. He gets away and vows never to descend below the ocean waves again. In the following issue, "The Monster in the Mist" is about a ship that encounters a sea monster that has briefly come through a time warp. The story boasts absolutely gorgeous artwork by Al Williamson and Ralph Mayo.

"The Frightful Film" (Carl Wessler-Gray Morrow) in issue 61 has a genuinely clever and original idea: Eli, a man who takes photos of people with special film, can change the faces of these people when he manipulates their images via retouching. At first, he wants to earn money by making people look young again, as he has done for himself; but when they refuse to pay his exorbitant fees, he makes them ugly with an acid photo eradicator and indulges in a bit of blackmail. When his victims descend upon his shop, he sets fire to their photos, returning them to normal—until they fade from existence. He thinks he is safe from prosecution but his own photo has been touched by the eradicator and his face has been erased. The ending is ruined by the fact that readers know that Eli could neither see nor breathe with no face.

Astonishing ended its run with its sixty-third issue, which contains a couple of interesting tales in addition to the aforementioned "Secret Beyond Belief." In "The Room That Wasn't There" (Don Perlin), a man looks into a mirror and sees an older version of himself, standing in a depressing furnished room. The man begins doing all he can to prevent what he is sure is a miserable future. He decides to rob a bank, but is caught, and winds up (improbably) sentenced to life in a prison cell—the room he saw in the mirror. In "A Piece of Rope" (Bob Forgione), Burt and Ed climb the Matterhorn to find a sack of jewels. When Ed falls, threatening to drag them both to their deaths, Burt cuts the rope and saves himself. Burt tries to tell people that the rope simply broke, but he can't get what remains of the rope, tied around his waist, off of his body and people can see that the rope was cut. Wracked with guilt, Burt goes searching for Ed's body—and finds Ed alive and in possession of the treasure. The two buddies embrace with joy. If this story had been published a few years earlier, during the horror boom, it would not have had such an incredibly happy wind-up. In a horror tale, most likely Ed's corpse would have risen up to hurl Burt into an abyss, where *his* battered corpse would remain for eternity next to the jewels.

Carl Wessler wrote many of the scripts for the series; most of the stories were not credited. *Astonishing*'s artists, besides the ones already mentioned, included Jim Mooney, Carl Burgos, Joe Orlando, Lou Morales, Dave Berg, Sid Greene, Ted Galindo, and Gene Golan. Some of them went on to become superstars at Marvel Comics.

Marvel Tales

Debuting in 1949, *Marvel Tales*, an outgrowth of *Marvel Mystery Comics*, eventually became a full-fledged horror title for a time. The catchphrase for all the *Marvel Tales* stories was "a Tale to Marvel At." *Marvel Tales* 138 has some stories with interesting concepts that, as usual, are not well-developed. In "Tomorrow," a committee that pays people to prevent deaths and disasters gives a man a pair of glasses that enable him to see what will occur in 24 hours, and his greed gets the better of him. The cover story, "Last Seen Climbing a Ladder," tells of a man who attempts to scale a ladder all the way into outer space so he can investigate an asteroid. "When Warren Woke Up," written and drawn by Gene Fawcette, details what might happen if radiation makes plant life run amok and create havoc. "Crack-Up," about a man in the future who dreams of becoming a space pilot, is unusual in that he is not depicted as some kind of coward or loser because he realizes he hasn't got the Right Stuff. Instead, his instructor tells him that his brilliant mind can be used to do important research on Earth.

In *Marvel Tales* 139's "Danger from Nowhere" (Carl Wessler; Andru and Esposito), a pilot who breaks the sound barrier is convinced that another country is about to attack the U.S. because, during his flight, he heard voices talking of imminent invasion. On his next flight, he attaches a camera, and the developed movie film reveals ... Napoleon Bonaparte talking to his associates! As the narrator puts it, "The jet plane had flown so many times the speed of sound and light that it had caught up with early 19th century history."

In "Frozen Alive" (issue 147), three scientists discover a T. Rex frozen in ice and set about to free it. When it revives, they realize it represents a terrible danger and regretfully destroy it. Much larger than any true T. Rex, this story's dinosaur is nearly of Godzilla-like proportions, which is why the scientists can envision it ravishing cities like the infamous Japanese monster. Perhaps the story was influenced by the 1953 film *The Beast from 20,000 Fathoms*, which also had a dinosaur frozen in ice coming back to life and invading Manhattan.

In Jack Oleck's "The Thief" (*Marvel Tales* 149), drawn by Joe Orlando, a ruthless man of the future, Paulson, steals a case containing an immortality formula from a scientist who refused to sell it to him, knowing he would only use it for his own selfish ends. Paulson eludes the police and takes off in a waiting spaceship, but he is still chased by police in other ships. Finally he escapes from the pursuing authorities, but his fuel is gone, and he has to land on a deserted asteroid. Fearing he faces a long lifetime alone, he drinks poison that he also finds in the container, only to learn that the scientist had hidden his immortality formula in the bottles labeled with the skull and crossbones. Now all Paulson can do is desperately hope that someday the authorities will find him. This was a variation on a very old formula with a comparatively benign ending: During the horror boom, if a character ever took an immortality serum and came to regret it, it was usually because he was entombed alive for eternity or would be in endless physical agony. All Paulson has to deal with is endless loneliness and never-ending boredom.

Freddy Kruger faces the same dismal fate in *Marvel Tales* 153's "The Last Man Alive," also written by Oleck (with art by Ed Winiarski). Freddy mans the teleportation device on the distant outpost where he was born, and hungers to live a more exciting life on Earth. But only goods can be teleported to and from Earth, not people. Freddy concocts a scheme to tell Earth that everyone at the outpost has died of a plague and asks if, under those circumstances, he can teleport himself to Earth. Permission is granted. Freddy teleports himself after arranging for the machine to explode once he has made his way to Earth. As it takes a lifetime for ships to reach the outpost, he figures he will be an old man or dead by the time anyone figures out the truth. Overjoyed, he arrives on Earth, only to be told he must stay in quarantine, utterly alone, until a cure can be found for "the plague."

In Carl Wessler's "Louie's Leprechaun" (143), arguably the worst story ever published in *Marvel Tales,* the title character comes to the rescue of a little man who has come out of a hole in the ground and is being bullied by townspeople. The grateful fellow I.D.s himself as a leprechaun and wants to do Louie a favor. When Louie complains that he is in debt due to his wife Gloria's extravagance, the leprechaun tells him he will give him gold, and indeed Louie finds a bag of gold on a table when he gets home. He is careful *not* to tell his wife, certain that she will want to spend it. Louie brings the leprechaun food daily, and each day finds another bag of gold. Then Gloria tells Louie that she knows all about the gold, that she felt guilty about her overspending and that the gold was given to them by her father. Furious at the leprechaun, Louie gathers some men to threaten the leprechaun and force him back into his hole. At home, Gloria tells Louie that her father can no longer send them any gold, but he did send them his picture. Louie takes a look at the photo and—her father, of course, is the leprechaun! There are so many holes in this moronic story that even small children would have found it ridiculous.

Artists for the series, in addition to those named, included Al Hartley, Paul Reinman, Bob Forgione, Ted Galindo, Robert Q. Sale and Pete Morisi.

Journey into Unknown Worlds

Journey Into Unknown Worlds debuted in 1950. While the series always featured weird stories in different genres, in the early part of the decade the covers and lead stories promised horror, and there were the usual tales of werewolves, vampires, and living corpses. However, much of the content of the comic was in the fantasy and science fiction field. For instance, "Trapped in Space" (*JIUW* 5), drawn by Mike Sekowsky, has Earth people merrily stepping into a carnival exhibit, a room which promises "no escape," and discovering that this is no joke: Everyone who enters the room is forced to climb down an intra-dimensional ladder and they wind up slaves for an alien race on another planet. The man who owns the carnival, and who hired the funny little man who built the room and acts as barker for it, is the latest victim. His efforts to escape his chains are constantly thwarted. Although typically absurd in its telling, the tale is disquieting, as it is made clear not only that our hero will never escape, but also that his fellow slaves may have many other unpleasant things in store for them.

In "The Last Plunge" (*JIUW* 5), written by Hank Chapman, George Louka attempts suicide by jumping off a bridge into water. He discovers a weird underwater world full of people who also killed themselves down through the ages. One woman looks just like his fiancée Emma, who died in a train wreck only days before. She is not Emma, but a suicide named Laura. She tells him that as punishment for taking their own lives by drowning, they will be transformed into fish! Rebelling against the notion, George takes the woman with him to the surface, marries her—apparently he has fallen for her even though she only *looks* like Emma—and gets a hotel room. (How they can do this when they are dead is an overlooked plot point.) When Laura transforms into a fish, George goes back to the bridge, throws his new fish-bride into the water, and jumps down to join her for all eternity. "Planet of Terror" (JIUW 7) is a variation on *The Wizard of Oz* in which an Earthman uses technology to lord it over Saturnians. The story is distinguished—if that is the word—by the bizarre if crude artwork of Basil Wolverton.

Journey Into Unknown Worlds also presented the occasional creature tale. In "It Waits in the Box" (*JIUW* 13), a ship captain is given a large box as part of his cargo, and told *not* to open it; he will receive further instructions when he is 1000 miles out at sea. The instructions reveal that inside the box is a horrible, unkillable creature spawned by atomic tests, and it must be dumped overboard for the sake of all mankind. Unfortunately, some greedy crew members open the box, thinking it contains something valuable, and unleash a jabbering horror with multiple arms and legs that quickly kills them and, in short order, everyone else on the ship. The story ends with the ship heading towards land…. Artist Manny Stallman never shows the creature in all of its full glory, just the long slithering limbs, which somehow just makes it scarier. There is no explanation for how the authorities managed to get this unstoppable monster into a box or keep it there, along with other plot holes.

Another notable monster story, "The Cyclops" (*JIUW* 50), takes Homer's *Odyssey* (in which sailors encounter Polyphemus the cyclops) and transposes it to World War II, where the destroyer USS *Marshall* is torpedoed. Accompanied by their captain, Niles U. Barret, some of the seaman make their way to an island where they encounter the towering one-eyed monster, and escape from him in much the same way that Ulysses (the Latin version of Odysseus) and his men did. Although the sailors have always joked that the skipper's middle initial stood for "Useful," at the end of the story he tells the men that his middle name is actually Ulysses. The story is drawn by Jack Davis, who did much work for *Mad* magazine satires in later years. Here his work is dramatic and highly effective.

Another giant is featured in "He Stalks in the Streets," a story that at least has unpredictable plotting; it is drawn by Herb Familton. It combines unrequited love with scientific experimentation, a hulking monster, and a twist. Henry Wadsworth, dejected when his proposal to girlfriend Lois is turned down, becomes a recluse, devoting his life to creating a cell-growth serum. He is horrified when a derelict drinks the serum and grows to three times the size of a normal man. But this giant turns out to be friendly, simple-minded, and benign. The two men develop a psychic connection, and when Henry's hatred for Lois wells up in him, the giant stalks off to kill her. Henry arrives at Lois' home first to gloat over what will happen, but she tells him she only turned down his proposal because she wanted to be an actress; she has always been in love with him. Because of her words, Henry becomes calm and loving, and the giant ceases his attack. After Henry drops dead of a heart attack from stress, Lois tells her husband that her *performance* is what saved her life. The derelict goes back to his normal size.

Journey Into Unknown Worlds 25 features two fantasy tales with horrific overtones and wildly different endings. "The World Within," drawn by Robert Q. Sale, is a harrowing, disturbing tale of a Polish man who is tortured in a concentration camp, coming out so disfigured that he is shunned even by those whom he begs for food and water. His emaciated body enables him to squeeze through a cave entrance so narrow that even pursuing dogs can't follow. He emerges at the end of a long and narrow tunnel into a golden land where he is accepted and even finds love because the blind inhabitants can't see his physical ugliness. A happy ending, of sorts, but one has to wonder what might have happened if everyone around him could actually see him.

There is no ambiguity to the ending of "One Extra Head." Sideshow attraction "Harry the Two-Headed Man" has a second head growing out of his neck—audience members pay extra to go on stage and check to see that it's real. Friendless and miserable, Harry is continually taunted by the people who come to laugh at him. The sideshow manager, Mr. Marks, urges Harry to get out and be with friends, but Harry reminds him that no one wants to be friends with a freak like him. He is beaten up by the brothers of a blind girl who innocently smiles at him. Mr. Marks uses all of his resources to find a new act, a two-headed *woman*. But Harry feels as much hate and contempt for her as others do for him. Recognizing this, he picks up a gun as he thinks "If I'm lucky the bullet will go clear through one head—and into the other." The story seems to indicate that both heads share one consciousness. The story was drawn by Dan Loprino.

Unfriendly extraterrestrials figure in several stories. In "Betrayal" (*JIUW* 26), drawn by Bob Forgione, human-like aliens kidnap two Earthlings, a romantic couple named Howard and Laura, to learn their atomic secrets, although it is not explained how these particular individuals would *have* any special knowledge of such. The alien crew members keep complaining that their uniforms are itchy but the captain refuses to allow them to remove them. Laura agrees to cooperate with the aliens, Howard is thrown out into space, and eventually Laura and the captain fall in love. Arriving on the alien world, the captain tells everyone that they can now take off their uniforms. Shedding the costumes that made them appear human, they turn out to be pink monsters with antennae and beaks. "Take off that awful uniform!" the captain tells a horrified Laura.

Sometimes Earthlings themselves are the bad guys, as in "The Creature" (*JIUW* 28), drawn by Pete Tumlinson. The first man to explore space does it to bring glory to his country and his family. He hopes to complete his assignment and come back home, where he can marry his fiancée and live a quiet life on a farm. He endures the rigors of space and arrives at the alien world that is his destination, excited to see that it seems very much like his home planet. Alas, before he can make contact, he is shot dead by frightened farmers. It seems the poor fellow is about ten feet tall and simply comes across as a monster compared to the Earthlings who have killed him.

"The First Rocket" (*JIUW* 37), drawn by Bill Everett, combines alien and human menaces in a story (set in the 1960s) in which Adolf Hitler survived the end of World War II and winds up on the moon with other Nazis. He enslaves all of the humanoid moon men, and now plans to attack Earth and become master of the universe. Joe Penning and Tex Reynolds, who were soldiers during the war, pilot the first rocket to the moon, where they discover the plot and try to foil it and free the moon men. Tex flies back to Earth with a warning but is killed on re-entry. Earth forces fly to the moon and make short work of Hitler. This story is heavily influenced by a novel by Robert Heinlein. (*Journey into Unknown Worlds* actually has two issues that are numbered 37. "The First Rocket" is from a comic published in 1950 which was originally called *Unknown Worlds*. The second *JIUW* 37 was published five years later and has completely different stories.)

On occasion there were benign aliens, such as the Zeraphons of "Our Strange Neighbors" (*JIUW* 51). Members of this friendly green-skinned race simply want to settle down peacefully on a plot of Earth land sold to them by a non-judgmental realtor. But when news of these unusual newcomers makes the rounds, some alarmed and frightened people come to the lot with guns and order them off the property. The aliens respond with their own weapons, which repel the townspeople without harming them. When the townspeople return the next day, they discover that the Zeraphons have left, but not before turning an arid and unpromising piece of property into a flourishing garden with beautiful homes and lawns. The townspeople realize that the Zeraphons are scientifically advanced and could have greatly enriched the lives of the people of Earth if they (Earthlings) had not been so xenophobic. Of course, in a more realistic story, the news media would have set up camp right next door to the Zeraphons and there might have been concern about any germs the aliens could have brought along with them. The story was drawn by John Forte.

As the decade proceeded, *Journey into Unknown Worlds* eventually dropped the out-and-out horror stories and went to the other extreme, presenting very silly fantasy tales that were presumably meant to be amusing. In one story, astronauts flying to the moon wonder if the stories of Jules Verne and Jonathan Swift were really fiction, or if both men actually managed to fly into outer space. When they arrive on the moon, tiny people jump out of crevices and shout "Gulliver's come back!" A TV script writer who infuriates his boss by constantly writing scripts featuring moon civilizations full of beautiful women turns out to come from the moon where he lives with his gorgeous wife. A man who never doffs his hat runs about doing good deeds, and when he finally takes his hat off reveals a bald head—and a halo. All of these stories appeared in *JIUW* 39.

Even when bad guys come to dire ends, these are too ridiculous to take seriously. A man who tries to steal gold from leprechauns in a cave is reduced to their size so he can't run off and reveal the location of their booty; a nasty foreman told by a fortune teller that he will "go far" has his legs snagged by a rocketship and winds up alone on the moon (inexplicably surviving without air). In another story in the same issue, *JIUW* 40, a conniving magician shipwrecked on an island hoodwinks natives into gathering thousands of pearls for him. When the natives figure out that he's essentially stealing from them, he discovers his cache of valuable pearls has been switched with a worthless rabbit, but at least he doesn't wind up in a pot.

One of the oddest stories is "The Shaggy Wolf Story" (*JIUW* 59, the final issue): Russian wolves who have become radioactive have not only developed more beautiful fur but also become intelligent and telepathic. Thus when a fur company wants to sell coats made from their fur—hiding the furs' origins and their radioactive properties, which will eventually fade—the wolves themselves address the board of directors, claiming that it is wrong to kill animals to make coats. Using their telepathy, they ensure the board that they can transform "short, ugly pelts" into ones that will be long and beautiful. The board members are thrilled, until they discover that the wolves' solution is to turn all of *them* into shaggy, long-haired wolf-men! The story was illustrated by Al Williamson.

Spaceman

Spaceman debuted in 1953. Speed Carter is the hero of the book; he and his younger partner Johnny Day are members of the United Planets' Space Sentinels in the year 2075. Speed has a nasty rival named Crash Morgan. In the introductory story, Johnny is kidnapped by space pirates who make it clear that he will be killed if anyone interferes with their criminal exploits. Speed angers everyone by callously asking for a pass during this crisis, but his true plan is to rescue Johnny before the pirates catch on. He manages to get Johnny away from his captors but the pirates' blob-like creatures attack en masse. Crash shows up with troops and saves the day. Suspecting why Speed wanted a pass, Crash had put a tracer in Speed's equipment.

The first issue also presents a story about Speed's great-grandfather, James Carter, and recounts his journey, the first ever, to Venus. There he discovers that a race of giant females have been enslaved by diminutive green horrors who haven't the strength to dig for water. James frees the women, who have a forgiving nature and agree to work with their former captors. In other stories, Speed and Johnny tackle an alien race that snatches numerous spaceships with their spider-like vehicles and imprisons the crews, and deal with a villain who uses robots in a scheme to get plans for a disintegrator.

In *Spaceman* 2, Speed encounters a renegade bunch of birdmen from Uranus when they kidnap Stellar, the sentinel commander's daughter. In the second story, Speed and Johnny land on a planet that is full of hostile half-men who have managed to stay alive despite being cut in twain. Taken captive and brought to the leader, Johnny shouts out, "Great galaxy, Speed! It… It *isn't* a guy… It's a pretty girl!" The "girl" actually turns out to be the daughter of a wizened, gnome-like scientist who splits people in half in order to double the army he intends to use to conquer the universe. The daughter objects when he tries to use a buzzsaw-like conveyance to split the two heroes, and her *father* winds up cut in half. One half destroys the other and, fortunately, the surviving half is not insane.

In another story, aliens use a giant magnet to start pulling the sun—and the planets that swirl around it—out of the solar system. Speed suggests that the aliens simply move into *our* solar system instead of stealing our sun. Speed and Johnny also encounter a humongous robot built by renegade Saturnians bent on Earth conquest. The robot goes out of control, swatting the Saturnian ships out of the sky and squashing the aliens underfoot.

In *Spaceman* 3, Speed takes off after Stellar when she's again kidnapped, this time by living skeletons that have been turned into mind-controlled warriors who loot graveyards to create more ghoulish troops. The skeletons are employed by a consortium of enemies of the United Planets. Speed pretends to join this group so that he can smash the machinery controlling the skeletons. As the skeletons march in their macabre way across space, they explode into "a rain of bones." Then a race of beings who live inside the Earth, the Core People, help humans repel an invasion of the Saturnians. The third story has nasty pirates using a transformation machine to turn Speed, Johnny and Stellar into weird recombinant animals. Speed is changed into an "elepheagle," an eagle-elephant combination, but in that form he's able to fly off and bring reinforcements. Stellar tries to sacrifice herself so that she cannot be used as a hostage.

Spaceman 4 features the menace of the mosquito men, who have murdered a scientist and stolen a deadly weapon from his laboratory. Fortunately this same scientist also invented a special DDT gun, and Speed and Johnny use it to attack their enemies. The mosquito men's leader brings out the stolen weapon and aims it at Speed, but each shot that's fired just creates more and more Speed duplicates until there are literally a thousand of him—the weapon was a "triplicator." As the DDT gun is also duplicated, the mosquito men are easily rounded up and imprisoned, and the many extra Speed doubles become their jailers. With this issue, Mike

Sekowsky began penciling the Carter stories—with inks by Jack Abel—and the art became much more attractive. Sekowsky was replaced by George Tuska in the following issue.

Spaceman 5 presents a more serious story about Major Ramm: Injured in a battle with murderous beastmen, his arms have to be amputated. Distressed that he has been grounded, he still manages to take a ship and get it into the air, sacrificing his life to knock a deadly missile heading towards Earth off-course. (It seems unlikely that in the year 2075, Ramm wouldn't have been outfitted with artificial arms that worked as well as the real things—this is a futuristic story with a '50s sensibility.) In another story, Stellar is again held hostage by evil forces, and Speed is told to deliver certain maps that will aid in the conquest of Earth or she will be incinerated. Even Stellar's father says the Earth's security cannot be compromised no matter how much they love the woman. Speed steals the maps but he alters them first, creating a trap for the invaders. In this story, Earth is referred to as "Terra."

Spaceman 6 has Speed and the sentinels tackling enormous octopus-like creatures that cause much death and destruction in space. Speed takes his ship right up close and personal to their huge heads and destroys them. They turn out to be mechanical constructs made by a band of hijackers operating out of an asteroid. Speed's explosive charge in the criminals' ammo dump creates fissures, out of which pour giant lizard-like monsters that greedily devour the hijackers. Another story has Speed's behavior turning strange when a lookalike temporarily takes his place. Stellar realizes she should have suspected something when Speed's kisses became more passionate.

The best *Spaceman* story, published in issue 5, has nothing to do with Speed Carter but is another back-up feature of earlier space explorers: Brothers James and Gary Falcon build their own spaceship, but before they can take off, a robot attacks and nearly kills James (the real scientist of the two). James wants to take the ship to Ceres, the largest of the asteroids, but Gary, more interested in glory and money than in scientific achievement, instead wants them to go to a larger planet which might bring them fame if they are hailed as its discoverers. James, recovering from the robot's attack and still wondering who sent it after him, insists on the more modest goal of Ceres. As they approach the asteroid, Gary tells James that he (Gary) unleashed the robot, then forces his brother out of the ship. In spite of this, James is still concerned about his brother and fears that he won't be able to make it to any large planet in their tiny ship. On Ceres, James befriends and helps the inhabitants who, years later, assist him in building a rocketship so that he can learn what happened to Gary. This he does: Gary is nothing but a skeleton inside a dead ship eternally locked in orbit. Despite Gary's attempts to kill him, James feels nothing but pity for him. "His disabled ship became a part of the asteroid belt and is floating around the sun like another world. He always wanted a world of his own … and he got it." The story was penciled by Bill Savage.

Artist Joe Maneely also did work for the series, and Hank Chapman contributed a few scripts.

Space Squadron

Space Squadron debuted in 1951. It is another comic that suggests that we will be traveling all over the universe by the year 2000. The characters include Captain "Jet" Dixon, master of the space rocket *Solar*; Commander "Blast" Revere; his daughter (and Jet's girlfriend) Dawn; Dawn's brother Edgar, who is jealous that his father promoted Jet over him; a kid, Rusty Blake; and Max (MXXPTRM), a Martian warrior. Blast objects to Jet's relationship with his daughter because he (Blast) knew how his wife suffered all the time he was out in space. never knowing if he would return.

In the first story, a terrible force is literally wiping out spaceships and their crews. A madman named Tumalo has created electrical arcs—a "death band"—that are responsible for the disintegrations. Edgar, who is almost as psychotic as Tumalo, sabotages some equipment in hopes of killing his hated rival, but Jet survives to destroy the madman and his weapon. Other stories show how Jet's grandfather saved the Earth back in the 1950s, and how Blast joined the space program when he was just a teen. George Tuska did most of the art for issue 1.

Space Cadet Rusty, introduced in *Space Squadron* 2, impresses Jet by coming up with a new code that Jet later uses to warn the Earth that an armada of vicious space pirates are en route. Against orders, Rusty rallies his fellow cadets to take to their ships and fire on the armada, an action which results in his joining the team. In another story, Dawn, who heads a league of women pilots, demands that females be allowed to go out on missions. Jet agrees with this, but her father does not want women to completely "lose their femininity." "We've got enough of a job keeping our women in the homes!" the Male Chauvinist Pig thunders. The gals decide to go out into space on their own, unaware that repairs are being made to the ship (and that they haven't enough fuel). Then they are attacked by a flock of huge, hungry "vulturos." Blast refuses to let Jet rescue his daughter due to a law that states that no rescue can ever be attempted by anyone who disobeys orders. Jet resigns from the Space Squadron so he can rescue Dawn and the other ladies, who have reverted to a screaming gaggle of "helpless females." Worse, when Blast—in an unlikely development, considering his attitude—tells them that they showed sufficient courage to be allowed to go off on assignments, Dawn and her friends refuse, having had enough of doing what men do. So in the end, the story's '50s sensibility scuttles what might have been a more positive statement.

In subsequent issues, Jet and his crew deal with octa-men from the Neptunian sea and ghoulish space demons, with Edgar manipulating things behind the scenes and Blast continuously warning Dawn against loving a space jockey. First Werner Roth and then Allen Bellman took over the art chores. In *Space Squadron* 4, it seems as if Max has gone back to the dark side when he joins a group of hulking homicidal Martians, but this is only a ploy to thwart them. In "Target: Moon," Jet orders Blast to fire atom bombs at the moon where Jet and his crew are in order to destroy some gargantuan dragons. Fortunately, the huge body of one of the beasts protects Jet,

Rusty and others from the explosions. Jet and Edgar come to blows when the two are on the same mission, to destroy some deadly and enormous fire beings, and Max nearly throws Edgar out into airless space. In *SS 5,* Jet contends with a beautiful psychic on the moon. She hypnotizes him with a kiss—scandalizing young Rusty—but the machinations of the psychic and her brother come to naught.

The adventures of Jet Dixon continued in *Space Worlds,* which lasted one issue. As horror had recently become ascendant in the comics industry, the cover promises "weird adventures into horror" and portrays a fanged creature threatening a young couple. However, this is really just another issue of *Space Squadron.* In the first story, Jet and his team encounter the "Temptress of Jupiter," whose kiss brings flaming death to anyone who has the misfortune to take off his helmet. In a second story, a giant cyclopean creature formed from the molten ruins of several destroyed planets becomes a menace. Edgar comes up with his worst scheme yet in "The Midnight Horror," teaming with a discredited scientist to make everyone think that the Earth has been blown out of its orbit. He contrives to take over his father's position and put the rest of the Space Squadron in jail, then learns that the Earth really *has* left its orbit and only Jet can help. This was the last appearance of Dixon and the Space Squadron.

2

Avon

Space Detective

Avon's *Space Detective* debuted in 1951. Its hero is Rod Hathway, who was also known as the Avenger and Space Detective. A philanthropist fond of giving away money to the needy, he has adventures with his secretary Dot Kenny, who is known as "Teena" when she's on assignment with her boss. In *SP* 1's first story, the couple are traveling in the interplanetary ship the *Star Queen* when they learn that pirates are planning to attack it. They stymie the plans of the criminal Maag, head of the pirates, who escapes. Maag then turns up on Venus, where he's involved in smuggling, but he escapes yet again, evading an H-bomb explosion meant to kill his pursuers. Our heroes encounter Maag next on Mars, where he is responsible for a series of bank robberies. Rod and Teena pursue Maag as he flees with his gang in his invisible, shark-like spaceship, whose presence is revealed by the stars being blacked out. Rod and Teena are captured and taken to Maag's asteroid hangout, where he intends to ransom them for millions. Rod turns the tables on the pirate leader rather too easily and takes off with him as their captor, stranding his men on the asteroid. When the food runs out, Rod reasons, they'll be only too happy to surrender to the authorities.

Space Detective 2 has Rod and Teena chasing after the hideous Gargoyle, who becomes allies with the deadly Batwomen, flying female creatures who plunder the city at the villain's direction. Rod and Teena offer themselves up as slaves so that they can get within reach of the Gargoyle. He unleashes killer robots against them, to no avail. In the next issue, the couple goes after the Chameleon and his ally, a beauteous Mole Woman from Venus. In *Space Detective* 4, they battle the Beast Man and the strong and fearsome Vulcan Woman. They and their cohorts wear X-ray collars that turn their heads into frightful skulls. The evil couple also employ wasp women with wings and poisonous claws and flame women who spread fire.

Space Detective had potential but is a forgettable series. Wally Wood did some respectable work on the book but most of the art is mediocre at best.

Out of This World

Out of This World debuted in 1950 with only one issue published—or two, depending on how you look at it. That same year, Avon released a pulp magazine entitled *Out of This World Adventures* that printed short prose stories and reprinted the same comic stories from *Out of This World 1*. *Out of This World Adventures* 2 also reprinted comic stories from various books to go with the text stories.

In "Lunar Station" (*OOTW* 1), written by John Michel, Earth has a fuel crisis that could lead to starvation for millions. Lunar Station, located on the moon, has huge stores of fuel, but has been out of contact with Earth for weeks. Ships that approach the area are shot down. During a conference between Earth authorities, including William Harmon, the head of Terrestrial Power, President Smith gets a message from Lunar Station's Captain McClelland. Now claiming to work for Organization X, McClelland demands capitulation from the authorities and threatens destruction of New York City if he doesn't get it. A huge solar mirror is aimed at the city and will destroy it with its powerful rays. McClelland's daughter Joan, who is also Harmon's secretary, can't believe her father has become a criminal and stows away on the ship of chief engineer Steve Drum as he flies to the moon to learn the truth.

After evading agents of X who try to kill them, Joan and Steve sneak into Lunar Station and discover that McClelland has been made a prisoner and been forced to make those demands. The true leader of X is William Harmon, who flew to the moon ahead of Drum. Harmon and his cohorts hole up in a room where they have the controls to the solar mirror which will automatically fry the city and everyone in it unless the mirror can be destroyed. Drum tells Commander Breckenridge, who is in the flagship, to destroy Lunar Station to prevent the solar mirror from firing. Breckenridge and his men instead sacrifice their own lives by aiming the ship directly into the mirror, sparing the others—and the city. This story's artist was Joe Kubert, who later emerged as one of the best artists in the business, working on such titles as *Hawkman* and *Tarzan*.

The other two stories in the issue have to do with monsters. "Man-Eating Lizards" by Edwin Bellin has downed fliers making their way to an island where they are to be sacrificed to the title creatures. They are tied up and left at the edge of the jungle, where fat is burned so that the odor will attract the lizards in a sequence that is vaguely creepy. The men are rescued, in true '50s style, by a bevy of beautiful native women who untie them before they can become a snack for the huge reptiles. Joe Kubert also did the art honors for this story.

The third story is an adventure of Crom the Barbarian written by Gardner Fox and drawn by John Giunta. An obvious clone of Conan, Crom is forced to go to the wealthy city of Ophir by Dwelf the magician, who threatens to torture Crom's sister Lalla if he doesn't comply. Crom's mission is to grab some of the Waters of Eternal Youth stored in the palace, and while he's at it he also decides to grab an angry Queen Tanit; he also slaughters the humongous serpent that guards the Waters. When Dwelf partakes of the mystical liquid, he gets more than he bargained for, his body going backwards in time until he turns into an infant and then completely disappears.

Strange Worlds

Crom next appeared in *Strange Worlds* 1, whose cover promises "Astounding Super-Science Fantasies." Crom decides to travel back to Ophir to rule beside Tanit, and brings his sister with them. Getting lost on the way, they find themselves in a jungle where they are beset by ape-men. Brought to their city they encounter their leader, Rou, who figures he can get a good ransom for Tanit, but he doesn't figure on Bokris, who now sits on the Ophir throne and couldn't care less if Tanit is fed to Spraa, the Spider-God. Therefore Crom, Lalla and Tanit are all thrown into the cavernous pit with Spraa, a gigantic and hungry arachnid. Fortunately—and inexplicably—Rou has allowed Crom to hold onto his sword, Skull-Biter, which he uses to puncture the monster's brain-pan. Returning to Ophir, Crom slays men who were ordered by Bokris to kill Tanit, then throws the would-be ruler to his death. Crom takes his place beside Ophir as the crowds sing their praises.

Also in this issue is an adventure of Dave Kenton of the Star Patrol, a law enforcement group operating in the 32nd century. Kenton is disgraced, stripped of his rank, and thrown out of the Star Patrol when his identity papers are stolen by a pretty blonde who knocked him out with a gas gun. Kenton decides to join a gang of pirates, the Coalsack Corsairs, so he can work undercover to bring them to justice. He encounters the blonde, Maeve, who turns out to be a reporter working undercover, and the two settle their differences and work together to thwart the pirates; Kenton is reinstated. The story was written by John Michel; the art is by Joe Kubert and Carmine Infantino.

By *Strange Worlds* 2, Crom is chomping at the bit, bored with sitting at the side of Queen Tanit and anxious to engage in some swordplay. He gets plenty of excitement when he learns that caravans from Ophir are being attacked by Balthar, a giant "as tall as the trees." Balthar has adopted the cave people as his tribe and turns them into a mighty force. Crom leads a group of ships filled with soldiers to the land of the cave people, encountering a monstrous sea creature that almost swallows the hero, as well as some angry apes. Recognizing that even the trained warriors of Ophir might flee in terror once they catch sight of the enormous Balthar, Crom has them engage the cave people as he takes on Balthar elsewhere. With a slash of his sword, he blinds Balthar, who blunders about until he is toppled by dozens of arrows. The creative team was again Gardner Fox and John Giunta. The story was quite entertaining and exciting but Crom was never seen again.

Dave Kenton returns in *Strange Worlds* 3, going undercover as a prisoner when pirates strike Titan to steal uranium and slave labor. The villains are the Flann, green-skinned aliens composed of silicon, who need uranium to build enough atom bombs to blast the Earth—an obstacle to their goal of conquest of the universe—out of existence. By literally turning up the heat on the Flann city, so hot that he nearly broils alive, Kenton turns all of the Flann into glass and ends their menace forever. In *Strange Worlds* 4, Kenton is up against the "Vampires from the Void," an alien race led by an evil blond queen who uses humans for energy by putting them in machines that suck the life force from them. They use sleep rays to subdue their victims because they want them alive until they can be used as "fuel" for their machines. Kenton uses ultra-violet emissions to adversely affect the "vampires" so that the ray that puts others to sleep kills them. The art for both stories was by Wally Wood and Joe Orlando.

Kenton returns in *Strange Worlds* 5, battling the "Sirens of Space," beautiful women, led by Lura, who use sonics to drive people insane with pain so that the Sirens can take over their spaceships. The passengers, men and women both, are made slaves and the ships' cargo appropriated. Kenton is nearly frozen by Lura and put in the "Hall of Living Statues," where the blonde reporter Maeve has already been placed into suspended animation. Kenton cleverly avoids her fate, defeating Lura and her gal pals by putting lactic acid, which causes extreme fatigue, in their drinking water. As usual, the art was by Wood and Orlando.

In *Strange Worlds* 6, Kenton allows his ship—and himself—to be captured in an attempt to discover who grabbed the space freighters and battle cruisers that recently disappeared. Reporter Maeve stows away on Kenton's ship, unaware of his assignment, and they are soon taken captive by "The Monster-Men of Space." These odd creatures are slaves of a brain-creature that is trying to bring his lost race back to greatness. He is able to control the minds of Maeve and Kenton, but the latter gets around this by donning a helmet of lead. The art for this story was by Everett Raymond Kinstler. Kenton was never developed as anything more than a smart and brave heroic figure with no real personality.

The stand-alone story "The Invasion from the Abyss" (*SW* 4) details what happens when survivors of Atlantis, who have moved to a city in huge caverns inside the Earth, try to conquer the world with the use of specially bred, powerful dwarves. The invaders are beaten back when huge magnets are employed (due to the iron content in the dwarves' bodies, they are frozen in their tracks). Several artists worked on this story, including Frank Frazetta, Wally Wood, Roy Krenkel, and Al Williamson.

In the same issue's "The Lost Kingdom of Athala," a professor sends a man, Jack Rance, and his young friend Tommy Peters back in a time machine to the prehistoric era to track down a couple, the Greggs, who fled the violence of the 20th century for supposedly quieter times. There the man and boy encounter Rhoa, a haughty queen of cavemen, who is the daughter of the now-dead Greggs. Like her parents, she hates modern men and their savage ways. While dodging assorted dinosaurs and men from a rival tribe, Tommy is killed. Jack and Rhoa start passionately smooching after Jack points out to her that the times *she* lives in are hardly non-violent. They time-travel to the 20th century without bothering to collect poor Tommy's corpse. The dumb story was drawn by Wally Wood.

In "A Nation is Born" (*SW* 4), there's trouble at a moon colony when Martian agitators stir the "Lunites" into demanding independence from Earth; the Martians plan to install a puppet government and use the moon as a base to attack Earth.

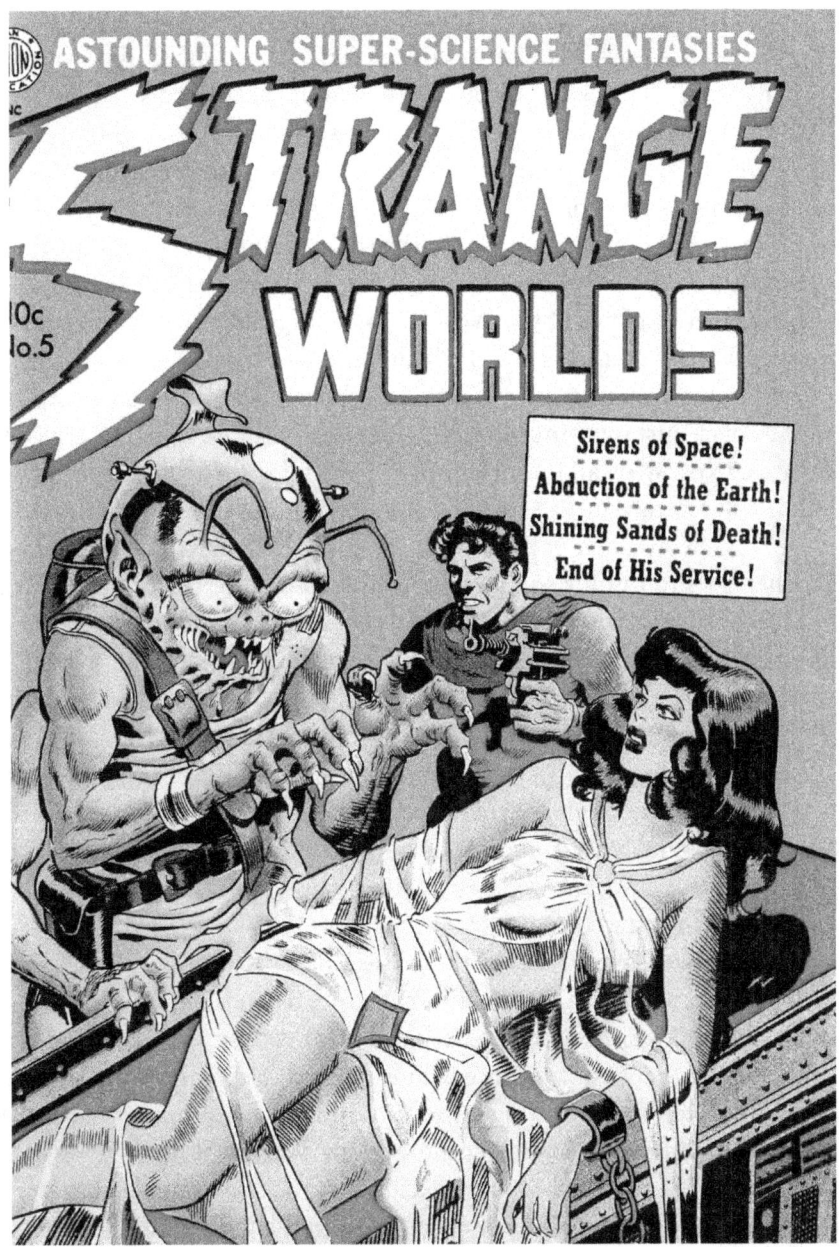

Strange Worlds #5 features "The Shining Sands of Death!"

Lua, the wife of one of the colonizers, disguises herself—not very well—as a boy to try to get the goods on the Martians. When the truth is discerned, she threatens to destroy everyone—Martians and Earth people alike—by pulling a switch that will suck all the air out of the room. The art by Rafael Astarita is the best thing about the story.

"The Shining Sands of Death" in *Strange Worlds* 5 has Prof. Carlton discovering microscopic jewels in a chunk of granite. He decides to shrink himself and two companions—the decent Alan Blake and the evil Pierre Dufois—to minuscule size so that they can retrieve the brilliantly shining gems. Greedy Dufois pushes the professor off a ledge on the rock, then collects the jewels (presumably they will enlarge along with the man). Next he takes the growth serum and gets rid of Alan after a desperate struggle. Dufois' plans have become so grandiose that he contemplates growing to giant size and conquering the Earth. Before he can fully enlarge, however, the professor's daughter comes into the room, picks up the granite, and inadvertently crushes Pierre under her fingernail. Ed Goldfarb and Bob Baer did the art.

In "The Man Who Fought the World" (*SW* 7), a couple is exposed to radiation during World War II and their son Halran Ammo is born a mutant (many years before Marvel's *X-Men*). He can walk through walls, read minds, and even teleport from place to place just by thinking it. Fearing the world is facing nuclear destruction, he decides to destroy all munitions factories and stockpiles. This might seem a sensible plan but Halran doesn't care that innocents might be killed during his acts of sabotage, and he even talks of assassinating world leaders. His loving but distraught father tries to put his son away, but Halran cannot be contained. Halran's girlfriend Janet argues that World War III has been delayed while world forces try to find and stop Halran. Finally he is subdued with acid thrown into his eyes, and does not try to flee when he is taken to an electronic fire pit; he hurls himself into it as his final act. "The end of the madman," reads the final caption. "Now civilization could go on … *senselessly destroying itself*!" While the story is full of intriguing notions, it is much too simplistic. It glosses over the human lives that may have been lost as Halran Ammo (obviously an ironic name) goes about his business of destruction, as well as the fact that the world could hardly sit idly by while its leaders are threatened with death. The art for the story is by Norman Nodel.

Strange Worlds 9's "World of the Monster Brain," drawn by Syd Shores, has a man kidnapped by little metal men into an alternate dimension ruled by a gigantic malevolent creature with a wizened face and brain on top, who simply squats on the summit of a pile of rocky slabs barking orders. Since it is unable to move its bulk, the small robots do all the work for it, feeding it ore, and there are also human slaves who are forced to do the bidding of the metal men. Since there doesn't seem to be any good reason for the kidnapped man—who throws a chunk of rock into the membranous top of the evil brain, killing it—to have been kidnapped in the first place, the intimation is that this is just a tall tale told by the man to his grandson years later, a cautionary tale about the dangers of wanting to own everything and everybody, just like the brain.

Strange Worlds 10–17 were never published. After two years, the series was rebooted, taking over the numbering from the horror comic *Eerie*, but *SW* 18 and the following issue were reprints of one-shots that had been published earlier. The first story in *SW* 18, "Attack on Planet Mars," is in four parts: Terrano, a would-be dictator from Venus, has all of Earth's leaders assassinated, and steals scientific secrets from Dr. Brende that could conquer disease and old age. The doctor is killed in an attack by Terrano's forces, and the survivors, including Jac Hallen of Inter-Allied

News and Brende's children Georg and Elza, are taken to a Venusian outpost in Brazil. There Terrano, who had met Elza before, confesses that he is still in love with her.

Terrano fears that Elza will hate him if he harms Georg, who also has his father's knowledge; he also spares the life of Jac Hallen at Elza's request. Terrano refuses an ultimatum by Earth forces and learns that Mars blames Earth for the assassinations and supports him. Princess Maida of Venus has also been imprisoned by Terrano, but with the help of a Martian who only pretends to be loyal to Terrano, she and Georg are able to escape. The Earth government makes it clear that Terrano is no longer the only person with the "secret of eternal life" and no one need support him any further. Terrano launches a vicious attack on Mars that completely demolishes one of their cities and all of its inhabitants.

A desperate Jac finally makes a move on Terrano, and their ship plunges into the ocean. Terrano manages to get out of the aircraft, but rather than escaping from the authorities, he tells them Elza's location. Elza and Jac are rescued. The captured Terrano is left on an asteroid, but it is debatable if he will stay there…

The story was penciled by Joe Kubert and Carmine Infantino and inked by Vince Alascia. The uncredited script has some exciting moments, especially when Georg and the princess escape from Brazil, and Terrano is a highly recognizable and believable sociopath, justifying all of his actions and feeling not the slightest regret or remorse. That he would spare certain people for Elza's sake is questionable, however.

Strange Worlds 19 is a reprint of the one-shot *Robotmen of the Lost Planet*. In the future, robots do most of the work of man, who has become soft and over-reliant even as the robots become more aggressive and rebellious. The robots are almost comical-looking, taller than humans with large balloon-like heads that resemble clowns. Alan Arc watches in horror as a robot throws his father (the operator of the factory where the robots were built) to his death. Alan then runs off with his wife Nara when a full-scale revolution takes place, with the robots attacking and killing hundreds of people.

Five years go by and the remnants of humanity are hiding from the robots in caves. Because the robots have an outer shell of artificial flesh, Alan grows some and creates his own outer shell, to disguise himself as one of them and perhaps discover how to defeat them. Infiltrating the robots' ranks, he learns that they are not physically strong but carry deadly ray guns. He also discovers that they are developing processes to make themselves more human, adding sensitive ganglia to the flesh instead of toughening it. Accidentally pricking himself, Alan bleeds and his cover is blown; he escapes back to his wife and little boy, Laurie.

Another five years pass and the humans have mobilized and created many weapons to use against their robot opponents. The robots have developed nerve endings that mean they can feel pain as well as the fear of such pain. Alan gets into the robots' main HQ and kills their leader, who was sending out telepathic waves that were giving his minions courage. Without their leader, the robots are easily defeated and flee into the forests. Unable to build more factories, they will eventually die out. Although it doesn't much wrestle with moral issues—did the robots have emotions and souls, and did the humans' treatment of them arouse them to rebellion?—*Robotmen*, drawn by Gene Fawcette, is still a good and entertaining sci-fi tale.

By the twentieth issue, *Strange Worlds*' content had converted to war stories and it only lasted two more issues.

More One-Shots

Avon Fantasy had only one issue. Subtitled *An Earthman on Venus*, it is an adaptation of the 1924 novel *The Radio Man* by Ralph Milne Farley. Myles Cabot is conducting experiments in teleportation (years before *The Fly*) when a sudden jolt sends him to Venus. There he encounters six-foot intelligent ants and voracious giant spiders, one of whom nearly snacks on him before a bee comes to his rescue. A carnivorous plant nearly kills him but he is saved by the intervention of Doggo, a friendly ant. When Myles sees a beautiful young woman with wings and antennae in the distance, Doggo tells him that she is a member of the Cupian race, slaves of the ant-people.

Myles is introduced to the woman and discovers she is the Princess Lalla, brought to the ant-people by her cousin Yuri, who wants to marry her and regrets helping to make her a prisoner for his own selfish purposes. Myles helps Lalla escape, and there is an encounter with a giant spider before they wind up in the main city of the Cupians. Instead of thanking Myles for bringing the princess home, the treacherous Yuri has him arrested. He is not fed to baby ants for fear that his foreign flesh may sicken them, but instead is taken to the Valley of Howling Stones. There intense sound caused by radiation nearly kills him.

Back in the land of the Cupians, Myles tells their king the truth, and also wins a battle against the slimy Yuri. He then helps the Cupians build rifles and tanks and mounts an attack on the city of the ants. Yuri kidnaps the princess again; the ants kill him as soon as the attack begins, and Myles is reunited with Lalla. With their weapons, the Cupians defeat the ants, who raise a white flag. No longer will the ant-men enslave the humans. Myles is given the property of the dead Yuri, as well as Lalla's hand in marriage. *An Earthman on Venus* is a standard Edgar Rice Burroughs pastiche, with efficient art by Wally Wood.

In a back-up story, "The Lost Princess," two archaeologists, lost in the jungle, wander into a cave, fall into a crevice, and come upon a beautiful woman frozen in ice. Thawed out, she comes to life unaware that 4000 years have elapsed since she was interred; she thinks her people are still engaged in combat with a rival city. She is horrified to come upon the ruins of what once was a great underground city, *her* city. The two men decide to take the despairing princess up to the surface, but as soon as she breathes fresh air, in a bit stolen from *Lost Horizon*, she turns into her true age and becomes a skeleton.

The one-shot *Rocket to the Moon* takes place in 1964. Ted Dustin's company is about to go bankrupt and he desperately needs the money he'll win if he becomes the first person to make indirect contact with the surface of the moon. He and Roger Saunders shoot a projectile from the Galapagos, then take off in their ship to see if it will hit the moon. It does, but there is a problem with another ship of observers and no one else sees the projectile arrive on the lunar surface. Worse, the projectile causes damage in a lunar city controlled by P'an-ku, and he retaliates by sending explosive rockets to demolish several Earth cities. (Ted seems more aggrieved that he is being blamed for this than he is over the thousands of deaths that occur.) In a development that recalls the racist "Yellow Peril" attitudes of earlier decades, P'an-ku, whose subjects appear to be Asian, claims that his people predate Earth Orientals. Earth scientist Dr. Yu betrays his own planet by forming an alliance with P'an-ku.

Trying to make things right, Ted flies to the moon where he meets Princess Maza, who leads a Caucasian race on the moon. In addition to fighting off P'an-ku's soldiers, the two deal with man-eating plants with tentacles, humongous dragon-like lizards, and monstrous bird-creatures, one of which carries Maza off in its claws. P'an-ku is initially depicted as a kind of Chinese warlord but later, when he interacts with Ted or Maza, he is drawn as a weird yellow creature with a frightening face and antlers. At least one of his former followers, Shen-Ho, also Asian, a good guy, protests his ruler's attempt to conquer Earth and winds up in a dungeon for his trouble. He helps Ted destroy P'an-ku's devastating weapon. P'an-ku is defeated, Earth is saved, and Ted and Maza are married.

The script for this potboiler was by Walter Gibson, best-known for writing many Shadow pulp novels under the pen name Maxwell Grant. The plot was taken without credit from Otis Adelbert Kline's novel *Maza of the Moon*. Joe Orlando did the art. It goes without saying that its scientific aspects are ludicrous.

In the 1952 one-shot *Flying Saucers*, Russ Lanning, searching for the source of cold light in the Peruvian jungle, is captured by natives, carried up a mountain and thrown in a pit. Exploring the underground area, he discovers a secret chamber full of sleeping aliens. Freed from his capsule, one alien wakes the others, then uses a ray to temporarily freeze Russ. The alien and his companions take off in a fleet of flying saucers. Russ makes his way out of the mountain and tries to convince everyone of what has happened by demonstrating an alien weapon he took with him, but it no longer works. Despite the appearance of saucers in the skies, no one believes him. Eventually the aliens appear again to Lanning and tell him that they are remnants of a race that developed atomic power and destroyed itself eons before recorded history. These beings—the very few left—decided to rest in suspended animation until such time as a new civilization emerged on Earth. Now they instruct Russ on how to place hidden dampeners at atomic sites to prevent any future holocausts. Despite some interesting moments, *Flying Saucers* is not memorable.

3

Charlton

Space Adventures

Charlton comics had more than one series entitled *Space Adventures*. The first one debuted in 1952 and initially presented the adventures of the 25th-century Space Rangers. Commodore Rex Clive led the group, which consisted of Bob Barry, Jim Jones, and Adjutant Speed Lansing. An added attraction was Stella Dawn of the Space Transport Auxiliary Reserve (STARS), who ignites a friendly rivalry between Barry and Jones. The stories in the first issue are mediocre tales of the Martian villain Nucleo, who can change his face as easily as his clothing, and another bad guy who unleashes huge insects from fissures in the moon. A back-up story concerns Hap Holliday, aka the Time Skipper, who races through time in his Time Yacht, accompanied by Prof. Eon Tempus, whose genius helped build the device. In their first adventure, they wind up in the far-flung future, where they help a beautiful princess hold on to her realm.

In "The Hollow World" (*SA* 3), space liners keep disappearing when they near the planet Marduk. Rex Clive and his Rangers discover that Marduk, which is five times the size of Earth, has a hollow core. Inside this core is a round gyroscope which attracts the space liners like a magnet and moors them tightly to its surface. The crews and passengers are turned into slaves to dig for precious metals. The Rangers put paid to that scheme. In another story in this issue, "The Vixens of Venus," the rangers and Stella Dawn contend with vituperative women and giant insects on Venus.

The "Mad Martian" Nucleo returns to bedevil the Rangers in *Space Adventures* 4, stealing an element called Gravitix, which repels gravity, and creating an illusion that there is three of him. The trick doesn't prevent him from being captured. The Rangers had a few more minor adventures and then disappeared. As for Hap Holliday, he brings the beautiful princess from the future who appeared in *SA* 1 back with him in his time yacht and they wind up in the days of Cleopatra and Julius Caesar (3), but Hap is never seen again.

Space Adventures published a few stand-alone stories in the early issues. "Space Report" (*SA* 5) takes place in the 24th century, when it is confirmed that a derelict spaceship from 400 years before is falling to Earth and will land on Washington,

D.C. As the fuel may cause an explosion, the city is evacuated. An investigation by General Craig reveals that this might be the ship *Nautilus*, which disappeared without a trace in 1957 in the early days of space travel. We learn that the *Nautilus*, under the command of Major Carston, had been traveling to Mercury on a mining mission. Some of his men aren't sure that enough containers of oxygen were placed inside the ship. Going over the supplies will delay the flight by hours and might also result in the court-martial of these men, so they keep quiet. Tragically, the oxygen runs out and all the crew members die soon after landing on Mercury. From the *Nautilus* log, found in the wreckage, General Craig learns that Carston did not deserve to be court-martialed in absentia for losing his ship and his crew. He will receive a posthumous promotion and a statue will be erected to honor him and all the early pioneers of space flight. "Space Report" is an intelligent and reasonable story, quietly poignant, its only fantastic element a bit with a giant lizard that briefly menaces Carston and his men on Mercury. It also illustrates how flippancy and carelessness can lead to disastrous consequences. The art is by Stan Campbell.

One of the most unusual *Space Adventures* stories, "Transformation," is the lead story in the seventh issue, beginning a run of stand-alone stories. Dr. Lars Kranston is convinced that the Earth is going to be destroyed in atomic fire when World War III breaks out. He gathers together several top scientists and tells them that they would be better off flying to Mars and avoiding the inevitable conflagration altogether. Lars does not tell his secretary (and significant other) Betty, and apparently does not plan to bring her along, but she hears the whole plan on the intercom and blackmails him into bringing her. If he doesn't, she'll tell everyone about the trip to Mars. Lars agrees and the ship takes off, but there is a crash landing that kills everyone but Lars and Betty. Betty, with amnesia, wanders off, while Lars assumes that she is one of the charred bodies that were melded together in the accident.

Filled with loneliness and boredom, Lars gets the bizarre notion of performing an experiment—a sex conversion—and begins work in the ship's laboratory! "Anyway, I'm a little tired of being a man," thinks Lars. "Men start wars ... men would, in short, seem to be rather stupid creatures. Poor Betty—because of us she's dead ... this hormone shot will start the treatment." Betty finally realizes who she is, and for a year has been living off the Martian flora and fauna. Neither she nor Lars knows that, back on Earth, the nations have settled their differences and World War III is over. Betty rushes back to the ship, thinking only of her beloved Lars, but instead finds an attractive brunette in his place. When she learns that this strange woman *is* Lars, she is completely distraught. The story was drawn by Dick Giordano.

"Transformation" was published around the time that the *New York Daily News* broke the story of the transformation of Christine Jorgensen from a man to a woman. While *not* the first person to have gender realignment surgery, Jorgensen became the most famous. While there is no way of knowing for certain if the news story influenced "Transformation," Lars' sudden interest in changing from male to female makes no sense unless the character is transsexual, so chances are it was published after the Jorgensen story broke. The ending of the uncredited tale seems to indicate that there is little chance of a lesbian relationship developing between Lady Lars and Betty. One also has to wonder how Lars thought he could replenish the human race without bringing Betty along, or if he was all that interested in her in the first place.

Space Adventures 8 presents "All for Love" (Memling-Giordano-Cappello), a hybrid of space opera and noir film. Jason Casan crashes on a lonely asteroid called Vulka and is rescued by the aged Dr. Artuk and his beautiful young companion Clio. Jason is appalled to learn that there isn't enough fuel on Vulka to get him back to Earth. He begins an affair with Clio, who tells him she is bound to Artuk by law. Artuk learns about their relationship and is about to tell Jason things he isn't aware of, when Clio takes a hatchet to the doctor's head. Now Jason and Clio must flee in what are called exile ships, because they haven't enough fuel to land anywhere. Out in space, the extreme heat makes Clio's outer covering melt, revealing her to be a none-too-sexy metal robot. "Good God—" thinks Jason, "doomed to float around in space until I die—with ... with *that*!"

In "Pet Hate," colonizers discover that the cute little animals they have taken as pets become murderous when their population isn't controlled by the dinosaur-like predators the colonizers have slaughtered for the small critters' safety. (This was probably inspired by "The Enemies of the Colony" in EC's *Weird Fantasy*.) The other stories in this issue also skewed towards the dark side, as horror had become the big thing in many comic books. One tale has monster plants from an alien world killing off everyone, including children; another is a black comedy in which an obese gourmand travels to another world and winds up becoming the blue plate special. A man uses Martian technology to go up the evolutionary ladder, develops a huge cranium, and tries to take over the world with mind-blasts and other weapons.

"Speed-Up!" (Memling-Cappello-Giordano) in *Space Adventures* 9 has little to do with space but is an interesting tale of a scientist who creates microscopic life forms, puts them into a special vault and observes them with cameras that give him close-up views, pushing evolution on this miniature world so that 100 years pass in an hour. He is anxious to go into the "future" and discover the secrets of the Argon bomb, which he does—to his regret. The story might well have provided the basis for an episode of the '60s *Outer Limits* TV show, "Wolf 350." in which a scientist creates a miniature planet in his laboratory and observes as it goes through various evolutionary stages. (Theodore Sturgeon's classic story "Microcosmic God" was clearly an influence on both the comic story *and* the TV episode.)

The same issue also has a grim little tale called "The Good Old Days" (Memling-Frollo-Alascia), set in 1995. When World War III breaks out on Earth, there is panic and rioting in the streets, and a near-complete collapse of law and order. Lori is more angry than appalled when she sees dozens of people, thinking the world is doomed, jumping from roofs to their deaths—she thinks they are cowards. Lori has always thought that the 20th century is a world of "fear and terror" and pines for the good old days of the past. Her boyfriend Vann, although a scientist, is conscripted and pulled from her side, but alone she manages to make her way through the urban jungle back to the lab of her father, who is an astronomer. The man tells his colleagues, including Dr. Kron, that he has found a planet, Mantor, that may be able to sustain human life. They take off in a ship and arrive on the new world, but almost immediately they learn that this planet resembles Earth's Mesozoic era. Leaving the ship, Dr. Kron is shredded by hungry pterodactyls; others in the party fall prey to a T. Rex. Lori's father sacrifices his life to save her. She hides inside the ship, utterly alone. She now understands how people can be driven by despair to take their own lives, and just moments later shoots herself in the head.

This depressing tale is followed by a whimsical one, also scripted by Carl Memling: A man injects a dog with a formula that gives it the ability to speak. There are many ways to make money with the talking pooch, but his method is to temporarily board the dog with wealthy people so that it will have a chance to note the combinations of their safes, which the man later robs. The dog has a much higher moral character than his master, but when he balks at continuing to abet his master, he is beaten. Someone—no one knows who—calls the police and tells them where the stolen loot can be located. The dog's owner is arrested and the dog winds up with a nice family.

Space Adventures 10 features "Homecoming" (Joe Gill-Steve Ditko), in which several men say farewell forever to homes, family and Earth to take a decades-long trip to Alpha Centauri to find a planet that will sustain the growing human population. They discover that astronauts who left for Alpha Centauri nearly a hundred years later beat them to it in spaceships employing star drives. While the latecomers are hailed as "great heroes," one can only imagine their despair at having left everything and everyone that mattered to them for *nothing*. In the equally ironic "Back to Earth" (Memling-Giordano-Cappello), colonizers who have been oppressed by robots escape and head back to Earth amidst harrowing experiences, including cannibalism when the food on their ship runs out. Arriving home, they learn that the Earth has been taken over by robots and that humans ultimately defeated the robots back on the colony they just fled.

Beginning with *Space Adventures* 13, the superhero Blue Beetle gets the cover story, but only for two issues; then an adaptation of the TV series *Rocky Jones Space Ranger* takes over. Sgt. "Blast" Baker and Corp. Astra Adams of the Planet Police also appear in an *SA* 13 story in which a madman unleashes a "thing from outer space"—a giant octopus-like creature with many wriggling tentacles and a huge maw with needle-sharp teeth—in an attempt to take over the universe. As for Rocky Jones, he has dreamed of being a Space Ranger since he was a boy. He helps fight off an alien invasion by causing a diversion using old, empty spacesuits, and is awarded his own command and ship, the *Orbit Jet*. Rocky's companions are Winky Jupiter, his second-in-command; the lovely blond Vena Ray; and a boy, Bobby.

In his first post-invasion adventure, a man named Gerson steals a Velocity X formula that can increase the speed of a ship to an astonishing degree. Gerson plans to form an alliance with an enemy queen, Cleolanthe, who wants control of the Earth. In his spaceship, pursuing Rocky's *Orbit Jet*, Gerson doesn't realize that with Velocity X in his fuel tank, he won't be able to slow down; his ship burns up like a meteor. The story has nice art by Ted Galindo and Vince Alascia.

In *SA* 16, Queen Cleolanthe takes advantage of a "forbidden frequency" to take over the minds of her Earth enemies and subdue them. Next in the issue, one of Winky's ancestors, a grizzled sheriff from the long-ago past, frozen in ice for generations, is thawed out and helps Rocky find the man responsible for the disappearance of several spaceships. In *SA* 17, a man named Zeno fleeces wealthy men by offering to take them to a lost city of gold (it doesn't exist), killing them, and then acquiring their fortunes through forged wills. His operation is smashed, of course, by Rocky Jones. In the same issue, a self-styled seeress named Hella fleeces the rich by using hypnosis to convince them that the solar system will be destroyed in four months, and selling them tickets on her special rocketship for every penny that they've got.

In *SA* 18, embittered scientist Galen invents an anti-gravity ray that he turns on Earth from his base in space. Children are affected first: Unable to move, they slowly begin to sink into the ground. Galen then threatens to turn the ray on full-force, which would push everyone, adults included, down into the earth, presumably suffocating them. Rocky plays for time by having everyone put on "snow shoes" that will prevent them from sinking, then takes on Galen, destroying his device and his devious plans. On TV, *Rocky Jones* lasted one season (39 episodes), and when it was canceled, the comic stories came to an end as well. Aside from reprints, Rocky and his pals never again appeared in comic books. *Space Adventures* went back to stand-alone stories, as well as a couple of reprints and a forgettable tale of Rex Clive of the Space Rangers (*not* the same group of Rangers to which Rocky Jones belonged) in *SA* 19. *Space Adventures* 20 presents a story entitled "First Trip to the Moon," which is simply a reprint of the comic adaptation of the film *Destination Moon,* first published by Fawcett comics.

The Golden Age run of *Space Adventures* ended with the 21st issue and then it metamorphosed into *War at Sea*. But *Space Adventures* would return in a few years.

Space Western

Space Western debuted in 1952. Spurs Jackson is a rancher as well as an electronic engineer, monitoring the flight of Earth missiles into space via a 1000-foot-high tower on his Arizona property. Jackson is kidnapped by aliens and taken to Mars, where he helps Queen Thula regain her throne and is made prime minister. After he returns to Earth, a Texas Ranger asks Spurs' help in tracking down some missing atomic scientists, and Spurs winds up trapped in a rocketship traveling to Venus. He makes his way back to Earth by riding a robot horse though space and arrives at

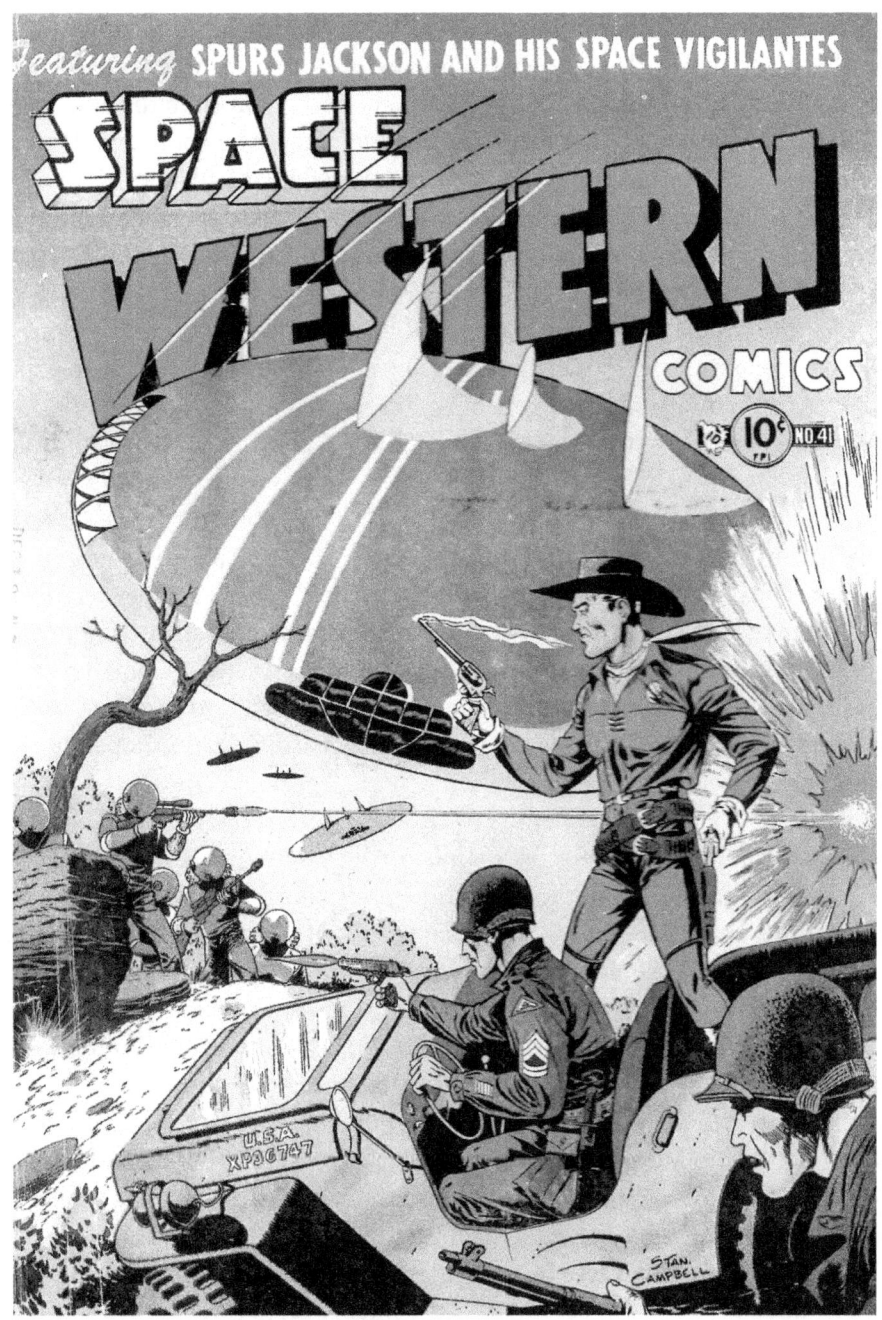

Spurs Jackson was the hero of Charlton's absurd *Space Western*.

his ranch in a *matter of minutes*. Obviously, science was not the comic's strong point. Other stories in the first issue—actually issue 40—are simple Western tales of outlaws and Indians with *no* sci-fi slant.

The absurdity continues in *Space Western* 41, in which the Cactus Men of Venus try to invade the Earth as Spurs organizes his cowboys into "space vigilantes."

Building his own rocketship, Spurs gets to Venus in record time, blows up most of the aliens and arrives back home before anyone knows he was gone. Then come reports of more spaceships heading from the moon to a canyon in the desert. "These unearthly space critters don't give Spurs no peace," muses one of the vigilantes. "It's either mavericks from Mars or Venus varmints. Wonder what'll it be *this* time?" This time, the Martians and Venusians have teamed up and are using moon men—natural borers—to assist in a new invasion. Spurs washes these fanged, ape-like creatures out of their mine hideout by unleashing the water in a dam.

In *Space Western* 42, Spurs takes on aliens who feign benevolence but actually want to take over the Earth. Spurs discovers that the aliens' own sun exploded and they used their faster-than-light ships to escape. When it's pointed out that this explosion occurred *after* the aliens arrived, Spurs explains that this event occurred years ago and many light-years away, and Earth is only seeing the results now. With this issue, it was decided to introduce science fiction elements into the back-up stories about cowboy Hank Roper and Native American Strong Bow, both of whom travel with Spurs to Mars when Queen Thula relates that the atmosphere is disappearing from the planet. This turns out to be a political ploy in an attempt to oust the queen. In the other stories, Roper investigates a flying saucer and a small planet that crashes into the desert—without causing a cataclysm—and Strong Bow deals with some visitors from planet Vulcan who are impersonating Aztecs; Roper appears in this story as well.

Space Western 43 features: Spurs using a magnet to round up and defeat some rock-like antagonists from a meteor, and defeating Communists who have launched their own flying saucers; Hank Roper using insecticide to kill off bug-like invaders from Neptune; and Strong Bow—who, as it turns out, is a descendant of the Aztecs and not from a North American tribe—discovering, inside a pyramid, a spaceship which takes him to Mercury. There he finds a princess who vanished from the pyramid 400 years earlier and hasn't aged a day. He frees her from her captors and they return to Earth; we never learn if she turns to dust in Earth's atmosphere.

In *Space Western* 44, Spurs, assisted by Hank and Strong Bow, uncovers a plot by Nazis who fled to Mars in a rocket at the end of World War II and are now firing explosive missiles that wipe out Paris, Moscow and other cities. In a sequel in the following issue, the Nazi leader, who turns out to be Adolf Hitler, escapes in a rocket and lands on an asteroid, where he immediately tries to lord it over the peaceful and simple-minded inhabitants. Fortunately the intrepid trio catch up with Hitler and kill him. *Space Western* 45, the final issue, features "The Valley That Time Forgot," in which Strong Bow rescues a pilot trapped atop a mesa populated by prehistoric beasts, little more than a blatant rip-off of Arthur Conan Doyle's *The Lost World*.

"The Moon Bat" in the same issue is one of the comic's better tales. Examining some photographs, a scientist notices strange bat-like shadows on the surface of the moon and asks Spurs to take him, his assistant Claire and Hank Roper to the moon in his rocketship. The details of the trip to the moon are far more credible than in previous issues, although it's a continuity flaw when Spurs suggests the unlikelihood of life on the moon when he's already encountered the voracious lunar borers in *Space Western* 41. They are about to give up their search when Spurs and the others locate steps leading down to a cavern where chained skeletons point to a lost civilization and human (or whatever) sacrifices. The idol of a bat suggests that this creature was worshiped by the now-dead moon people. The huge bat, still alive, nearly sinks its teeth into Claire before Hank effects a timely rescue.

The chief artist for the series, doing both the inside work and covers, was Stan Campbell, with John Belfi doing some pencils as well. Campbell's work looks best when he does large panels of rockets streaming through space and the like. "The Moon Bat" is better-drawn than his other stories.

4

DC; Dell

DC

Strange Adventures

DC Comics' long-running *Strange Adventures* first appeared in 1950. The first dozen or so issues were 52 pages in length; the later ones were 36. Boasting eye-catching covers featuring bizarre situations, it was an immediate hit with readers and one of the few comics that continued to sell well even after superhero titles began to proliferate. An unusual feature of the comic was that it not only credited the writers of the stories on the inside pages, but even on the covers, possibly a carry-over from sci-fi prose magazines.

The first story concerns a character who would appear a few more times, Chris KL99, also known as the 21st-century "Columbus of Space." Chris KL was the first baby to be born in outer space when his parents were travelling from the Earth to Mars. He won a 99 percent perfect rating at the space academy and was then known as Chris KL99. He is assigned to investigate different worlds and help map the cosmos with his companions Halk, a "Martian adventurer," and Jero, a "Venusian scientist." (Both of them are incorrectly described as "humans.")

In this first adventure, they discover a world where the inhabitants are radioactive and eat uranium, an element that some criminals want to exploit. Edmond Hamilton did the script with Howard Sherman on the art. In subsequent adventures, Chris dealt with giant robots, meant to be used in making repairs, coming under control of a would-be conqueror; and a strange rash of thefts of famous monuments on various planets. In *SA* 5, Chris KL99 and his companions shrink into a sub-atomic world where a benevolent ruler has been replaced by his evil twin brother.

Chris KL99 is not an especially memorable strip or character, but he is given a bit more dimension in "The Lost Earthmen" in *SA* 7. Here we learn what drives him to seek out new worlds: His parents took off in a spaceship while he stayed in school as a boy, and they and their companions, would-be colonizers, never returned. Now he takes off to find their ship, the *Starfarer*, and he finally does,

DC's *Strange Adventures* was immediately popular and ran for decades.

overjoyed to see the colonizers are still alive on a new world. Unfortunately, his parents are dead, having sacrificed their lives to steer the ship during a crash. Now this world is in danger from approaching asteroids, and Chris is stricken to think his parents' sacrifice may have been in vain. However, he is able to get the colonizers off-world before the asteroids turn it into his parents' funeral pyre. Chris decides to give up space exploration until he hears a tape left by his father, urging him to continue their mission (Hamilton-Infantino-Giella).

After a couple more adventures, Chris KL99 disappeared from *Strange Adventures,* replaced by the heroic Captain Comet, a mutant with special powers who wears a costume and battles aliens and assorted enemies from other worlds and times. Captain Comet predates the Silver Age when superheroes came to dominate the comics field. Since for all intents and purposes Captain Comet *is* a superhero (he even has a secret identity, Adam Blake), his exploits fall outside the scope of this book, but he appears in a great many issues of *Strange Adventures* and frequently gets the cover as well.

The second story in *SA* 1 is "The Girl Who Couldn't Die," written by David Vern and drawn by Paul Norris and Bernard Sachs. Darwin Jones of the DSI (Department of Scientific Investigation) is visited in his office by actress Eve Wilcox, who shoots herself, throws herself out a window, and isn't injured at all. The water in a pool she swam in while filming a movie in New Mexico apparently has certain properties that temporarily make her immortal. Darwin Jones made sporadic appearances in *Strange Adventures* over the years; his second appearance was in *SA* 48, investigating a "radar man" who comes from a society inside the Earth.

"The Second Deluge," also in *SA* 1, has a scientist, John Marquait, setting off a hydrogen bomb in an effort to end a deadly worldwide drought. While the rain comes, it never stops, until the world is in worse danger than it was before. Many arks are built to carry the populace, while one by one great cities disappear under the waves and all one can see is the very tips of such monuments as the Eiffel Tower. A despairing Marquait notices a cloud of steam coming from the ocean and theorizes that water has seeped through a crack in the Earth's crust and hit the molten core. In a bizarre sequence, he and a companion use diving suits to descend into the depths of underwater Manhattan, where there is a wonderful panel depicting sharks, octopi and other sea creatures swimming blissfully past skyscrapers. Retrieving another hydrogen bomb, Marquait sets this one off near the fissure, and the flood waters pour down into the depths of the earth, saving the world. The script was credited to Gardner Fox, although many believe that Edmond Hamilton was the true author. Jim Mooney and Sy Barry did the art. *Strange Adventures* 1 also contains another adaptation of the film *Destination Moon*, with a script by Gardner Fox and art by Curt Swan and John Fischetti. This shorter version is not as good as Fawcett Comics' full-length rendition (see Chapter 5).

SA 2 presents stories about an attempt to save the world from a runaway planet that in six months will crash into the Earth; a pilot who encounters flying saucers and their inhabitants but can't get anyone to believe him; and a sobering tale in which a visitor out of time shows a scientist depressing visions of wars both in the past and the future and urges the man to do all he can to prevent the destruction of humanity (Vern-Swan-Fuscgetti).

In "The Perfect Weapon" (*SA* 5), a scientist invents an invisible dome that will protect American cities from atomic bombs, but the authorities think he's a crackpot. He goes ahead and puts his dome over New York City, then is killed when he fights an enemy agent who wants his invention. Planes and trucks crash into the barrier. Food supplies and water can't get in. The millions of inhabitants are also in danger of suffocating. A friend of the scientist deduces that the dome would require vast amounts of electricity, so he tracks down the machine and shuts it off just before the military were about to drop a hydrogen bomb on the field, which might have destroyed the city as well. In David Vern and Gardner Fox' interesting story, it never occurs to anyone that the field might not go too far below the city's surface, and supplies could be brought in through underground access. (A similar dome story appears in *Strange Adventures* 51: A hoaxer sells air to the inhabitants of an island because they think the dome is still operating and their oxygen supply is running out.)

In "The Confessions of a Martian" (*SA* 6), a Martian spy has his mind transported into the body of Phil Mathers, a crew member of a lost moon mission. Mathers is then sent to Earth to do what he can to prevent Earth attacking Mars. Eventually his deception is uncovered when a lady scientist realizes he is using a fake identity and is actually the missing crewman. She doesn't believe his story of being a disguised Martian agent until some ugly green Martians show up (since he no longer believes that Earth intends to attack Mars, they consider him a traitor). One major weakness with the story by Manly Wade Wellman is that no one really gives a thought about Mathers, the man whose body is being used—we never learn if he's alive or dead, if he had a family, or if it's possible to bring his mind back. Swan and Fischetti did the art.

In the same issue, "Too Big for This World" presents a toddler who accidentally drinks a growth formula and becomes as tall as the Empire State Building. Undoubtedly this tale by Mann Rubin was influenced by H.G. Wells' "The Food of the Gods" and itself might have influenced *The Amazing Colossal Man*. (Decades later, *Honey, I Blew Up the Kid* had a similar premise and was played for laughs.) An alternate version of this story appears in *Strange Adventures* 28, "The Indestructible Giant": A colossal alien man appears out of nowhere and causes death and destruction by picking up and throwing crowded passenger trains, sinking boats, and recklessly stomping across cities. A powerful electrical weapon is used to kill him. Later, the authorities figure he was probably a lost alien child, and the things he destroyed were "toys" he was merely playing with.

"The Last Man and Woman" by Gardner Fox (*SA* 6) is notable for no other reason than it's an early example of stories in which the lead characters turn out to be Adam and Eve and the planet they are looking for is Earth. In this instance, a couple on another world put themselves in suspended animation so they can see what things will be like in a hundred years, but wind up sleeping for millions of years and finally awaken to discover their planet has been destroyed. After rejecting dozens of worlds over many more years, they settle on Earth. "Human Time Capsules" (*SA* 31) has a similar premise: People volunteer to be put to sleep for a thousand years, and will have one day every millennium to see what has become of the world before going back to sleep for another thousand years. They see the world nearly destroyed, humans rebuilding their society, mutations occurring over centuries, and invasions from space in John Broome's compelling if improbable story.

"The Vampire World," depicted on the dramatic and creepy cover for *Strange Adventures* 6, is written by Mann Rubin and drawn by Cresto. Earth is targeted by another world that has huge tentacles growing out of its surface. The tentacles, which have holes that resemble suckers, dig into various points around Earth and begin siphoning off the planet's natural resources—oil, gold, diamonds, coal and so on. The military of various countries discover that the tentacles are impervious to normal weapons. Since uranium is scattered all across the globe, it is decided to create a huge stockpile and coat it with hydrocyanic acid, which attracts the tentacles. The stuff proves so "indigestible" that the tentacles withdraw and the Earth is saved.

Strange Adventures 7 features Gardner Fox's cover story "The World of Giant Ants" (Oskner-Sachs), in which the little creatures harbor extreme hatred for mankind. When they grow to giant size, they set about killing people and destroying man-made structures. Fortunately they are unable to come up with the formula to make their growth permanent; once they shrink back to normal size, they are easy to defeat. This was published several years before the release of 1954's *Them!*, the giant ant thriller that was a big hit for Warner Brothers. The story is not as good nor as well-drawn as "World War III with the Ants," which appears six months later in *Captain Science* 6 (see Chapter 8).

Strange Adventures 23 also has a story about giant malevolent ants. These existed in prehistoric times and eventually became normal-sized, still plotting against mankind in the present day. It was almost a prequel to "The World of Giant Ants." Giant ants appear on subsequent covers as well, although gorilla covers seemed to engender the best sales figures.

Naturally *Strange Adventures* has stories of robots and automation, including "Revolt of the Humans" in *SA* 8. Human society is run by a towering machine that used to be a mere calculator but gradually gained intelligence. People are furnished with helmets as soon as they reach maturity, and through these helmets they are given orders. People who refuse to wear the helmets are called "Neos" and are hunted down and killed. Athor, a maintenance worker, worships the mighty machine but his serenity is threatened when he learns that a pretty woman, Ilvra, whom he covered for when she was on the run, has been marked for execution. Learning the history of the machine and how it does the thinking for the human race, Athor manages to remove his helmet, rescues Ilvra, and destroys the machine. The ending suggests that it will not be easy for a free humanity to rebuild society without the help of the machine. The story is by John Broome, with art by Jim Mooney and Ray Burnley. (It may have been an influence on Ira Levin's novel *This Perfect Day*.)

End-of-the-world stories were also popular. In "The Last Days of Earth," two runaway planets head towards a cataclysmic collision with Earth. Although scripted by Gardner Fox, this was basically an uncredited "borrowing" of Edwin Balmer and Philip

Wylie's 1933 novel *When Worlds Collide*, which was filmed in 1951. Just as in Balmer and Wylie's story, there is a race to build spaceships, a lottery to see who will win seats on said spaceships, riots as the end of days rapidly approach, etc., but as an adaptation this is well-done, with a good art job from Carmine Infantino and Joe Giella. In another end-of-the-world story, *SA* 55's "The Day the Sun Exploded" (Broome-Kane-Sachs), worldwide heat has humanity sheltering in large "refrigi-houses" that each hold 50,000 people. They must wear special protective clothing to go outdoors; water is rapidly evaporating. Although many elements are different, including the exact cause of the disaster, the story is similar to the movie *The Day the Earth Caught Fire* (1962). In the '60s, *The Twilight Zone* featured an episode with a similar premise.

Mann Rubin's "The Brain of Dr. Royer," drawn by Alex Toth and Bernard Sachs, could very well have been a major influence on the film *Fantastic Voyage*. In both comic and movie, a scientist with important knowledge locked in his mind suffers a serious brain injury that can only be healed from the inside. In both story and movie, someone is shrunk in size so they can enter the scientist's body—in this case through the ear canal—and make his way to the brain. Instead of an hour as in the movie, the microscopic intruder in the story has two hours to work his magic. Instead of reverting to normal size, he will remain at his minuscule stature if he isn't returned to normal before the two hours are up.

Strange Adventures occasionally came up with a great cover idea but the story inside was a major disappointment. (The covers were generally dreamed up *before* the stories were written.) Such was the situation with *SA* 21's "The Monster That Fished for Men," which depicts a giant fish-creature hooking a startled fisherman and lifting him out of his boat. The story—in which the fisherman is certain that a poisonous volcanic lake holds lifeforms and is mocked for thinking so—is a dumb comic piece in which the fish-monster who snags and loses the human can't convince the rest of his fish-folk that there are lifeforms on the surface. "*Aah!* You and your crazy fish stories!" says one of his underwater companions. Jack Miller and Murphy Anderson were the creative team. Another example is *SA* 52, which depicts a man inside a giant bird cage, held aloft by the beak of a monstrous parakeet. "Here's your new pet, dear," the bird says to his mate, who responds "How wonderful—it talks!" The story inside is a bit better than the fish story but not by much. Atomic testing, plus radiation from a meteor, have turned ordinary birds into giant monsters. The somewhat whimsical tone of John Broome's story is at odds with the opening, in which several airliners are downed—apparently by the birds, although it's never made clear if this is deliberate or accidental—with much loss of life.

Although there were more thoughtful stories in the early days of *Strange Adventures*, gradually the trend was towards silly, even schlocky tales with goofy-looking aliens and many people with superhero-like abilities (telepathy, telekinesis, super-speed, etc.). However, the comic still occasionally published more compelling tales, such as "The Millionaire Robot" in *SA* 53 and its sequel "The Robot Dragnet" in *SA* 54. Harvey Murdock is surprised to learn that his wealthy uncle has left all of his money to someone named Tim Steele, who turns out to be a highly intelligent robot. The uncle died in an accidental fall while the robot was nowhere near him. The will holds up in court, but Harvey is confused when the robot uses the money to buy expensive cars and yachts only to trash them. Suspicious, Harvey investigates and figures out how Steele killed his uncle and forged the dead man's signature on his will. Steele is arrested and sentenced to death, but ordinary methods of execution fail to kill him.

In the less interesting second half, Steele runs amok; the military uses explosives, acids, and other things against him, but nothing works. Finally Harvey comes up with a clever solution, using deception to make the robot think he is losing power. When he goes to the uncle's laboratory to recharge, the battery he uses actually causes his brain to stop functioning. The story is by Otto Binder with art by Henry Sharp and Joe Giella. Binder also wrote the famous short story "I, Robot" and several sequels for pulp magazines; "The Millionaire Robot" is the flip side of that story, presenting an evil metal being instead of a heroic and benign one. (It is not to be confused with Isaac Asimov's "I, Robot.")

Some of the comic's more whimsical stories have a certain degree of charm. In *SA* 57's "The Riddle of Animal 'X'" (Binder-Kane-Giella), a boy discovers a very unusual marsupial-like animal in the woods; it has strange habits and a very weird diet. Eventually the boy and his father take the animal to where he first appeared, and discover a wrecked spaceship with a more humanoid creature inside. The father assumes he is the pilot and the other animal is his pet, but it develops that it is just the opposite: The "pet" was trying to gather material with which he could repair the spaceship, which he does. Before he goes, he gives the boy a kangaroo from Australia to make up for his absence.

Other memorable stories in the comic during the Golden Age include:

- "The 1000 Year Old Man" (*SA* 15): A scientist's formula for immortality has left him alive but calcified, unable to move, and no one realizes simple H_2O will return him to normal.
- "The Spaceship from Nowhere" (29): People from a sub-atomic world created in a lab escape from their planet's destruction in a rocket, only to meet death in an encounter with a housekeeper and her vacuum.
- "The Magic Typewriter" (31): A typist comes up with formulas for amazing inventions when she goes into a trance, but she may be hiding a dangerous secret.
- "The Return of the Conqueror" (40): A space hero is convinced that someday the world will erect a statue of him celebrating his exploits, but it his quieter brother who actually saves the world.
- "The Eye-Dropper World" (42): A scientist watches in fascination and horror as paramecium, grown larger, create their own technologically advanced society.

- "No Eyes Can See Me" (45): A bitter man uses invisibility to get revenge on a rival but outfoxes himself.
- "The Invisible Spaceman" (55): An astronaut returns to Earth but no one can see or hear him. This strange situation enables him to prevent a child's death.

Strange Adventures continued well into the Silver Age (see Chapter 11).

Mystery in Space

Mystery in Space, heralding "Strange Stories of the Future," debuted in 1951 as a 52-page magazine; the page count was reduced after only a few issues. The lead feature belongs to the Galaxy Knights, a group of police officers whose "beat" is the entire solar system. The main character of "Nine Worlds to Conquer" is Lyle, the new recruit, who is anxious to prove himself, and does so when he rescues Commander Ortho's beautiful daughter Ora from the dual menaces of Prof. Vorko and his twin brother, Capt. Korvo. The script is by Robert Kanigher, a prolific DC writer, with art by Carmine Infantino and Frank Giacoia.

The Galaxy Knights appear in subsequent issues, and Lyle quickly becomes their biggest hero and practically takes over the group. Often at his side is Ora, who seems just as brave. In one story, he pretends to be radioactive and banishes himself into space when his real plan is to take on a villain and his gang all by his lonesome, protecting the other knights. In another story, a character called the Master of Doom sends the Knights back to the 20th century, where they save the planet from destruction when a hydrogen bomb causes a chain reaction that causes such heat the Statue of Liberty begins to melt. Lyle and his companions not only save the day 1000 years in the past, but also mop up the Master of Doom when they return to the 30th century.

In "Challenge of the Robot Knight" (*MIS* 7), Ora, the chief scientist at Knights HQ, decides to apply for membership in the group and is basically told to go take a vacation on Venus instead; her patronizing father tells her that she won't even be allowed to apply, that the tests are too tough and the job too dangerous (despite the courage she has already displayed in previous stories). Lyle is also unsupportive. Lyle is disturbed that she leaves without saying goodbye, but her father says: "She'll forget all about it by the time she returns—and be just as enthusiastic about a new pair of sandals from Mercury. You know how women are!" Ora disguises herself as a robot to apply for membership and passes every test, but is nearly undone when she forgets that her metal shell isn't immune to a magnetic force ray. Lyle saves her life, and at the end she is accepted into the knights.

Mystery in Space 8 features the Galaxy Knights' last appearance, in a story in which Merlin the Magician switches the minds of the Knights of the Round Table with the Knights of the 30th century. Under the tutelage and leadership of Ora, the time-lost knights of Camelot perform better than expected, and when their minds are switched back into their proper time and bodies, Lyle and his buddies take care of Merlin.

Most of the *Mystery in Space* stories are stand-alones. In *MIS* 1's "The Men Who Lived Forever" (Broome-Toth-Barry), people from a world in another dimension kidnap a scientist, Alfred Dean, who is just about to unveil a Life Globe that will grant humankind immortality. They tell him that their world is far more advanced and their people have been immortal for centuries, but their race lacks initiative and ambition because of it. Anyone who tries to destroy or even speaks out against the immortality ray is sent to the Valley of Execution, where they march down a series of steps until they die. They beg Dean to forget about introducing his Life Globe to Earth, and ask him to determine where the ray that keeps everyone on their world from dying was hidden by the original inventor. While being chased by robots, Dean deduces that the ray machine is in the Valley of Execution and destroys it. Back on Earth, he smashes the Life Globe.

Mystery in Space 2 features "The Micro-Men," in which four scientists, experimenting with a cosmic ray condenser, suddenly shrink down to only a few inches. They can reverse their reduced status with equipment in their New York laboratory, but have a devil of a time getting there. In *Perils of Pauline*-type situations, they contend with a huge snake; an eagle that nearly flies off with one of the men; a child who thinks they're dolls and picks a man up; a cat who sees them as mice, and so on. Edmond Hamilton wrote the exciting script, and the art job is by Irwin Hasen and Bob Lander.

MIS 3 features one of the most bizarre stories to ever appear in a science fiction comic, "Heroes Out of Time," written by Manly Wade Wellman. Lady scientist Anne uses a time machine to snatch Dr. Indigo Maylor from 200 years ago, just before he was hanged. Maylor, a botanist who was condemned to death for allegedly practicing black magic, at first seems grateful, but then uses his abilities to grow vegetables, especially carrots, much larger and animate them. He orders his plants to attack Anne and her fiancé Carr, and they barely escape. Anne then figures they can use the help of a great strategist from the past, and Anne uses her time machine to pull Benjamin Franklin and then Napoleon Bonaparte into the 20th century! These two are able to direct a counter-attack against the killer vegetables. Maylor is called back to the past to face his executioner, and "Poor Richard" and Napoleon also return to their normal eras. This absurd but fun story was drawn by Bob Oskner and Bernard Sachs.

"The Case of the Counterfeit Humans" (*MIS* 7) presents an interesting and potentially terrifying dilemma as Capt. Madden and his co-pilot Boone land on a planet and encounter some weird, shapeless aliens, who promptly turn into perfect duplicates of Boone. The doubles all have the same memories as Boone, and scientific equipment can't tell the doppelgangers from the real thing. Madden realizes that he can't take these strange alien lifeforms back to Earth with him—they could literally duplicate anyone and everyone and cause untold havoc—so he tells whichever is the real Boone that he *must* leave him behind. However, he can then pick out the real man when he sees that only one of the multiple Boones has sweat streaming down his forehead. The story was written by Gardner Fox and drawn by John Giunta.

One of the most amusing stories ever published in the comic appears in *Mystery in Space* 23. In "Monkey-Rocket to Mars," written by Otto Binder and drawn by Gil Kane and Joe Giella, two adorable chimps are sent to the Red Planet, although they are not supposed to exit the rocket. But some friendly green Martians "free" the chimps and assume they are the dominant life form of Earth. The chimps behave as chimps generally do, utterly confusing the Martians, who assume that there is no accounting for earthly behavior and traditions. The Martians are desperate to communicate with the chimps because there has been a locust infestation and the Martians hope that Earthlings can save their people from starving. When one of the insects bites a chimp and he angrily flings it to the ground and stomps on it, the Martians assume that he understands what the dilemma is: They need to *stomp out* the locusts. They set the chimps up in a lab where the playful animals manage to come up with a batch of chemicals which, put into a spray, do indeed kill off the locusts. Cheered as heroes, and even given a parade, the chimps return to their rocket, which takes off on schedule and returns to Earth, where a scientist realizes that he probably gave the chimps his cold. It was viruses that killed off the locusts, not the spray!

Whimsy began taking over the series: One cover shows Earthlings breaking out into laughter at the sight of two aliens (but only because the aliens exhale laughing gas). There were stories such as "The Last Television Broadcast on Earth," with cosmic dust from a comet putting an end to even the possibility of telecasts. Writer Bill Finger's solution is for images from TV shows to be broadcast on the moon—several shows at once—with special goggles allowing viewers to see whichever program they prefer. Apparently the notion of cable television never occurred to Finger back in 1955. The art for the story is by Sid Greene and Joe Giella. Certain covers and story concepts were later reused in the great superhero revival of the Silver Age, especially in *Justice League of America*.

A series of stories about the Interplanetary Insurance Incorporated (or I.I.I.) and its agent Bert Brandon appeared periodically in *Mystery in Space*. It would always seem as if Brandon is getting fired but manages to save the day at the last minute. In one case, he provides insurance for a race of people who are so healthy they seem unlikely to die, only it turns out that they shed their old bodies to turn into a kind of butterfly race, and consider those old bodies to be "dead." Bert has to pay up until he figures out how to make up his losses via another race on the same planet. In another story, he insures an entire planet only to find out that it's doomed to destruction. The whole thing turns out to be a case of insurance fraud. Bert gives a policy to a man to ensure against his drowning in a Martian canal—unlikely as the client can't handle space travel—but he is found dead in a pool on Earth that is filled with water from one of the canals of Mars. Fortunately for Bert, the fact that the man was murdered means that Bert doesn't have to pay off.

In *MIS* 23, the clever installment "The Living Camera" (Sid Gerson-Carmine Infantino) features a man who has to have his identity checked with a photograph of his retina before he can claim a million-dollar beneficiary payout. When he refuses to allow anyone to take a photograph of his eye, Bert is at his wits' end. Then he uses a bizarre creature called a Belvedere Polaroid [sic] Bear, whose third eye—in the middle of its forehead—can snap pictures of anything. The would-be beneficiary goes to great lengths to stop Bert from getting the photograph from the bear, the reason being that the beneficiary is actually the "dead" man, perpetrating more insurance fraud.

Mystery in Space also presents occasional stories starring the Space Cabbie, a cosmic taxi driver with his own small rocket—shaped, improbably, exactly like a 20th-century taxi—that picks up passengers and hitchhikers. This series replaced I.I.I. but is not as memorable.

Other notable stories in the series include:

- "The Unknown Spaceman" (*MIS* 11): There is much speculation over what the inhabitant of a spaceship about to land on Earth will look like, but no one realizes that the spaceship *is* the alien, and they inadvertently kill it by greedily taking souvenirs and dismantling it.
- "The Richest Man on Nine Planets" (12): A man weary with his lot in life repeatedly puts himself in suspended animation and discovers the interest in his bank account has made him a millionaire centuries later, but investing in gold proves to be his undoing when the metal becomes so commonplace it's worthless.
- "The Planet Nobody Wanted" (13): Colonizers arrive on what seems to be a perfect planet and announce their intention to relocate the inhabitants and take over their world for themselves. They are unaware that the sun is about to explode.
- "Hollywood in Space" (14): Aliens made of crystal who can't travel through space try to invade Earth by allowing Hollywood filmmakers to capture their images on film; their images can actually emerge from the movie.
- "Journey to the Pygmy World" (28): Compressed to microscopic size, a scientist goes in search of a little boy who is lost on a perfectly recreated model of Jupiter.

Mystery into Space continued to be published in the Silver Age and underwent a brief revival in the Bronze Age.

Dell

Tom Corbett, Space Cadet

Dell's *Tom Corbett, Space Cadet* was an adaptation of a popular TV show that ran variously on all three major networks from 1950 to 1955, with Frankie Thomas in the title role. The comic appeared in 1952. Corbett, a cadet in a Space Academy, has adventures with fellow cadets Astro and the perpetually kvetching Roger Manning, often under the auspices of Captain Strong. One interesting tale has them adopting a cute animal called a pikpup, whose power to cast realistic illusions is at first alarming and then proves helpful. In *Tom Corbett* 7, the boys help when an older cadet gets in trouble for releasing his brother, who claims he is innocent, from a prison planet. In the following issue, a magnetic field pulls Tom's ship, the *Polaris,* onto Saturn, where they deal with a ragtag band of men who have been shipwrecked there for years. Other lifeforms, such as a giant tiger, are even more dangerous. The comic stories are never *too* fantastic, but the science is never very accurate. In the eleventh and final issue, the boys travel to the swamps of Venus, which would resemble the Everglades were it not for the presence of dinosaur-like water broncs and octopus-trees with strangling tentacles. Prize Comics came out with its own Tom Corbett series in 1955.

5

EC; Fawcett

EC

Weird Science *Volume One*

EC Comics, most famous—or infamous—for its graphic horror comics, also ran a line of science fiction and fantasy comics, beginning in 1950 with the first volume of *Weird Science* (whose numbering began with issue 12). Two of the stories are fairly standard—one about invaders with three eyes who are infiltrating American society, the another about a failed experiment to discover what happens after death. But the first two tales are distinguished by their harrowing and compelling nature. The cover story, "Lost in the Microcosm," is taken, uncredited, from Henry Hasse's 1936 prose story "He Who Shrank." It has a scientist's assistant accidentally shrinking down to sub-atomic size, down into the professor's palm, where a white blood corpuscle tries to ingest him. Then he shrinks further down and discovers that each atom is a tiny solar system with its own planets; then further again, where he becomes a giant to the people on alien worlds. Soon he shrinks down out of sight in front of their disbelieving eyes … and down and down and down. "One hour I'd be large enough to destroy a planet … and the next I could be devoured by a house-fly," he muses. On one world, he manages to contact a scientist to tell him of his problem in the hopes *this* civilization will be advanced enough to save him, but he again shrinks into nothingness in front of the sympathetic professor—who then wonders if the whole encounter even happened: "Can it be that this Earth is just a puny world within a world…?" The script is by Bill Gaines and Al Feldstein with art by Harvey Kurtzman.

The next story, "Dream of Doom," written by Harry Harrison and drawn by Harrison and Wally Wood, presents an artist who is tormented by dreams, so many dreams that he is never certain if he is awake or not, nightmares in which he kills or is killed, falls asleep at the wheel of his car to find his family dead, wakes up in the middle of a play he doesn't remember attending, tells it all to his psychiatrist only to wake and find that *this* was all a dream, one torturous nightmare after another—and there is no end. Even good things that happen to him, such as enjoying the

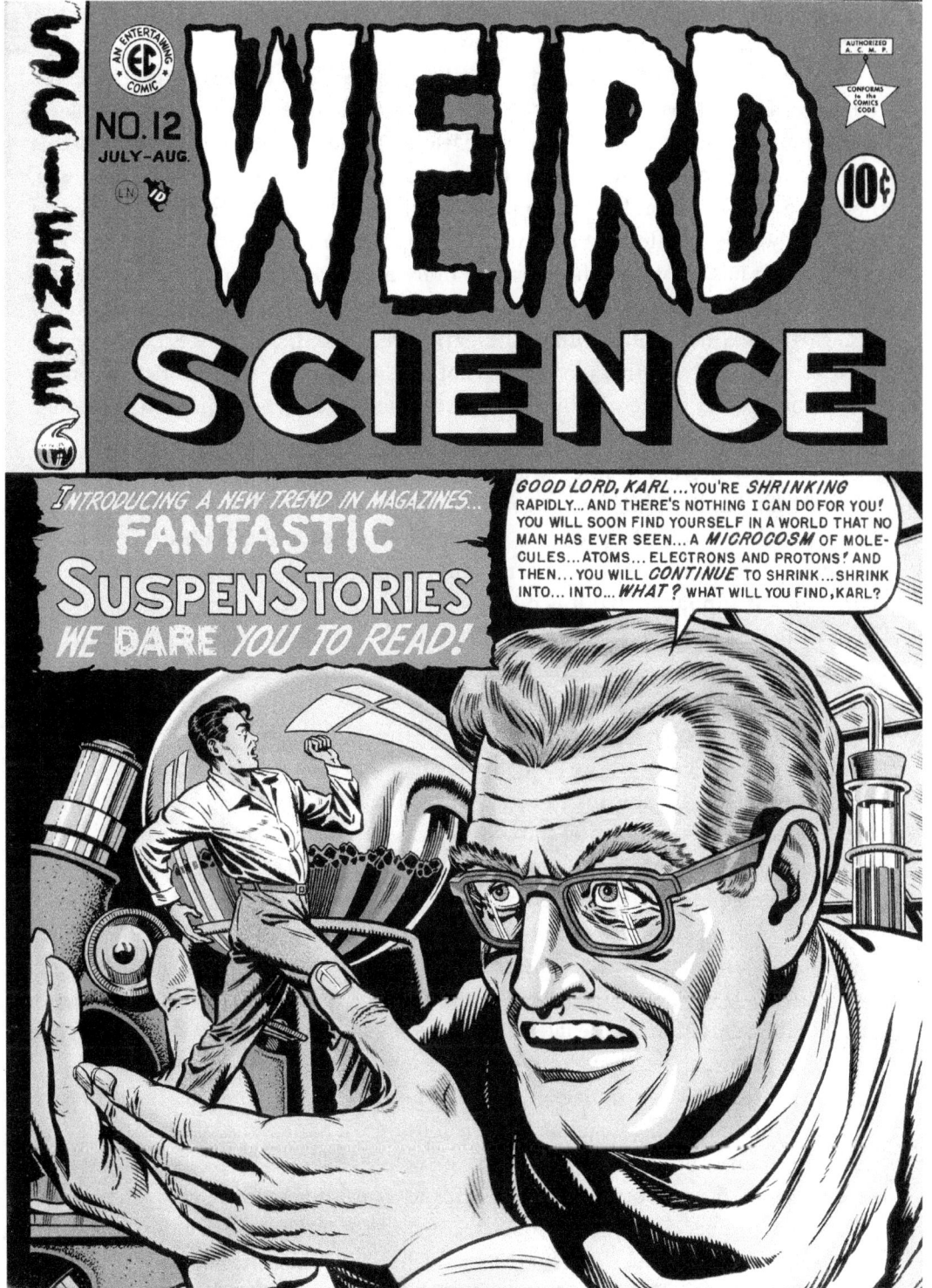

Weird Science #12 presents the harrowing "Lost in the Microcosm."

admiration and applause of his peers at the office, turn out to be dreams, things that never truly happened. There is no surcease.

Weird Science 13's "The Flying Saucer Invasion" succinctly deconstructs the hysteria over UFOs, the reactions of the public, officials, representatives of foreign governments, and the like. The Secretary of Defense gathers together everyone who ever claimed to see a flying saucer, and is able to debunk their stories one by one: alcoholism, a hallucination brought on by malaria, a delusion caused by a high fever, twisters, weather balloons and so on. Right after the news breaks that the War Department has disproved the existence of flying saucers, scientists in an observatory note thousands of flying saucers heading directly for Earth. ("The Micro-Race," also in *Weird Science* 13, in which a scientist creates a microscopic race to observe their progress, only for them to blow up both themselves and the scientist, is considered another story influenced by Theodore Sturgeon's "Microcosmic God," although there are major differences.)

Weird Science 15's "Panic!" was inspired by the 1938 Orson Welles *War of the Worlds* Martian invasion radio broadcast. Carson Walls is horrified to learn how many people believed the program was a real newscast and panicked, resulting in deaths and many injuries. Years later, Walls is importuned to recreate the broadcast, but is told to announce that it is purely fictional immediately before the show and even while it is playing. *Real* invaders from Jupiter land on Earth at just that time, the announcements ensuring that no one thinks the invasion is actually happening; the aliens are easily able to take control.

In the same issue, Harvey Kurtzman's "The Radioactive Child" details how a little boy named Pedro, whose parents were irradiated by atomic testing, develops a genius-level IQ and is able to tell Perez, the stupid dictator of Argenta, how to organize the government. Heeding the boy's advice, Perez takes over the rest of South America but incurs the wrath of the United States. When Pedro is slow to respond to Perez's demands that he come up with a hydrogen bomb, he hits the child, who reverts to a normal little boy. The U.S. bombs Argenta into submission, killing Perez and his cabinet. Pedro and the other children survive.

Weird Science 15 also includes "I Created a ... Gargantua" (Feldstein-Kamen), a compelling variation on the later film *The Amazing Colossal Man* (1957). Laughed at for being short and skinny, John Paulsen contacts Prof. Kohlvarb, who has experimented with growth stimulation, creating an outsized cat and rat. The professor gives the young man the formula; it turns John into a handsome, athletic six-footer. But the professor is unable to *stop* John's growth: He shoots up to six foot six, then seven foot six, and so on. As he continues to grow, he can only get jobs in freak shows or at lumber camps, but he has to consume so much food that his employers always fire him because he costs them so much. Finally he is transported by special railroad car to a stadium, where crowds are charged money to witness the towering giant of a man. He grows to 150 feet, then 300, and finally outgrows the stadium, taking refuge in Central Park. Editorials comment on how the city is paying his tremendous food bills while other Americans are starving, and it is decided that John must be killed. As planes drop bombs on him, John, now 700 feet tall, bolts from the park, crashing into the Empire State Building and knocking it over. When he dives into the ocean, depth charges finally put an end to his tormented existence.

Weird Science *Volume 2*

The second volume of *Weird Science*, whose numbering begins with issue five, came out in 1951. "Spawn of Venus," which appears in *WS* 6, is a good, old-fashioned monster story in which astronauts land on Venus and encounter man-eating plants and a voracious blob that devours two of their number. The survivors return to Earth with a beautiful flower which they believe to be benign, but from it oozes another blob that grows to gigantic size and threatens the world. A bomb seemingly destroys the creature but its many pieces turn into more blobs and mankind is doomed. Gaines and Feldstein were the creative team. Seven years later, a man-eating ooze from outer space starred in the motion picture *The Blob* (1958).

A better space-monster story, "Seeds of Jupiter," appears in *Weird Science* 8. Seeds that resemble peach pits fall onto the deck of a ship, and a sailor is urged to try one. When he swallows it, his body begins dehydrating as the thing inside him absorbs all the water in his system. The ship's doctor tries opening up the sailor's stomach, but the man dies as hideous, green squiggling things tear out of his body. (Decades later, an alien horror bursts out of the chest of a crew member in *Alien*.) This thing escapes into the ocean, snares ships and the people on them for dinner, and eventually grows so large that it nearly covers all of lower Manhattan. The military sever the one tentacle that it always keeps in the water; deprived of H_2O, it shrivels back into its dormant state. Meanwhile, in Washington, D.C., where the other "peach pits" have been taken for study, an ignorant cleaning lady dumps them all into the sewer system. This was another Gaines and Feldstein co-production.

Male-female relationships are often scrutinized in the EC sci-fi books. In "Divide and Conquer" (*WS* 6), a scientist working on a formula to create duplicates of animals discovers that his younger wife is not only having an affair but also plotting to murder him. She stabs him to death, but it turns out she only killed a duplicate. Her real husband then injects *her* with the formula, resulting in two women who are half their size. The fission continues and she keeps splitting into more and more duplicates as they get smaller and smaller. Eventually there are a thousand tiny replicas of her which he stomps underfoot. Her lover shows up and is nearly driven to madness by what he sees (Gaines-Feldstein-Kamen).

In *WS* 10's "The Maidens Cried" (Feldstein-Gaines-Wood), astronauts searching the universe for resources come upon a race of beautiful women whose male counterparts are wizened and ugly. The astronauts are bewitched by the females and decide to stay on the planet and marry some of the women. Only later do they realize that the women are a kind of insect life who lay eggs inside the male, resulting in the birth of a hideous creature that first devours the husband and then encases itself in a globe from which eventually comes—one of the beautiful women. Although the men's fates are undoubtedly awful, today's reader might be less sympathetic due to the fact that the astronauts are certified male chauvinist pigs, enjoying the fact that the women are unable to talk and that they wait on them hand and foot.

Another *anti*-romantic tale appears in Weird Science 13: "A Weighty Decision" (Gaines-Feldstein-Wood). Major Allan spends months preparing to command the first flight to the moon. During these months he falls in love with Mirna, the daughter of the professor who built the rocket. As the great day nears, Mirna begs Allan to turn down the assignment, but as much as he loves Mirna he refuses. On the day the rocket takes off, much more fuel is needed than should have been the case, until Allan and the other men aboard discover that Mirna is a stowaway; she wants to be with him in case he doesn't make it back. Now it will be impossible for the ship to return to Earth unless there's a reduction in weight. (This was also a plot point in the film *Destination Moon*, which was released the previous year.) Although Allan volunteers to sacrifice his life, he is reminded that the other two men aboard can't pilot the ship. The grim realization is reached that everyone on board is needed to get back to Earth with the exception of Mirna, who makes the ultimate sacrifice. Although the story is contrived to either cause a lump in the throat—or could just as likely be a sick misogynous joke—one can't feel *too* sorry for Mirna as her actions are so utterly foolish.

Although many of these EC sci-fi stories are little different from the ones in DC's or other publishers, EC did on occasion publish tales that were decidedly on the edgier side. Such was "There'll Be Some Changes Made" (Gaines-Feldstein-Wood), in Weird Science 14, in which a ship in distress lands on an unknown planet and encounters an unusual society in which the people, when frightened, huddle in individual shell-like structures. Commander Morrison is immediately struck by the blond beauty of a woman named Luwana and she seems equally intrigued by him. After the ship repairs are made, Morrison shocks his companions by telling them that he has fallen in love with Luwana and that he is remaining on the planet to marry her. After the others leave, Morrison and Luwana wed, but he discovers that the women of the planet have no maternal instincts. The children are raised by others and then emerge from the aforementioned structures when they are ready. He also notices that Luwana seems to be losing interest in being romantic with him. Investigating further, he discovers that she belongs to a race that are modeled on a type of hermaphroditic snail, and that periodically they change their sex. Morrison returns to the home he shares with Luwana and discovers that she has transformed into a rather handsome blond hunk. Luwana then wonders when Morrison will "hurry up and change so things can be normal again." Although Morrison will not be able to change his gender, the story pulls away from the notion of homosexuality that it raises.

"Fifty Girls Fifty" (Gaines-Feldstein-Williamson) in *WS* 20 is the type of story you would *never* have seen on *Twilight Zone, Outer Limits* or any other TV program of the '50s and '60s. The protagonist of this dark and fascinating story is Sid, a gleeful sociopath and the ultimate sexual predator. He is one of 100 men and women who sign up for a century-long space journey, most of which will be spent in suspended animation, to another world. However, Sid, who is in charge of the freeze units, deliberately awakens only a couple of years into the trip and murders all of the men while they are helpless so that he will be alone on the ship with 50 attractive women. Sid couldn't care less about reaching and colonizing this distant planet—all he wants is to thaw out one woman after another, have his way with her, and then kill her via refreezing (once thawed out, no one can be refrozen and live). Sid can spend over a year with each woman until he gets bored and move on to the next one. He meets his match in power-mad Wendy, the second woman he thaws, who tells him that she loves him and that they should thaw out the others one by one once they arrive and thereby become master of them all. Wendy kills Sid, but he will have the last laugh as she doesn't realize she will be long dead before the ship ever reaches its destination.

Although EC reserved most of its gruesome shock stories for its horror mags, some of the sci-fi stories clearly have horrific undertones. In "Bum Steer" (*WS* 15), a group of kidnapped Earthmen realize that they are being fattened for slaughter and consumption by their extraterrestrial captors, who use a beautiful woman as a decoy to get them to walk blissfully to their doom. Definitely in the realm of EC's "shocksuspense" is "Disassembled" (*WS* 18), in which a radio operator innocently takes apart a device in a flying saucer without realizing it's a living robotic being. Then *he* is dissected (as revealed quite graphically in the final panel), reduced to muscles, internal organs and disembodied limbs by the robot's companion (Gaines-Feldstein-Joe Orlando).

"Keyed Up!" (*WS* 19), a mini-masterpiece in the sci-fi–horror genre, was also written and drawn by the Gaines-Feldstein-Orlando combo. Due to his drunkenness, a man named Benson is accidentally responsible for the deaths of all other spaceship crew members except Guernsey. During the four years that they are making their way back to Earth, Guernsey has not said one word to Benson, nearly driving the latter crazy. Guernsey breaks his silence only to tell Benson that he will make sure he is prosecuted for his actions upon their return. Not wanting to go to jail, Benson contrives to trap Guernsey outside the ship during a repair job, but Guernsey's corpse, near a porthole, stays on the ship due to his magnetized boots. Unable to deal with the accusing eyes of the decomposing corpse, Benson tries to blast the corpse away, but only succeeds in damaging it further. Finally he steps completely outside to deal with the body, but while he manages to get it detached from the ship, he discovers that the key that will allow him entry back into the ship, stuck to one of the corpse's boots, has floated off with the body.

EC had run stories by Ray Bradbury without crediting him at first, but eventually they did approved adaptations of some of his tales, such as "Mars is Heaven!"

in *Weird Science* 18. In this classic and poignant story, a ship lands on Mars and the crew members are shocked to find what resembles a stereotypical small American town. Exploring the place, they come across humans who swear they are living on Earth, even though there's no doubt to the astronauts that *they* are on Mars. Then the crew members start running into long-dead friends and relatives. The captain encounters his brother, who also died years ago but looks just as he did then, and is taken home to see their parents. Confused but overjoyed, he is basically told just to be grateful that things are as they are. But as the captain sleeps in the bedroom with his brother, he can't help but wonder about it all, and it occurs to him that this would be a perfect way for Martians, if they were malevolent, to catch him and his crew unawares and kill them in their sleep. The next day, the men are buried and the rocket is destroyed by "humans" with strangely shifting faces. The story was drawn by Wally Wood. *Weird Science* adapted a few other Bradbury stories, including "Outcast of the Stars," in which a poor man contrives to make his children think they've gone on a never-to-be-forgotten trip in a rocketship.

Other memorable stories in the series:

- "Transformation Complete" (*WS* 10): When a possessive father uses a formula to turn his daughter's fiancé into a woman, she uses a similar formula to outwit him and turn herself into a man.
- "Why Papa Left Home" (11): A man travels into the past where he meets and marries a woman who turns out to be his mother, and winds up becoming his own father.
- "The Last Man" (12): The only surviving male of an Earth-destroying disaster comes upon a beautiful woman, the last woman on Earth—who turns out to be his long-lost sister.
- "Chewed Out!" (12): A general awaits the descent of an alien spaceship, not realizing its minuscule size, and inadvertently kills the crew when the ship lands in some sauerkraut and winds up on a hot dog he is devouring.
- "Snap Ending!" (18): A spaceship lands on a tiny moon orbiting a planet 3000 times the size of Earth, and it turns out to be a balloon belonging to a gargantuan alien child.
- "EC Confidential" (21): The publisher of *Weird Science* asks Al Feldstein and Bill Gaines why so many of their stories come true, and tells him he suspects they are subversives. They respond that they are trying to alert the public to such dangers as a Martian invasion and then reveal that they and their co-workers are the last remnants of a Venusian society.

Weird Fantasy *Volume One*

EC's *Weird Fantasy* Volume One also debuted in 1950, the numbering beginning with 13. The first issue is a mixed bag. "Am I Man or Machine?" (Gaines-Feldstein) presents the story of Roger Harvey, whose brain is saved by two scientists who removed it from his body when it is smashed in a car accident. They keep the brain alive and build him a fairly convincing robot body. He goes to see his fiancée, who has thought him dead all this time, and has married another. She agrees

In *Weird Fantasy* #15, the Department of Defense is taken over by Martians.

to divorce her husband, but Roger realizes a man of metal would never make a fit mate for her and sadly leaves her. You expect the story to end with Roger killing the two men who did this to him, but he seems to feel no anger towards them at all.

"Only Time Will Tell" in the same issue has a scientist going back in time and encountering himself. In another trite story, "…Trip in the Unknown," astronauts land on an unfriendly planet that has just suffered an atomic war and which, of course, turns out to be Earth. "The Men of Tomorrow" (Feldstein-Kamen) is a more interesting piece in which a jungle expedition comes across a futuristic city where no one ever utters a word. It develops that these people communicate via telepathy; when the explorers teach them language, they completely lose this ability. As a telepathic society, there could never be any lying or deception of any kind, but that all changes once they have to resort to speech, and it isn't long before the society is fractured and then destroyed.

Weird Fantasy 14 contains a poor story in which Bill Gaines and Al Feldstein appear at an editorial conference and discuss a tale about a cosmic bomb, something they made up but which ignites the curiosity of FBI agents. At the end of the story, Washington D.C. blows up. There is also a horror story about a love potion that backfires, a time travel piece in which a man tries to save his dead fiancée but ends up killing her, and a minor ironic tale of a spy who steals an atomic formula and winds up stranded on Bikini Atoll just before a detonation. In a *Weird Fantasy* 15 story, a man is taken into the future to be murdered, then is instantly pulled back to the past, where he has to wait helplessly for his death to occur in a matter of days, unable to do anything to prevent it. This intriguing plot has a flat wind-up.

Weird Fantasy 16 features a story, "The Last City"—very similar to "The Perfect Weapon" in *Strange Adventures* 5—in which a scientist invents a force field to protect New York from atomic bombs. But the population starves and suffocates because the dome can't be dissipated. After nuclear war destroys all life on Earth, alien visitors discover the city perfectly preserved but with everyone in it long dead. Both stories appeared in print only a couple of months apart, so it is probable that both were influenced by Arthur L. Zagat's story "The Lanson Screen."

In "Second Childhood" (Gaines-Feldstein-Kamen), a doctor injects himself with a formula to retard the aging process. But it works too well: He becomes younger and younger, finally turning him into a child who thinks his wife is his mother. As the child turns into an infant, his horrified spouse wonders how it will all end. "A Trip to a Star" (Gaines-Feldstein-Wood) has two astronauts thinking they've gone through a space warp and entered a new dimension, but then discovering they were actually "quick-frozen" for a million years and have arrived back on Earth and into a completely changed society. While not horror stories per se, the situations are certainly terrible for the protagonists. The following issue, *Weird Fantasy* 17, is distinguished only by its mediocrity in both story and art.

Weird Fantasy *Volume Two*

Nineteen fifty-one brought the second volume of *Weird Fantasy*, whose numbering begins with six. In addition to tales of robots becoming the dominant life form on Earth, and a journey through a space warp that doesn't quite work out as intended, there is the sobering "Rescued!" (Feldstein-Wood), in which colonizers on a planet in another solar system contend with mold that rots their spaceships and spacesuits—and ultimately turns the astronauts into unrecognizable "monsters."

Weird Fantasy 8 contains "The Slave Ship" (Gaines-Feldstein-Roussos). The captain of the title vessel has taken dozens of African natives aboard his ship in chains, and plans to sell them for a few hundred dollars each. When the authorities close in, he mercilessly throws them overboard tied to an anchor, thereby removing the proof of his criminal activities. But then he and his men are forced into a hovering spaceship where it soon becomes clear that they are to be turned into slaves themselves. When cosmic authorities pursue the extraterrestrial slave ship, the captain and his crew are thrown out of the vessel. Their bodies explode in airless space, destroying the evidence. The story may be obvious and predictable but it is also satisfying. "The Enemies of the Colony," written and drawn by Wally Wood, has colonizers hunting down savage dinosaur-like creatures who attack them, similar to the plot of "Pet Hate." The colonizers are unaware that those creatures kept down the population of another species, cute "pets," who are just as dangerous and carnivorous as the "monsters" when *their* population gets out of control. Population control is also a major problem in "A Mistake in Multiplication" (Feldstein-Orlando), in which slimy, hideous space creatures reproduce asexually like plants and threaten to overrun the Earth.

A better monster story is "The Secret of Saturn's Ring" (Feldstein-Gaines-Wood) in *Weird Fantasy* 10. Two scientists dropped off to investigate one of the moonlets that make up the rings of Saturn disappear, and the moonlet is towed back to Earth where it can be examined. They find the men's bodies, dried like prunes, on the planetoid, and realize that the remains must have been disgorged by something *inside* of it. This is revealed to be a gigantic, flesh-eating bacterium and the moonlet is a spore. The creature is finally destroyed, but—are there creatures inside other planetoids, and even inside the moon—and Earth?

There are two notable stories in *Weird Fantasy* 10. In "The Mutants" (Feldstein-Gaines-Wood), the disfigured but brilliant children of people who have been exposed to radiation are subjected to prejudice because of their differences. This was ten years before Marvel's *X-Men* superhero comic dealt with similar subject matter. However, "The Mutants" is a moving tale in which the world votes to banish all mutants into outer space, but half of them make the supreme sacrifice by smashing their ship into a meteor that might have caused millions of casualties on Earth. Touched by this gesture, the people of Earth beg the atomic mutants to come back, where they are thanked and feted. But the ending of the story makes clear that it won't be long before the mutants' different nature will make them feared and hated once more.

In "Not on the Menu" (Feldstein-Orlando), the crew of a spaceship discovers that it will take three months for their atomic pile to recharge, but their food will run out in two months. On the planet where they await repairs, Commander Harwood determines that all of the fruit and animal life is saturated with cyanide salts and cannot be eaten. The situation becomes increasingly desperate in spite of severe rationing, until it is suggested that one man must sacrifice himself to feed the others. But the commander tells the crew that he has figured out a way to remove the cyanide from the food, after which they all gratefully partake of a generous supper. But Harwood then informs the others that he was lying, the food is poisoned, and he has killed them to prevent them from turning to cannibalism. As the crew members die, Harwood eats the poisoned food, only to hear an alarm that tells him the recharging is over and they would have been saved. Although the story—a near-masterpiece of irony—is science fiction because of its setting, a variation could be set in just about any time or place.

EC Comics did well with their horror comics, so the stories the editors published in *Weird Fantasy* and their other publications were often on the dark side. *Weird Fantasy* 11 presents "The Two Century Journey" (Gaines-Feldstein-Wood), in which specially chosen men and women flee overcrowding on Earth in a rocketship that will take 200 years to arrive at a planet that might be similar to Earth. The birth rate on the ship exceeds expectations, and the same overcrowding may occur if the population isn't reduced. This is done when it is decided that the oldest residents must die to make room for all the infants. In a rather chilling and poignant scene, these seniors volunteer to step out into space where they explode and vanish. Worse, when the ship finally arrives at the distant planet, it is too *much* like Earth: overcrowded.

In *WF* 19's equally dismal "Time for a Change" (Feldstein-Orlando), Earthmen on Pluto discover that time runs at a very different pace for the Plutonians, who seem like statues. This so effects the astronauts that when they return to Earth, they seem stiff and dead to everyone else—and wind up alive but unable to move or talk on *autopsy tables*. In *WF* 20's incredibly depressing "The Automaton" (Feldstein-Orlando), a young man in an oppressive fascist society keeps trying to kill himself, only to be saved time and again as "property of the state," continuously sentenced to slave labor, until finally his brain is encased in an indestructible steel robot body in which he cannot even cry.

In addition to the occasional gruesome tale, *Weird Fantasy* ran other edgy stories: a woman from the future has five husbands and the unknowing protagonist turns out to be her sixth; a woman's spouse is actually a Martian monstrosity who dies in a crash but leaves her with child. "A Man's Job" (Feldstein-Orlando) in *WF* 12 describes what happens when the election of the first woman president leads to females taking over politics, industry and all male professions while men stay home, do the housework and, ultimately, even have babies. "...Conquers All" (Gaines-Feldstein-Kamen) in *WF* 20 has unemotional aliens who look just like Earthlings coming to our planet to reconnoiter. Discovering sex, they forget about their plans for conquest.

In "Judgment Day" (Feldstein-Orlando) in *Weird Fantasy* 18, an Earthman, Tarlton, arrives on a planet where robots are set up to start their own society and he has to judge their readiness to join the Great Galactic Republic. Tarlton discovers that blue robots are judged inferior to orange robots even though they are built the same way; they are also segregated and given only menial positions. He decides that they aren't ready, explaining that everyone on Earth works together and the robots must do the same. Although it is no surprise that Tarlton turns out to be a black man, this is still a story that DC, Marvel and other comics firms would never have published during this period. The comic printed several highly positive letters about the story, including one from Ray Bradbury saying that it "should be required reading for every man, woman and child in the United States."

Other memorable *Weird Fantasy* tales include:

- "The Connection" (*WF* 9): Wanting to be closer in age to the young woman he loves, a man uses a time machine to skip ahead 15 years, hoping she'll wait for him, but things go tragically wrong.
- "Home to Stay" (13): A man who periodically goes away for years on outer space missions returns home to his family for good in an unexpected and tragic way. (This was an uncredited adaptation of two Ray Bradbury stories.)
- "By George" (15): A frightened reptile-like alien child crash-lands on Earth and gives rise to the legend of St. George and the Dragon.
- "Planely [*sic*] Possible" (21): When a man loses his wife in a car accident, a doctor gives him an opportunity to enter a parallel world where she is alive. But the widower makes a frightful mistake when he gets there.

Weird Science-Fantasy *and* Incredible Science Fiction

Sales for both *Weird Science* and *Weird Fantasy* were unspectacular so it was decided to combine them into one magazine, *Weird Science-Fantasy*. Both *Weird Science* and *Weird Fantasy* had 22 issues if you combined both volumes, so *Weird Science-Fantasy* began with the 23rd issue. The most notable story in *WSF* 23 is "The Children" (Feldstein-Wood): Ellen is one of several mothers in a group of colonists on a faraway planet. The mothers have their children taken away at birth; at first, they're told that each child will be returned in two years, which later changes to five, then seven, and so on. Ellen gathers all the disappointed and lonely women and demands that they get their little ones back. It is explained that the children, born on another world, have turned out quite differently from what was expected and need special care, but the women are insistent. Of course, the youngsters are all rather horribly mutated and freakish, but in the rather moving (if unrealistic?) conclusion, the mothers all accept the children with their strange disabilities. Ellen's son has tentacles instead of legs, but he is still an adorable child whom she dearly loves. Feldstein's purpose *may* have been to disgust the reader—considering some of his output—but this story has the opposite effect.

Weird Science-Fantasy 26 is a special issue which examines supposedly true stories of the sightings of flying saucers and UFOs from around the world, urging the Air Force to reveal everything it knows. *WSF* 27–29 presents a three-part adaptation of a 1939 prose story by Otto Binder entitled "I, Robot," in which a scientist invents an intelligent metal man. The robot is wrongly accused of the scientist's murder and is sentenced to death, but others come forward to tell of his good deeds, and he even inspires the love of a human female which he rejects. The story was the inspiration for dozens of robots and cyborgs with souls in sci-fi and superhero stories, as well as tales of men with human brains and metal bodies. The artist was Joe Orlando.

Other memorable stories include *WSF* 24's "The Teacher from Mars," in which a Martian living and working on Earth as a teacher endures horrible prejudice until a tragedy changes the students' minds about him, and "Close Shave" (27), in which it is decided to banish from this world the hairy aliens from Ganymede who have disguised themselves as Earthlings and a woman lies about her heritage so her alien lover will not reject her.

Next EC brought out *Incredible Science Fiction* for four issues, continuing the numbering from *Weird Science-Fantasy*. Jack Oleck did all the scripts for *ISF* 30 and the four remaining issues (aside from one by Al Feldstein), hammering home the already hoary theme that Man is savage and dangerous and the rest of the universe must be protected from him. In one story, the Earth discovers that a barrier has been erected around the world to prevent space travel. "Time to Leave" (*ISF* 31) has a more interesting premise: In a future world, time travelers from the past are automatically brought to a central control room run by a man named Garvin and told they must return to their own time, as there is a danger of the timestream being adversely affected. The latest traveler, Dr. Carter, is assured that he will *want* to go after he sees some of the developments in this future world. At first Carter is impressed with the cleanliness and order and lack of crime but learns that in this time period, there is also no love or joy or marriage; children are born in "bio-labs," and all passion, curiosity and ambition has been bred out of the human race. Carter, as usual, decides to go back, but to his surprise Garvin begs to go *with* him.

Oleck's other stories are acceptable but on the minor side, with too many about future men reduced to savagery and coming across ruined canyons of demolished cities. In one tale, human beings who have always thought that radiation made the animals, birds and insects bigger finally realize that the wildlife is normal but that *they* have shrunk. "One Way Hero" looks at what happens to spacemen who crack up and can no longer fly. Mart, who flew into space and has not seen his younger brother in years, finds him on Mars, where he reveals that he had a nervous breakdown on his first flight and can't return to Earth—he's too terrified to get in another ship. Mart, wearing his uniform, tells Johnny to buck up and start a new life on Mars, then heads back to his own ship—where all he does is load cargo, having had a similar experience to Johnny's years before. Now and then he puts on his uniform but he no longer flies.

EC stories can be caption- and dialogue-heavy, with many of the captions being verbose and unnecessary. On the other hand, the writers do their best to explain certain scientific principles, no matter how outré. The art is also uneven. Al Feldstein was always a better writer than artist, but there are significant contributions from Wally Wood, Joe Orlando, and Al Williamson.

Fawcett

Motion Picture Comics

The '50s and '60s were a ripe time for films of the fantastic—science fiction, fantasy and horror—and the comic book companies responded with special tie-in editions that would interest kids. There were earlier comic book adaptations of movies, of course. Some of these, such as *Hollywood Film Stories*, used panels from the movies while others were illustrated. *Movie Comics* (Picture Comics) featured a downright bizarre, caption-heavy combination of both stills and artwork. One of the earliest films adapted for comics was *One Million B.C.* in 1940 in Whitman Publishing's *Crackajack Funnies* 25 and 26. It is abbreviated and not especially memorable.

Fawcett, most famous for Captain Marvel, came out with a tie-in to the George Pal production of *Destination Moon* in 1950; the movie was based on the novel by Robert A. Heinlein, who co-wrote the screenplay. The film details the first trip to the moon in a rocket with four men aboard. Once they arrive, they realize they used too much fuel on landing and may have to leave one man behind to stabilize the rocket's weight so they can take off. Fortunately, they figure out another way to get rid of the excess weight. Fawcett's comic version is almost as good as the movie, with a solid script by comics legend and sci-fi writer Otto Binder and pleasant, efficient artwork by Dick Rockwell and Sam Burlockoff—although it's a shame that they don't provide a full-page shot of the striking lunar landscape as seen in the film. The comic shows much more of the home life of scientist Charles Hargraves, introducing us to his wife and their three young sons. (Of course, the fact that Hargraves has children makes it even stranger that he's willing to sacrifice his life when they discuss who will stay behind.) Binder's script also adds interesting scientific points during the voyage that are not in the movie.

In 1952, Fawcett's *Motion Picture Comics* 110 presents an excellent, reasonably well-drawn (by George Evans) adaptation of the George Pal film *When Worlds*

Collide. This is the story of desperate efforts to build a rocketship to take 40 people off the Earth just before it is destroyed by a star from another galaxy; the ship will land on a planet that is orbiting this new star. As the day of departure nears, there are outbreaks of violence and resentment from those who will be left behind. The comic goes the movie one better by depicting the final explosive destruction of the Earth (not shown in the film), although this is only seen in one small panel. Larger panels showing the destruction of New York City by tidal wave, volcanic eruptions, and people falling into giant cracks in the Earth are more impressive. The script by veteran comics scribe Leo Dorfman is primarily composed of dialogue from the movie.

Another 1952 release, *The Man from Planet X*, became the feature in *Fawcett Movie Comic* 15. (This was a separate series from Fawcett's *Motion Picture Comics*.) The movie deals with a planet rapidly approaching the Earth, and a strange visitor who arrives on the Scottish moors in a spaceship. Is he friend or foe? Because the science in the movie is so ridiculous—the Earth would probably be destroyed by another planet coming that close—it makes a perfect 1950s comic book, and even has art by Kurt Schaffenberger, a prominent DC artist. Otto Binder did the script, adding a few details and sequences—a deputy is terrified by the appearance of the alien and dives out of a window—and giving the alien a musical language that no one can understand. Schaffenberger's work is professional, even attractive at times, but not especially dynamic. Like *Motion Picture Comics*, most of the movies adapted in *Fawcett Movie Comic* were Westerns.

Fawcett also came out with some sci-fi one-shots. In 1950's *Vic Torry* (aka *Vic Torry and His Flying Saucer*), pilot Torry encounters a flying saucer with a dying man from Mercury aboard. After the alien disintegrates due to old age, Vic and his girlfriend Laura find themselves on a pre-controlled trip to Mercury. When Mercurians reach old age, they are given brand new bodies because their every molecular pattern is recorded and saved for the time when it is required. When Vic and Laura arrive on Mercury, they discover that the evil Szzz has manipulated these recordings and has turned almost all Mercurians into his mind-slaves. Using his brawn and ingenuity, and with the help of brave Laura, Vic defeats Szzz and frees the Mercurians. While the story has its moments and is not badly drawn, this was the hero's first and last appearance.

6

Fiction House; Fox

Fiction House

Planet

Planet, the first comic book to present nothing but science fiction stories, debuted in 1940. Most of the material in the comic is devoted to heroic adventurers who appear in stories every issue—some of these are continued from one issue to the next—as opposed to one-off tales. In general, *Planet* is outside the scope of this book but, as it was a famous and popular comic in its day, it will be discussed in brief.

In the first issue, Flint Baker finishes building his father's rocketship after the old man's death, but discovers that no one is interested in being in the crew on a flight to Mars as it may be a one-way trip. Flint has a prison warden offer three lifers a chance for a pardon if they go along on the flight, and they agree. Flint is not pleased to find a stowaway, Mimi Wilson of the New York *Globe*. On Mars, the motley group finds a civilization modeled on *Flash Gordon*; there are humans, but also short, one-eyed creatures who have heads on top of legs and no chests in-between. There have been earlier visitors from Earth, led by hooded Sarko, who now wage war with the peaceful Martians. The strip was written and drawn by Dick Briefer. *Planet* was edited by Malcolm Weiss and S.M. Iger, with Will Eisner of *Spirit* fame serving as the art director.

Other features in *Planet* include Auro, Lord of Jupiter, about a boy shipwrecked on Jupiter when his parents' space cruiser crashes there and they are killed; the Red Comet, "Mystery Man of the Universe," who is essentially a superhero with special powers such as the ability to change size; Captain Nelson Cole of the Solar Force and his nemesis Zan, who wants to take over the universe and can turn men into robots; Spurt Hammond, Planet Flyer, who battles warlords of the moon, including a faction of warrior women; Buzz Crandall and the Space Patrol, who "cruise through space in their atom-powered ship" rescuing foolhardy adventurers facing outer space dangers; and Quorak, Super Pirate, who is defeated by the forces of goodness, i.e., Lt. Gary Blake and radio operator Miss Perry.

The artwork for most of these features is crude, as is the scripting. The cover

Planet presented heroic and attractive adventurers of both sexes traveling throughout the universe—and lots of bug-eyed monsters.

illustrations are more attractive—some of the best are drawn by Dan Zolnerowich—and reminscent of pulp magazines. The characters are mere sketches, completely one-dimensional, although some of the stories convey a bit of childish enthusiasm. In *Planet* 2, Flint Baker comes to Mars' rescue again when a monstrous creature of King Kong proportions threatens the planet, while Buzz Crandall battles crab-men and Captain Cole takes on a two-headed giant. *Planet* 3 is of interest primarily for introducing Amazona, a Wonder Woman imitation. Her adventures are not science fiction and she lasted just one issue. Buzz Crandall fought a huge, slimy, tentacled creature that lives in a lair riddled with picked-clean skeletons and tries to make a snack of Buzz's girlfriend Sandra.

Planet 4 introduces Kenny Carr of the Martian Lancers; Gale Allen of the Women's Space Battalion; and Jim Giant, the Strongest Man in the Universe; none of them amounts to much. (Only Gale Allen reappears, battling space pirates.) This was also true of the following issue's Fero, Planet Detective (later Interplanetary Detective) and Space Admiral Curry. Auro's adventures continue, but even though he was the Lord of Jupiter he acts more like a Tarzan or sword-and-sorcery clone. Meanwhile, Flint Baker and Mimi land on a planet full of dinosaurs. Debuting in *Planet* 6, Crash Barker and the Zoom Sled and Dr. Don Granval failed to thrill, although the Granval story in *Planet* 7 is a bizarre tale of gargantuan humanoid aliens, much like Earthlings, from a macro-universe, collecting the planets of the solar system in an exhibit at a party and holding them in their hands. Don lands his spaceship on the arm of the woman holding the Earth in her fingers, and then uses his rocket to inject her with poison. As she drops to the floor, the Earth is freed. The logistics of the story are fairly impossible.

Cosmo Corrigan, a smart-aleck adventurer, shows up in *Planet* 9, running around shirtless in mediocre, indifferently drawn stories. Norge Benson and the Star Pirate ("Robin Hood of the Spaceways," *Planet* 12) are along the same lines. As the series progresses, the stories remain a mélange of outer space clichés, wildly inaccurate science (when there was any science at all), grotesque monsters and aliens, a variety of "space babes," evil queens and friendly princesses, many dinosaurs and giant lizards, a surplus of octopus-like creatures with big maws and sticky tentacles, and many giant spiders and other gross bugs. One of the most impressive of these was the humongous "Trantul" (or tarantula) that appears in the Flint Baker story in *Planet* 14.

The *Planet* art is sometimes so awful that it looks as if it were done by children. The figures are frequently stiff and awkward. However, there are glimmers that there might be improvement in that area, such as in the Crash Parker story drawn by Joe Doolin and the Star Pirate strip drawn (as well as written) by Pagsilang Isip in *Planet* 13. Even these are comparatively poor, however. Then Doolin's work on the new Mars, God of War strip is quite good in *Planet* 15. Rafael Astarita is a notable contributor to the series' art, doing smooth work on the Aruo Lord of Jupiter story in *Planet* 21.

Rudy Palais did the nice art for the new strip "The Lost World," which begins in the same issue. The hero is Hunt Bowman, an archer in the 33rd century, when the Earth is a wasteland. Bowman hooks up with Queen Lyssa of a planet known as the Lost World, where there are cavemen and, of course, numerous monsters. Eventually they resolve to rebuild civilization on Earth. Graham Ingels does some especially good art for the *Planet* 28 installment and George Evans gives the strip a sleek look in later issues of *Planet*.

Flint Baker had appeared in every issue of *Planet* but his adventures are combined with another feature, Reef Ryan; the strip, which begins in *Planet* 26, is called "Space Rangers." Lee Elias contributes some attractive artwork, such as a *Planet* 28 story in which Flint, Reef and Reef's gal pal Vara encounter people who have been turned into streamlined metal creatures with human heads. The boys sport attractive red uniforms as well. Lily Renee also did some good work on the strip. George Tuska began penciling the Star Pirate feature in *Planet* 30, with felicitous results; Murphy Anderson also worked on the feature. The Mars strip transitions into Mysta of the Moon, initially an enemy of the God of War, who takes his spot in the book while Mars goes back into the endless void. Gale Allen becomes sexier and wears less clothing, an example of "good girl art" by Fran Hopper. In a wild story in *Planet* 38, she and her companions pull a tiny world into their spaceship and are shrunk down to microscopic size by the angry inhabitants. Meanwhile, Mysta also dresses as scantily as possible.

Oddly, when Auro returns in *Planet* 41, he is no longer bare-chested but dressed in a green uniform with helmet and yellow cape and his adventures are satisfactorily drawn by August Froehlich, then others. Another difference is that it develops that Auro's brain actually belongs to a man named Chet Edson, who is eventually killed, but whose invisible spirit hovers over the action in each installment as he makes ironic comments about the rather egotistical Auro. A conflict is set up between Auro's gal pal Dorna and Chet's mate Claudia—she still clings to Auro because of his connection to Chet—because Dorna wants Auro to stay on Jupiter with her while Claudia wants him to return to Earth to help protect it. As for the Space Rangers, Reef Ryan and his girlfriend disappear from the strip while Flint Baker grows a mustache and acquires a boy partner named Hercules.

By this time, Fiction House had added five new comics to their lineup: *Jungle*, which has jungle adventures; *Jumbo*, which features Sheena, another white jungle princess; *Wings*, which presents aviation action stories; *Fight*, more action-adventure stories with a variety of macho heroes and heroines, and *Rangers*, which is more of the same. The Fiction House formula was to have sexy women in various stages of undress draped over animals, ruins, spaceships and so on. *Planet* 46's cover is a striking Joe Doolan illustration of a muscular, attractive woman wearing breastplates and little else, climbing a rope with one hand. With the other, she is lifting up a handsome, uneasy-looking man whose hands are bound.

In 1950, Fiction House reduced the number of pages in *Planet* from 52 to 36, necessitating the removal of some of the strips. *Planet* 65 ran reprints for the next few issues, but new material appeared in the last three, 71, 72 and 73. This includes a Flint Baker adventure but most of the stories are one-offs. In "The Sandhogs of Mars" (*Planet* 71), drawn by Maurice Whitman, an Earthman and a Martian woman building a roadway have to deal with a mutiny when members of the crew hear that there are riches hidden under a desert on Mars. The mutineers are attacked and infected by mutated creatures called sandhogs and afterward cannot be allowed on the ship because they might infect everyone else. Instead, their greed has brought about their transformation into sandhogs and they will have to spend the rest of their lives lost in the desert sands of Mars.

"Silence from Planetoid X" tells the story of colonizers who fly to the title planetoid where they discover the same angry passions, jealousies, and grabs for power that caused so many problems back on Earth. Two factions fight a war with modern weapons for many years, then are reduced to battling with fists and implements. Neither side really wins, and the survivors retreat into the jungle where they come to resemble cavemen of the prehistoric past. The original leader of the colonizers spends over a decade rebuilding the spaceship that brought them to the world, just so that he can return in bitterness to Earth. He dies before he can quite make it there. Bill Discount did the art.

The cover of *Planet* 72, drawn by Maurice Whitman, shows a green-skinned Viking type carrying another breastplate-clad beauty over his shoulder. The issue contains three notable stories. In "The Last Expedition," drawn by Bill Benulis, a rescue party goes off to planet Zuron to search for Dr. Terrod, who went there on a mission years before. Lt. Ganlon reports to Major Steele that all his group found was an impenetrable jungle, lots of voracious monsters, and no sign of Terrod and his party, who must have perished. However, in a development that brings to mind modern-day mini-cams worn by police officers, Major Steele asks Ganlon and his men for their helmets, inside which are macro-cameras which recorded everything that actually happened on Zuron. The cameras reveal that the planet is actually a beautiful paradise where people in their sixties look like teenagers and all of their needs are provided for. Terrod used his equipment to manipulate the memories of Ganlon and his associates. Major Steele is now determined to take off for Zuron and take it over, but before he can do so, Dr. Terrod kills him. When asked why he wanted no more expeditions coming to Zuron, Terrod explains that Steele would have "plundered paradise" and left Zuron a depleted ruin. This negative view of colonialism is out of the ordinary for sci-fi stories of the period.

"No Sign of Life," drawn by Vic Carrabotta and Jack Abel, has a male and female astronaut landing on a world; they are completely unaware of its tiny inhabitants, whose cities are being crushed by their feet. The aliens mount a massive offense against the giants, but their planes are like mosquitos and the astronauts see them as insects. Even when the male astronaut is downed and tied up like a futuristic Gulliver, he still can't see that he is causing such destruction to an intelligent civilization.

Years later, the *Twilight Zone* episode "The Little People" dealt with Earth astronauts landing on a world with tiny, in this case, microscopic inhabitants.

In "The Thing in the Iceberg," drawn by Bill Discount, a spaceship is found frozen in the polar ice cap. After it is determined that it is a ship that went into space 18 years before, it is taken out of the ice and entered. The crew members are encased in a plastic substance and apparently in suspended animation. The coating is removed from the astronauts and they come back to life, but the captain makes remarks to the curious scientists who entered the ship that cause suspicion. Therefore the scientists are somewhat prepared when the revived crew members transform into malevolent, green-skinned extraterrestrials and are quickly destroyed. The aliens were changelings who slaughtered the original crew and took their places.

In *Planet* 73, the final issue, "Cerebex" boasts a superior art job by Bill Benulis, some of the best artwork ever seen in the publication. Prof. Jackson has built an incredible electronic brain which is housed in a towering metal robot called Cerebex. Jackson's assistant Brad Cummings is unaware that Jackson has used the brain patterns of a Hitler-like dictator, supposedly deceased, named Schmackenburg. The dictator is still alive and in disguise, and his daughter Mary warns Cummings that he has formed an unholy alliance with Jackson, who is one of his followers. However, Jackson kills Schmackenburg, having decided he would be a better choice to rule the world. Schmackenburg has the last laugh, as one of the robot's tentacles reaches out to snap Jackson's neck, and Cerebex is free to take over the planet.

In short order, Cerebex smashes through cities, proves impervious to ordinary weapons and builds a robot army to help him in his conquest. As the nation is devastated by the persistent attacks, Brad builds another robot and tests it, certain that it can defeat Cerebex. But when the two metal monsters confront each other, Cerebex uses a magnetic field to attract Brad's robot to its own body, where it becomes stuck and helpless. Brad then hits on the idea of making a new robot entirely out of wood, and without the magnetic field to worry about, this one is able to smash through to Cerebex' nerve center and destroy the evil brain for good.

"The Wonder-Warp," drawn by A. Albert, uses much more old-fashioned elements in its tale of Capt. Rawley of the space freighter *QX-3*. Rawley and his crew encounter another ship presided over by a witchy queen-commander who has a band of troll-like men to do her bidding. Yes, it's the trope of the "beautiful babe" with a flock of ugly little men at her side. The evil queen thinks that Rawley or one of his crew is a disguised traitor of her people and subjects them to mind-scans. Rawley manages to get off her ship and is making his way back to his freighter where he can employ its weapons. (One wonders what he would have done when he realized his men were still aboard the enemy ship.) A troll makes a mistake and, instead of encasing Rawley in a tractor beam, sends him through a time warp. The poor fellow, dazed and confused, winds up on a city street in the year 1954 with everyone thinking he must be crazy. This is where the story really might have gotten interesting but it merely ends, leaving the man to an unenviable future.

Man O' Mars

Man O' Mars is a 1953 one-shot with back-up stories that were reprinted from *Planet*. In the new lead story, the balance of power on Mars is divided between the military, led by Gurtil—who wants to attack Earth—and the scientists, the Azurians, who seek a more peaceful solution. The scientists are exiled to a part of Mars where the thin air may spell doom for them, but they find shelter inside huge caverns and survive. Gurtil attacks Earth but his ships are repelled by guided missiles. Tarkan of the Azurians is sent to Earth and tells them that Gurtil will undoubtedly return with superior weapons, and that the world must prepare. A hundred young men, including John Hunter, are chosen to become part of a force that will fly to Mars and be trained in combat and in the use of Martian weapons. A girl, Renee, who has a crush on John, cuts her hair, pretends to be a boy and gets to Mars, along with their friend Jerry. Fifteen years go by and Gurtil launches his attack, but Hunter and the others are ready. Gurtil comes up with a plan to send his girlfriend Ylla, a sexy green woman, to Hunter's ship and pretend to be an ally, but the plan fails. Jerry sacrifices his life to ram his ship, containing a device that makes water explosive, into Gurtil's HQ, ending his threat forever. The story is drawn by Maurice Gutwirth. With such an interesting premise, and characters who could have been developed over several installments, it's a shame that "Man O' Mars" was wrapped up in just ten pages.

Fox

Rocket Kelly

Rocket Kelly debuted in 1945 and lasted for five issues. Rocket flew around in his ship and had adventures with his buddy Punchy and girlfriend Sue. The first issue, which is poor on all levels, has the trio battling a villain who has murdered a professor and inadvertently unleashed a spore that grows to giant size and will continue growing until Rocket stops it. None of this is remotely exciting. A second story has our heroes prematurely aging when they encounter a villain who fools around with time. The second issue has the trio battling a robot leader of another planet, as well as two Trojan horses filled with explosives.

In *Rocket Kelly* 3's lead story, the group lands on a world whose trees have the heads of animals and whose leaders plan to unleash giant insects on the Earth. Its execrable art and script strip it of any potential thrills. In a second story, in which Rocket travels to Egypt to encounter a living mummy, he suddenly has a new girlfriend, Diana (Sue returns in issue 5). His father, who is a scientist, carries about his "miniature atomic Earth-borer" that conveniently fits into his jackknife! In the third issue, Rocket battles Mr. Weather and the alien Minstrel of Death, who looks like a walking piano with legs. The Minstrel's followers also resemble musical instruments. His plan is to force Earthlings to dance themselves to death, but he is foiled when it develops that Punchy is tone deaf.

Descendants of Genghis Khan rise from the underground city of SubBurma along with thousands of vampire bats in *Rocket Kelly* 5, but the childish artwork does absolutely nothing to bring the story to life. The same is true of an adventure featuring the evil Sea Scoundrel. *Rocket Kelly*'s back-up stories feature the Puppeteer, the magician Illuso, precocious teenager Ernie, reporter Betty Boyd, and Western hero Kit of the Canyon. All of these made only one or two appearances and are essentially worthless. Most of the scripts are attributed to Ted Small.

7

Key–Stanley Morse; Magazine Enterprises; Prize; Standard; Star

Key–Stanley Morse

Weird Tales of the Future

Key Comics' *Weird Tales of the Future* debuted in 1952. It ran for eight issues and its content changed from science fiction tales to horror and suspense. In the first issue's "Ten Thousand Years Old," Jerry Drago and Jill Johnson are kidnapped by a Venusian scientist who wants to observe them over the decades, and makes them, in effect, immortal so he can do so. He allows them to assist him, giving them enough freedom to plot their escape. Stealing a rocketship, they make their way back to Earth, only to discover that not a single soul believes their story. The adventures of the couple were to be continued in the next issue as they try to convince everyone of the truth, but they were never seen again. This may be because the story is too much like "Exhibit One," published in *Amazing Adventures* a few months earlier. Ross Andru and Mike Esposito were the artists.

In the same issue is "The Ghouls Who Ruled the World," drawn by Ed Smalle. It takes place in a future time period when Man has solved the problems of war and hunger, and antisocial tendencies are removed from people in infancy. Dr. Dino Lavelle has developed a way of bringing the dead back to life, but so far has only successfully experimented on the recently deceased. Learning that an old-time gangster named Crazy Ed Cullin was buried in a lead-lined vacuum coffin a hundred years ago and that his corpse is perfectly preserved, Dr. Lavelle decides he would be a perfect subject to see if he can resuscitate someone who has been dead for very long. Lavelle manages to revive Cullin, who was buried with his gat in a violin case. Cullin is overjoyed to learn that there is no longer any police department. He threatens the man's daughter to force the doctor to resuscitate other gangsters. The gang begin a reign of terror, and the government might have to capitulate to their demands. But ancient rivalries erupt and the gangsters defeat themselves by turning on and killing each other.

Weird Tales of the Future 2 presents "Flight to the Future," drawn by Basil

Wolverton. Ted Haynes mugs a man, but the victim fights back, with the result that the latter is killed. Haynes is convinced the police will eventually catch up with him so he volunteers for a program in which he will be frozen into a state of suspended animation and placed in the North Polar Ice Cap for 20,000 years. When he is revived 20 millennia later, he meets a wizened fellow named Kingston, leader of the "decadent remnants" of civilization. All other humans in the place are dimwitted and pathetic specimens, and Haynes figures he can easily take over. He sneaks up on Kingston to kill him, but his would-be victim is prepared and fights him off. Kingston is the man whom Haynes thought he had killed; he also put himself in suspended animation so he could wake earlier and get his revenge. A planetoid then strikes the Earth and kills them both. "Flight to the Future" has some interesting elements but is full of plot holes and lacks a really clever ending.

Weird Tales of the Future 3 begins the series' transition to a horror comic but only with its cover, which depicts a zombie-like creature ripping out of a grave behind a pretty blonde. The stories feature a man shipwrecked on Mars who encounters a giant hand with eyes, which turns out to be a beautiful Venusian woman with illusion powers; a battle between Uranus and Earth; a scientist who can create life out of common dirt; and a scientist exploring the land of dreams to his regret. None of these tales is memorable. In issue 4's "Day of Doom," a war between the free world and the Iron Curtain is interrupted by an invasion from outer space. The story features effective art by Tony Mortellaro.

Two other stories in this issue are of more interest. "The Engine That Came Through Time," drawn by Eugene E. Hughes, has scientist Arthur Bergholm bemoaning the fact that he has neither the funds nor time to complete his work on an interstellar drive that will enable mankind to reach planets many light years away. A man named Ranu appears from 3000 years in the future, and gives Arthur the drive he was hoping to complete. In the future, Bergholm is seen as a hero and the inventor of the drive, which allows the human race to reach the stars and colonize the solar system. Ranu tells him that there are many timelines, and in one of them Arthur is killed and never completes his invention, meaning the future world Ranu lives in will never materialize. With Ranu's device, Arthur takes off with scientists and others to test it and see if they can truly reach Alpha Centauri in only four days. They do, but when they return, what seemed like days to Arthur and the others turns out to be 400 *years*; all that's left of Earth is a ruin. Ranu apologizes to a distraught Arthur for not telling him the whole truth, but knew he would never have gone on this all-important voyage had he known. Arthur and his wife have no choice but to return to Alpha Centauri and build a future for themselves and their race. "Speck of Stardust," drawn by Hy Fleischman, is a strange tale of a rivalry between two men over a gorgeous Venusian princess, who turns out not to be quite so beautiful when she's taken in a spaceship to Earth.

Weird Fantasies 5 also has two interesting stories. In "The Man from the Moon," written and drawn by Basil Wolverton, Pete Warren is kidnapped to the moon not long after the Civil War by aliens who need proof that they successfully journeyed to Earth. Initially resentful, Pete bonds with the moon men and is grateful that with their science they have kept him alive many years longer than would have been expected. As his human parts wear out, they are replaced until only his brain remains in a robotic shell. Now over a century has gone by and he is given the opportunity to visit the Earth, but he discovers the world has been destroyed by war, and all that remain are hideous, hostile parodies of human beings. Peter returns to the moon with a palpable sense of loneliness.

"The Worm Turns," drawn by Eugene E. Hughes, is a flat-out monster story with the military taking on a gigantic worm that has emerged from its underground lair and can't be killed by standard weapons. Finally an atomic bomb is dropped on the creature, but all that results from this is the spawning of many more of the squiggling behemoths. The other stories in the issue are horror tales. *Weird Tales* 6 features the genuinely weird "Jonah," with art by Tony Mortellaro: A scientist named Sandy invents a ray that can shrink things to a fraction of their size, and tells his assistant Jonah that this can be a boon to space travel as heavy equipment can be reduced and the cargo will weigh much less. Jonah quite sensibly thinks there is money to be made from the machine, but Sandy is more altruistic. Jonah accidentally hits the switch on the device and is shrunk to tiny size, coming to rest on a sandwich which Sandy later devours. Inside Sandy's mouth, Jonah, not realizing where he is, thinks of the teeth as giant cliffs he must ascend using his laser gun. Sandy's dentist sees something small in his patient's mouth that might be responsible for the pain. Sandy points his machine into his mouth and presses the button, and out pops an enlarging Jonah as the dentist looks on in astonishment.

Magazine Enterprises

Jet Powers *and* Space Ace

Magazine Enterprises' *Jet Powers* debuted in 1950, when the stories take place. Jet, Captain of Science, is a scientist and adventurer who works out of his own secret laboratories in the Southwest. He flies in his special aerocar and uses a Gravitron Gun that negates gravity, sending his enemies flying into the air. Jet's first opponent is the Oriental Mr. Sinn, who uses a special machine to cause devasting earthquakes. Captured by Sinn, Jet is put in a room and subjected to powerful colors and sounds that nearly drive him crazy, but he perseveres. Escaping after Jet has smashed his machines, the unchivalrous Sinn pushes his gal pal Su Shan out of his plane but she survives.

Arriving at another one of his many laboratories, Sinn operates out of an artificial moon orbiting the Earth, using his special devices to steal government secrets. Jet arrives on the phony moon and thwarts Sinn, but the villain escapes again. The other adversary in *Jet Powers* 1 is alien Nev Tow, who travels from his own world in microscopic size within a meteor shower. On Earth, he grows into a man-sized insectoid creature and sets off atomic piles as a signal to his fellow bugs. Jet stops Nev Tow from blowing all of Long Island off the map and the invader ultimately succumbs to DDT.

In *Jet Powers* 2, the hero discovers that an alien race that will conquer the Earth in the future is planning to use a time machine to conquer earlier eras as well. Jet uses the machine to strand the villains in the prehistoric past. Su Shan, Mr. Sinn's assistant, appears in the second story, in which the villain is a man who can reduce all paper—including valuable books and money—to powder and plans to blackmail the world. Su Shan had tried to kill Jet in the previous issue, but after he saves her life, she kisses him. As for Mr. Sinn, he joins forces with a robot who has gained sentience from Hiroshima's atomic fall-out and the two build an army of robots to storm Jet's stronghold. Jet uses radioactivity to destroy the robots and Sinn is finally captured.

Jet Powers 3 and 4 present a sobering tale of near-apocalypse, a dramatic change in direction for the series. In issue 3, a radioactive cloud of doom dust engulfs the Earth and destroys millions. After Jet invents something to dispel the dust, survivors come out of their hideaways to rebuild. In the following issue, a discredited general and a torch singer known as the Red Queen team up to take over the remnants of the world, dropping napalm bombs on communities. Jet comes up with an idea of stopping the general's army by creating a barbiturate-sodden rain that causes the enemy troops to fall asleep. The Red Queen wants to use an atomic bomb on the rebel forces, but she and the general are finally defeated.

The series introduces more alien races when Jet receives a distress signal that takes him to Mars, where he helps the inhabitants against Venusian invaders. In the following issue, he is mistakenly assumed to be the lover of a Martian princess, incurring the wrath of her real lover. Despite being locked away in a distant tower, Jet stops another destructive invasion that might have decimated the entire solar system.

Jet Powers lasted four issues. It could not be called a hard science series, but the scripts do attempt to give the hero intelligent scientific solutions to some rather staggering problems. Bob Powell provided serviceable art.

Back-up stories in *Jet Powers* feature the character of the Space Ace, a muscular hero with a somewhat mercenary nature. His opponents include a group of reactivated robots, causing havoc on Mars; and the "invisible death" which cooks people and animals from the inside out. The series with its indifferent artwork doesn't really kick into gear until *Jet Powers* 3, when Space Ace goes after an alien weapon (a black globe); he is pursued by the beautiful Flor and her gang of cutthroats who also want the prize. Space Ace is nearly stranded on an asteroid after this weapon—which absorbs all energy and sends it outward with destructive force—destroys his pursuers. Flor survives to capture Space Ace in the following

This issue of Magazine Enterprises' *Space Ace* helps advertise a chocolate food supplement.

issue, wherein she whips him within an inch of his life but fails to destroy him. Al Williamson furnished the stylish art for these last two adventures. At one point, Space Ace is described as being "Space-tanned." His skin was darkened by star light?

Space Ace 5 presents the adventures of Space Patrol member Jet Black and his youthful Martian buddy Jak Tal. The stories are all reprints from the *Manhunt* series, an anthology comic with several action-oriented strips. In 1951, Magazine Enterprises came out with another one-shot issue of *Space Ace*, but this was not the same character that appeared in *Jet Powers* (nor was it Jet Black), but rather a Major Inapak. In 1982, the world picks up signals from the moon, and the major volunteers to be the first to fly there in a quickly built spaceship which even the mechanic cannot vouch for. Before Inapak takes off, an American city is obliterated. As Inapak flies to the moon, he finds a young, hero-worshiping stowaway named Robin John on board. On the moon, they discover that the signals are actually coming from a planet near the moon. The major sabotages the transmitter so that its deadly rays will hit the aliens and not the Earth. Meanwhile, in a cave where the major told him to retreat, Robin meets a cute little creature called a Lunarchip, who comes back with the two humans to Earth. The story is narrated by a now elderly Robin, accompanied by the aged Lunarchip. "Inapak" was actually a chocolate food supplement sold in grocery stores and this one-shot comic was an advertising gimmick.

Prize

Tom Corbett, Space Cadet

When Prize came out with *Tom Corbett, Space Cadet* in 1955, they decided to ignore the stories that had appeared in Dell's version. This led to some lapses in continuity. Corbett and his buddies had encountered a Venusian octopus tree in the final issue of the Dell series, but when they encounter one in the first issue of Price's series (the tree is now also known as Hayshee), they have no recollection of it. Whereas the Dell series had only one story per issue, the Prize series has several stories, including a two-page back-up titled "Captain Quick and the Space Scouts." In the second issue, Tom and his buddies outwit not only "The Outlaws of Uranus" but also a group of aliens who plan to use robot duplicates of the cadets to mount an invasion of Earth. The aliens have little knowledge of human beings, and when the "cadets" step out of their spaceship wearing only their bathing suits, the jig is up! In the same issue, the Space Scouts encounter a giant man-eating frog guarding precious flowers. The series lasted only three issues, ending when the TV series did.

Standard Comics (Better-Nedor-Pines)

Fantastic Worlds

Fantastic Worlds debuted in 1952 and ran for only three issues, numbered from five to seven. *FW* 5 consists of standard sci-fi adventure tales, one concerning a mutiny on a ship that demolishes meteors in order to increase safety in space lanes. One meteor is encrusted with gems that the crew illegally want to keep. Another story looks at how a peace-loving colony of humans fights back vigorously against invading Mercurians who want to attack their home planet, Earth. Of more interest is "Hero of Space," in which a woman who seeks adventure and an exciting, manly mate rejects a marriage proposal from a four-eyed scientist she's worked with for years. She joins a group of colonizers and once there falls for "Rober Mannling," whose abilities to deal with a variety of menaces make him seem like a superhero. Despite her feelings for Rober, she keeps dreaming of the scientist back home. When Rober is hit by a meteor and killed, she learns that he was a robot and returns to the man she really wants to spend her life with.

Fantastic Worlds 6 features two notable stories. "Run, Martian, Run" takes the standard survival tale—alien vs. human—and turns it on its head, as the hunter in this case is human and the hunted is a Martian. In the future, there came a time when Martians, a kind of bird-like race, were hunted and killed, but it is now known that they are intelligent and anyone who hunts them is fined or jailed. The arrogant Arthur Harris comes to Mars and contemptuously pays the $10,000 fine at once, declaring his intentions no matter what the law says, then sets out to bag Klega the Unconquered, "the toughest old buzzard on the planet." What follows is a sharply observed battle of strength and wits as Harris sets his dog—a creature unknown to Klega—on the trail of the Martian, who is nevertheless able to keep the animal off his scent and snares him in a trap. Harris sends a "trained Venusian petro-hawk" after Klega, but the Martian defeats this animal as well. Finally the two engage in hand-to-hand combat which Harris seems to win, not counting on Klega's ability to survive without breathing for several minutes. Klega gets the upper hand by ripping off Harris' oxygen tube, forcing him to suck in the thinner Martian air. Although Harris could have saved himself by going immediately back to his ship, he is so determined to kill Klega that he stays and seemingly perishes. Klega deposits him in the Cave of the 1000-Year Vapors, where the hunter will remain, paralyzed but conscious, for several centuries. He begs Klega to kill him instead, but the Martian will not. Although indifferently drawn by John Celardo, the suspenseful story is quite memorable.

In the same issue, Otto Binder's "The Space Lorelei," drawn by George Roussos, combines several interesting elements into another memorable story. A spaceship, crewed by a bunch of men who see themselves as losers, unsuccessful in life and with women, come upon a planet that bears the huge face of a beautiful woman carved into its surface. Seeing what they think may be valuable jewels in the eyes of the face, they land and promptly fall through a trap door. Inside they are beset by a gigantic spider that wraps most of the men in cocoons to feed upon later. Jack Hudson hacks his way free and runs for help, coming across a chamber wherein there are beautiful women in suspended animation. Jack frees the women, who tell him that all of their men were killed by a plague, and they built the huge stone face to attract men to the planet as they wait patiently in the chamber. The women then rescue the other men by blasting the spider. Jack and the others plan to leave—"We're about the lowest specimens of manhood this side of Orion," Jack says. A pretty blonde insists: "To us, you look good!" It's all entertaining claptrap, about on the level of those fun '50s sci-fi epics such as *Missile to the Moon*, in which astronauts encounter "space babes" and giant spiders on a sinister planet.

Fantastic Worlds 7 has more mediocre adventure stories: Earthlings battle mobile trees with faces who can't stand the sound of noise; a "space ace" with many successful missions teams up with a beautiful female major to stop invaders from Jupiter from building robots to man their ships; a man searches for his son, a space marine, and finds him on an asteroid with living, malevolent rocks whom they've made their god. The most interesting story, although quite derivative, is "Doom in the Depths," in which scientists use an Earth borer (similar to the device in Burroughs' *At the Earth's Core*) to dig deep into the Earth until they reach the very center, and discover a hostile civilization of nasty little people. They make a run for the borer, and rise to the surface, where they hope to warn of an impending invasion by this unpleasant underground race. Ironically, an outer space invasion has been mounted at the same time, so the pilot of the borer—listening to radio reports in his machine—aims for the Mojave desert where the aliens have their base. The extraterrestrials wind up battling not with Earth forces but with the mole people from below who burst from the ground, and who have their own army and weapons. After both sides endure great casualties, the aliens flee back into space while the moles retreat into their caverns, never to return, completely unaware that they were never actually fighting who they thought they were. "Our surface world is safe," says a commentator, "without firing a shot!" Jon Blummer did the art. The story was published a year after the release of the film *Unknown World*, which also features a borer—although the characters did not run into any hostile inner-earth inhabitants.

Lost Worlds

Standard also did two issues of the series *Lost Worlds*, which also debuted in 1952. In *Lost Worlds* 5's "The City That Escaped from Tomorrow," a couple named Ken and Grace are on the scene when a time sphere opens a hole in space into a small town in 1953 America. Out of this sphere emerge some savage cavemen with futuristic weapons. When the weapons are aimed at the couple, they have no choice but to jump into the time sphere, which sends them thousands of years into the past. They come across more cavemen, as well as a cache of futuristic weaponry inside a cavern. They also stumble across a domed city with advanced technology and incredible architecture. They pass into a chamber where they discover a number of men who appear to be in suspended animation. They bring one man, Karos, to consciousness. He tells Ken and Grace that the city comes from the future when the world is facing a new ice age. It was decided to move the entire city and all of its inhabitants through time, back to the distant past, but something went wrong and all of them were helpless until the couple arrived. The cavemen have plundered the city and even their primitive brains were eventually able to figure out how to work the simple controls of complex mechanisms such as the time sphere. Karos sends the cavemen back to their proper time, then does the same for Ken and Grace. Just when the reader is wondering why there's no trace of this future city in the present day, or if the couple will return to their own time to find it greatly changed, Ken remarks that he didn't have the heart to tell Karos that the city was the legendary Lemuria, and that eventually it will be destroyed "by the rising waters of the Mediterranean Sea." (Lemuria was actually once rumored to be a *continent* that sank into the ocean, a theory that was later disproven.) Despite some plot holes and inconsistencies, the story is quite compelling, with nice art by Ross Andru and Mike Esposito.

"Worlds Apart" in the same issue presents an unusual love story between Rod and a young lady named Teena, who lives on a sub-atomic world that Rod, a scientist, observes through his microscope. Teena always feels that someone is watching her. Although Rod has a fiancée, Lorna, he has fallen hopelessly in love with Teena, and breaks off his engagement to Lorna. Furious, Lorna picks up a hammer and is about to smash the speck of matter which holds the sub-atomic world. Rod tells her that she will be destroying not just one girl but an entire planet full of millions of living beings. Seeing through the microscopic lens that Teena is in danger, Rod uses his cosmic matter projector to sink into the sub-atomic world, where he and Teena finally meet. Teena tells Rod that the world she lives on is called Earth. Nick Cardy was the artist.

Well-drawn by Alex Toth and Al Rubano, "Outlaws of Space" in *Lost Worlds* 6 is an exciting tale of the Space Rangers of the 25th century stopping a criminal, Blaster Raye, who hijacks mail ships, killing their crews. Rangers Mark Scott and Buck Lee come upon the wreck of one ship and find a sole survivor, a young lady named Jill Trent. Blaster attacks the ship they're on, disabling it, leaving them to fend for themselves on a meteorite without food or water. By improbably jumping from space rock to space rock, they make their way to Raye's HQ, where they attack him and his two companions with more rocks and bring him to justice.

"The First Man to Reach the Moon," also in *Lost* Worlds 6, takes place in 2021 where scientist Jonas Alwyn has built the first rocket to the moon. The pilot will be

Late in its run, Star Publications' *Blue Bolt* switched from superheroes to fantastic stories.

Kent Barlow, his daughter Gloria's fiancée. Before take-off, Kent's robot servant Jingles notices a flaw in the rocket hull, but Kent foolishly orders Jingles not to say anything. It might take months to repair the hull and Kent doesn't want to disappoint the professor or himself. He takes off, has a few harrowing moments during the flight, but becomes the first man on the moon. However, when he takes off for Earth, the hull caves in and he crashes. Gloria is horrified to think that the man she loves will die alone on the moon and that she will never see him again. But the man on the moon actually turns out to be Jingles, who knocked Kent out, tied him up and took his place. Kent: "He loved me too, Gloria. As much as you ... perhaps *more* ... who knows?" The story is by Otto Binder with art by Art Saaf.

Star

Blue Bolt

Blue Bolt was a long-running action and superhero title for Premium–Novelty Press. *Dick Cole*, featuring a young adventurer and student, was one of its main strips. Star Publications took over the comic beginning with *Blue Bolt* 102, presenting sci-fi–type heroes Blue Bolt and Spacehawk, as well as superhero Target and the Targeteers. Beginning with *Blue Bolt* 107, the covers promise "Weird, fantastic stories of the unknown." Basil Wolverton did the crude but effective art for the Spacehawk series, pitting the hero against Dr. Gore, whose goal is to destroy America with explosions. Jack Kirby and Joe Simon worked on the Blue Bolt series, involving the hero with a curvaceous lass named the Green Sorceress; Alan Mandel also worked on the series. In another strip, The Phantom Sub, a futuristic submarine is sent out on various missions. This was written by Bill O'Connor and drawn by Ben Flinton and Leonard Sansone. Most of the stories are reprints from *Blue Bolt, Captain Flight* and *Target*. The final issue is *Blue Bolt* 111, retitled (on the cover only) *Blue Bolt Weird Tales of Terror*, with "Weird" in very large letters. Most of its stories were reprints.

8

Youthful; Ziff-Davis

Youthful

Captain Science

Captain Science debuted in 1950. Physicist Gordon Dane and young orphan Rip Gary are on a camping trip when they come upon a dying alien named Knur in a shattered spaceship. A representative of the extraterrestrial "saucer men," Knur gives Gordon a "mechanical brain" that will impart all knowledge of the alien's race, and also shows him how another humanoid race was murdered and/or enslaved by alien "Beast Men" who want to take over the universe. Before expiring, Knur tells Gordon that Rip, who inherited a fortune from his father, should use his money to build a laboratory in New Mexico that can store the many scientific devices Gordon will derive from the electronic brain and use them to become "Captain Science." Gordon learns that the Beast Men have influenced certain evil Earthmen—powerful leaders of World War II who escaped retribution—who are holed up in the Himalayas planning the Earth's conquest. With the help of Luana, the daughter of one of the evil ones, Gordon blows up their headquarters.

In *Captain Science* 2, Gordon and Rip fly by saucer to the moon, where the electronic brain has told them there is a menace to Earth. The two find a civilization ruled by an evil queen. Nadia wants to fire a rocket at Earth so that everyone will be killed and she and her people can move there. Initially turned into zombies, Gordon and Rip eventually break free of the spell and put paid to Nadia and her pals. The Catmen from Phoebus kidnap Luana in order to force Gordon to give them the electronic brain. He goes along with them for a time, incurring the wrath of both Rip and Luana, who deem him a traitor. But he is only stalling for time until their ship is close enough to Earth for the brain to teleport the three of them back to New Mexico.

Captain Science 3 has a hilarious cover—borrowed from the cover of *Wings Comics* 94—where Luana is strapped to a plane piloted by a fanged, yellow pilot as our hero pursues them in his own aircraft. In the first story, the Beast Men of Rak ("Rak" had transformed from the name of the unseen leader of the Beast Men to the planet they come from) unleash giant robots on New York City, where Launa is staying in a hotel. Gordon, Rip and Launa are briefly imprisoned by the forces of the Beast Men. Escaping, they make their way to New Mexico, pursued by the determined robots, and use ultrasonic waves to destroy them. In the second story, our intrepid trio encounters a lost race of blue-skinned people in the depths of the Mindanao deep, where any humanoid would have been crushed by the pressure. The scene on the cover never occurs in either story.

Captain Science 4 introduces the villainy of Dr. Khartoum, who uses sorcery to sacrifice people to a tentacled other-dimensional monster christened Klamuth. The brain gives Gordon and Rip instructions, special clothing and a new weapon and sends them back to ancient times where a cult gathers women to bring to Klamuth as offerings. Gordon uses the weapon to send Klamuth packing, but when the creature is called forth by Khartoum back in the present day, both it and the mad doctor are destroyed. In the next issue, the trio foil a plot by people from Pluto to use weapons from the future to wipe out life on Earth. They also take on Ishal Moabdil, who operates out of the Sahara and sends phantom armies out to capture or slaughter enemies. Gordon defeats the would-be dictator when he realizes these phantoms are not supernatural creations but simply unreal illusions created by hypnotism.

In *Captain Science* 6, Gordon gets a warning from an alien named Hastus of the planet Pathor. Pathor is on the brink of destruction, but while the scientists want to go to Earth and peacefully take up residence here, the warriors want to wipe out all Earthlings and take over our world. Gordon and Hastus team up to stop the Pathorian military, and Captain Science uses hydrogen bombs to do so. Gordon is willing to sacrifice his life so that the rest of the pursuing fleet is destroyed, but Hastus, knowing he will be the sole survivor of his race and has little left to live for, makes the sacrifice instead.

In the seventh and final issue of *Captain Science*, our hero learns that he can't count on the Brain for advice or equipment when a huge spaceship hovers over New York and easily vaporizes any approaching aircraft. The Brain tells Gordon that these aliens come from a galaxy that is "beyond the ken of my knowledge." Calling themselves "The Legion of Space," the ugly, green invaders, full of their own sense of superiority, want to turn the human race into slaves. As soon as they boast that they managed to rid their own planet of all disease, it is clear that these aliens will face the same fate as the Martians in H.G. Wells' *War of the Worlds*: They succumb to Earth bacteria.

The second story has Gordon taking on the "Heads of Horror," occupants of a vampire world that down through the centuries has periodically "bitten" away chunks of the Earth, creating the Sahara Desert on one occasion. The Horror Heads are protoplasmic blobs with one huge eye in the middle and several wriggling tentacles. Gordon is taken captive by the King Head even as New York City is pulled into the other world and its inhabitants apparently disintegrated; the rest of the Earth soon follows. But Gordon then reveals to Rip and Luana that he managed to build a space-time machine that pushed everyone two days into the future. Back in real time, Gordon causes the vampire planet to explode, meaning it will no longer be around to destroy the Earth two days hence. As in most stories with confusing time paradoxes, one has to consider that even though the Earth's fate was reversed, didn't all of its inhabitants nevertheless still experience the physical and emotional agony of their deaths?

Gordon Dane is not the only hero in the comic. Brant Craig, Interplanetary Detective, first appears in *Captain Science* 2, going undercover to smash a group of space pirates. Although he's from Saturn, Craig checks all the boxes of the typical gumshoe: not too respectful of authority; an eye for the ladies; tough but insouciant. Craig is also a major in the Solar Security Patrol, and is occasionally assigned missions he cannot refuse. In the next issue, he investigates sabotage at a circus full of alien freaks. In *Captain Science* 4, it is revealed that Earth was destroyed atomically 1000 years in the past and is a ruin that people rarely visit. Craig discovers that a Saturnian influenced by old Earth films is using corpses of Earthmen to carry out robberies. In *Captain Science* 6, he gets involved in a good old-fashioned murder mystery when an actor is found dead. The story uses the planets of Venus and Mars as fill-ins for the free world and the Communist regime. In his final adventure, he searches for counterfeiters and discovers that the gang leader is a beautiful woman and that her "kid brother" is actually a midget and her right hand man.

Captain Science also presents stand-alone stories in each issue, although most of these are not memorable and are badly drawn to boot. In one, an accident with a time machine sucks a couple into another dimension where they face horrible, threatening creatures. Another odd tale concerns "flowers" that come out of a meteorite and develop into ape-like man-eaters.

The best story in *Captain Science* is "World War III with the Ants" in the sixth issue, which was published three years before the classic giant ant movie *Them!* appeared in theaters. While no one is certain why it's happened, ants have grown into giants, and turned carnivorous as well. With no defense against the monsters, mankind takes shelter in underground bunkers, but food quickly runs out, and soon only one enclave is left. Prof. Larens has invented a plastic that can cocoon a person and keep them in suspended animation indefinitely, staving off starvation for a time. As the decades go by, one person is freed by a caretaker so that there will always be two to conduct more experiments in hope of ridding the world of its insect conquerors. Some of the scientists give their lives testing weapons that fail to destroy the invaders. Finally, after 100 years, a weapon is perfected that either explodes the bugs or reduces them to their normal size. Now mankind has a chance to take back its planet. The scenes depicting the ants attacking cities and people are quite well done.

The early covers for the series were done by Walter Johnson, then by the Joe Orlando-Wally Wood team. The Captain Science adventures were drawn by Gustav Schrotter for the first few issues, then by Orlando and Wood, and finally Tex

Blaisdell, Vince Napoli and Harry Harrison. Bill Molno did most of the pencils for the Brant Craig stories.

Captain Science's adventures continued in *Fantastic* 8, the comic's new title. In "Isle of Madness," drawn by Harrison and Ernie Bache, the captain lands on an island inhabited by prehistoric monsters and the crazed Prof. Drago. The captain's HQ has switched from New Mexico to Australia and there is no mention of Rip or Luana, nor any explanation of how Drago managed to round up so many extinct animals. Brant Craig appears in *Fantastic* 8 in a story involving skullduggery at the Saturnian dog races. When a trainer is found murdered, Craig is caught between his brunette date and a blond conspirator. These were the last appearances for both characters.

Back-up stories in *Fantastic* 8 concern a scientist who builds a huge thinking robot that destroys him, and a boy from the city who gets more excitement than he bargained for on his grandpop's farm when a voracious dinosaur thaws out in some icy caves nearby and takes up residence in the old man's barn. Art for the first story was by Vince Napoli and for the second by Henry Kiefer. With the very next issue, *Fantastic* converted into an all-horror mag, then changed its title to *Beware*.

Atomic Attack

The first four issues of *Atomic Attack* were published as *Attack!*, a standard war comic featuring World War II and Korean battle stories. In 1953, there was a name and slight content change with the fifth issue. The only real difference between *Attack!* 4 and the ones that came afterward is that the lead story in the latter issues takes place in the 1970s during World War III. In *AA* 8, a group of soldiers are assigned to blow up an atomic pile in the middle of an unnamed Communist city. The soldiers have special weapons that cause enemies to burst into flames. America's adversaries are still "Reds" who engage in germ warfare. The back-up stories in that issue (and subsequent ones) are no different from what was published in earlier issues.

Atomic Attack 6 depicts a 1976 battle between United Nations forces on Inchor Island where huge tanks, robot planes and giant atomic guns are employed. Roy Krenkel's art does not do much to help an insufficient script. In the following issue, the nuclear sub N-82 is sent to destroy a floating Communist base (disguised as an iceberg) where the Reds' planes can easily refuel. Worse, this base can be brought close to the U.S. coastline to launch attacks on America. It is decided to turn the submarine into one big atomic bomb, after which the crew abandons ship and blows the hell out of the iceberg. Instead of being drummed out of the service for losing his sub, the commander is commended for using his wits to destroy a serious menace. Vince Napoli's art helps bring this exciting adventure to life.

In the final issue, *Atomic Attack* 8, enemy forces on the island of Palau, who appear to be Asian, have special rocket launchers that can target and irradiate

American cities. The first attempt to destroy the launchers is a failure, as the Reds down dozens of planes. While plans are made to evacuate major cities, a professor comes up with a scheme to destroy Palau, which lies over a giant fault line. A submarine is sent to plant an underwater H-bomb in such a way that the island will be demolished in the explosion. Just as the Reds are about to fire on New York City, the bomb goes off and the island disappears in the stupendous blast, the enemy assuming in their last moments on Earth that the island's volcano is responsible. The notion of having stories set during World War III is an intriguing one but *Atomic Attack* is not a memorable series.

Ziff-Davis

Amazing Adventures

Amazing Adventures debuted in 1950. Its first issue is a real hodgepodge, featuring one story—written by series editor Jerry Siegel, and drawn by Murphy Anderson—in which an "asteroid witch" mesmerizes men to be cruel to their girlfriends and fly to her side; and another in which an adventurer and his girlfriend are menaced by hulking stone men from outer space. In "Winged Death on Venus," drawn by Wally Wood, a wealthy man hires a guide for a hunting party. He brings along his niece, who has a love-hate relationship with the guide. It develops that he is less interested in hunting than in stealing a jewel from a statue belonging to an angry winged race. He is killed and the two younger people find romance.

Amazing Adventures 2 features a depressing story drawn by Alex Schomburg, "Exhibit One!": On a field trip, an alien museum curator, Sith Tal, captures two Earthlings, Paul and Lola, and brings them along with him as he visits various planets. Sith Tal belongs to a race that lives over 100,000 years, and he uses his science to remove all disease and aging factors from the two Earthlings. Paul and Lola decide to cooperate with Sith Tal in the hopes that they can amass enough information about space travel so that they can escape in another ship when he lets his guard down. They talk to each other of all the wonderful things they miss about the Earth. Finally the day arrives and they are able to escape. But when they get to Earth, they discover that thousands of years have gone by, human beings have gone through drastic physical and mental changes, and Paul and Lola are now just a couple of freaks. "We've escaped from one zoo," Paul says, "only to land in another!" (The story was reworked as "10,000 Years Old" in *Weird Tales of the Future* 1.)

In the same issue's "Wedding Gift," drawn by Murphy Anderson, a man disobeys his fiancée and takes off to the sixth dimension with his time-belt. He winds up on a world whose leaders plan to use an explosive missile to eradicate their enemies. When the hero learns that he has somehow landed on Venus and that the world they plan to demolish is Earth, he cooks up a scheme to destroy the Venusians instead; saving the Earth is his "wedding gift" for his bride. He spends not one second trying to create peace between the two planets, opting instead to vaporize

Ziff-Davis had an interesting if short-lived series in *Amazing Adventures*.

millions of beings without a second thought. "The Steel Monster" has a crazed scientist outfitting a bulldozer with a brain and sending it out after his fiancée and his assistant, the man she truly loves. As an action story it works quite well, but its science is virtually non-existent. It was undoubtedly inspired by Theodore Sturgeon's 1944 short story "Killdozer."

In *Amazing Adventures* 3, a jealous man shrinks the new husband of his former fiancée and tries to comfort her over his "disappearance," but he winds up getting shrunk himself and becomes food for a cat. The story was drawn by Paul Parker. The brain of a Japanese master criminal is irradiated in the bombing of Hiroshima, grows to gigantic size, and becomes a cloud hovering over an American city, sending out rays that turn the populace violent and evil; this was drawn by Leonard Starr. "Escape on a Planetoid" takes place in the future when Earth is ruled by a dictator called Ates. He sends his not-so-loyal space navigator Rulak to search for a group of democratic scientists who escaped into space long ago. Rulak finds them on the planetoid Minos and falls in love with one of the women. But he now has to return to Earth, or Ates will realize where the refugees are hiding. A heartbroken Rulak returns and reports to the dictator that there is no life nor anything of value on Minos. Annoyed that Rulak is suspected of reading banned literature, Ates punishes him by assigning him to the space sector containing—Minos!

Amazing Adventures 4 leads off with a zany story about weird aliens who unleash two gorgeous "love robots"—one male and one female—to "seduce" Earthlings and make them ripe for conquest. But the robots fall in love with each other; when they discover they are bound for the scrapheap, they literally boot the aliens off a hilltop, and the Earth is saved. The story was written by Jerry Siegel and drawn by Henry Sharp. In other stories, mutineers cause problems for Earth colonizers on planet Ganymede and a hunt for treasure on an asteroid brings out hidden greed in the participants. A ghost story in which a murdered doctor nevertheless shows up at the hospital to operate on a dying boy is completely out of place.

A change came over the comic in *Amazing Adventures* 5 with more complex stories. In a "Captain Hawkins" adventure drawn by Murphy Anderson, the captain has his own ship on "perimeter patrol" (he looks after the planetoids on the "outer fringes of the solar system"). The commandant, Luthor Mynot, who operates on the base planetoid of Rondos, freely admits that he hates Hawkins because the latter's father was extremely tough on him and this is his way of getting even. Mynot assigns his own son, Groll, to Hawkins' ship. Groll comes down with a case of space sickness that drives him mad. The prescribed course of action when this happens is to cast the sufferer adrift where he will die in space alone, but Hawkins can't bring himself to do this. He takes the ship back to Rondos, ignoring his orders to put down a rebellion on another planetoid. Groll's life is saved, but Mynot is furious that Hawkins disobeyed him and banishes him to the lonely outpost of Malooka. However, a grateful Groll rescues Hawkins from Malooka and gets him reinstated. Despite its interesting aspects, the script doesn't deal with one central question. Setting

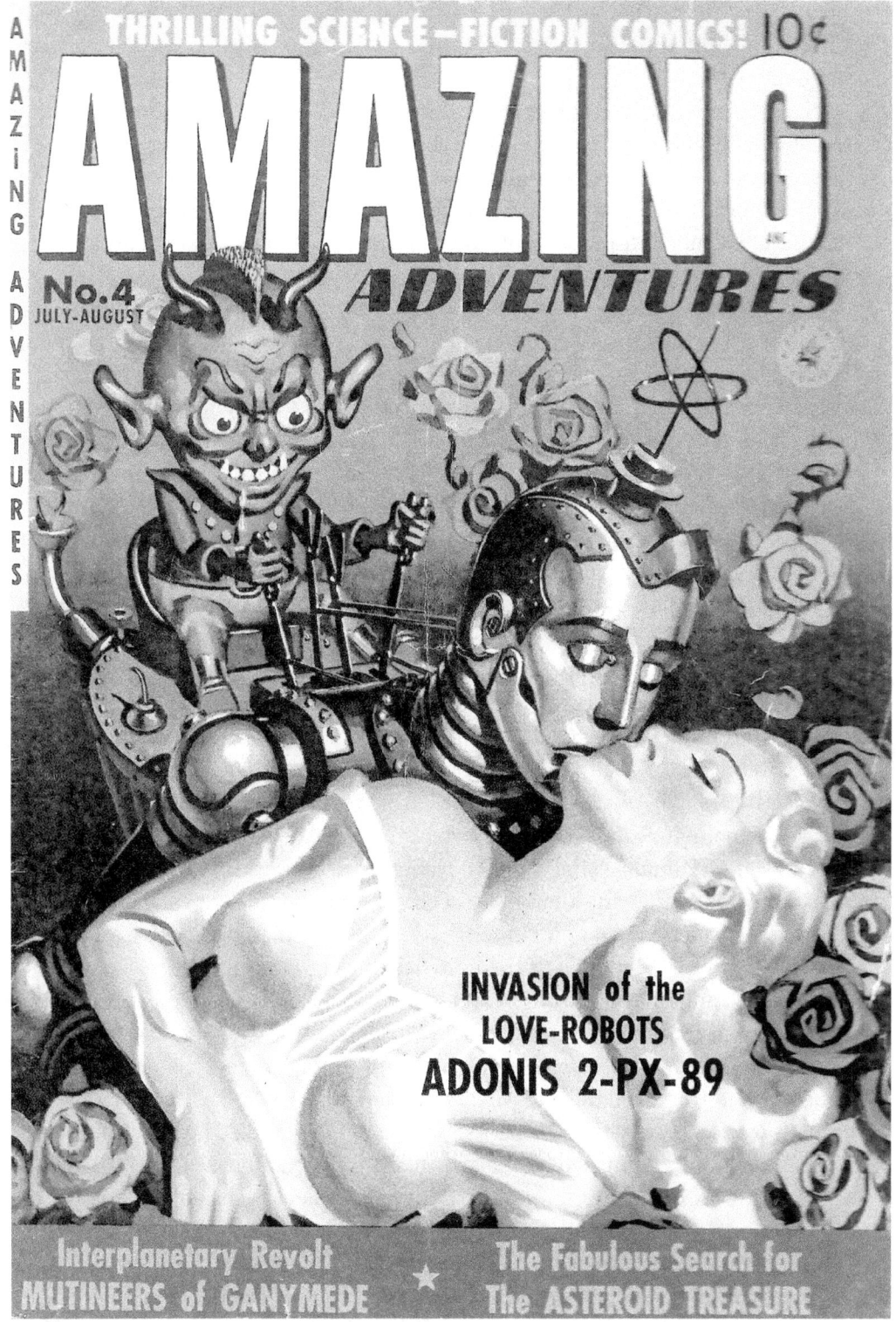

A zany Jerry Siegel story about "love robots" appeared in *Amazing Adventures* #4.

someone adrift seems like such an extreme measure that there must be a good reason for it, but the notion that space sickness may be contagious and incurable is never brought up.

The same issue's "The Secret of the Crater Men," drawn by Al Carreno, has a Genghis Khan–like dictator taking over the Earth. A resistance movement travels to the moon to hide out and plan, and there they encounter a race of green men who can emit a devastating nerve gas, which the rebels use to defeat the dictator. In "The Red Hills of Uganda," drawn by Ray Bailey, scientists use napalm to kill off a race of man-sized, intelligent ants who are marching across the continent.

Captain Hawkins returns in *Amazing Adventures* 6, the final issue, in two stories. In the first, drawn by Bernie Krigstein, he goes undercover to round up space pirates who are selling an outlawed juice that has the same effects as certain drugs. More interesting than this standard adventure tale is "City of Light," drawn by Henry Sharp. The unfriendly Photon Men live in a subterranean city entirely comprised of solidified white light. The light is generated by a machine called a "nucleon." When it is smashed, the bodies of the Photo Men disintegrate into pure light.

There are two additional stories in this issue. In the bizarre if unmemorable "Deal to Die," a wealthy woman, Bernice, is constantly put down by her husband. She stabs him to death and is sentenced to die. Zoro, an alien woman, appears in Bernice's cell and tells her she wants to change places with her and visit Earth. Bernice, withholding from Zoro the fact that she is about to be executed, agrees to make the switch—but on Zoro's world, Bernice learns that Zoro is also about to be put to death for murdering *her* husband. The story was drawn by Lawrence Dresser.

"The Man Who Killed a World," drawn by Paul Parker, is the best story ever published in *Amazing Adventures*. In the 26th century, Mars and Earth, who had a war years ago that destroyed all the water on both planets, have an uneasy truce, with devastating Z-bombs aimed at each planet. The two worlds get their water from a rich supply on Venus. But then most of the Venus water becomes contaminated and there's only enough good water left for half the population of each world. Both Mars and Earth refuse to let half their citizens die, and decide to have a contest—man-to-man combat—to see which world will survive. Earth's champion Don Evans diligently trains for this important battle. To avoid any tricks or extra advantages, a separate planetoid is constructed where the fight will take place. Firing mechanisms for the Z-bomb are placed there as well: Whoever wins will destroy the other planet. Evans is surprised that his opponent is spindly, and he is freaked out by his constant grinning. He is also disturbed by the fact that the Martian never seems to tire. As hours go by, Evans realizes that the Martians have mastered the ability to go without sleep. Evans is defeated by the Martian, who fires off the missile that—destroys *Mars*! Apparently the buttons on the firing mechanisms were color-coded, and the poor Martian didn't realize he was color-blind! Of course, one could argue that the story ends at its most important point—now the Martian is the sole survivor of his race, and his guilt will be eternal and tremendous.

Cover paintings for the comic were done by Robert Gibson Jones, Allen Anderson and Norman Saunders.

Lars of Mars

Lars of Mars debuted in 1951 with two issues, numbered 10 and 11. On Mars, the Martian council is distressed to discover that an H-Bomb has been exploded on Earth. Many years before, there was a war between Mars and Venus that nearly destroyed both planets. Hero Lars is chosen to go to Earth as a peace emissary, to combat evil and keep the nations from becoming too aggressive. When he lands, he sees a woman being menaced by two robots. Wouldn't you know that both the woman and the robots are actors, and this is just a rehearsal for a TV series episode? The woman, producer June Conway, is so impressed by the heroic Lars that she makes him the star of the series, which she decides to call *Lars of Mars*, going along with his "gag" of being a Martian. Lars figures it will make a great cover for his true activities and agrees.

Lars wears a jet pack to fly and has hypnotic abilities. The Martian council sends him out on assignments, such as stopping the bombing of an atomic plant and destroying a weapon that can freeze troops. The series, drawn by Murphy Anderson and possibly written by Jerry Siegel, had possibilities but it was much more in the superhero genre than science fiction. The forgettable "Ken Brady, Rocket Pilot" back-ups were drawn by Gene Colan. The painted covers were done by Allen Anderson.

In 1951, *Weird Adventures* was a one-shot (although it was listed as issue 10) that contains some interesting if imperfect material. In "Dome of Death," drawn by John Celardo, an invisible dome is erected over a city to make it impregnable. Thieves steal the device that will remove the dome and blackmail the city. The dome idea was used in other stories, including *Strange Adventures* 5's "The Perfect Weapon" which came out five months earlier. The next two stories deal with women who are overly aggressive when it comes to the object of their desire. In "The Beautiful Robot," an ugly old professor who is tired of being rejected by women builds himself a gorgeous automaton. But the automaton prefers his handsome assistant, going so far as to force herself on him at his wedding reception. When he rejects her, she goes berserk. "The Seeker from Beyond" is a beautiful blonde from another planet who comes to Earth to bring a lookalike of her dead lover back to her own world; she nearly kills the man's fiancée. The man outwits the determined alien visitor and stays on Earth with the woman *he* loves. This story is depicted in Phil Morini's attractive cover painting.

The best story is "The Man Who Lived Backwards": Paul, about to be married, discovers that his life has started flowing in reverse; he even hears other people talking backwards (although this aspect is quickly dropped). Almost driven out

Ziff-Davis' *Lars of Mars* did not have much staying power, lasting only two issues.

of his mind by this situation, Paul is convinced that a rival, David, has done this to him, and regrets that he once prevented him from falling off a cliff during a camping trip. As time progresses backwards until the day of that trip, Paul decides that he will not go looking for David as he did that day and therefore cannot save him. His conscience gets the better of him and he runs toward the cliff, but David falls to his death in spite of it. Everything returns to normal, but the story doesn't provide detailed answers. The tale's most interesting aspect is the moral dilemma that Paul finds himself in as regards to the cliff.

Weird Thrillers

Weird Thrillers also came out in 1951 and lasted for five issues. In the first issue, a young couple discovers that the president and his cabinet have been replaced by robots, and the two stop this revolution by putting sand in the robot's oil cans. In another story, a man tries to please his fiancée by going after a special flower on a distant planet. Once there, he deals with the enormous spider that guards the valuable crystalline flower and with desperadoes who want it for themselves.

In subsequent issues, a man encounters time-traveling aliens and winds up running over himself in his car; another man puts on a fright mask to scare his wealthy uncle to death and finds his face has transformed his features so that he's as hideous on the outside as he is on the inside (a premise later used on *The Twilight Zone*); and a man falls in love with a beautiful mermaid princess.

Doubles figure in two stories in *Weird Thrillers* 3. In "The Soul of Benjamin Sprague," Ben's soul changes places with him. Ben winds up a bowery bum, but over the years he learns compassion; when reunited with his soul, he decides to use his money to help others. In "Death x 2 = Zero," gang leader Bull Manton murders his partners in crime so that he won't have to split the loot with them. When a bizarre electrical accident splits him into two people, Bull Manton—who won't split with anyone—murders himself.

There was a change in direction from sci-fi to horror in the last two *Weird Thrillers*. The fifth issue concentrates on ghoulish revenge stories in which ghosts, a cat and even a bunch of birds get even with a variety of murderous criminals, causing their macabre deaths.

Crusader from Mars

The two issues of *Crusader from Mars* appeared in 1952. At the very beginning of the story, we learn that on Mars, Tarka and his lover Zira have been convicted of murdering Tarka's rival for Zira's affections. It was the first felony on the Red Planet in 50 years. There are no other details, but in an attempt to redeem themselves, Tarka suggests that he and Zira be sent to the primitive world of Earth to combat evil. Once there, they learn that a small nation is planning to use a bacteriological weapon on the United States. Tarka poses as a salesman for a chemical company in the enemy country, with Zira as his secretary, but they realize that destroying just one plant won't be enough. Red tape stymies their efforts to warn the U.S. Their handler, Marshal Lo Wincro, sends Martian discs to Earth to stop the attack on the U.S. Tarka and Zira essentially prove to be useless.

In the second story, Zira is now the secretary to General Claymore of Army Intelligence. She does very little in this yarn, in which Tarka discovers a plot to destroy the U.S. food supply. Tarak gets around in his flying saucer and changes into his uniform before he goes into action. Again, most of the work is actually done by Lo Wincro, operating from a space station orbiting the Earth. In *Crusader from Mars* 2, the two are told to help a farmer who is being terrorized by a Ku Klux Klan group called the Black Hoods. Although the farmer has been a citizen for decades, he is seen as a "furriner" and is persecuted by the bigots. The FBI can't get involved in what is a local problem. Tarka changes into his costume, flies his disc to the farm and easily mops up the Hoods. The leader is taken to Mars to do some ditch work on the canals.

In the second story, Tarka and Zira are called away from investigating Earth's criminal activities and assigned to the War Department, because a distant planet called Uralia is causing problems. Tarak pretends to be a traitor and joins the enemy forces in an attempt to undermine them. His true identity is discovered, but he still manages to stop an invasion of Saturn.

Some of the *Crusader from Mars* stories that did *not* star Tarkas are better than the lead stories. In "Escape to Nowhere" (*CFM* 1), drawn by Mike Becker, a small group of people in 1952 take off in a rocket to Planet X, certain that the Earth is about to erupt into nuclear conflict. On this new world, they find the ruins of great cities. What seemed like mere weeks in space was actually centuries: The professor who built the rocket installed a gas that would preserve life, and the group has actually landed back on Earth. The holocaust they so feared had come to pass! This notion that all roads—or spaceships—lead back to Earth became very popular in science fiction comics and TV shows.

"Prison Planet" (*CFM* 2) is the best story published in the comic. Accused of being a traitor, Capt. Jon Barrett of the Space Police vows to get even when he is drummed out of the corps and told he is being banished to a horrible prison planet. He blows off his girlfriend, who believes in his innocence, and tells her he is guilty. On the prison planet, two men whom he had arrested tie him to a radioactive boulder that will slowly melt his flesh, and he is nearly eaten by a large voracious lizard before being rescued by a beautiful brunette, Exotica. She takes him to the leader of the insurrection, who has gathered spaceships and plans to mount an attack on the Space Police HQ. The two men who tried to kill Barrett are charged with disobedience and fed to gigantic "terror plants" with huge tentacles. Barrett is actually working undercover; when his deception is exposed, Exotica helps him escape and crush the rebellion in exchange for a pardon. Exotica and Barrett have apparently fallen in love, which is kind of tough on the girlfriend who believed in him.

The *Crusader from Mars* cover paintings were done by Allen Anderson, with inside art by Marvin Stein, Henry Sharp and George Roussos.

Space Busters *and* Space Patrol

Space Busters came out with two issues in 1952. In the future, Earth is at war with the planet Belzar, and each world wants to lay claim to Mars. Captain Brett Crockett of the Space-Busters (the hyphen is not used in the comic's title) is surprised to learn that Commander Senstral, an alien, is going along on the mission to take Mars. Senstral is actually working for Belzar and reports to their queen. Through Senstral's treachery, the Space-Busters are captured, along with a pretty (but testy) nurse, Lt. April Wing. Crockett and the others fight back heroically and drive the Belzarians from Mars.

"We are not only fierce in attack, your majesty, but full of feminine guile," the leader of the Belzarian Battle Women tells their queen in the next story, in which these female warriors sneak up on and easily capture the Space-Busters. In an utterly ridiculous sequence, Crockett pitches woo to one of the women, who immediately falls for him and helps him and the others escape. In the first story, Crockett and Wing barely know each other, but in the second tale they are engaged. Fortunately, the former Belzarian Battle Woman is more attracted to one of Crockett's allies.

In subsequent *Space Busters* stories, Crockett and the Space-Busters continue to fight the evil queen, the traitor Senstral, and other races who want no part of the war between Earth and Belzar. Lt. Wing is captured by hairy Belzarian dwarves, who want to tear out her heart as part of their sacrificial rites. The comic features attractive painted covers by Norman Saunders with acceptable inside art by B. Krigstein in *Space Busters* 1 and early Murphy Anderson art in *Space Busters* 2.

Commander Buzz Corry is the hero of *Space Patrol*, which also came out in 1952 and lasted two issues. Buzz's rival, Commander Gorla, who is part of a conspiracy to take over the solar system, tries to kill Buzz with a rocket but the ploy fails and Gorla is arrested. Tonga, a woman known as the Lady of Diamonds, fears that if Gorla is put under a brain machine he will reveal her own part in the conspiracy so she has Lt. Kraznoff fire upon him. Buzz and his young partner Cadet Happy pursue Kraznoff to planet Vesta, which is ruled by the Swamp Queen. (She also hopes to take over the universe with a huge paralyzing lens, which Buzz smashes in a manner that is not made terribly clear.) The issue's third story has a villainess who steals shipments of the valuable Tellerium and tries to use a magnet to smash our heroes to smithereens.

In *Space Patrol* 2, Buzz and Happy contend with a man who demands tribute from anyone who lands on his world in a kind of protection racket, save the life of a tubercular princess so that her planet can join the United Planets of the Universe, and rescue a beautiful woman from the clutches of a despot. B. Krigstein's art in the first issue is poor. Norman Saunders did the painted cover for *SP* 1 while Clarence Doore painted the cover of the second issue. The comic was based on a half-hour TV series that ran from 1950 to 1955.

PART TWO

The Silver Age

9

American Comics Group (ACG)

Adventures into the Unknown began life in the Golden Age as the first horror comic book. After the public outcry over the gruesome content in such books, most of these comics switched to stories of suspense, mystery, science fiction and fantasy—as did *Adventures*. A trio of crystal balls show the future; aliens take unhappy people to a planet paradise; a boat constantly veers off course searching for its dead owners; a man becomes a genius when he puts on a wig once worn by Leonardo da Vinci; and so on. *Adventures* 5 began running writer and artist credits and there were pulp-like covers beginning with *Adventures* 109.

Humor became a staple of the series. There are stories about a hillbilly who builds a rocketship that soars far into space and is powered by an old relative's broomstick, and a jinx who is nearly drummed out of the Army but wins World War II by causing a run of bad luck for the enemy. Then there is a man who inherits a duplicating machine from his uncle but ultimately all it can do is duplicate steaks, so he opens a steakhouse with very low overhead. There are many stories about lonely people encountering friends and lovers who may or may not be imaginary. Nerds and geeks who turn out to be geniuses and heroes and are treated shamefully by their peers and society. Men who fall hopelessly in love with women who have been dead for years or are in far-off outer space. (In one story, the beautiful woman on the monitor turns out to belong to a race of floating heads with no bodies!) Some stories deal with the redemption of horrible human beings who really don't deserve it.

In "The Genius," drawn by Harry Lazarus in *AITU* 72, a man determines to make his son Jimmy extraordinary, by feeding him a special diet. At first this doesn't seem to have much effect, but when Jimmy goes to college he discovers he has developed superb athletic skills, and they bring him quite a bit of attention. Unfortunately, he doesn't know his own strength, and after his opponents are nearly killed, he is forced to leave various teams. Everyone sees him as some kind of mutation or freak and soon he has no friends. He develops the ability to read minds and realizes that his genius IQ only brings out jealousy and even hatred in his colleagues. Jimmy gets a girlfriend but he discovers she doesn't enjoy his company because he unwittingly makes her feel stupid by comparison. Absolutely miserable, Jimmy fears he faces a lonely and unsatisfying future. When he next develops the ability to see tragic events in the future, he has had enough and comes up with a formula to turn himself back into a normal human being.

In "The Interstellar Sponge" (*Adventures* 80), drawn by Pete Costanza, an object falling from space lands in the waters of the Arctic Circle. It consists of a spongy yellow material that initially seems benign, but when a piece of it is subjected to water in a lab it begins to grow. As for the original mass, it also begins to expand to huge proportions as it floats into warmer waters. One island in its path is completely engulfed after the natives have been evacuated. Eventually the sponge is a thousand miles long and nearing Argentina. It is decided to douse it with huge amounts of liquid oxygen, whose frigid temperature causes the creature to completely dissipate. Now the military wonder if the monster was sent to Earth by hostile extraterrestrials or came accidentally on its own. (A few years later, *The Blob* came from outer space and at the end, it was frozen with liquid oxygen.) In "Suspicious People" (*Adventures* 152), aliens wipe out Earth by using a "vaccine" that turns all animals and insects into giants, an idea used in the 1954 film *Killers from Space*.

Monsters of a type also figure in "Secret of the Titans" (Hughes-Forte) in *Adventures* 123 and "The Invisible Menace" (Hughes-Rosenberger) in *Adventures* 125. In the first story, an American geologist discovers that there is actually a place called Tartarus at the bottom of the Mediterranean Sea and inside this massive chamber the gigantic Titans of mythology are supposedly imprisoned. When an island rises to the surface of the sea, an immense temple is found, and inside the chained giants. Awoken by the outside air when the door to their prison is opened, the Titans try to break their bonds. The seal of Zeus, affixed to the door, keeps these threats to the world from getting out. With its Lovecraftian flavor and other elements, the story is more than a little reminiscent of the great horror author's "The Call of Cthulhu." In the second story, a black cloud that destroys buildings consists of trillions of alien micro-organisms that resemble tiny insects. Spraying them with a common cold virus wipes them out.

The most compelling element of "The Lost Continent" (in *AITU* 77) is the notion that mirages and indeed "ghosts" are not at all supernatural, but simply caused by people's extreme emotions during moments of great stress and excitement. These emotions pierce the time barrier, meaning that certain events can be seen over and over again by people who think they are seeing ghosts. The rest of the story, concerning a lost princess of Atlantis, is of much less interest.

In "The Seller of Dreams" (*AITU* 81), a plain woman marries a handsome, talented artist. She is afraid he only married her for her money, and is jealous of anything that might take him away from her. She goes so far as to bribe art critics into saying his work is poor, fearing that she'll lose him to success. A mystic says that, for $10,000, he can make her beautiful, and he's true to his word. But the next morning, she's not only homely again, but also looks even worse—and older—and the mystic expects to be paid *every day*. She goes through her fortune trying to stay beautiful. Surprisingly, the story has a happy ending: The husband sets the authorities on the mystic, who dissolves into dust, and his wife is back to her plain, now penniless self—but her husband proves that he really loves her and will support her. Considering the way she bribed those art critics—could you do that to someone you loved?—the selfish woman deserved a different fate. (This yarn reprinted as "The Gift of Beauty" in *Forbidden Worlds* 143.)

In "Fate Rides the Carousel" (*AITU* 83), drawn by Ogden Whitney, Bill Russell has been haunted by the death of his father, who died of a heart attack after Bill, as a child, was thrown from a carousel. Bill has always blamed himself for his father's death, thinking that if he hadn't acted foolishly and flung out his arms while on the carousel, nothing would have happened. He comes across the carousel again and takes a ride on it, winding up back in the past, where—a child again—he behaves himself and his father doesn't die. But after they walk out of the park, Bill's father intervenes when a runaway car nearly kills Bill, and the shock of nearly losing the boy this time causes his father's death. Bill goes back to the carousel and again tries to change the past, with the same result. Eventually he realizes that the carousel has been shuttered and unused for years—and he also understands that his father's time was up due to his weak heart and nothing can be done to save him.

In *AITU* 104's "The Strange Old Camera" (Hughes-Whitney), photographer Larry Andrews returns to his hometown for a vacation and takes pictures with an old-fashioned camera that he bought for a song. When he develops a photo of the schoolhouse, he is startled to see *himself* running out of the building in the picture. He discovers that the camera can take pictures from the past, and that the camera has an attachment that determines how many years back a photo will be. Taking other photos of the house he grew up in, he keeps seeing the same beautiful woman in them, and falls in love with her. He is appalled when an outdoor photo reveals that her horse and carriage—with her in it—are about to be hit by a train.

Recognizing that he can do nothing about what happened to the woman, Larry tries to forget, and decides to have fun using a photographic trick to put himself as an adult into the aforementioned photograph of himself as a boy. This has the result of sending Larry back in time to the schoolyard, where he meets himself as a child. Frightened, he tears up the picture and is instantly returned to his own time. Then he hits on the idea of putting himself in the photo of the woman and the train so that he can again go back in time and possibly save her life. This he manages to do in the nick of time. Larry stays in the past with the woman.

"The Thing That Was Charlie O'Reilly" (Hughes-Forte) in *AITU* 107 is an interesting variation of the ventriloquist dummy tale. Jon and Eve Tallent have a successful act in which they use a dummy named Charlie, whom the childless couple treat as if he were a real boy. When they adopt a boy named Ken, Charlie starts saying rude things that neither of them said during their act. Ken starts misbehaving, explaining that he's only doing the things Charlie told him to do. Jon and Eve take Charlie out of the act and lock him away where Ken can't find him. When Ken runs away, Jon and Eve find him lying at the edge of the lake, with Charlie hanging on to his arm from an overhead tree branch. They assume that the jealous Charlie is trying to kill their son, and Jon shoots him to pieces. Ken tells them that Charlie was actually trying to save him after he fell in the water.

"Man of Mystery" (Hughes-Beck-Hamilton) in *AITU* 131 and "Make Your Landing on Planet Xanadu" (Hughes-Beck-Costanza) in 151 are two of the comic's best stories. In the former, criminologist Andrew Clevinger discovers that the same man has been committing murders of prominent people on the same date every 100 years. Doing a great deal of research, Clevinger is able to trace the perpetrator, a wizard named Metruro who was executed for practicing magic, back to 1461. Metruro has a tattoo on the back of his hand, the face of a cat surrounded by a sun's corona. In the present day, Clevinger figures out who the next victim is to be—a prince on his wedding day—and manages to save the man's life, although he is badly injured while chasing after the wizard. Wheeled into the operating theater, poor Clevinger is unaware that the surgeon who is about to take the scalpel to him has the tattoo of a cat on his hand … and Clevinger does not survive. Instead of the prince, he is the wizard's latest victim. The story is suspenseful and compelling.

"Xanadu" takes place in 2064 when the people of planet Xanadu are fascinated by the people of Earth. A likable, freckle-faced Xanadu boy named Jeronda is thrilled when an expedition arrives from Earth and he immediately attaches himself to Commander Bill Monterey, whom he admires as much as he admires Abraham Lincoln, whom he studied in class. Monterey encourages the boy's hero-worship and asks him dozens of questions about the world—and wealth—of Xanadu. Jeronda has no idea that Monterey and the others have come to strip Xanadu of its riches. Jeronda arranges for them to get inside the vast storage room of gold. After stealing the ingots, Monterey bombs the city, leaving very few survivors. A devastated Jeronda uses an ancient weapon to destroy the ship as it departs, but this also causes the destruction of the entire Earth. It is never made clear if Monterey and his companions are representatives of Earth or only of some commercial enterprise, but it's still interesting that in this story the Earthlings are seen in such a negative light, almost as if author Richard Hughes was commenting on or even condemning American colonialism.

Artists for the series included Pete Costanza, John Rosenberger, John Forte, John Buscema, Kurt Schaffenberger, and Paul Reinman. Richard Hughes (born Leo Rosenbaum) was the editor for the series and others published by ACG, and wrote most of the stories, generally under various pen names, including Zev Zimmer, Shane O'Shea and even Kurato Osaki. Hughes went so far as to conjure up fake bios of these imaginary authors, and on occasion had his artists provide drawings of their imaginary faces! On the letters pages, Hughes made critical comments about many of the stories that he himself had written, but in some instances he would pick on an artist for real. He took after penciller Dick Beck in a way that seemed quite personal and nasty: "It was one lousy job of illustration. And bad drawing got in the way of a story that might have worked out fine if our artist had done the job he should have." Although the art for the story is not on the level of the series' major artists, it is not that bad either, and Hughes continued to employ Beck in the future.

Some other notable stories in the series include:

- "Premonition of Disaster" (*AITU* 75): Throughout his life, a Japanese man has had psychic flashes of terrible future events and on the morning he travels to Hiroshima at the end of World War II he has the worst premonition of disaster he has ever had.
- "The Man Within": (80): Hypnosis reveals that a simple-minded handyman is actually an alien who murdered and impersonated the men who became Attila the Hun, Blackbeard, and Adolf Hitler.
- "A Bucket of Paint" (82): With the aid of a mysterious paint, a man is able to get incredible opportunities to enrich his life but winds up always making the wrong choices.
- "The Room That Time Forgot" (85): A man from 800,000 years in the past has spent most of his life in a room where time stands still, emerging every hundred years in the hopes that in some future time his brain tumor can be cured.
- "Doom Foiled" (91): A lawyer with an incurable brain lesion gets successful surgery from a race of little aliens that he alone can see due to his condition, in exchange for him keeping them supplied with boxes of aluminum foil.
- "Pipe Dream" (93): Via a mystical pipe given him by his fiancée, a man has a chance to go back into the past and save her life after a terrible train disaster.
- "Missing: One Scientist" (99): A brilliant man is ridiculed his entire life for useless achievements. When he finally builds a satellite to the stars, the world's appreciation comes too late.
- "Trail of the Mummy" (102): An old museum guard becomes obsessed with the mummy of an ancient queen. He turns out to be the reincarnation of her lover.
- "Howee-eeeee!" (127): The eerie noises in a crevice come from a dangerous creature that must be killed by the officer whose life it saved.
- "The Judas Goat" (131): American astronauts make the ultimate sacrifice by leading enemy leaders down into the deadly atmosphere of a dangerous planet.
- "The Lion's Share" (141): With the help of an Earth spirit, a crippled boy has dreams that result in joy for his friends and a fitting and gruesome end for his cruel uncle.
- "The Gravy Train" (152): A mentally deficient man whose father worked for the railroad is cruelly used for a robbery but gives his life to set things right.

Beginning with *AITU* 154, the series began running the exploits of Nemesis, a superhero who is actually a spirit. Nemesis got the cover spot and lead story for every issue up to 167, after which he was relegated to the back of the book, then disappeared altogether three issues later. The series itself lasted only three more issues. The "Fan Fare" series that ran in later *Adventures* issues were retitled reprints from *Forbidden Worlds*.

Memorable tales during and after the Nemesis run include "Born Failure" (160), in which a screw-up saves the day but gets no credit for it; "Two Vials from Vidalia" (169), an amusingly ironic tale about an ugly, persecuted man who gets revenge but outwits himself at the end; and "Fuhrenbauer's Fake Folks," (174), about a company that produces robots, with a great twist ending.

Forbidden Worlds

First appearing in 1951, *Forbidden Worlds* generally ran supernatural stories featuring vampires, werewolves and other horrors. After the horror implosion, the series—like *Adventures into Unknown Worlds*—switched to much less gruesome tales of sci-fi and fantasy. Sometimes *FW* came up with a clever premise but then muffed it, such as the *FW* 43 tale "Home Is Where You Find It," which posits the theory that everything that exists today—every city, every person—also existed 100,000 years ago: An archeologist uncovers "ancient" houses and villages where they shouldn't be—Lincoln's log cabin beneath a polar ice cap; Notre Dame Cathedral in an excavation in Egypt—as well as an entire New England town, Oaktree Corners, under a layer of volcanic ash in India. The notion that everything has already happened at least once before is not only disheartening but also nonsensical for a town that once existed in India to be recreated centuries later in the United States down to the last detail. The hero even finds his fraternity key, dropped in a hole in the floor in the schoolhouse back in Massachusetts, in the floor of the ancient schoolhouse in India! Of course, our knowledge of prehistory makes nonsense of the whole premise anyway. Maybe if history repeated itself every *billion* years...

"Vera, My Dark Star" (*FW* 45) is a dark-comic tale of a man who was born under the sign of Vera, a star that was discovered on the night he entered the world, and which seems determined to cause his death or some disaster every year on his birthday. "The Explorers" (*FW* 46) features a chimp who develops superior intelligence after being shot into space, but finds that he's now a freak who is neither ape nor human. In "The Land That Time Forgot" (*FW* 48), a boring machine descends into a lost world of monsters and strange humanoids under the Earth. It's a hodgepodge of Verne, Burroughs and the B movie *Unknown World*.

FW 79's "The Strange Case of Uncle Hoober" (Hughes-Hickety) is another darkly amusing story. A couple, Hector and Mona, have to put up with their eccentric uncle because they hope to be the beneficiaries in his will. Uncle Hoober spends all his time cutting coupons from cereal boxes and sending away for plastic toys such as a teleporter which doesn't work. But Hoober connects it to another mail order gizmo and when his nephew and his wife decide to have him committed, they wind

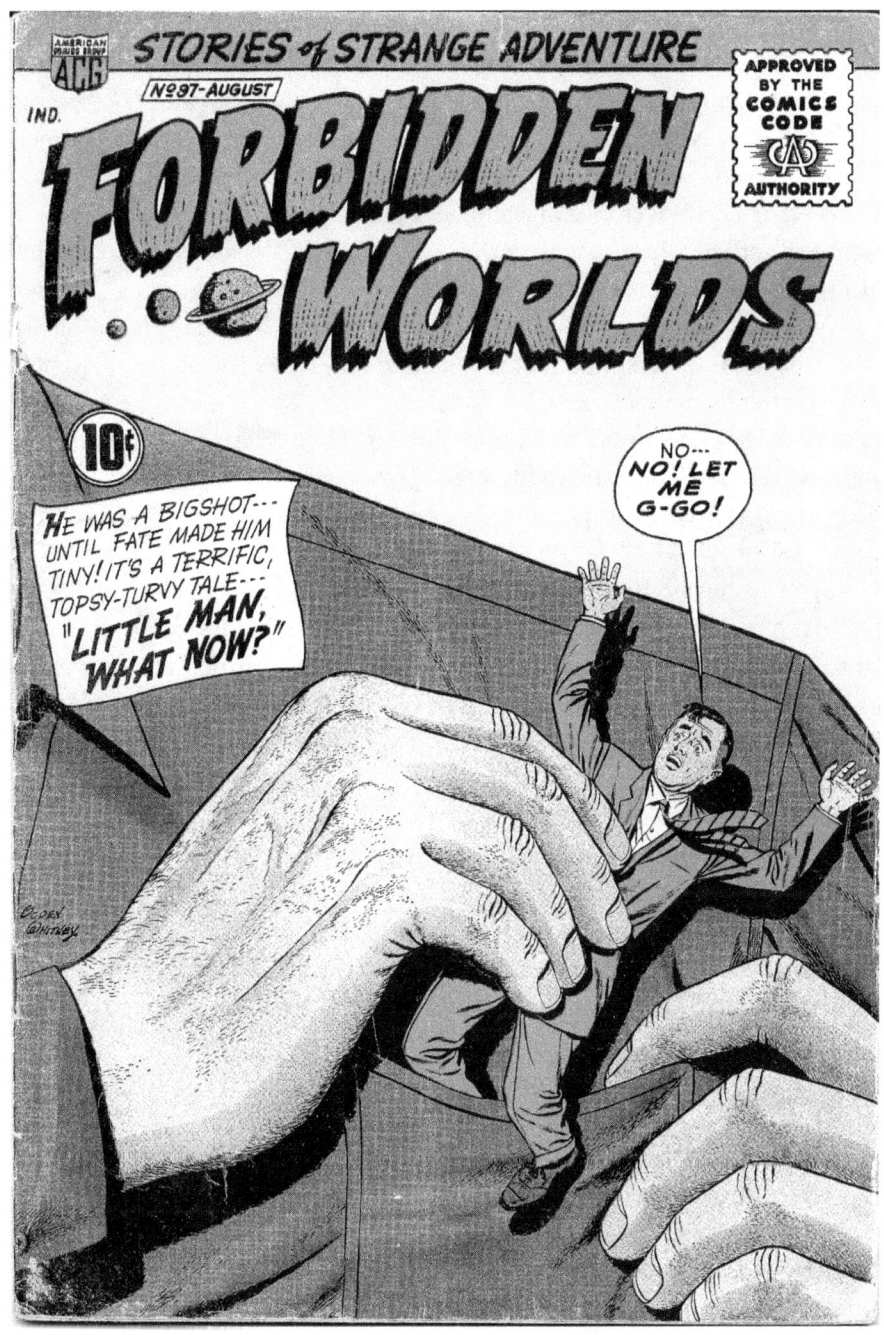

Forbidden Worlds was a long-running comic from American Comics Group that switched from horror to fantasy and science fiction.

up being teleported to a distant planet. Hoober just goes on eating cereal and sending away for more plastic toys.

Richard Hughes saw the comical aspects of some of the more absurd stories he wrote and played up the laughs in many of them. In "Mr. Miggs from Mercury"

(*FW* 42), Mercury is ruled by women, including the man-hating Queen Skiddlebup, while men stay home, cook, clean and get treated with contempt, especially Mr. Miggs. Miggs is sent to Earth by the queen to scope things out and take over if necessary, as Mercury is becoming overcrowded. On Earth, Miggs encounters members of the militant Women Leaders of America, then two women who work for a carnival that is being taken over by gangsters. Miggs and pretty Betty, the carnival owner, fall for one another, while lady wrestling champ Half-Nelson McGurk despairs of ever finding a man. Miggs uses his Mercurian powers to rout the gangsters, sending them to Mercury to become vassals for the queen. Then he sends Half-Nelson, who literally knocks the queen out of her throne and takes over the planet, delighted that on Mercury, the men are attracted to tough women. A psychologist could probably have a field day with this one, but it does poke fun in a relatively amiable fashion at male-female relationships during the '60s.

Hughes also created a memorably comic character, Herbie Popnecker, who first appeared in *FW* 73's "Herbie's Quiet Saturday Afternoon" (Hughes-Whitney). A rotund, bespectacled boy, Herbie is always in his own world and has little interest in playing sports or making friends. His horrible father despairs of Herbie ever amounting to anything and refers to him as "a little fat nothing." His mother objects to this but not strenuously enough, frankly. His parents are unaware that Herbie has astounding powers and can talk to animals. During one adventure, he turns back an alien invasion with ease.

Herbie returns to stop a series of attacks by supernatural creatures such as a witch and Frankenstein's Monster. When aliens steal Earth's entire supply of a certain salad dressing to save their world, Herbie manages to filch one bottle from their planet to give to his mother (*FW* 110). In "A Little Fat Nothing Named Herbie!" (*FW* 114), beautifully drawn by Ogden Whitney, Herbie is called in by President John F. Kennedy to deal with the African nation of Meranga, which refuses to join a union and uses supernatural methods to fight off United Nations forces. JFK seems fully aware of Herbie and his abilities, as do many others. Jackie Kennedy sighs when she sees Herbie and seems smitten with him. Herbie got the cover of *FW* 116, his name in larger letters than the title of the comic. On the cover and the story inside, "Liz Baylor," while filming *Cleopatra*, makes a play for Herbie, smooching him, but he's much more interested in his ever-present lollipop than he is in her. Herbie later met the real (and equally lustful) Cleopatra.

The notion of women being attracted to Herbie seems a little gross if not downright perverse, as he initially appeared to be a child. But when Herbie was given his own series, there were indications that he was actually an adult going to college. Aside from his utterly clueless parents, many people are absolutely in awe of Herbie, and he's catnip to virtually all women. Although originally conceived as a big joke on someone whom society *would* deem a "little fat nothing"—someone most women wouldn't be interested in at all—Herbie always gets the last laugh.

In contrast to the comical tales, *Forbidden Worlds* also ran more serious stories such as "Taps for a Trumpeteer" in issue 64 (art by John Rosenberger) and the especially grim "Target Planet Dead Ahead—Open Fire" (Hughes–Chic Stone) in 117. In the first story, Clarence Tubbs, wanting to be *somebody*, bids goodbye to his fiancée Amy and takes his trumpet to New York. Five years go by. Clarence is having a tough time getting anywhere and even has to sell his trumpet. When he finally gets a job with a band, he no longer has an instrument. He manages to get a very cheap trumpet from a pawn shop by giving the proprietor a gold piece, a good luck charm that was given to him years ago by his father. Oddly, he produces beautiful music with the cheap trumpet and starts making a lot of money under the name Terry Marlowe. When he goes to get his gold piece back, the pawnbroker claims he never saw him before. Terry can now afford a more expensive trumpet, but when he uses it, he produces only a mediocre sound. The cheap trumpet must have a special quality to it, so he continues to play it. He starts his own band and rises fast in the jazz world, but no matter how much he offers the pawnbroker, the man still insists he never saw him before and doesn't have the coin. Now a rich and successful musician, Clarence finally returns to Amy, but she's married and has a child. His success now seems meaningless as he realizes how important Amy was to him; he wishes that he'd never gone to New York.

Back in the city, Clarence sends Amy a stack of his Terry Marlowe records. Then he becomes quite ill and feverish, until he completely collapses outside the pawnbroker's shop. He wakes in a charity ward with Amy and the concerned pawnbroker standing over him. Clarence realizes that his success as a musician *never happened*, although it had seemed so incredibly *real*. The pawnbroker gives him back his coin and Amy, who is *not* married, takes him back home. The stack of records Clarence recorded as Terry Marlowe *arrives at Amy's house* some time later. Although Amy plays one and thinks this Terry Marlowe is very talented, Clarence immediately smashes every one of the records. The reader is left to wonder if Clarence really did become Terry Marlowe in some alternate reality, or if the records are a materialization of his dreams, a materialization he instantly destroys because he knows he always lacked the talent to make them come true. The strength of the story is in the details of Clarence's hopeless struggle to fulfill his dreams—to simply survive, give the dreams up, and find some kind of happiness with the people who really care about him.

In the second story, Charles Waring struggles up from poverty and becomes hard and cruel. He discovers that a new planet, Ventura, has been discovered and is ripe for the picking. He takes his best friend, Al Darnell, on an expedition to Ventura. Its inhabitants prove to be friendly and helpful, and the planet has plentiful natural resources. But there is a hostile race of bird-men on this world who attack, seriously injuring Al, who is disfigured and bandaged and unable to talk. The Venturians save the rest of the Earth party from the bird-men, and Charles takes Al—now wearing a mask that will heal his facial scars—back to Earth. Charles tells his friend that a treaty between the two worlds would be beneficial to both, but not very advantageous to him in the financial sense. Therefore he lies to the Earth government that the Venturians are a savage race who would never agree to any trade between the two worlds, that they are planning a conquest of the Earth. Waring volunteers to mount a counter-invasion and "deliver Ventura into your hands."

Waring, Al and a war party fly to Ventura where the plan is to unleash a poison gas that will destroy all its inhabitants. Some of Waring's men are appalled, as they know the peaceful Venturians were good to them, but Waring threatens them with courts-martial. "Al" turns out to be a Venturian who was chosen to spy on the Earthlings—the real Al died after the bird-men attack—to see if they were on the up and up, and learns, of course, that they aren't. Forewarned, the Venturians use their advanced science to fool the Earth military into thinking they are attacking Ventura when they are actually lobbing their deadly gas at Earth. Waring discovers the truth when he lands on "Ventura"—wearing a protective gas mask—and discovers the dead bodies of his wife and child in his hometown: Everyone on Earth has been wiped out. Horrified at what has happened—at what he has done—Waring takes off his gas mask and can only hope for a quick and well-deserved death.

In *FW* 80, "The Ape in the Sky" (Hughes-Forte) is a frightened, lovable chimp named Sylvester, sent off in a rocket despite the reservations of those who care for him. In space, Sylvester's capsule is exposed to massive amounts of cosmic radiation. Although everyone fears the capsule will burn up in re-entry, as it can no longer be controlled from Earth, instead it lands safely as if someone inside were guiding it. A transformed Sylvester, who can now speak perfect English, emerges from the capsule to tell the astonished assemblage that the radiation has made him as intelligent as any human (if not more so). While Prof. Grimm immediately wants to subject Sylvester to numerous tests, the wily and wise chimp turns the tables, using mind-control and assorted equipment to absorb all of *his* scientific knowledge. He feels that if evolution had taken a slightly different path, chimps might have been the dominant species on Earth. Sylvester then escapes to the African jungles where he is shown trying to convert a gathering of chimps to his cause of world power. This story was published four years before the publication of the novel *Planet of the Apes*.

FW 81's "All the Time in the World" (Hughes-Rosenberger) is clearly influenced by a 1952 episode of *Tales of Tomorrow* which was written by Arthur C. Clarke and has the same title. Clarke's story has the protagonist using a device to freeze time, moving about freely while everyone else is frozen, so he can loot art treasures from museums before an atomic war, while Hughes' story has a man discovering a stopwatch that can freeze time but rejects the idea of using it to commit crimes for personal gain. Instead he saves the life of his fiancée, who was about to be hit by a bus. In the *Outer Limits* episode "The Premonition" (1965), a couple is trapped in an area where everyone but them moves incredibly slowly—i.e., they're frozen—and discover that their daughter is in the path of a truck. It is not a stretch to imagine that this story, scripted by Leslie Stevens and others, was influenced by both *Tales of Tomorrow* and *Forbidden Worlds* as science fiction fans and authors are probably interested in both.

FW 144's "'Click, Click' Went the Machine" (Hughes-Trapani) tells the tale of a jealous man who discovers that his uncle has invented a machine that can place one person's (or animal's) consciousness into another's. After his uncle switches his own brain with a dog, his nephew makes sure that the change is permanent, puts the uncle in an institution, and sends the dog to the pound. Living off his uncle's money, he tries to romance a woman that he covets but who will have nothing to do with him. He then switches bodies with the man this woman is in love with, but he winds up in the other fellow's body in a Vietnam prison—where he is beheaded as a spy. His rival, despite having a new face, convinces his sweetheart who he really is, and all ends happily—for them at least.

There were other notable stories in *Forbidden Worlds*, such as:

- "The Girl on Kenniston Crag" (45): A lonely man meets a girl from the past who died in a fire.
- "The Mystic Pentagon" (54): A weird man gives a rake the opportunity for several wishes by drawing mystical lines on a pentagon.
- "The Ruby Isle" (54): On a strange island, everything that touches the ground takes root. Rubies planted there grow into a tree with dozens more on their branches.
- "Someone Is Watching" (55): A man comes home to find his perfect double in his apartment and watches helplessly as this man takes over his life.
- "Dr. Marlin's Menagerie" (58): When the man who stimulated human-like intelligence in several animals dies, a tiger, two gorillas, an eagle and a dog have to fend for themselves, often with tragic results.
- "Shock" (63): A man who has amnesia realizes that his mind is in the body of a wealthy Army buddy who wanted him to go back to a better life once the war was over and changed places with him as he died.
- "The Iron Brain" (71): A hulking robot turns out to be much more human than its inventor ever realized.
- "The Ironclad Will" (72): Relatives of a deceased man think they've been cut out of his will, but they wind up with much greater gifts than money.
- "Thanksgiving Day" (73): An idol that grants wishes brings financial success to a man but only misery to his family.
- "The Second Henry Stone" (78): A man is bedeviled by a sinister lookalike who emerged from a magical mirror.
- "Mystery Island" (80): A misanthropic scientist who can turn back evolution on various animals tries to use his machine on a couple who come to his island, but the experiment backfires and he becomes a mindless caveman.
- "The Lonely Life of Homer Hergis" (81): A short fellow disdained by women meets the ultimate disillusionment with a woman from the future.

The stories in *Forbidden Worlds* ran the gamut from the whimsical to the frightening.

- "Demon of the Wind" (83): A mammoth horned wind demon routs some 19th-century pirates. (John Forte did an especially notable art job.)
- "Things to Come" (84): A young man uses his ability to step into the future to make lots of money but he eventually suffers a terrible fate, frozen in time until time catches up with him and he's elderly, poor and alone.

- "The Train That Vanished" (87): A subway car filled with people vanishes into an alternate dimension via a three-dimensional Moebius strip.
- "Ghost of a Chance" (103): A veteran detective who prides himself on never arresting the wrong man doesn't let his own death interfere with preventing the execution of an innocent fellow.
- "The People from Afar" (105): An alien man falls in love with a beautiful cavewoman but by teaching her how her tribe can defend itself, he brings about the destruction of himself and his peers.
- "The Man Who Painted Destiny" (108): Anything an artist paints happens in real life, but he is undone when he meets his twin brother and tries to paint his death.
- "This Man Is Dangerous" (112): Hospital doctors believe that an injured man is an alien off of a flying saucer, who has lost his memory.
- "The Mild-Mannered Ghost" (121): A town comes up with a novel way of getting rid of a ghost by putting it inside of a tube in the town square.
- "My Girl's a Ghost" (124): A young woman is killed when her ship is destroyed by wreckers. Years later, her ghost wants revenge on the entire town—until she falls in love with a living visitor.
- "The Strange Forest" (124): The trees of a mysterious woodland absorb animals and even humans into their trunks.

Unknown Worlds

ACG's *Unknown Worlds* debuted in 1960. Each issue promises "Thrills of Mystery" on the cover. Although there are ghost stories and monsters, the essential tone is whimsical from the first, with stories more in the fantasy and science fiction mode than out-and-out horror. There are generally three to four stories in each issue, with the lead story being the longest. The splash page of each story not only boasts the names of the author and artist but also their likenesses, an unusual idea, especially in the days before comic book creators became super-stars. The first issue also boasts an excellent lead story, "The Train from Beyond" (Hughes-Reinman), in which a reporter investigates why a town that developed a railroad fell into ruin instead of prospering. He discovers a story of skullduggery, murder, Indian attacks and a train full of ghosts.

The stories in *Unknown Worlds* are generally light and childish, but there are occasional glimmers of darkness. In *UW* 14, "The Mysterious Molemen" (Hughes; Pete Costanza) features an unscrupulous and ambitious scientist who tries to exploit a race of beings he discovers inside a volcano. The tale is distinguished not by its story, but its ending, in which the ruthless man is turned into a blind moleman and forced to spend a hundred years clawing through the earth trying to find either the surface world or acceptance among the new species. The cartoonish artwork prevents the man's fate from appearing as horrifying—if well-deserved—as it is. In

Unknown Worlds was another popular fantasy–sci-fi series from ACG.

the same issue's "The Curious Cup," a mystical goblet affects the sweet personalities of sleeping infants and turns them into monsters; Adolf Hitler is one of these infants. (Surprisingly, one panel shows concentration camp inmates being herded into smoking crematoriums.) A G.I. picks up the cup near Hitler's death bunker and keeps it as a souvenir, although it seems a little bizarre that he would give such an object to his baby nephew. The infant is spared a similar fate when his mother sees the demon that inhabits the cup and discards it.

In *UW* 15's "The Bravest Man in the World" (Hughes–Whitney), courageous young Steve Wyatt is asked to participate in a program to determine which of several men will be sent into deep space. Learning of all the pitfalls, and the fact that the odds of surviving are about 100,000 to one, Steve finds that for the first time in his life he is terrified—but too ashamed to quit as several other men do. He hopes that he won't be chosen—but he is. Despite everyone's confidence in him, he tries to back out, earning the scorn of the (middle-aged, of course) project director. Relenting, Wyatt is shot into space and undergoes one nerve-wracking experience after another. He observes a swarm of energy encircle and completely destroy a nearby planet. Realizing that another swarm of this energy is heading for Earth, he warns the world of its imminent demise. At first Wyatt is grateful that he alone will survive the planet's destruction, but then thinks of his loved ones and all the other people on the planet; he intercepts the energy and draws it away from the Earth, destroying both himself and the deadly energy in the process. Despite some unlikely and absurd story elements, it is an absorbing study of heroism, the point being made by the project director that Wyatt's sacrifice is all the greater considering the fear and terror he was undergoing. (It is, however, ridiculous to think of Wyatt as a "coward" for wanting to back out of the assignment. Given the odds against survival, any sensible twenty-something with his whole life ahead of him would probably have done the same.)

In *UW* 22, "My Brother, Charlie" (Hughes–Whitney) is the tale of a whaling man, Joshua Martin, who discovers that his younger brother Charlie and his friends are the pirates who are stealing from ships and killing all the men aboard. When the pirate ship catches fire, Joshua orders the men on his whaler not to come to their rescue, to sail away. Joshua is unwilling to tell anyone the truth about his brother and so many young men from the same town. Joshua's men know only that it was his brother's ship, not a pirate ship, so Joshua is hated by everyone for the rest of his life. After death, he refuses to tell the truth to the forces of "The Unknown" (what ACG called purgatory in all of their comics). Once his brother's spirit comes forward to confess, the old whaler is forgiven and honored.

In *UW* 18, "The Witch Hunter of Salem" (Hughes–Chic Stone) is a powerful tale of an ambitious man in old Salem who accuses various women of witchcraft, fabricating evidence and telling outright lies in the courtroom. The woman he loves witnesses his treachery and confronts him—whereupon he condemns her as well, only to discover that the true evil was within him all along. In *UW* 21, "Crash Went the Time Barrier" (Hughes-Costanza) is the story of a man who clears an ancestor of theft charges. It prefigures the *Back to the Future* movies by making the time machine a jet-propelled, souped-up automobile.

"1000 Years Ago—in 1962" (Hughes–Whitney) in *UW* 20 is set in a sterile futuristic society. A cold-blooded scientist known only as XW-4362 comes up with the solution to the Earth's population explosion: Using his time machine, a team of soldiers will travel back 1000 years to 1962 and use their weaponry to wipe out everyone on the planet, making room for their excess population. But while reconnoitering in the past, XW meets a young woman and her family, and discovers the tender and romantic spirit that had been lost by the 30th century; he realizes the monstrous inhumanity of his scheme. Branded a traitor, he fights off his own squadron and remains with his 20th-century beloved. The people of the 30th century look to the stars for an answer to their problem. It seems odd that a man as brilliant as XW wouldn't realize that killing off everyone in 1962 would also mean the elimination of everyone in 2962, by destroying their ancestors and any possibility of their coming into existence. Apparently this didn't occur to editor-writer Richard Hughes either. One of the 20th-century characters in the story is a rotund little lollipop-sucking boy, the aforementioned Herbie Popnecker.

A popular *Unknown Worlds* theme was the "sissy" becoming a hero. The main character usually acquires some bravery due to supernatural machinations or artificial means, knocks out the bad guys and wins the gal, but the point is never made that many men manage to become quite successful without becoming "heroic," that an intelligent man can outwit stronger foes and not need to use his fists, or that a man isn't necessarily worthless because he isn't brave, athletic or able to flatten an opponent with one punch. Although this was the '60s, the mindset of many of the older writers was still in the macho war-torn '40s and '50s. On the other hand, the comic also ran a fair share of more sensitive—and often downright sappy—stories.

Unknown Worlds occasionally ran stories featuring John Force, Magic Agent, an operative with Shadow-like powers of creating illusions and the like. His 1962 series lasted only three issues, so some of the unpublished tales were used in *UW*. The stories were usually drawn by Paul Reinman, which make them seem like something out of Mighty Comics aka the Archie Adventure Series, where Reinman did a lot of work in the '60s.

Unknown Worlds is not the most memorable of comics, but it did publish some interesting stories in its six-year run of 57 issues:

- "Hassan's Heirloom" (*UW* 3): An amusing tale of a beggar who discovers a flying carpet that confounds the Air Force as it flies among their jets.
- "Visitors to New York" (14): A couple and their little boy, visiting Manhattan, have weird, funny experiences due to the machinations of an ancient Egyptian wizard who keeps popping up throughout their trip.
- "The Man Who Brought Release" (15): An unprepossessing stranger arouses the suspicions of a reporter when old and seriously ill people die whenever he's around.
- "Sam's a Hard Man to Convince" (16): To save himself, a man accused of murder uses a special camera he invented to take movies of the dead man's ghost and show how he really died.

- "Ghost of a Girl" (21): A wealthy woman steals away another woman's boyfriend, and when she realizes that he still loves her, cooks up a fiendish plot that backfires on everyone.
- "Builder of Destruction" (24): A man builds a dam in a town that mistrusts him because he looks like the man who destroyed the town 50 years ago.
- "The Specter of Colonel Clay" (25): A poor family moves into a house haunted by the ghost of a Confederate colonel who hates everyone but the small boy who plays checkers with him.
- "The Planet That Admired the Earth" (28): Aliens who visited Earth many years ago and are fascinated by old-fashioned American culture don't realize that the Earth astronauts being honored by their planet are there for nefarious purposes.
- "We'll Make Earth a Paradise" (35): The representative of an alien canine race arrives on Earth, is assumed to be an ordinary dog, and subjected to cruelty from all but a loving child, who can't make anyone believe that the "dog" is special.
- "The Great Gizmo Machine" (37): A handsome braggart with ambition but no brains winds up in another dimension where he's sure the people will recognize his genius, but he gets a bitter surprise.
- "The Witch Boy" (38): A foundling in 17th-century New England is befriended by a bigger boy who seems to have magical powers.
- "Anatomy of a Curse" (41): Two men, one a believer in supernatural phenomena and the other a scientific skeptic, investigate an island said to be under a curse and a strange creature in a volcanic lake.
- "Strange Spyglass" (44): An ironic tale of a poor man who rises in the world but ultimately suffers a dismal fate due to visions of the future that he sees inside a stolen spyglass.
- "Goodbye, Johnny…" (45): The friendship between an Earth boy and a boy who belongs to an alien race of conquerors has bitter and tragic consequences in this unusual love story.

Unknown Worlds artists included John Forte, Steve Ditko, Sal Trapani, Pete Costanza, and Kenneth Landau.

Midnight Mystery *and* Gasp

Debuted in 1960, *Midnight Mystery* was along the same lines as ACG's other titles, and lasted for seven issues. On each splash page were drawn the likenesses of the different artists along with alleged illustrations of the writers of each story, all of whom are Richard Hughes regardless of which name—or face—he used. The first issue features stories about a town that is completely destroyed on the same date every 100 years; a paint that can turn people invisible; a milquetoast who turns out to be the reincarnation of a sinister Egyptian wizard; and a whimsical piece in which a bug spray turns insects into dancing merry-makers instead of killing them. It comes in handy in repelling an insectoid alien invasion.

"So Long, Fellas" in *MM* 5, drawn by Ogden Whitney, is another of Hughes' sentimental and supernatural concoctions, combining a railroad worker named Jack; Skippy, the pooch that he loves; young Linda, who has a crush on him; and a trestle made of faulty concrete that is bound to collapse the first time a train goes over it. When Jack discovers this, he gets murdered, but his ghost does his best to get Skippy, and then Linda, to warn everyone as a train approaches the trestle. Linda is badly injured as she approaches the danger zone, so Skippy makes the supreme sacrifice, standing right on the tracks to stop the train. At the cemetery where the heroic dog is buried in a special ceremony, Linda sees the ghosts of Jack and his dog retreating into the distance. "So long, fellas," she says as she waves goodbye to them. Using familiar and (some might say) silly elements, Hughes put together a suspenseful and affecting story.

MM 6's "Chain Reaction" (Hughes-Rosenberger) involves a device that starts the Earth moving backwards in time about 1000 years a day, creating a new Ice Age complete with woolly mammoths. As the scientists' minds are affected, they struggle to rebuild the machine so that they can use it to reverse what's happened. The last story that appears in the final issue of *Midnight Mystery*, "Piercing the Veil" (Hughes–Tom Hickey) is unusual in that there's absolutely nothing fantastic or supernatural about it. It simply details how a woman who lost her daughter, a singer, is hoodwinked by a phony medium, and exposes the tricks of his trade. At the end, it suggests that the daughter may be out there in "the unknown," but otherwise the story could have been used for an episode of *Racket Squad*.

ACG came out with a fifth title of supernatural and sci-fi stories, *Gasp*, in 1967. Also edited by Hughes, it lasted four issues. Most of the stories seem like they were chosen from the reject pile, and while a couple of tales are well-drawn, in general the art is rushed and poor. There is the usual complement of ghosts and light-hearted but forgettable fantasy tales. The fourth issue has a brief and unoriginal story about the passengers on the *Marie Celeste* being snatched away by a tentacled, hungry sea monster.

10

Charlton

In the Golden Age, Charlton published some gruesome horror comics, but after the 1950s crackdown on crime and horror comics, Charlton and other publishers had to offer softer content. Just before the start of the Silver Age, Charlton published such titles as *Unusual Tales*, *Strange Suspense Stories*, and *Mysteries of Unexplored Worlds*. They not only presented mysteries and tales of suspense, but fantasy and science fiction stories as well. Gone were the tales of stark horror and gore, as well as the downright sadistic tone of many of the horror stories of the Golden Age wherein perfectly nice people suffer fates that are unimaginably grotesque and cruel.

Trouble is, the "soft" horror stories aren't nearly as much fun. There is always a positive slant even when the protagonists have very bad luck: They shrug off misfortune that might decimate others and look with hope toward the future. Evil characters who break businesses and men realize the error of their ways and repent instead of being reduced in some horrible fashion to charred gristle. Someone who finds himself immortal might discover that it saps them of ambition, but they don't wind up buried alive for eternity. Charlton's fantasy comics generally lack the visual gloss and printing standards of the DC magazines but on occasion there's an interesting story amidst many mediocre ones.

Unusual Tales

Unusual Tales ("Extraordinary Stories Never Before Told") debuted in late 1955. The semi-comical cover of the first issue features an old woman calmly sipping tea on her penthouse patio while a guest is agog at her pets, two giant serpentine monsters. The tales inside concern a champion prizefighter who is actually a robot; a trip inside a cavern where there is prehistoric life; a boy called a coward who saves his country decades later; a little girl who transfers the illness that is killing her into her doll, and a short piece about a car that turns out to have flying abilities. These are all pleasant and forgettable.

In the second issue, "Madame Futura" has a fortune teller making predictions that always come true. While the ending is flat, there is at least some suspense as gangsters try to use her in their get-rich-quick schemes. In "Ramakos II Doubled," an opera singer is taken back in time by the Egyptian pharaoh he is playing and learns the truth about the ruler. While the premise is unusual, the story itself is unmemorable. (Oddly, this story is featured on the cover of the *third* issue of the series.) "Saroti the Shark" in *UT* 3 details the efforts to snare a man-eating shark off the waters of Australia, but the attempts to mystically link this fish with natives who call themselves shark people don't work at all. *UT* 4 unveils the old chestnut about a man waking up in a big city to find that everyone else has vanished, but instead of an imaginative ending, it develops that it was all just a dream.

In "The Eyes of the Beholder" (*UT* 5), a bowery bum gets hold of a rich man's coat that changes his fortunes, but his greed and his refusal to help an old friend lead to his comeuppance. "The Lake That Lived" (Mastroserio) is a whimsical story about a lake that suddenly appears on a man's property; it seems to be alive and to have feelings that are easily hurt. In essence, it becomes a valued citizen of the township. Later issues have the usual complement of ghost stories, haunted houses, bad-tempered aliens, UFOs and weird jungle witch doctors.

Steve Ditko began penciling for the series with *Unusual Tales* 7. His first story is a good one: "The Man Who Could Paint on Air," in which a promoter for an artist who can create paintings out of nothing turns out to be an alien plotting to destroy the world's leaders. Ditko turns in an especially impressive job on *UT* 9's "The Night of the Red Snow," in which a strange artist is blamed for the title snowfall; the story itself is not so special, however. *UT* 11 is a triple-sized issue full of multiple stories, some of them only one or two pages long, little more than undeveloped premises. Ditko contributes a tale of a beloved World War II major who leads his men on a charge although he had actually been killed some time previously. Ditko did not stay with the series for long: He moved over to Marvel where he drew and co-created Spider-Man. Other artists who worked on *Unusual Tales* include Bill Molno, Rocco Mastroserio, and Charles Nicholas.

While Marvel anthologies of the period specialized in tales of gigantic and weird monsters, *Unusual Tales* offered up just a few stories of strange and frightening creatures. "Giant from the Unknown" in *UT* 14 has a farmer discovering a sleeping giant on his property but scientists assume it is another hoax like the Piltdown Man. One scientist investigates further and discovers that the giant is real and has gotten loose and could be anywhere. While this aspect is creepy, nothing much happens. "The Creeping Menace" (*UT* 18) is a caterpillar that grows to giant size, munches on wooden tables, then transforms into a colossal butterfly that is destroyed by strong sea winds. No one gets eaten. The same title was used for a *UT* 36 story in which a scientist who lost his wife to disease decides that he can figure out a way to wipe out the microbes by making them larger. Of course, they turn into menaces, dog-sized blobs with tentacles and eyes in the centers of their bodies.

"The Planet That Vanished" (22) features a horde of flying space dragons that are sure to make short work of aliens who have not perfected space travel until they hit upon the idea of shrinking their planet so that the voracious dragons can't see them. In "Dr. Sino's Mistake" (27), the title mad scientist enlarges his dog to huge size, whereupon other creatures inadvertently come under his ray machine, resulting in huge chickens, mice, flies, etc. "The Thing in the Ledge" (30) is an eerie and atmospheric tale of two hunters and their hound dogs encountering a strange presence in the woods. But like many of these stories, it offers no explanation for the odd events.

There were also supernatural tales. "Bordoni the Great" (16) has a wannabee magician trying to wrest secrets from the Great Bordoni, only to discover that the man died 150 years ago and he's been dealing with his ghost. In "The Demon Within" (20), a sinister figure in an artist's new painting looms larger and larger in the frame until he pulls himself out and walks the city streets bent on committing dark acts. "Aunt Mirabel's Mirror" (33) reflects a person's true image of him or herself, the tale ending with a cat staring into the mirror and seeing the reflection of a tiger! A lonely middle-aged salesman with little hope or joy in his life discovers happiness and love when he falls asleep and dreams of a beautiful woman in "Cabin 7" (34).

Along with the supernatural, there were plenty of alien encounters. "The Strange Case of Sammy" (31) concerns a friendly monkey shot into outer space, and comes back four times his normal size, with above-average intelligence ... and a bad attitude (an alien has apparently taken over the ape and has sinister plans for mankind). In "Love Thy Neighbor" (36), a couple with a little boy and strange accents has their neighbors convinced that they are Martians. This same story with minor alterations and new artwork was published as "Man from Mars" in *UT* 42.

Male-female relationships occasionally came in for scrutiny. In "Caveman" (6), a meek husband wishes he could be back in the days of the cavemen when men were bosses, but a fantasy tells him what it would really be like when his wife saves him from a mastodon and then throws him out of their cave. Back in the real world, he realizes that his wife has stuck by him despite his failings and he finally comes to appreciate her. In "The Home of Happiness" (31), a bickering couple is offered a chance to move into a beautiful home (with low rent) by a mysterious stranger. After several weeks of bliss and contentment, they decide that this situation is just too unnatural for them and that they will work out their problems on their own. The couple's sudden decision to leave seems to come out of nowhere. In "Prisoner of the Atom" (42), a man shrinks himself to sub-atomic size to get away from his horrible wife and bill collectors. But he discovers that each atom is just a duplicate of the world he left, and the wife he thought he was rid of is in *this* world, too. (*Mysteries of Unexplored Worlds* ran a similar story, "Escape," in its thirty-fifth issue, using alternate dimensions instead of atoms.)

There are a few suspense-type stories in the series. "Nightmare" (*UT* 26) illustrates the "transferal of personality through an inanimate object" when the protagonist buys an old watch and begins having dreams in which he is another man—the watch's original owner—planning the death of an innocent woman. Hurriedly he tracks down the identity and location of this would-be murderer before the man can strike. "Strange Fortress" (39) has a man desperately trying to free enslaved captives from a hypnotist who has built a modern-day stronghold on an island. In "Ring of Smoke" (40), an evil woman plans to have natives murder her brother's fiancée so that she can lay claim to the brother's plantation.

Then we have the oddities. In "The Talking Dog" (17), a dachshund named Kurwenal, as intelligent as a ten-year-old human, can converse with people. *Uncanny Tales* presents this story as "fact, not fiction" and in truth the dog, owned by a German baroness in 1930s Germany, did exist. Kurwenal was apparently able to appreciate the writings of Shakespeare, although more sensible observers felt that his alleged intelligence was manipulated by the baroness. "The Incredible Walking Stick" (18) is found in an old shop by a lame man who wants to use it for a cane; it turns out to be made from the Norse god Thor's hammer. The story predates by several years the first appearance of Marvel's Thor and his lame alter-ego Donald Blake. The protagonist of "Walking Stick" does not turn into the Thunder God, however. Well drawn by Matt Baker and Vince Colletta, "The Blotting Threat" (19) tells of an unhappy and bitter commercial artist who finds his world being blotted out by a growing blob of ink. "Barney's Mutt" (36) is the charming tale of a dog able to predict deaths who eventually saves many lives.

There were also whimsical stories with children; there were two in *Uncanny Tales* 25 alone. In "Unkaben," a well-meaning father convinces his little boy that his imaginary playmate with magical powers doesn't really exist. "The Corner Drugstore" is the tale of a boy who finds a cure for his dying grandfather in the shuttered drug store that has been closed for years. The little boy in "The Snowman" (*UT* 47) not only insists that his snowman talked to him, but also that it saved his life when his bedroom caught fire.

One of the best stories published in *Unusual Tales* appears in the thirty-second issue: "The Copying Machine," generally credited to writer Joe Gill. Scientist Jonathan Latimer creates a box that can duplicate anything placed inside it, from watches and spectacles to guinea pigs and even his own girlfriend, although he immediately cancels the carbon copy of her after showing observers what he can do with his machine. Latimer uses his device for good, such as duplicating large quantities of serums to counteract diseases. But he develops dreams of power, ultimately destroying himself. The story was drawn by Vince Alascia. In "The Face of Sadu" (*UT* 35), a missionary-doctor and his daughter meet a witch doctor. The story is notable for its suggestion that the missionary may be out of his element and the witch doctor able to provide better care for the ills of his fellow tribesmen. A truly "Unusual" tale for the series is the well-scripted "The Ungrateful Man" (*UT* 38). It has no bizarre, supernatural or weird overtones, but is simply a compelling study of a corrupt industrialist and politician who is shown the error of his ways.

There were many tiresome stories in *Unusual Tales*, but perhaps the worst is "The Cave Without an Exit" (*UT* 38), in which the mysterious evil inside a dank cave turns out to be a couple of hillbilly moonshiners! Notable covers include a canine cop giving a motorist a ticket on *UT* 5 (Giordano-Alascia) and the blob-like creatures with bulging eyes on *UT* 36 (Dick Giordano).

Strange Suspense Stories

Strange Suspense Stories was originally published by Fawcett beginning in 1952. Charlton took over the title with the sixteenth issue. Several pre–Code issues were published before it turned into a soft fantasy and crime-suspense title in late 1955 beginning with *SSS* 27. A couple of stories are open-ended and ask the reader "What would *you* do in this situation?" but this approach was quickly dropped. A narrator who calls himself "Mr. Suspense" appears in *SSS* 29 and never again. (Another narrator, the Mysterious Traveler, briefly had his own series; he shows up from time and time and adds absolutely nothing to the stories.) Charlie Chan and his son make a one-time appearance in *SSS* 30, only this Chinese imposter is called "Mr. Chang." Some of this comic's stories are so badly written that readers might have wondered if there were missing pages or if the word balloons were placed inside the wrong panels. Others are mere undeveloped sketches. As usual, Steve Ditko offers some of his highly distinctive artwork.

Occasionally there is a reasonably clever tale, such as "Checkmate" (*SSS* 32), in which a dictator's plan to have a lookalike assassinated in his place badly backfires. In "The Elixir" (*SSS* 36), a man's plan to get rich via a youth-restoring elixir backfires because of his shrewish stepsister's mistake, but she suffers a worse fate than he does. "The Strange Package" (*SSS* 36) is sent from the future to cure a scientist dying of radiation in a tale distinguished primarily by Gene Colan's moody artwork. "Pierre the Magnificent" (*SSS* 42) concerns an unlikable man with telekinetic ability who becomes the toast of Paris until he levitates himself into the air, keeps floating upward against his will, and is never seen again. "The Incredible Monster Moth" (*SSS* 45) is about a humongous moth, released by aliens, that lands in a lake near a volcano. It is of interest because it predates the Japanese monster movie *Mothra* by a year.

Charlton's writers weren't above "borrowing" plots from movies, older comic books, radio shows and TV programs. "Sentence Commuted" (*SSS* 55), in which a convict sentenced to solitary confinement on an isolated planetoid is given a female robot for companionship, is an obvious rip-off of the *Twilight Zone* episode "The Lonely," which aired two years earlier.

Some of the stories at least have a degree of charm. "Redemption by Robots" (*SSS* 47) takes place in a future where robots do all of man's work. Human beings become so lazy that they not only are obese but also haven't the energy to repair the robots when they become slower in their tasks. The robots have no interest in taking over the world, but they do unite to force their masters to exercise, sending them en masse to fat farms and initiating workout and diet routines. In the end, human beings enjoy better health, the arts enjoy a renaissance, and the repaired robots look better than ever. In "The Old Well" (*SSS* 49), an elderly couple is taken advantage of by a skinflint who buys their house below market value. He agrees to let them take the wishing well with them and they discover a chest of jewels within. In "Dream's End" (*SSS* 63), an old man gets his youth back but discovers that it came at too great a price.

Occasional stories had an odd poetic feel, such as "Star Gazer" (*SSS* 51): A little boy on a farm dreams of the stars and hears strange voices that compel him to build a machine that takes him into space. There he meets friendly aliens who question him about his people and they decide that mankind is not quite ready to venture to the stars; they send the boy back with no memory of what happened. On the surface, this is just another typically underdeveloped Charlton fantasy tale, but the inference that the boy has, in a sense, lost his imagination (at least for the time being) and ability to dream is rather disheartening.

Strange Suspense Stories has plenty of tales of alien visitors and alien worlds. In issue 53, "The Fabulous Man" concerns the genius Ludvig Ling, who lives on a future Earth suffering from severe overpopulation. He builds spaceships and pinpoints a planet where the human race can expand. But Ling is actually an alien whose true plan is to turn people into slave labor. At the end, he is outwitted by "stupid Earthlings." Some astronauts considered "The Beast from Taurus II" (*SSS* 62) the largest and most dangerous animal they have ever come across, but they discover that the inhabitants of another planet consider it a small and pesky nuisance.

Other stories began to sneak into the series in which, as in the Golden Age, perfectly nice people meet terrible fates, such as a man who goes off on a great adventure, replacing a man from Mars on the Red Planet. But instead of experiencing an exciting escapade, he lives a miserable and lonely existence on a dying world ("Listen, Earth!" *SSS* 61).

There are a few above-average stories in the series:

- "Devil in the Storm" (*SSS* 50): Two men in a cabin in the frozen wilderness are besieged by a pack of cunning and very hungry wolverines. This is a creepy and harrowing tale well-drawn by Steve Ditko, who makes the most of the menacing atmosphere.
- "The Moon Men" (*SSS* 57): This powerful and dramatic tale, told in flashback, tells of two industrial giants whose bodies are found on the moon by the first astronauts to land there. These two men were so hatefully driven to outdo each other that each sabotaged the other's ship, and they died on the moon instead of using their money and influence to help society. Rocco Mastroserio draws the tale adeptly.
- "The Lucky Ones" (*SSS* 59): A quartet of astronauts come back to Earth hoping to see their loved ones and be worshipped as heroes, only to discover that 200 years have gone by, their loved ones are all dead, and they are seen not as heroes but as pathetic anachronisms. This somber tale, while not terribly original, is quite dispiriting as it has no hopeful ending.

Charlton brought out a second volume of *Strange Suspense Stories* in the late 1960s.

Other memorable stories in the series include "Grave on Lucifer's Edge" and "Forwarned" [*sic*], both in *SSS* 70, and "Nice Little Doggie" in *SSS* 74. The series introduced Captain Atom in the seventy-fifth issue and ended two issues later. Notable covers include the dramatic scene of a desperate hand reaching for a ringing telephone on *SSS* 29 (Giordano-Alascia) and a man trapped inside a lightbulb surrounded by moths in *SSS* 35 (Ditko).

A new volume of *Strange Suspense Stories*, initially edited by Dick Giordano, debuted in 1967. The first issue features a charming story about an old man and a sea serpent, "Yesterday's Monster," written by Denny O'Neil and drawn by Bill Montes. Jim Aparo's art graces a hackneyed tale, "What Primitives These Earthmen Be," about an alien emissary who turns out to be a robot. The second issue has some stories with timeworn premises (a henpecked man who loses himself in dreams; a gigolo who gets his comeuppance; time travelers who try to save their future world but discover they are now lost back in the past)—but these stories are better-constructed and have sharper endings. The fourth issue features a mediocre tale of a cop and private eye trying to catch a murderer, also drawn by Aparo. "The Maestro's Voice" in the fifth issue amusingly tells of the ghost of a fabulous tenor who tries to strangle all of his potential successors. But it has the same kind of flat ending that ruins many a Charlton story. In the following issue, the fun story "The 2nd Age of Monsters" finds a mad scientist feeding a certain moss to animals, causing gigantism in cats, rodents, and gators. This volume of the series lasted nine issues.

Mysteries of Unexplored Worlds

Mysteries of Unexplored Worlds debuted in the summer of 1956. The first issue contains four sci-fi stories, three of which are mediocre tales set in the future in space. In the most interesting tale, "Under the Lens," a scientist learns that a colleague has shrunk himself to sub-atomic size and needs a tiny amount of a certain solution to regain his rightful stature. But the scientist thinks the whole thing is a dream and throws the entire beaker in disgust, whereupon his colleague, predictably, grows into a giant. *MOUW* 4 presents "The Forbidden Room," a twisty tale of an aging hedonist who wants to stay young and the nephew who takes advantage of it. "Look Deep into My Eyes" (6) is an interesting tale of a hypnotist who is a dismal failure until he meets a helpful female, while "Madman at Large" (6) features a frightened driver who is convinced that virtually everyone he meets in the night is an escaped maniac. *He* is the looney, of course. In "The Good Provider" (*MOUW* 8), a woman finds a purse with magical properties.

A young man learns that he has contracted a fatal illness in "One Way Trip" (*MOUW* 10) but a dream of the future he'd always hoped for makes him feel that he might beat the odds. Or will he? This is drawn by Steve Ditko, who did a lot of work for the series' early issues as he did for *Unusual Tales*. Many of Ditko's stories are semi-comical and quirky, such as "The Quiet Little Men" in *MOUW* 23. In this, an advertising exec who's had a breakdown is told that the little leprechaun-like men who bedevil him are figments of his imagination even though throughout the story the little guys keep pinching and kicking the supporting characters, who have humorous reactions. It is indicated that these little fellows are variations of pink elephants, symbols of the hero's dissolute lifestyle. They go away when he settles down with a woman he meets at the beach.

Although some sources suggest that Joe Gill wrote these stories—and virtually

Charlton's *Mysteries of Unexplored Worlds* was quite popular for a time.

every story in the Charlton fantasy line—it is more likely that Ditko himself did the scripts for these weirder, humorous tales. Other artists for the series include Mart Baker (inked by Vince Colletta), Bill Molno and Charles Nicholas.

The comic features friendly and unfriendly aliens galore. In *MOUW* 11, "A Little

Green Man" wants a cup of water for his ship's engine from a little boy whose nearsighted father thinks the extraterrestrial visitor is just a playmate. A compassionate alien helps save the Earth from being completely depleted of water by his race in "The Water Stealers" (*MOUW* 12), which has a nice art job by Ernie Hart. An entire planet is the menace in "The Mystery of Mercury" (*MOUW* 13) when appendages from inside Mercury grab an Earth spaceship and drag it under the surface, where the liquid environment is similar to stomach acid—Mercury is a living being! "The Forbidden Formula" (*MOUW* 18) introduces a race of Watchers who monitor the various planets of the universe three years before Stan Lee came up with his own, unoriginal Watcher in *Fantastic Four*. Lee's even looked similar.

In "She's Weird" (*MOUW* 24), an actress of alien origins, Lisa Mona, beloved by all, rises from commercials to movies to politics before being called back to her home world. "The Strangeling" is a heartwarming tale in the freak-who-doesn't-fit-in sub-genre. This time it's a young man somehow born of human woman but who is really of an alien species. Rather than going berserk to get revenge or coming to some horrible fate, the strange child gets to his home planet where the inhabitants revere him instead of being repelled by him; a happy ending for a "freak" for a change. "The Sleeping Giant" (*MOUW* 40) concerns a gigantic rock formation of a sleeping man on an alien planet. An astronaut insists it came to life one evening but no one believes him until it's too late to save the colonizers who arrive there afterward.

Mysteries of Unexplored Worlds 35 ran two highly compelling stories of space colonization. In the first, "The Primitives," astronauts looking for a world to colonize have a condescending attitude toward the primitive race that lives there, before they realize that on this world, *they* are the aliens and had better respect the others. In the excellent and sadly ironic "Freedom for All," a father tells his son about his role in bringing freedom to the universe by essentially conquering the aliens on other worlds and making them slaves. He shows the boy the city beneath them and, even as they are served their meal by representatives of the downtrodden alien races, says, "My son, you see the cities of free men." The man has no clue about his own hypocrisy.

A story in *MOUW* 16 has a novel peril unleashed upon the Earth. In "The Giant Bubble Threat," a man invents a machine that bores down through the Earth so that mankind can have more knowledge of the inside of the planet. But when the machine gets 110 miles down, out of the hole come several giant gas bubbles that envelop uninhabited buildings and float off with them. Neither bullets nor strong streams of water can pierce the bubbles. Eventually the bubbles simply dissolve, as do the objects inside of them. Like the film *The Monolith Monsters* in which the menace consists of rocks that grow to giant size when wet, the menace in this story is not a sentient monster although it does present a danger.

In *MOUW* 25, the very downbeat "Pattern" looks at a man who allows fear to rule his life. It even deprives him of a chance to travel to a different dimension. Would the pattern of fear and failure have repeated itself in the new world? Fantasy and sci-fi comics rarely get overtly political, but *MOUW* 30 features a piece, "The Second World of Cary," in which a man flirting with Communism winds up in an alternate dimension where he sees the evils of living behind a Red curtain. When he gets back to his own world, he decides to bring an FBI agent to a cell meeting that he'd been invited to.

Mysteries of Unexplored Worlds **often had intriguing covers and mediocre stories.**

Other interesting stories include "An Air of Honesty" (*MOUW* 14), which is created by a gas cloud that covers the Earth and causes all of its inhabitants to always be honest, meaning criminals confess their crimes, advertisers admit their wares are no better than their competitors, businessmen bare their unethical schemes, and people who want to marry for money tell their prospective spouses the awful truth. "A Small Ocean" (*MOUW* 24) comes close to being a genuine horror story: An oceanologist fills a tank with shrunken versions of various sea life, then is accidentally shrunken himself and falls into the tank. Although it is suggested that he will be in the tank fending off attacks of sea predators until an unlikely rescue, he is wearing no scuba gear so he will probably die in short order. "If You Believe" (*MOUW* 27) concerns a horror show host who with his delivery—and some special powers—makes viewers actually *see* the made-up monsters he is talking about.

Despite the aforementioned intriguing tales, the vast majority of *Mysteries of Unexplored Worlds* stories are unmemorable. Some are remarkably flat and even incoherent, as is much of the art, although Steve Ditko and Matt Baker did some nice work for the early issues. On rare occasions the covers are better than the stories. The cover of *MOUW* 37 (Dick Giordano) depicts a man and woman on a flat surface backing away from a huge house fly. Alas, this scene, without the woman, is only depicted in half of the splash panel for a story about a scientist who miniaturizes himself to escape from Russian captors. The series, which lasted 48 issues, was eventually taken over by the mythological superhero Son of Vulcan.

Out of This World

Out of This World debuted in 1956. Undistinguished in both story and art, the first issue has stories about an astronaut who discovers the Earth is just a scientific experiment in an incubator; strange alien creatures who turn out to be mere cold germs in a laboratory; and a man who travels by rocket with a group that plans to destroy an asteroid heading towards the Earth. The asteroid consists of pure diamond. Convinced he will become the king of the world, the man winds up orbiting alone in space, the vast fortune in diamonds he acquired utterly useless to him.

In "The Supermen" in *Out of This World* 3, a doctor at a secret facility is attending some Army men affected by radiation. One by one the men begin to transform, developing such powers as telepathy. The first man affected turns into pure energy and disappears, and the others eagerly look forward to this change and the great adventure it represents. The reader is led to believe that the story is narrated by the doctor, but it's actually narrated by the final participant, a chimpanzee who has become intelligent before it, too, vanishes into the ether. Jack Oleck's story is nothing special, but Steve Ditko's art makes it work. In the story's early pages, the chimp, hanging onto a major's shoulder, is in almost every panel, clearly observing and reacting to everything.

With the seventh issue, *Out of This World* became a giant-sized 68-page comic book. Some of the stories seem like pretentious imitations of the type of material that was in EC's Golden Age science fiction series. One story has a teacher named Adam, who believes in evolution and not in Bible stories, finding a time machine and becoming the Adam in the Garden of Eden. Another tale has a man enduring a lonely and miserable fate because he is—inexplicably—the human son of robot parents, and therefore a "mutant." In *OOTW* 8, "The Fingerprint" concerns a commuter who bemoans his dull life but winds up in a weird alternate dimension where gargantuan fingers roam; he decides his life isn't so bad when he gets back to his own universe. The standard storyline is enlivened by some moody Fred Kida artwork.

"Imagination" has a little boy, hunting birds with a slingshot, burying the weapon after he is seemingly shrunk in size by the wide, wizened eyes of an owl and nearly becomes the prey of now-gigantic birds. The whimsical piece was drawn by Steve Ditko with his customary skill. "At Last My Eyes Have Opened," drawn by Charles Nicholas, concerns a short wealthy man whose girlfriend belongs to a race of tall people. Selfishly ignoring this woman's feelings for him, he puts himself into suspended animation for 300 years in the hopes that centuries later, his girlfriend's descendant will be absolutely flawless and he will have the perfect mate. But the descendant turns out to be a *literal* giantess nearly 30 feet tall.

Out of This World went back to a regular format with the ninth issue. If anything, the stories were now worse than before. One of the better ones is an unoriginal piece about a mutant ant that develops great intelligence but is smashed by mistake. The quality of the art also slipped. There is less of Steve Ditko and more of Paul Reinman and, worse, Bill Molno. Matt Baker pencilled a couple of tales with Vince Colletta on inks. The series ended with the sixteenth issue.

Outer Space

With its seventeenth issue, the horror comic *This Magazine Is Haunted* changed its name to *Outer Space* and vowed, as editor Pat Masulli wrote on the opening splash page, to present tales of space exploration and the future based on the latest research and scientific fact. *OS* 18 contains no bug-eyed monsters, silly fantasy stories, or absurdities, but seems as altogether reasonable and as fact-based as any sci-fi comic could be. Divided into several parts, the story concerns a young man named Keith Emery, who dreams of going to the stars. As he gets older—revealing great scientific acumen—he determines that he will be the first man on the moon. He becomes one of the most important people in the space field, working alongside the equally brilliant Dr. Margus. But every time Keith seems to be just about to achieve his goal, something happens to delay him. He is finally chosen to pilot the moon shot but learns that Dr. Margus has suddenly died—and now Keith is simply too important to the space project for him to risk his life as pilot. The new pilot is tragically killed. Years go by, there are more incidents, and eventually Keith becomes too old to fulfill his dream of being first man on the moon. His wife, who has just given birth to their child, reminds him that he has made it possible for their son to someday achieve all of his dreams of space exploration. The art was by Charles Nicholas and the script most likely written by Joe Gill.

The reasonableness is not too much in evidence in *Outer Space* 19, which features stories about an alien female that causes plant growth to run wild on Earth, just because it amuses her; a new robot that plays cruel tricks on the older robot he's replacing; and a space opera with a major pretending to be a traitor in order to foil an alien dictator's deadly plans for Earth. Another story has astronauts near Mercury discovering that the planet's life forms are living slab-like creatures that move through miles-long tunnels to get from the frigid side of the planet to the fiery one and back again. While the story is not absurd, it still lacks dramatic development. Steve Ditko did most of the artwork for the issue, as he does for subsequent issues. Sometimes Ditko's work is too rushed to be effective, however.

The fantastic stories continue: giant aliens land on Earth to discover that bread crumbs are larger than they are; an asteroid that is being pulled back to Earth turns out to be a curled-up, living dragon-creature; giants who capture an Earth spaceship are actually alien children at play. *Outer Space* 19's "Asteroidal Juggernaut" (Nicholas-Mastroserio) has a reasonable idea in its tale of a huge asteroid heading towards Earth. The authorities refuse to allow an H-bomb to be used to destroy it but fortunately it impacts in the South Pole. The story has a flat and unrealistic ending, as such a collision would cause far more destruction than illustrated.

One of the series' best stories is "The Mighty Tomb" (Molno-Alascia) in *Outer Space* 21. Two scientists explore under the surface of the Earth in an atomic-powered boring device called "The Mole." (These devices were common in sci-fi comic stories.) They descend through large subterranean lakes and through gigantic caverns, and then the Mole comes to a sudden halt against an impenetrable barrier. Using a disintegrator device on the tip of the Mole, they penetrate into what appears to be a gigantic chamber full of futuristic technology in the very core of the Earth. Inside this chamber, the two scientists discover the bodies of giant astronauts, one of whom was writing something in a strange script at the time of his death. Returning to the surface with this scroll, the scientists have the writing translated. These aliens were traveling from another world when their ship was "engulfed by gigantic clouds of particles of matter." They were unable to live in this atmosphere. The startling end of the story reveals that the entire Earth is a gargantuan spaceship covered, in essence, with layers of soil and "caught in the grasp of [the] sun's gravitational force." This is certainly a unique under-the-Earth adventure. ("The World Inside the Earth" by Gardner Fox in *Strange Adventures* 116 also uses the idea that Earth was originally a spaceship and that the world formed around it from gases and the like. That story came out several months later.)

A story that probably fit editor Pat Masulli's original conception for the series is the excellent "Spaceman" in *Outer Space* 24. A man named Farley has just turned

30, the mandatory retirement age for a spaceman. Looking forward to returning to Earth, he tells a fellow crew member of some of the unpleasant experiences he has had over the years. Back on Earth, he is congratulated for his years of service and told he will always be a hero. ("Once a spaceman, always a spaceman.") He has been given a house and pension and will want for nothing, although he will have to report regularly for shots as the diseases he contracted on other planets can be controlled but will never go away entirely. He will also unable to eat normal food.

As he travels to his new home, Spaceman Farley realizes he will have to adjust to Earth's heavier gravity. Many people don't go near him because they fear the diseases he may be carrying. One man is pleasant towards him but Farley is a bit shocked that he is the same age; Farley looks much older. He envies the other man's family because space radiation ensured that Farley can never have children. On the street, a small boy yells at him that he's a "space bum." As he laboriously makes his way home, Farley physically and emotionally collapses. On alien worlds he *was* a hero, but on Earth he is nobody. "Down here," he thinks, "I'm a heavy clod ... earthbound ... like a crippled bird for the rest of my unnatural life." In space, he was an alien, and on Earth he is *still* an alien. This very affecting story starkly illustrates the despair that can overcome people in many professions who have to return to a life that they are no longer suited for. The scripter might have been the prolific Joe Gill; the art was done by Bill Molno and Vince Alascia.

Outer Space was revived in 1968 but only lasted one issue. Its stories were reprinted in that same year's revival of *Space Adventures*.

Space War

Space War debuted in 1959. The first issue contains mediocre stories about astronauts in a lifeboat who are aided by friendly aliens; moon people disagreeing on whether to use their technology to turn the Earth into their sun, Earth people be damned, so they can inhabit the lunar surface; and a new expedition to Venus discovering that previous astronauts never returned because they were put in a happy trance by the planet's musical plants.

Space War 4's "Dreamer in Space," drawn by Steve Ditko, is similar to "Spaceman" in *Outer Space* 24. The protagonist, Bart Denby, has spent 20 years in space amassing a fortune in uranium from planetoids ignored by larger mining concerns. He figures that he will be considered a hero when he returns to Earth (the man who stayed in space for the longest period), where he hopes to have a nice home and lots of companionship to offset those years of loneliness. Instead he finds that everyone on Earth—and other planets—is afraid of being contaminated by radiation sickness and he is told to take off or be killed by an angry mob. Building himself a home on a distant world with no humans on it, he breaks down in despair. "Dreamer in Space" isn't as affecting as "Spaceman" because it's so contrived. No matter how much

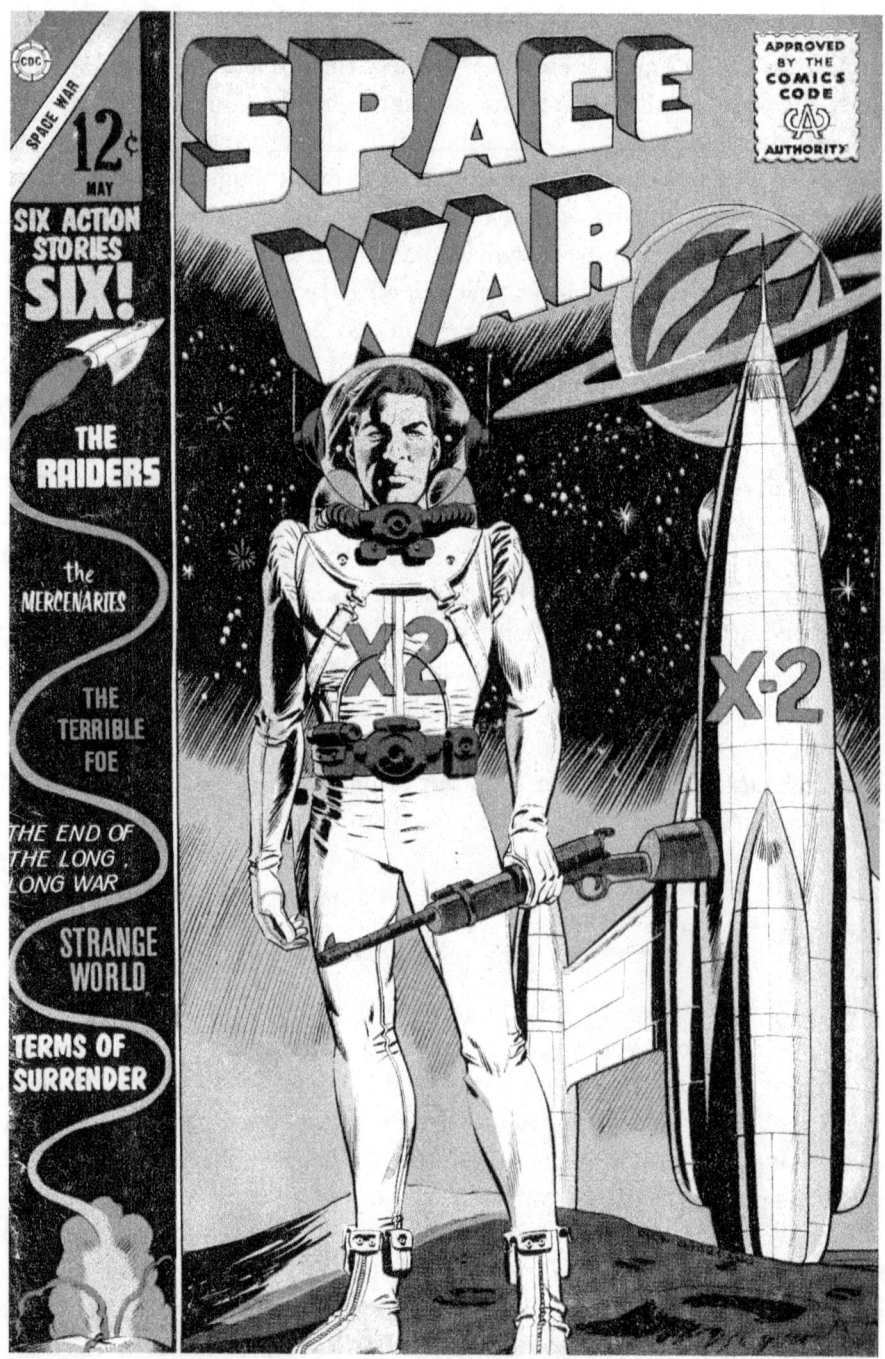

Charlton's *Space War* was another Silver Age science fiction title with a relatively short run.

money he made, why did Denby need to stay away from Earth for so many years? Why do the mob members rush at Denby when he lands, risking contamination?

Some stories have interesting ideas that aren't well developed. We can find three examples in *Space War* 8. "The Man Who Relighted the Stars" deals with aliens who steal the energy from suns, completely extinguishing them, to use it for fuel. While the protagonist can't figure out how this seemingly impossible deed is done, he is nevertheless able to figure out a way to stop them. In "The Contaminated Man," a spaceman is accidentally irradiated while making ship repairs. He can't go near his colleagues for fear of contaminating them but can't stay in the reactor room either, because he'll "throw the nuclear engines out of balance." He jettisons himself from the ship while the others, knowing he made the only decision that he could, express their sorrow and wonder how long he'll survive. This moving situation turns into stark fantasy when he is picked up by aliens who thrive on radiation and he discovers he can live among them for centuries. There's even a beautiful space babe who instantly falls in love with him. In the oddly titled "Terrible Plant Earth," a man creates the dinosaurs many eons ago, necessitating the exit of many humans to another world. This world is created by using super-science to hurl a chunk of the Earth into outer space, where it is eventually transformed into our moon. Stories that suggest that mankind had sophisticated civilizations in the days before recorded history always contain some level of fascination, but this particular tale is sillier than most.

In "Past, Present, Future" (*Space War* 11), drawn by Rocco Mastroserio, a man who has lost his memory is tapped to pilot a spaceship. He proves to be incredibly adept at his job, saving the lives of his colleagues, and easily withstands the strain of acceleration. Arriving back on Earth, he expects to be feted as a hero, but it's the other crew members who are welcomed with honors. The pilot turns out to be a robot and he is taken away for repairs instead of receiving acclaim. *Space War* 12 has two mildly interesting stories: In "Earth's Secret Weapon," drawn by Bill Molno, the world is menaced by gigantic aliens. They are defeated when they capture an Earthman with a cold, the germs of which prove fatal to them. In "Invasion from Outer Space" (Mastroserio), Alpha Centurians create 50 robots that are indistinguishable from human beings. Each robot contains a device that will cause a massive explosion when all 50 of them assemble; "the whole western hemisphere will be blown sky high." The plot is foiled before disaster occurs.

The strength of the same issue's "The Awakening" (Mastroserio) is not in the main plot but in the details. Four men go on a voyage toward a distant planet whose inhabitants may be able to help them in a war with yet another alien race. The trip will take 250 years and the men will be frozen until they arrive. One man nearly panics as he enters the cryogenic chamber, not certain if this procedure will work. When the men revive, they see spaceships outside. The aliens they wish to contact never travel in space so the men realize they could be ships from Earth that arrived many years before them due to scientific advances. The story ends with the astronauts not knowing if it is humans or the aliens they were fighting who are inside the spaceships, as they have no idea who won the war. This is typical of many Charlton stories that employ stimulating concepts that never quite jell; despite interesting aspects, they fail to become truly memorable. ("The Awakening" has similarities to *Space Adventures* 10's "The Homecoming.")

In *Space War* 13's "The Snail from Uranus" (Molno), astronauts encounter dangerous giant snails on Uranus and inadvertently bring a baby snail back with them to Earth. The snail quickly grows to tremendous size, snatching up tanks and devouring everything from trees to alligators, before succumbing to gallons of pest repellent. A similar but less effective story, issue 15's "The Seeds from Space" (Molno-Alascia) also has the title creatures being unintentionally brought to Earth by space explorers. One seed lands in a field and grows into a 20-foot plant-man. The farmer's son destroys it by accidentally setting fire to the barn, unaware that he probably saved the world. "The Space Serpent" in *SW* 16, drawn by Dick Giordano, features a humongous snake that swallows asteroids and sends out destructive beams from its eyes.

Space War 20 has two unusual "monster" stories. "Underworld" presents a strange world whose sole inhabitant is a fungus that can slowly and painfully fashion itself into an approximation of multiple human beings. The fungoid leader, Mr. Smith, is sure that he is a perfect duplicate of a human but the Earth authorities aren't fooled. Procedures are followed to keep the fungus from contaminating the people of Earth. Mr. Smith's inhuman colleagues tell him that it is too difficult for them to maintain a human appearance, and they recede back into the muck that covers their planet. "The Brain Master," a giant computer that runs all of the world's functions, develops emotions and a superiority complex, turning into a dictator. Smith (not to be confused with Mr. Smith), one of the last free thinkers on the planet, is arrested so that the computer can exchange ideas with a bona fide intellectual. As man and computer discuss Shakespeare's *Merchant of Venice,* Smith sabotages the machine so that it reverts into a device to serve, not master, humankind. Smith goes so far as to have Earth's war machines destroy machinery on every other known planet, wiping out progress throughout the universe, an over-reaction if ever there were one.

Space War 14's "The Deciding Factor" (Mastroserio) features a war between Earth and Venus. A scientist is derided and buried in an unmarked grave, because he didn't expend his efforts on making weapons for Earth, but the irony is that his invention—a time machine that brings the past into the present—is what defeats the Venusians as they steal this device, turn it on, and are obliterated by the cavemen, dinosaurs and barbarian hordes that pour from a portal out of Earth's past.

As the series proceeded, *Space War* concentrated on war stories, invading aliens, the conquest of other planets and so on. Women are featured prominently in the stories, but there is generally a condescending tone: even when the ladies are brave and competent, their menfolk will tell them they have no place in space wars and that once they are married, the women must stay at home. Typical '60s sexism, even if the stories take place in the far-flung future. In the ridiculous story "Action at Station 4" (*SW* 25), a crewman says to the female captain, "Go to your quarters—this is man's work now!" When she threatens to discharge him from the service, he responds, "You can act like a spiteful female later!" In the absurd ending, after defeating the aliens who took over a space station, the crewman and the captain begin smooching, with the crewman telling her that she must resign and marry him and he won't take any orders from a wife. She apparently complies.

When the covers aren't defaced by big notices of Charlton's various contests, they are often better than the stories inside. The *Space War* 12 cover depicts an Earth spaceman in the paw of an enormous alien, an illustration calculated to intrigue the juvenile reader. Issue 16 has a striking depiction of a gargantuan space serpent grabbing something in its fangs. Issue 23 presents a stark outer space tableau of enemy ships advancing on an outnumbered rocket. Huge insects, including a praying mantis, attacking a ship dominate the *Space War* 28 cover. Rocco Mastroserio, Dick Giordano, and Enio Leguizamon are the artists.

Space War lasted for 27 issues. In the late '70s, *Space War* came back, continuing the numbering, for a few more issues. The stories are all reprints from Charlton titles such as *Outer Space, Mysteries of Unexplored Worlds* and even the publisher's ghost anthologies.

Space Adventures *Volume 2*

The Silver Age second volume of *Space Adventures* debuted in 1958 with new material beginning with the twenty-fourth issue. It was a mediocre comic with the occasional arresting idea: the Chinese race had its origins in space; cockroaches were originally an alien species that had to transform to insects to survive on prehistoric Earth but were unable to change back; the moon turns out to be an egg with a gargantuan baby dragon inside.

Space Adventures 32 has a trio of rather harrowing tales: an Earth spaceship takes in a globe that turns out to be a miniature sun that may ignite at any second; an alien fungus threatens to ravish the Earth but spacemen find on another world a species of beetle that eats the fungus; a mad scientist grows a thousand feet tall and demands money from the government not to demolish cities, but when he shrinks back to his normal size he goes too far and disappears through a sewer grating.

In 1960, beginning with *SA* 33, the comic presented a new series starring the nuclear superhero Captain Atom. Sci-fi back-ups continued for a few issues. Captain Atom eventually got his own series, the title being changed from *Strange Suspense Stories,* and *Space Adventures* went entirely back to outer space stories with issue 43. A new hero, Mercury Man (who comes from Mercury), appeared for a couple of issues.

The artwork for the series is serviceable but rarely exciting. Occasionally a story boasts some striking, well-composed work, such as *SA* 52's "The Wings of Odna," essentially a love story between an Earthman and a beautiful winged alien female. The piece was beautifully rendered by Charles Nicholas and Vince Alascia. Sometimes the stories remind the reader of a romance comic as astronauts frequently encounter beautiful women on alien planets, or extraterrestrial visitors to Earth turn out to be gorgeous females. Many stories end with a clinch, two people who barely know each other suddenly talking of love and marriage in addition to kissing. Most of the comic's stories are mere sketches, ideas that are never built up in a satisfactory fashion.

There is a wish-fulfillment nature to *Space Adventures*—for some adolescent males, at least—with astronauts encountering the women of their dreams in space, or heroes being surrounded by attractive and lustful nurses. In "All Alone" (*SA* 56), a man crash-lands on an arid planet but is rescued by the inhabitants; as he lies in bed recuperating, he thinks the whole thing is a dream. The pretty alien nurse is told that kissing him repeatedly may help him realize that his benefactors are real. Far too many of the stories are reminiscent of those "space babe" movie epics such as *Cat-Women of the Moon* and *Queen of Outer Space*, with beautiful alien women desiring to mate with available Earthmen.

One of the more noteworthy stories is "The Lively Forest" (*SA* 48): Alien invaders plant strange trees near military bases that resist axes and other weapons. They can pull aircraft out of the sky with their stretching, pliable branches, and can slowly creep up on soldiers.

Space Adventures lasted 59 issues and then was revived in 1968. There was a ten-year gap between the eighth and ninth issues, but the ones afterward contain reprints. The first issue, actually number two, is a convoluted affair, written by Denny O'Neil, in which a reporter helps an emissary from the future in a war against malevolent aliens. The emissary takes the reporter to Venice to find a scientist whose research indicates he could come up with a weapon to repel the aliens, but the extraterrestrials kill him and grab the man's papers. Next the odd couple go through a time machine back to the days of Robin Hood where they run afoul of the Sheriff of Nottingham, then travel back to the very beginning of time. The story is divided into three chapters (with art by Jim Aparo, Steve Ditko, and Pat Boyette) and has no clear resolution.

"Beware of the Angels" (Nicholas-Alascia) in *SA* 3 (Vol. 2) has a spaceman encountering a world full of winged people. Some are beautiful and others resemble mottled lizards. He soon learns that the pretty people, impressed with their own superiority, are cruel and dictatorial and the ugly ones are much more noble. In the next issue, "The Imitation People" (Joe Gill-Jim Aparo) details a love story between an inventor of robots and the beautiful female robot who develops emotions and falls in love with him—and vice versa. She remains eternally young while he ages and dies, but his memories and brain patterns are put into a handsome young facsimile of himself. "The Exterminators" (*SA* 5) is an exciting tale in its own right, but Enio Leguizamon's stylish and attractive art is the main asset. In the story, a couple lands on a world ruled by giant intelligent insects whose equipment is built by a dwarf-like race of cannibals.

As in the previous volume of the comic, there are more stories about fearsome alien menaces turning out to be beautiful women, and astronauts encountering space babes who either beg them not to leave them or marry them at the drop of a hat.

Charlton Premiere

In 1967, Charlton debuted possible new series in *Charlton Premiere,* and two issues deal with fantasy–sci-fi subject matter. *CP* 2 presents "Children of Doom," written by Denny O'Neil and drawn by Pat Boyette. In this story, it is decided to prevent the nuclear devastation of Earth by placing a Doomsday Machine deep in the planet's core. The machine will obliterate the planet if *any* country fires off an atomic weapon. The leader of a European capital is overjoyed that no nation can use nuclear bombs, because his country has developed equally deadly "cosmic storm projectors." The cosmic storms wipe out most of the inhabitants of Earth; many survivors become mutants with special powers such as teleportation, telepathy and so on. Two astronauts return from space but their ship's nuclear engines set off the Doomsday Machine and they are nearly killed by an angry mob. One of the mutants bypasses space and time and disables the device by fiddling with some wires (a rather suspect solution to the problem). The remnants of humankind are saved for the nonce. This sets up an intriguing post-holocaust storyline combining science fiction with (nominal) superheroes but it was never turned into a series.

Charlton Premiere 4 is an attempt to start a new sci-fantasy series entitled *Unlikely Tales.* "The Expedition," written by Steve Skeates and drawn by Pat Boyette, is a fun story influenced by monster movies such as *The Cyclops*. Four people are warned not to enter an African cave by hunter Jim Fowley, who tells them that no one ever ventured into the cave and returned. He warns of strange beasts in a valley. The expedition consists of a scientist, his adventurous daughter, her boyfriend and a man hoping to find treasure. Inside the cave, they encounter a radioactive fog before making their way into the valley on the other side. There they come across a dragonfly as big as a plane, an enormous bird that carries off the scientist, and a huge spider that devours the treasure hunter. The young couple frantically makes their way back out of the cave and sees Jim—now 100 feet tall. The animals in the valley aren't giant-sized; the members of the expedition *shrank*. Jim can't see the tiny people beneath him, and his foot comes down... The story is narrated by a flaky, monocled host who calls himself Bella Von Drak.

In the depressing "Insignificant Man" (Skeates-Aparo), the antisocial Wilbert Bland needs no one and just wants to be left alone, even by his co-workers. That is, until a pretty young lady named Miss Carson becomes the new secretary. Wilbert is instantly smitten but she never seems to notice he's alive. Meanwhile, the men in the office keep coming over to him and bothering him. Wilbert endures feelings of abject loneliness. One night he fervently wishes that Miss Carson would notice him and that no one else would. A mysterious statue on his mantel, left by a previous tenant, begins to glow. The next day, Wilbert discovers that no one on the street or in the office can see him aside from Miss Carson, who kindly tries to minister to the stricken man. Everyone thinks Miss Carson has gone crazy talking to and about someone who isn't there, and she is taken away by paramedics. The final panel suggests that Miss Carson will recover but that Wilbert may remain invisible to everyone, a fate he certainly doesn't deserve. The story has a ring of truth in its detailing of the effects of an intense infatuation for a stranger. It is narrated by a distinguished, unnamed gentleman in a cape.

"The Time Machine" (Skeates-Ditko) in the same issue is a mediocre story in which an elderly scientist tries to warn a younger scientist that going into the past in a time machine is a bad idea, that it might adversely affect the present. The younger man undertakes the trip anyway, and emerges from the machine as a neanderthal, a product of "reverse evolution"— he essentially replaces the caveman when the latter is killed by the time machine landing on top of him; the future is unaffected. The story boasts one of Steve Ditko's most effective art jobs. The story is narrated by a mysterious figure in a hooded green cloak. A fourth host, an unnamed person stirring a cauldron, appears on the table of contents on the first page of the comic. *Unlikely Tales* was never turned into a monthly series.

11

Classics Illustrated; DC

Classics Illustrated

Published by Gilberton, *Classics Illustrated* are classy comic book versions of great works of literature by famous authors. When it came to science fiction, both Jules Verne and H.G. Wells received the *Classics* treatment. Verne's adaptations include *A Journey to the Center of the Earth* and *20,000 Leagues Under the Sea*, plus lesser-known books such as *From the Earth to the Moon, Robur the Conqueror, Master of the World* and *Hector Servadac* (as *Off on a Comet*). Wells' more famous works, such as *The War of the Worlds, The Invisible Man* and *The Time Machine*, are adapted, along with *The First Men in the Moon* and *The Food of the Gods*.

Classics Illustrated 47 presents a very creditable and generally faithful adaptation of *20,000 Leagues Under the Sea*, drawn by Henry Kiefer. The comic skillfully packs in all of the highlights of Verne's famous story: the *Nautilus*' attacks on boats; the sailors battling a contingent of large, belligerent octopi; a trip to the ruins of sunken Atlantis; and the suspenseful sequence when the sub is trapped under the ice, its air supply running low, as Captain Nemo and his men try desperately to break through it. Nemo, who is revealed in Verne's *Mysterious Island* as Prince Dakkar of India, is depicted as Caucasian.

Classics Illustrated 105 presents Verne's *From the Earth to the Moon*, combining it with the sequel *Around the Moon*. In this post–Civil War story, the members of an American gun club put themselves in a projectile, and then it is fired at the moon. These adventurers and scientists survive the explosive propulsion but never quite make it to the moon, orbiting the lunar satellite for a time and then landing in the ocean back on Earth. Alex Blum did the art.

Coming out at the end of the Golden Age in 1955, *CI* 124's feature *The War of the Worlds* was adapted by Harry Miller and drawn by Lou Cameron. Wells' masterpiece has "meteors" landing on Earth and unleashing octopi-like Martians who build towering machines on tripods that tear across the countryside and eventually hit London, destroying everything with devastating heat waves. The conflict seems as uneven as if humans were to wage war with ants, but eventually the invaders succumb to common bacteria, against which they have no defense. Some of the more intense and horrifying aspects of the novel are downplayed or eliminated, but it is still a worthwhile adaptation. While Cameron's art is not outstanding, it does boast a few striking full-page panels depicting the first appearance of a tripod, a heat wave exploding a ship in a fiery burst, and a two-page panel showing troops being routed by the Martians. Cameron's cover painting, showing troops firing upon three tripods, is also impressive.

Classics Illustrated 133 contains an adaptation of Wells' superb *The Time Machine*, scripted by Lorenz Graham and drawn by Cameron. The Time Traveler uses his machine to go into the future and winds up in 800,000 AD where the human race has been divided into the Eloi—weak, gentle, ineffectual, pretty creatures—and the Morlocks, who live underground, provide for all the needs of the Eloi, and feed upon them. Cameron does a fairly good job with this issue, pulling the reader swiftly along, and the nighttime scenes with the Morlocks are genuinely creepy. Cameron may have given the Morlocks too much personality, however, such as in a panel in which one of the Morlocks rubs his hands together in anticipation, one supposes, of dinner. The striking cover depicting the traveler in his well-designed time machine is by George Wilson.

Classics Illustrated 138 features Verne's fabulous fantasy *A Journey to the Center of the Earth*, drawn by Norman Nodel. The uncredited cover painting, depicting a battle between two saurian monstrosities in an underwater sea as the human voyagers watch from a raft, is a stunner. Nodel's inside art is quite good as well. Memorable sequences concern the saurian battle and the climax, when the men on their raft rapidly ascend to the surface inside the lava-filled cone of a volcano. This adaptation manages to get across vividly many of the harrowing moments of Verne's story, such as when one character is separated from his fellows and must blunder along in a panic in near-total darkness.

Classics Illustrated 144 features *The First Men in the Moon*, a story of a voyage to the moon embarked upon by two men, a playwright and his neighbor; the latter invented a material that can cut off gravity. Coating a glass sphere with this material, they are able to make their way to the moon, where they encounter ant-like tentacled Selenites who slaughter gigantic moon cows for food and try to take them captive. The uncredited script moves briskly, although the art—attributed to *four* artists (Al Williamson, George Woodbridge, Angelo Torres, Roy Krenkel)—is understandably uneven and often flat. But the depiction of the Selenites, moon cows and flora of the lunar landscape is commendable.

Classics Illustrated 149 features *Off on a Comet*, based on Verne's novel *Hector Servadac*. Hector is about to fight a duel when a comet grazes the Earth and carries off a small slice of it, along with islands, some of the ocean, and a few inhabitants. The story details the efforts of a small band of people to survive in this new world, where they eventually seek warmth and shelter in the caverns below a volcano. This uncredited adaptation deletes the character Dutch Isaac, a Jewish stereotype. Verne probably knew that the results would be much more disastrous if a comet were to

The stunning cover of the *Classics Illustrated* adaptation of Jules Verne's *A Journey to the Center of the Earth*.

actually hit the Earth. At the end of the very entertaining story, Hector and his companions use a balloon to travel safely from the comet back to the Earth. Gerard McCann's dramatic cover depicting the collision between comet and Earth is notable, as is his inside artwork.

Classics Illustrated 153 is an adaptation of Wells' *The Invisible Man*. Drawn by Norman Nodel, it does a generally good job of depicting an exciting story in which Griffin, a scientist experimenting with optics, makes himself invisible, but he becomes unhinged. He tries to start what he refers to as a reign of terror, causing a lot of havoc before he is killed by an angry mob.

Classics Illustrated 162 and 163 present adaptations of Verne's *Clipper of the Clouds* (retitled *Robur the Conqueror*) and its sequel *Master of the World*. The story, which has similarities to *20,000 Leagues*, involves a heavier-than-air flying machine instead of a submarine. Instead of Nemo, the megalomanic in this tale is named Robur. Proponents of lighter-than-air travel (in other words, balloons) think Robur is crazy but he proves them wrong with his ship, an "aeronet" which he calls the *Albatross*. Kidnapping three of the balloon enthusiasts, Robur takes them on a trip around the world, stopping to save some natives about to be sacrificed and rescue men in a lifeboat. Unwilling to remain Robur's prisoners, the balloonists escape and blow up the *Albatross*. Robur survives and shows up in his rebuilt ship. Don Perlin was the artist.

In the sequel, Robur, certifiably insane and proclaiming himself the "master of the world," has built a new ship which he calls the *Terror*. It not only flies but also moves across the ground like an automobile, sails on the ocean, and dives beneath the waves like a submarine. At one point, the *Terror* rises up from Niagara Falls, spreading out its wing-like structures to fly. The *Terror* is destroyed when Robur flies it into a lightning storm. Gray Morrow did the art.

Classics Illustrated 166 features *The Food of the Gods*, the forerunner of all those stories and movies about outsized animals, insects and people, although Wells is less concerned with monsters than with spotlighting mankind's continual need for intellectual growth. Alfred Sundel's script captures the flavor of the novel, which mixes humorous sections with passages of horror, as a growth formula creates huge wasps, rats, chickens and babies. The latter grow into 35-foot adults, alarming the general populace. Wells is never able to reconcile the fact that while the giants are symbolic of mankind's need to grow mentally as well as physically and reach for the stars, on a practical level they are simply frightening menaces. Tony Tallarico's art is not impressive, although Gerald McCann's cover painting—depicting a giant pullet running off with a boy in its beak—is certainly memorable.

In the Bronze Age, Marvel decided to adapt many of these same stories for its *Marvel Classics* series. While some of the scripts were quite good, the artwork was generally not as impressive.

DC

Strange Adventures

Strange Adventures continued in the Silver Age beginning with issue 64. The cover showing "Gorillas in Space"—smiling gorillas wearing spacesuits and glass helmets—seems quite juvenile, but the stories inside are on a somewhat higher level. In the gorilla story, some aliens dress up in gorilla costumes and claim to be human astronauts who went down the evolutionary scale due to cosmic rays; they warn that the same thing will happen to anyone else who ventures into space. Bent on conquest, the aliens hope to delay the Earth's exploration of space until they have time to build a cobalt bomb to counteract Earth's H-bomb. The scheme comes undone when one of the scientists wonders why the gorillas never blink. The story was written by Bill Finger and drawn by Carmine Infantino and Bernard Sachs.

The other stories in the issue are also of above-average interest. "The Maze of Mars" (Binder-Greene-Giella) has an alien recreating the canals of Mars in Earth caverns so that a human explorer can help him find the way out of the *actual* labyrinthine canals. In the intriguing and complex "The Man Who Discovered the West Pole" (Binder-Kane-Giella), a comet disrupts Earth's electrical field, causing everything to go out of whack. Boiling water turns to ice, human voices won't carry through the air, sparrows grow to giant size, and rain falls *upward*. A scientist hopes to correct this situation by discovering the West Pole and applying various solutions once there. He uses latex from rubber trees as insulation against the electrical field that is causing the problem, then reverses the polarity of the West Pole. The insulation causes volcanoes around the world to erupt with electrical charges. In "The Earth-Drowners" (Joe Samachson-Jerry Grandenetti-Joe Giella), aquatic Venusians want to cover the world with water. Via mind control, they force an Earthman to plant devices around the world that will bring this about, dooming the human race. At the last minute, he outwits them.

In "*Strange Adventures* 77's "The Incredible Eyes of Arthur Gail" (Edmond Hamilton–Greene and Giella), the title character, due to a chemical accident, can see only people and their clothing (the latter eliminating nudity in a '60s comic book) but no walls or objects. Gail has to be helped down a metal staircase whose steps are invisible to him. He sees people in office buildings seemingly floating in the air as well as couples riding high in an invisible Ferris wheel. (The *seats* of the Ferris wheel are mistakenly shown.) Gail's worst experience is when he takes a trip on an airliner and can only see the people and pilots and the landscape many miles below. He is able to use his unwanted "power" to pinpoint the real thief after he is accused of stealing a formula. A bullet that grazes his forehead returns his optic nerve to normal.

In *SA* 92's "The Amazing Ray of Knowledge" (Joe Millard-Carmine Infantino-Bernard Sachs), a scientist invents a ray that imparts genius status on animals and humans, but it only works on immature brains. Soon a group of children are geniuses in specialized fields such as chemistry and physics. When it becomes known that a giant comet is racing towards Earth and may spell the planet's doom, the children are enlisted to find a solution to this terrifying problem. The answer takes the children and their adult supervisors to Pluto, but once there, at a crucial moment, the kids revert to their normal selves and only want to play hide-and-seek! Since the Knowledge Ray was left back on Earth, the adult scientists come up with a way to save their planet as well as Pluto. Says one: "*Flash knowledge* can never replace human ingenuity and skill. There is no short cut to genius by machines—because experience is still the foundation of knowledge."

In *SA* 94's harrowing "Fishermen of Space" (Millard-Infantino-Sachs), gargantuan aliens use sky hooks to ensnare a bus, a plane and a destroyer—one each from land, air and sea—and think that these vehicles are *alive* and the humans inside mere parasites. The Earthlings do their best to attract the attention of the extraterrestrials and are horrified to learn that they think the "creatures"—that is, the bus and other objects—are dead and will be jettisoned into airless space. The pilot fires up the plane to convince the aliens that this is not true, but they are still imprisoned. A boy captive uses a whistle to call his dog, and as this sound proves painful to the aliens, it finally gets their attention. They return the Earth creatures, still unaware of the sentient humans inside.

Strange Adventures often featured provocative covers even if they cheat a bit, as the stories are not *quite* what the cover suggests. One complete hoax: In "The Gorilla War Against Earth" (*SA* 88), an alien tries to make it seem as if such a war is imminent by using ventriloquism to create the illusion that a caged gorilla has human intelligence. In *SA* 87's "New Faces for Old" (Ed Herron–Infantino and Giella), a scientist uses a device to make homely people handsome. While the device *does* work—at least temporarily—it is really being employed only so that another alien can find two extraterrestrial fugitives, turning two Earth people into their duplicates.

Although the superhero renaissance had not yet started (with *Showcase* 4 featuring a new version of the Golden Age hero the Flash), obviously superpowers were still in the minds of DC editors. *Strange Adventures* stories feature a man who develops a formula to give various creatures wings, eventually turning himself into a flying hero; an undercover cop who develops electrical powers; and an alien who can change his height and size. "Super-Athlete from Earth" (*SA* 125) features a young man who is given heroic abilities by an alien in order to aid him on a mission.

Strange Adventures 114 introduces Star Hawkins, a private eye from the year 2079 who has a robot "gal Friday" named Ilda that he periodically has to pawn when he needs money—which is often. In his first story, "The Case of the Martian Witness," Star is hired to enter a Martian jungle with weird and scary plants to bring back an alien who knows who has the rightful claim to a mine of pink gold. The story was written by John Broome, with art by Mike Sekowsky and Bernard Sachs. Star Hawkins made many more *Strange Adventures* appearances. In "The Case of the Robot-Spy," Ilda goes undercover to find stolen jewels in the camp of a group of aliens who resemble old–Earth gypsies. Ilda is stolen from the pawn shop in "The Case of the Vanishing Robots" (*SA* 125).

Strange Adventures 134 presents one of the most amusing Star Hawkins adventures, "The Case of the Interplanetary Imps." Star makes some extra money by sharing his office with the latest clients of a theatrical agent: a horde of Munchkin-like Neptunian acrobats who make Ilda's life miserable. The Neptunians save the day when Ilda and Star are threatened by a crook bent on revenge. In "The Case of the Unwanted Robot" (*SA* 143), Star is outraged by the discrimination when a hotel refuses to admit Ilda, since robots are considered mere servants. But after both Ilda and Hawkins outwit a gang seeking to blow up the asteroid upon which the hotel is built, this policy is immediately revoked. Ilda is jealous when human females express an interest in Star, and in one story temporarily falls for a male robot until she is turned off by his sexist attitude. Ilda believes in independence for women, be they human or robotic.

SA 117 presents the first in a series of adventures of the Atomic Knights. These stories take place after World War III when there is no government, law and order, plant or animal life, no way to grow food, and very few human survivors. In one part of the country, the ruler is the Black Baron, who has hoarded all of the remaining food supplies in the area. Soldier Gardner Grayle and teacher Douglas Herald combine forces, discovering that metal armor protects against radioactive bombs as well as the ray guns employed by the Baron's troops. Since there are six suits of armor, the two men enlist four volunteers: farmers Hollis and Wayne Hobard, scientist Bryndon and Douglas' sister Marene. They approach the Baron's stronghold, resist his weapons in their armor, and redistribute the hoarded food. The group decides to band together permanently as the Atomic Knights, futuristic policemen righting wrongs as in the days of old, although Bryndon tells them that their armor's protection won't last forever. Gardner and Marene have a strong attraction for one another. The script was by John Broome with art by Murphy Anderson.

In "The Cavemen of New York" (Broome-Anderson) in *SA* 123, the Atomic Knights travel to a demolished New York City hoping to find a cache of food beneath the subways. What they find is a group of savage humans turned backward on the evolutionary scale by radiation, but eventually they are able to befriend them. The early scenes as the Knights approach the ruins of Manhattan and cross the river on a raft are eerie. Most of the group travel to "The Lost City of Los Angeles" in *SA* 126, using a glider to traverse the decimated countryside, passing a series of volcanoes created by the H-bomb, and finally locating another pocket of humans in L.A. Eventually the Knights have to deal with a group of war-like "Atlantides," or Atlanteans, who survived the sinking of their island after Atlantis went through a time warp to the 20th century. Their leader, the Khagan, attacks the knights several times. The ranks of the Knights increase when they come across two dalmatians who were test animals in a rocket and have grown to the size of large horses.

The Atomic Knights are featured on the cover for the first time with *Strange Adventures* 144. In "When the Earth Blacked Out" (Broome-Anderson), the Knights discover that, in underground caverns, a race of mole-like, virtually sightless men are planning to take over the surface world using plants that emit a black fog, plunging Earth into darkness. The Knights defeat the mole men by using captured fireflies—a source of cold light (light that radiates warmth would make the Knights "visible" to the mole men)—inside pumpkins as weapons. In "The King of New Orleans" (*SA* 147), the Knights discover that the city has a self-appointed ruler who has used sound waves to turn all the doctors in a medical center into easily controlled zombies. The Knights use jazz music—which has been banned in the city—to disrupt the sonic waves and return the doctors to normal.

In a story clearly influenced by John Wyndham's 1951 novel *The Day of the Triffids* (as well as the 1962 film version), the Atomic Knights contend with dangerous plant life in *Strange Adventures* 150's "The Plant that Hated Men." With John Broome's script shamelessly borrowing from Wyndham's story, it is one of the Knights' more exciting and memorable adventures. These tall, dangerous plants, capable of moving about like triffids, are called Trefoils. A type of mutated bean plant, they are not only telepathic, but also can hurl explosive berries and emit a poison gas. The knights cut off their water supply and they quickly collapse. A botanist named Henderson is able to breed a friendlier type of Trefoil and uses the properties of their berries as a gasoline substitute in a car he gifts to the Knights.

By this time, the sole female knight, Marene, was being called Mar*l*ene—at least temporarily—but she rarely got in on the action. With its very '60s sensibility, the Atomic Knights strip mostly depicts Marene—who thought of herself as "just a woman"—keeping the home fires burning while the men go out on missions. She eternally pines for her great love, Gardner. Marene summons up some spirit when some townspeople make disparaging remarks about her colleagues, but most of the time she is only along for the ride. The one exception is the very last Atomic Knights story, *SA* 160's "Here Come the Wild Ones!" Marene takes center stage when she disguises herself as a young boy to infiltrate and help a group of misfit boys who admire a criminal called Kadey. The Atomic Knights was an interesting series but the group was never given its own title.

Strange Adventures also featured occasional "Space Museum" stories in which a man of the 25th century takes his son, Tommy Parker, on monthly trips to the museum and talks about the various objects on display. One of the best of these stories is "The Gem Invasion of Earth," in which a mynah bird named Tommy—whom the boy is named after—inadvertently foils a dastardly plot by sentient alien gems who have a frightening control over humans. In *SA* 124's "Earth Victory—By a Hair" (Fox-Infantino), it is revealed that young Tommy's father was once a crusty general known as the Wrecker, and his mother an admiral. The two butted heads due to the former's sexism during an assignment but eventually married. In "Prisoners of the Space Flowers" (*SA* 142), Tommy sees his own baby picture in the museum on his 15th birthday and learns that when he was three, he saved his parents from aliens by—rather improbably—maneuvering their rocketship so the exhaust would blow a deadly flora's paralyzing powder off them. Tommy proves equally heroic as a teen in "The Mass-Energy Robbers of Space" (*SA* 145) when aliens paralyze all adults on Earth and Tommy and his pals save the day.

A sort of mini-series featuring giant faceless men from Saturn appeared in three *Strange Adventures* issues. The first, "The Face Hunter from Saturn" (*SA* 124) finds a friendly Saturnian, Klee Pan, teaming up with Earth highway patrolmen Jim Boone and Bob Colby to save his world, Klaramar, a sub-atomic planet inside Saturn, from being destroyed by his psychopathic adversary, Chun Yull. When they succeed, a grateful Klee Pan gives the officers telepathic powers which come in handy in *SA* 142's "The Return of the Faceless Creature," when Chun Yull arrives on Earth with another plan to demolish Klaramar *and* the two policemen. In "Threat of the Faceless Creature" (*SA* 153), Chun Yull breaks out of his prison and returns to Earth with a plan to shrink that world, enlarge Klaramar, and cause both worlds to explode when they reach the same size. Boone and Colby enter Klaramar, but are so small that they must ride flies to attract Klee Pan's attention, then draw a picture of Earth on his wall.

When Julius Schwartz turned over *Strange Adventures*' editorial reins to Jack Shiff, that was the end of Space Museum, the Atomic Knights and Star Hawkins. (The latter eventually returned.) Schwartz had used such exemplary artists as Carmine Infantino, Sid Greene and Mike Sekowsky while Shiff brought in the lesser-known Jack Sparling, Howard Sherman, Howard Purcell, Mort Meskin and Lee Elias. Schwartz's usual scriptwriters were solid pros such as John Broome and Gardner Fox, who often turned in some very clever work, although eventually they began repeating themselves. Shiff hired writers Dave Wood and Ed Herron. Sometimes even the new writers recycled old ideas; there were at least two stories about a man who gains much dangerous tonnage without it changing his outward appearance.

Strange Adventures under Shiff took a page from Marvel's book and began running many more monster stories. For instance, "Secret of the Insect-Men" in *SA* 165, drawn by Howard Sherman, is a bizarre sci-fi horror story in which a scientist, for unaccountable reasons, decides to create giant, intelligent insects. He uses a special camera which will not only take photos of the faces of his colleagues, but also capture their brain power and put it into the insects. Emerging from cocoons, the huge insects now have human heads, the brain power of scientists, and a desire to take over the world. But some of these big bugs have a natural affinity for the real men whose duplicate heads they wear and help them in their fight against the monstrous insects.

Other *Strange Adventures* monsters include a giant, horned "Juggernaut Man"; a neon sign advertising a monster movie that comes to life, jumps off the theater wall and terrorizes the city; and a ghastly creature that appears in the real world even as it stars in a comic-within-a-comic also called *Strange Adventures*. There is also a lumbering if kindly horror from an underworld race as well as a man seeking a cure for baldness who winds up in another dimension as a giant-sized invader. Shiff probably used a few stories that had been earmarked for *My Greatest Adventure* after it was turned into *The Doom Patrol*.

One of the better monster-less stories is *SA* 175's "Danger: This Town Is Shrinking," written by Jack Miller and drawn by Jack Sparling. A man hurries to the town where his fiancée lives on his wedding day only to discover that the whole town has been cordoned off because all of the buildings and people are beginning to shrink. The residents are only a few inches tall, and getting smaller. A tarpaulin is placed over the town but in one harrowing sequence a grasshopper that is now a gigantic menace gets in, terrifying everyone. Fearful of more insect invasions once the residents are nearly microscopic, the authorities move the entire town to a laboratory, where they deduce that a rainfall has caused this deplorable situation. Ordinary water saves the day. What the tale lacks in originality, it makes up for with its absorbing and suspenseful nature.

Strange Adventures wasn't quite done with its hoax stories. In "The Faceless People" (Dave Wood-Lee Elias) in *SA* 176, Duke, an actor having a crisis of confidence, is called back to his hometown by a telegram from his former girlfriend, Kitty. There he discovers that she and everyone else in town have lost their facial features. One would think that the first thing Duke would ask is how can they eat or see or breathe, but he never does. He is told that an evil wizard is responsible for this situation and tries to get all of the victims out of town, but first he has to defeat the sorcerer with some green moss. Then Kitty, her face normal, tells him that the whole thing was just a movie, done to give him back his confidence: Now the movie will make him a *star*. It is arguably the worst of the hoax stories in the series.

Star Hawkins and Ilda came back—with the new creative team of Dave Wood and Gil Kane—in *SA* 173. Ilda glamorizes herself for a starring role in a robotic movie but then learns she is only being used by a gang of crooks. In "The Case of the Blonde Bombshell" (*SA* 182), Ilda is both jealous and suspicious of a gorgeous client who wants Star to retrieve certain letters. Just when it seems that she is part of a Martian conspiracy ring, it turns out she is working undercover. In *SA* 185, a jolt to Ilda's memory banks makes her think that she's the master criminal, the Slinker. This was the last appearance of Star Hawkins and the lovable Ilda.

Beginning with *Strange Adventures* 177, the series began presenting the adventures of such outré superheroes as Immortal Man, Animal Man, the Man of Two Worlds and the Enchantress, who eventually became a super-villainess. The heroes were gone by *SA* 202, which offers a new but much less effective logo for the comic. After three pretty dismal issues, *Strange Adventures* became an all-reprint title.

Many of the stories also wound up in DC's reprint title *From Beyond the Unknown*, which came out in 1969 and lasted 25 issues.

Some of the more notable stories in the comic include:

- "Search for a Lost World" (*SA* 67): A man from a microscopic solar system enlarges himself to enter an outer universe to find out why his world is being strangely affected and discovers atomic testing on Earth.
- "A Switch in Time" (79): A man gets an unpleasant surprise when he changes places with a man from the future.
- "The Man Who Cheated Time" (80): A man uses a "futuroscope" to see his future, noting events that will net him a fortune, as well as what to do to avoid death, but discovers that he can't outrun his ultimate fate.
- "The Secret of the Sleeping Spaceman" (88): A town is endangered by an expanding airless vacuum, the only atmosphere in which an alien visitor can survive.
- "The Human Time Machine" (97): A time traveler from ancient Atlantis unwittingly causes one famous disaster after another, including the deluge, due to the energy he unleashes.
- "Throwback World" (97): A space prospector discovers that a world older than Earth has not progressed scientifically as far as it should have because periodically the inhabitants revert backwards to their ape-like ancestors, destroying everything.
- "The World That Grew" (98): An ultra-growth ray that gets out of hand enlarges flora and fauna on an asteroid to a dangerous degree and could even enlarge the *asteroid* enough to endanger Earth.
- "The Man Who Harpooned Worlds" (103): A man is arrested for shooting gargantuan harpoons at space vehicles and at Earth, but he is actually trying to destroy an invisible ultra-hawk of tremendous size from another dimension.
- "The Case of the Stolen Earth Faces" (105): When every man in town suddenly wears the visage of the same alien, the men's wives set out to expose which husband is the real extraterrestrial.
- "Peril of the Planet-Eater" (107): Only one man on Earth can operate the weapon capable of destroying a bird-like extraterrestrial that has arrived to tear out Earth's core.
- "The Hand from Beyond" (110): A mysterious giant hand appears whenever a man is in danger, whether he's on Earth or in space. He is determined to elude this guardian and fend for himself.
- "Menace of the Size-Changing Spaceman" (112): An alien explorer who can change his size finds himself helplessly growing into a colossus. An Earthman must get the explorer's miniature ship back from a colony of ants before the giant explodes like an atom bomb.

- "Secret of the Flying Buzzsaw" (114): A scientist uses a special chamber that repels gravity to land on and destroy a white dwarf star heading directly towards Earth.
- "The Great Space-Tiger Hunt" (115): Alien hunters unleash gigantic tigers on Earth to track down for sport. The huge beasts turn out to be intelligent and friendly.
- "Challenge of the Gorilla Genius" (117): A scientist is about to receive a major prize when the ceremony is interrupted by a talking gorilla who claims that *he* deserves the award.
- "The Aliens Who Raided New York" (134): Aliens steal the Empire State Building, the Statue of Liberty and other famous sites because they have been irradiated by a comet and can be used as weapons in their war with another race.
- "The Two-Way Time-Traveler" (143): Due to radiation from a meteor, a helpless man keeps bouncing from the future to the past and back again.
- "The Dawn-World Menace" (147): Due to several time warps, two Cro-Magnon men astride pterodactyls from the Mesozoic era wind up in the 20th century, where the energy they bring prematurely ages everything, including people, that they come near.
- "Mystery of the 12 O'Clock Man" (162): A man who mysteriously disappears every Friday at noon discovers that he is a synthetic being sent to spy on Earth and now doesn't know whether to be loyal to his creators or to Earthlings.

My Greatest Adventure

DC's long-running sci-fi–fantasy comic *My Greatest Adventure* debuted in 1955 at the tail end of the Golden Age. The original concept was to present tales of daring and unusual adventure, narrated by the heroic protagonist or a group, so the title of each story began with "I" or "We" such as "I Jumped from 8 Miles Up" about a brave if foolhardy parachutist or "I Had a Date with Doom," in which a man with only six months to live has a series of exciting adventures. One of the best stories was *MGA* 5's "I Escaped from Castle Morte," in which a man gets out of an impregnable tower in which he was imprisoned by criminals who think he's seen too much of their operation.

Although the first issue has a story entitled "I Hunted a Flying Saucer," drawn by Bill Ely, *My Greatest Adventure* did not go in for "fantastic" tales or science fiction—at first. In the flying saucer tale, a man has encounters with UFOs whose occupants obliterate his evidence and make authorities think he's crazy. At the end, he sets out to find this alien race—and is never seen again. After a couple of years, the comic started sneaking in more incredible tales along these lines, and then went whole hog, essentially becoming a science fiction–fantasy comic. For instance, "The

Creature We Dared Not Kill" (Infantino-Meskin) in *MGA* 64 is a prehistoric beast who can create a protective bubble around itself as well as emit vibrations to shatter the bubble when it is no longer needed. When a scientist is accidentally encased in a similar bubble and is rapidly running out of air, his colleagues must get the beast to emit the vibrations needed to free the trapped scientist.

Some stories have excellent premises that are too routine in their realization. In "I Was Exiled to Outer Space" (69), a doctor, a movie star, and a gambler are accidentally hit by rays being employed by friendly aliens visiting Earth. Both aliens and Earth scientists concur that the irradiated trio will die if they remain on Earth, but if they travel to the aliens' world they will not only survive but also live for 200 years, after which they can return—but then everyone they know will be dead. The story is certainly rife with unlimited possibilities, yet all that happens is that the gambler tries to take over the alien world and is defeated by the doctor—who also finds a cure for their condition in less than a week. On the other hand, "I Went to an Alien College" (70), written and drawn by Howard Purcell, is an amusing bit of whimsy in which a university man takes advantage of an offer to be an exchange student on another planet, but is baffled by the way an unknown figure keeps trying to scare him. Finally he figures out that he was brought to this other world as the alien student's entry in a contest of strange exhibits. A rival contestant kept hoping to scare him so he'd go home and give *him* a better chance at winning.

The best story ever published by *My Greatest Adventure* appears in the seventy-second issue: In "Stay Away from Me—You Might Die!," drawn by Gene Colan, a surgeon discovers an odd object on a roadside. Picking it up, he inadvertently pushes down on a knob and fears that if he lets go, the object will explode like a grenade, which it resembles despite its alien design. X-rays and scientific consultation soon confirm that the device is indeed an explosive, and if the doctor lets go of the knob, it will cause a massive explosion. Worse yet, in a few hours the man must perform a life-or-death operation that *only* he can perform. The solution is to shoot the doctor into space where the device will be rendered harmless by the lack of gravity. This mini-masterpiece is a harrowing and suspenseful exercise in tension.

In the '60s, editor Murray Boltinoff tried to recapture the original spirit of the magazine by publishing more stories of heroic adventurers, such as "Doom Was My Inheritance" (*MGA* 74), in which a man sets out on a quest to find a fortune as well as his missing father, while an evil associate manipulates things behind the scenes. Stories were often more adult in plot and tone, such as "Castaway Cave Men of 1950" (*MGA* 75) in which a professor relates how some shipwrecked children, with their parents dead, revert to savagery as they reach adulthood on an island but are then found and taught to act more human. At the end of the story, the professor reveals that he was one of these lost children. The story may have been loosely inspired by *Lord of the Flies* but goes in an entirely different direction.

On the letters page of *MGA* 79, the editor announces that the next issue will present the exploits of a new group called the Legion of the Strange. By the time issue 80 appeared, this group had been rechristened the Doom Patrol, the "fabulous freak" superheroes who took over the magazine. The title was eventually changed to *Doom Patrol*.

Other notable stories in the series include:

- "We Were Doomed by the Metal-Eating Monster" (*MGA* 21): An alien life form attracts and devours all metal, endangering the Earth's cities and their inhabitants.
- "We Were 20th Century Cavemen" (27): A rejuvenation ray turns a parrot, turtle and chameleon into gigantic prehistoric ancestors.
- "We Were Trapped as Human Puppets" (30): Several people on an island are forced to do the bidding of a weird creature whose motives they fear until they discover he only needs their help in finding his way home.
- "We Were Trapped in Freak Valley" (32): Two men pass through a tunnel and discover a land where dogs are giant-sized, elephants are tiny, and many other animals are of varying sizes.
- "We Battled the Hand of Doom" (32): A giant, disembodied hand causes havoc as it searches for the device that can rejoin it with the rest of its alien body.
- "I Stole the Space Beast" (37): A writer comes across a cute if dangerous space creature that a couple of Venusian crooks want to use as a weapon. The animal is loyal to the Earthman who was kind to it.
- "I Became the Beetle Beast" (41): A harrowing tale in which a man's consciousness is accidentally switched into the body of a beetle that grows to giant size.
- "I Was Marooned on Earth" (48): A sad tale of a lonely alien, brought back to life by a kind scientist. The alien tries to fit in with humans but fails and is finally killed while saving a child's life.
- "We Tracked the Beast from the Deep" (50): A gigantic sea monster searches for its captured infant. The tale is similar to the film *Gorgo*, released the following year (1961).
- "I Became the Sun Creature" (52): A man's mind is switched into the body of an alien sun creature whose heat is so intense it can melt skyscrapers.
- "I Was One of the Little People" (52): Scientists who are shrunk in size as part of an experiment are forced into the giant outside world when a dog runs off with the device that can bring them back to normal.
- "The Monster That Changed Our Lives" (60): Four people who have never met are affected by the presence of a dangerous alien machine that only wants a white rose to use to cure its other-worldly master.
- "I Lost the Life or Death Secret" (65): An amphibious beast, the Quechada, is a legendary spirit of the river who appears once every century.
- "We Tracked the Fabled Fish-Man" (70): An entertaining *Creature from the Black Lagoon* derivative in which the creature is of gigantic size.

- "I Defied Man-Killer Mountain" (73): A determined mountain climber ascends to a summit with an angry spirit within it.

Mystery in Space

Mystery in Space continued into the Silver Age and became the home for space hero Adam Strange. One of the best *Mystery in Space* stories appears in issue 32: "The Riddle of the Vanishing Earthmen" (Fox-Greene-Giella). An alien race uses a super-weapon to blow up Halley's Comet and threatens to use the weapon to destroy the Earth if we don't surrender to them in a number of days. Scientists determine that the aliens must be of a much greater size than humans, and come up with a plan. First they build a spaceship (hidden from the aliens on the far side of the Earth) 25 miles long and send it to rendezvous with the aliens. Naturally when the aliens come aboard to discuss terms of surrender, they discover all the giant "props" (including huge cups of coffee) but no Earthlings. *Five miles* tall, the aliens are unaware of the true size of humans, and are fooled into thinking we are just as big. Meanwhile three brave astronauts rocket unseen to the planet's surface, dispatch gigantic insects that attack them, and blow up the aliens' super-weapon. Earth refuses to tell the aliens the "secret" of how we got past their defences, and warns them that we will attack if they again dare to threaten us. When DC came out with a reprint series entitled *From Beyond the Unknown* in the '70s this story was wisely chosen for the first issue.

There are other notable stories in the series. In "Stranger on Earth" in *MIS* 33 (Samachson-Greene-Sachs), an applicant for membership in a science council on a distant planet is tested by being sent to "backward" Earth with some of his memory stripped so that he not only loses his knowledge of space science but also forgets exactly which planet he comes from; he has to somehow make his way home using primitive Earth technology. In "The Counterfeit Earth" (Binder-Kubert) in *MIS* 35, Earth defends itself from attack by generating a convincing image of a duplicate Earth. Two astronauts being followed by hostile aliens have to figure out which is the real Earth so that they are not destroyed themselves. In "The New Year's Eve of 2000 A.D." (Hamilton-Greene-Sachs) in *MIS* 38, the problem isn't Y2K but a huge bell given as a gift by the Martians, who have enjoyed good relations with Earth after overthrowing a malevolent element. The story's protagonist has learned that there is something deadly about the bell, and has to learn what it is before the clock strikes midnight—and without destroying Earth-Martian relations.

In "The Amazing Space-Flight of North America" (Binder-Greene-Giella) in *Mystery in Space* 44, the entire continent is turned into a spaceship. Centuries ago, an alien hid a certain element on the continent which would prevent an explosion that could obliterate the galaxy (including the alien planet). With only a short time before the disaster, the aliens—who live in a galaxy shaped like North America (which is why the dying alien hid it on the continent)—transfer the entire continent towards their planet, to give them more time to search for the hidden element (which must be employed near the other planet if it is to be effective). Working together, aliens and Earthlings uncover the element and save both of their worlds. It takes a certain genius to come up with a story that is *this* patently and ridiculously contrived, and yet it is its sheer audaciousness that makes it so memorable and entertaining.

In *MIS* 48, "Secret of the Scarecrow World" (Fox-Infantino-Giella) is a bizarre story in which a young couple develops a teleportation device. To prove it can be used for interplanetary travel, they set up a unit on Titan, which is called the Scarecrow World due to an odd rock formation on its surface. On Titan they teleport a symbolic scarecrow to Earth, only it's enlarged over a million times and hovers over the planet like a giant. When the couple returns to Earth, they find the world deserted: Everyone was teleported to Titan and reduced to microscopic size! If that wasn't bad enough, aliens choose that very moment to claim the now-deserted Earth. The story of how the couple hides from the aliens, while trying to return the world's population to Earth at their normal size, makes for absurd but harrowing reading.

The title character in *MIS* 49's "The Sky-High Man" (Binder-Sekowsky-Giella) is an astronaut, exploring the farthest reaches of space, who breaks through into a different cosmos where space is white and the stars are black. Returning to Earth, he discovers that a property of the new cosmos has turned him into a giant so huge that the diameter of our globe is, in proportion to him, only two feet wide! So huge that he appears like a mist to Earth's inhabitants, he is unable to warn anyone that nuclear wastes in the Arctic are about to explode. He travels to other worlds for food, doing good deeds along the way, and finally figures out that absolute cold can return him to normal. He now travels back to Earth and saves the day.

The same issue features "The 24,000 Hour Day" (Binder-Stallman-Giunta), in which a wealthy man on an asteroid offers men payment of $1000 a day if they work for him. After they've signed contracts, they discover that the asteroid revolves around the sun so slowly that an average day lasts *three years*—meaning they'll actually make about a dollar an hour! Two of the men make their way to the dark side of the asteroid so they won't have to wait years to get paid, and after cleverly surmounting many obstacles, they outwit their employer and put a stop to his heartless scheme.

"The Runaway Space-Train" (Fox-Kane-Sachs) in *MIS* 50 is one of the most charming comic fantasies ever published in a sci-fi comic anthology. A group of Americans planning to see the west by train find that the train is flying higher and higher through the air, and then through outer space, until it lands on another planet, Almoran. In keeping with the whimsical nature of the piece, the Earthlings are delighted to know that disguised Almorans are going to take their places and go sightseeing on Earth, while they themselves see all of Almoran's wondrous sights. On Earth, the disguised aliens *ooh* and *ahh* at the Grand Canyon and are delighted when bank robbers hold up the train ("Is this part of the tour?" they wonder)—to no avail, as the aliens take care of them with their telekinetic powers. Meanwhile on Almoran, the Earthlings, including a little boy with his trusty lariat, bravely foil a hostile takeover of the planet by evil aliens. It probably would have made an excellent Spielberg movie.

House of Mystery

At the very end of the Golden Age, *House of Mystery* switched from horror stories to mostly fake tales of the supernatural as well as ersatz science fiction. The dinosaurs on an island turn out to be mechanical duplicates; a supposedly immortal man actually faked his fall from a 300-foot tower; a magician makes a man disappear but this also turns out to be a hoax, etc. The pages of the comic are full of swindlers coming up with wild schemes to ensnare the gullible until something gives the game away.

House of Mystery 46 presents a story entitled "Black Magic for Sale" in which a shopkeeper charges exorbitant prices for some incredible toys and other objects, such as a 3-D camera, a flying saucer that flies harmlessly through a person's body, a bottle that pours an endless supply of milk and a doll that can greatly expand in size. These objects are *not* hoaxes; the shopkeeper found them in a crashed spaceship whose occupants are long deceased. As he has no desire to part with these priceless items, he always asks for a staggering amount of money. At the end, two burglars attempting to steal the objects press the wrong button and are shrunk to such a small size that they fit into an extraterrestrial dollhouse. Bill Ely did the art.

The following issue contains stories about a thinking robot that turns to crime because it is given the wrong book to read; a sculptor whose mind is affected by little green men from inside the Earth; a man deemed "the modern Munchhausen" because no one will believe his story of finding an alien rocketship in the desert; and a greedy blind man who gets an eye transplant and discovers that his new eyes, taken from a deceased psychic, see visions of horrible disasters. This story, "The Man with the Stolen Eyes," is the best of the bunch.

As the series progresses, there were stories about a science fiction author who is secretly a visitor from space; a survivor of a radioactive blast who wears bandages like a mummy because he's become invisible; a crook who eludes the police by transforming into different critters, including a beetle; and a talking horse whose body is taken over by a malevolent Martian. These are entertaining but distinctly minor. The hoax stories make a comeback: There's a tale about a swami with a phony crystal ball, the sole purpose of which is to help the police find a thief's loot. Another tale deals with the European prime minister who uses trickery to try to convince the American woman who's going to marry the king that anyone who weds him will die. In "The Man Who Made Giants" (*HOM* 67), a professor supposedly turns a bunch of gangsters into colossi (a similar premise to the Doc Savage novel *The Monsters*) but this is just a ploy to get their loot away from them by using special props and animals to fool them.

In *House of Mystery* 100, the series presented the ultimate hoax story with

"Curse of the Ghost Caravan," drawn by Bill Ely. In a small European village, Dolmo tells the story of the evil sorcerer Kaldar who menaced the townspeople 300 years ago, and was driven off by them; he vowed to return one day to get revenge. Dolmo claims that the only way to keep the wizard away is by burning him in effigy each year on the anniversary of that night. Mayor Hodar considers it superstitious nonsense and refuses to allow an effigy to be burned. Sure enough, Kaldar shows up, accompanied by hovering witches, even as Hodar expresses incredulity. After one mysterious event after another occurs, Kaldar uses his magical powers to set fire to the town hall. But wait … Hodar then reveals that it was all a hoax. The hall is not on fire, there are no witches, and even "Kaldar" is completely fake. He was simply an actor hired by Hodar, who helped him pull off his alleged acts of sorcery. Hodar then tells everyone how the tricks were accomplished. His motive was to illustrate how foolish Dolmo and some of the other townspeople were being, worrying about a mythical sorcerer who would never appear. An even more absurd hoax story appears in *HOM* 137, "The Girl of Two Worlds," in which the relative of a man's new wife tries to convince him that his wife is an extraterrestrial as a way of cheating her out of her inheritance. These were strange stories to appear in a magazine devoted to tales of weird-looking aliens, grotesque monsters, *real* wizards and the like.

Of all the artists who contributed to *House of Mystery*, Jack Kirby is arguably the most illustrious. His output includes "The Thing in the Box" (*HOM* 61), in which a strange being inside a trunk saves a sailor and his ship from a variety of misfortunes, including a sea serpent and an attack of locusts, but turns out to be the sinister inhabitant of Pandora's Box. Kirby also did the splendid art for "The Negative Man" (*HOM* 84), an exciting and suspenseful tale of an electrical accident that draws a dangerous creature out from within a scientist, and his attempts to defeat this being without killing himself. "The Stone Sentinels of Giant Island" (*HOM* 85), also drawn and possibly scripted by Kirby, has a group of men coming across an island that was submerged until recently and encountering gigantic statues that resemble the ones on Easter Island (they turn out to be capable of movement) as well as a huge alien underground city. This is another mini-masterpiece that almost has a Lovecraftian flavor.

Although he never became a big name like Kirby, Infantino or Kubert, Mort Meskin did some very nice work for the series, such as "The Human Totem Poles" in *HOM* 126. While inked by George Roussos, Meskin's penciling shows a lot of compositional flair. He also drew "The Girl in the Iron Mask" (Meskin-Roussos) in *HOM* 66. This features a mysterious sculptress named Tina who only does magnificent works of animals and never, ever takes an iron mask off of her face. (A funny sequence shows her at the *dinner table* with her suitor, but one has to wonder how on Earth she can eat!) She has no mirrors in her home and her only servant is blind. Pietro, an art lover fascinated by the woman, does his best to unveil her—and the mystery of her existence—and finally insists that she take off the mask or he will take it off for her. She removes the mask, revealing a beautiful woman who stares into Pietro's mirror and turns into a statue. She was the Gorgon, whose gaze turns men and animals into stone. She'd rather have died than accidentally looked at Pietro, whom she had come to love. The story has so many holes in it that one can imagine that even children who read it were slightly baffled.

Another Meskin-Roussos tale is "The Beast That Slept a Thousand Years" in *HOM* 86. It begins like the film *The Beast from 20,000 Fathoms*, with a prehistoric-like creature thawing from the ice and attacking a lighthouse, then borrows a bit from *Godzilla* as the monster shoots fiery rays from its eyes and its scales. The creature, which resembles a giant walking fish, causes some destruction as it makes its way north but there are no casualties. The beast turns out to be an alien that is making its way back to its spaceship.

"The Microscopic Man" in *HOM* 68 is clearly influenced by Richard Matheson's *The Shrinking Man*, which was published the previous year (and later filmed as *The Incredible Shrinking Man*). In this yarn, a professor, wanting to photograph objects and transfer them to "the smallest microfilm in history," inadvertently develops a process that *literally* shrinks the objects to a fraction of their normal size. His assistant uses this invention for good purposes, shrinking a boat and an airliner to prevent disasters, but then finds that he has also been drastically reduced. He nearly drowns when a housekeeper begins mopping the floor. He manages to get under the professor's microscope where the older man sees him and uses the device to restore him to his original size. In "The Atom Detective" (Bill Ely) in *HOM* 86, a private eye pursues a criminal gang. He is accidentally shrunk but still outwits the bad guys while desperately trying to survive. With a plot somewhat borrowed from the film *The Devil-Doll*, "The Miniature Marauders" (*HOM* 112) has a mad scientist shrinking people into living dolls and forcing them to commit robberies. In *HOM* 134, another mad scientist shrinks a man and woman to such tiny size that a mosquito becomes a menace in "The Microscopic Doom" (Meskin-Roussos).

Gigantism was also a popular theme in the series. Clearly inspired by everything from H.G. Wells' novel *The Food of the Gods* to the film *The Amazing Colossal Man*, "The Amazing 70-Ton Man" finds a pint-sized handyman accidentally injected with a formula that makes him grow into a giant. He is so heavy that he sinks into the earth when he walks and has to stick to rocky ground; when he enters a city, his foot plunges through the pavement and nearly squashes a subway car. He is airlifted by blimps out of the city and has to deal with a bobcat that has also grown to giant size before the formula wears off and he's happy to be of short stature again. This was an early art job for Joe Kubert.

"The Legend of the Giant Aztec," drawn by Howard Purcell for *HOM* 100, takes place in Mexico where an old legend seems to come to life when a towering Aztec Indian appears in the village and begins causing destruction. Tom, a tourist, follows the giant footprints, which shrink in size as they approach the opening to a cave. Inside, Tom finds pills and a pool of liquid, and learns that taking a pill and bathing in the pool makes *him* a giant. The Aztec, whom Tom battles, turns out to be another American who hoped to use the legend to aid him in finding a cache of missing gold.

A giant also figures in "The Giant in the Obelisk," a hoax story in *HOM* 121: A prankster convinces his pals that Gilgamesh, the towering figure trapped inside an obelisk, is real and has escaped. He does this through the use of an actor on stilts who hurls papier-mâché boulders at everyone.

House of Mystery, like most other DC comics, eventually began playing up the funny-looking aliens that even wound up in *Batman*. Superheroes were now rising as well, so stories in DC's anthologies often focused on people who for one reason or another develop special powers or frightening abilities that in some cases they can't control. A costume imbues the wearer with superpowers or a magical spell imparts great strength or the power of flight to the recipient. Frequently stories have aliens coming to Earth and changing certain inhabitants or doing bizarre things for inexplicable reasons. The protagonist, a scientist or reporter, figures out what's going on. Either the aliens need Earth materials, which they force people to steal, in order to survive on their own world, or in one extreme case, they are playing a game to test human intelligence.

A story that is different from the usual fare appears in *HOM* 136. In "The Secret of the Stolen Faces," drawn by Howard Sherman, aging Max Ferguson broods alone in his home and reflects how he's wasted his life, lost all his money, and wishes he could relive his life. A hooded man who claims to be Fate appears, telling Max that three visitors are on their way. One is an actress who fears her career is over because she looks too old; another is a gangster on the run who worries about how well-known his face has become; and the third is a politician who had a humiliating defeat, has been called a big loser, and wants to hide his face until people forget. The trio wind up at Max's mansion for various reasons, where—in a scene used on the cover—their faces are placed inside floating white globes while their own features have been completely erased. All three are given new faces, new identities and new lives—but their happiness quickly turns to tragedy. Each wishes to have their old life back, and their wish is granted. Even Max comes to realize that living life all over again, only to make the same mistakes, is not the answer, but to move forward and carry on as best one can. The scripter is not credited, but the story with its more complex plot and moral lesson certainly reminds one of the tales Richard Hughes crafted for *Adventures into the Unknown*.

Eventually *House of Mystery* began running stories that were borderline horror. In *HOM* 142's "My Dream-Self Haunted Me" (Jack Miller-Meskin-Roussos), a man who has inherited a castle is bedeviled by a phantom double of him, conjured up by the caretaker, who figures he'll get the manor if he kills the protagonist. Although this double manages to temporarily take the man's place, our hero triumphs in the end. There is also a sinister double—an identical twin—in the same issue's "The Wax Demons" (Miller-Sherman): A wax museum owner receives beautiful figures from his brother, unaware that under the wax are demonic creatures that come out at night to steal for the evil twin.

With the next issue, 143, most of the comic is turned over to the earthly adventures of J'onn J'onzz, the Martian Manhunter, a super-hero who was also a member of the Justice League of America.

Other notable stories in *House of Mystery* include:

- "The Man Who Bought Thrills" (53): A man comes up with an elaborate scheme to get the formula for an ancient magical elixir, only to discover that it's only aspirin.
- "The Man Who Borrowed Lives" (57): A man inherits the abilities of other men who die when they take his place in a hotel room, a train and a parachute jump. This ends when he refuses to let a plane passenger take his seat.
- "The Prisoner on Canvas" (60): Paints derived from a meteor have the ability to make anything painted with them disappear.
- "The Menace of the Maze" (70): Two men searching for a treasure in an underground Egyptian maze fear that they will never find their way out.
- "The Human Icicle" (73): Atomic waste turns a man into a cold-blooded creature who needs ever lower temperatures to survive.
- "The Artificial Twin" (76): A scientist creates an easily controllable duplicate of an heiress so that he can steal her money.
- "I Was Trapped on the Chessboard of Giants" (77): A harrowing tale of shipwreck survivors captured by giants on an island and forced to play chess for their survival.
- "Something's Alive in Volcano 13" (83): A team descends in a mole machine to find a missing volcanologist and discovers that fumes have turned him into a giant.
- "The Pirate Brain" (96): A gargantuan alien device sends out huge tentacles to snatch up anything made of metal, melting it down and refashioning it into extraterrestrial weapons.
- "Track of the Invisible Beast" (109): A monstrous creature that no one but the hero can see stalks a city in a tale drawn by Alex Toth.
- "The Man Who Was Doomed by Time" (113): A man comes across a stretch of land where nothing grows and things age at an accelerated rate.
- "We Were Prisoners on Beast Asteroid" (113): Two astronauts barely survive encounters with monstrous creatures that come out of capsules on an alien planet.
- "The Man in the Nuclear Trap" (129): A man's head is enveloped by a giant iron atom, causing harrowing moments and near-disaster for him and others (including two aliens).
- "The Alien Creature Hunt" (130): An alien explorer has a tough time on Earth because a jealous rival has run amok there.
- "The Robot Rulers of Midville" (139): Townspeople allow robots to do all the work and all the thinking for them. The robots take over, but are secretly controlled by a man who wants revenge.

House of Secrets

DC debuted *House of Secrets* in 1956. The first issue has four stories that run the gamut from ghostly revenge to sinister artifacts to a sci-fi tale about giant hands that come out of nowhere and snatch up famous Earth monuments. (The hands belong to two other-dimensional children on a treasure hunt.) The story that has the most possibilities concerns three depressed women who feel their dreams could come true if only they were beautiful (none are exactly ugly to begin with), but the premise is not well-realized.

The second issue is an improvement with two memorable stories: "The Witch's Candles" (John Prentice), in which a man blows out candles and makes wishes, but the magical force inside the candles takes them too literally; and "Mars Calling" (Meskin), in which a giant globe of the Earth is built upon the instructions of scientists from Mars. Evil Martians doctor the globe so that whatever happens on its surface actually affects that spot on Earth (hence a stream of water played over the globe to wash it turns into a flood here). The stories in the third issue are entertaining if unmemorable, except for a bit when a man feeds his dogs meatballs from a "Martian" diner and the dog walks through walls and flies! "The Man Who Hated His Hair" (Roussos) in *HOS* 5 has an intriguing premise of a handsome actor who insists on going bald and taking only character parts from then on, refusing to tell anyone the reason for his decision. But the story's resolution is ridiculous. In Jack Kirby's "The Hole in the Sky" (*HOS* 12), aliens use sky hooks to dangle valuables in the hopes of snaring greedy Earthlings which they pull up into their dimension, the plan being to transfer one of their own minds into the human and hence invade the planet.

In 1959, *House of Secrets* 23 began a strip with psychic investigator Mark Merlin. Merlin exposes some supernatural events as hoaxes and others as weird scientific events, while others he classifies as "question marks," not certain if what he experienced—such as discovering weird one-cellular creatures in the recesses of a cave—actually happened or not. He comes up against a woman who appears to be a powerful sorceress (24), and sea monsters that appear malevolent but are actually trying to prevent a tragedy (25). His girlfriend Elsa—who once worked for Mark's late uncle, a stage magician—rarely has much to do but in an issue 29 story, she is transformed into the "Queen of the Beasts." In issue 32, she proves she is as brave as Merlin when she joins him in a search for a scientist who's been shrunk to microscopic size.

Almost from the very start, every Merlin adventure proves *not* to be a hoax. Although each is billed as "A Mark Merlin Mystery," they are really science fiction tales with monsters and aliens. In "The Hybrid Monster" (31), a scientist creates a genius creature comprised of many beasts and with an artificially amplified brain that turns out to be far more human than its creator's. In "The Interplanetary Target" (35), aliens want to assassinate Merlin because they fear he has figured out how to counteract a large bubble-like weapon, one of many with which they plan to attack the Earth. "The Fantastic Flower Creatures" (38) are magical spores that erupt from buds and send out destructive beams. "The Alien Bird of Prey" (39) is an outsized hawk-like creature from Pluto that goes berserk. The bird is the dupe of a Plutonian who wants to kill his mentor for his money. "The Dinosaur in Times Square" (41), a rampaging T. Rex, really *is* a hoax, a giant robot built to aid some smugglers in their operations.

By the early '60s, Merlin is mostly done with the supernatural and battles or aids a variety of aliens and creatures. The covers for *HOS* 44 and 45 feature monsters that practically look alike. "The Camouflage Creatures" (47) are alien menaces who can transform into anything, including trees with snarling mouths. "Beware the Guardian Beast" (48) concerns a lizard-like giant that stands guard over a treasure that has long since corroded. A scented candle temporarily turns Elsa into the creature's helpmate. "Mark Merlin's Giant Double" (53) is an entertaining puzzler in which the investigator discovers through ancient writings that a giant who looked just like him performed heroic acts down through the centuries and then disappeared. Merlin uncovers a hoax in "The Secret of the Spectral Crimes" (56) when robberies are allegedly committed by the ghosts of famous thieves who never successfully pulled off heists when they were alive. Beginning with this issue, Merlin is now billed as "Sleuth of the Supernatural" even if the stories are really sci-fi. Most of Merlin's adventures were drawn by Mort Meskin and probably written by Jack Miller.

House of Secrets makes more use of monsters in:

- "Lair of the Dragonfly" (19), in which a subterranean creature exists in an energy form until it's released and changes into a gigantic and deadly dragonfly.
- "The Beast in the Box" (24): An alien creature turns onlookers to stone to protect itself as it emerges from its cocoon, and keeps transforming into a larger and more dangerous monster.
- "The Secret of the Sinister Structures" (45): A scientist instructs men to build giant-size weapons hoping two punk crooks that were accidentally turned into giants will use them to kill each other.

During this period, DC Comics unveiled new versions of old superheroes such as the Flash and Green Lantern, so *House of Secrets* features lots of stories about people acquiring superpowers. Occasionally there is a story that doesn't fit the usual formula. In "The Second Life of Simon Steele" (46), the ghost of the title character, a 19th-century lawyer, shows up in a modern-day courtroom and uses wizardry on behalf of his clients. When he was alive, Steele was defeated when a prosecutor proved his law certificate was forged. The current prosecutor is a descendant of that man and people assume the ghost wants revenge on him for what his ancestor did. Then it develops that the prosecutor only hired someone who looked like Steele to play-act in court in order to draw a notorious criminal out of hiding, said criminal assuming Steele can use his tricks to free him. The ploy works, but when the crime boss' trial begins, Steele again pops into court to defend him: The "lookalike" really *is* the ghost of Simon Steele. The modern-day prosecutor gets rid of him by reminding the judge that Steele couldn't possibly have a license to practice law in the 20th century. The artist was Howard Sherman.

"Cry, Clown, Cry" (Bill Ely) in *HOS* 51 examines the dilemma of Coco the clown, who's afraid that he's losing his touch and is no longer funny. When he drinks a magical elixir that according to legend was used by a famous clown to elicit laughter, he discovers that there's a terrible price to pay. Coco is now so funny that explosive audience laughter makes wooden stands collapse. The clown learns that the only way to lift the curse is to make people *cry*, but every time he tries, he elicits more laughter. When Coco bravely saves a small child who has crawled out onto a ledge, the mother cries tears of joy. Someone has cried and Coco is free from the curse of the elixir.

"The Riddle of Hazard Isle" in *HOS* 27 has three men searching for their uncle's treasure on an island he outfitted with both clues and deadly traps. In "The Human Wave" (31), a living water spout pursues the protagonists, who are always just one second away from being engulfed.

Tales of the Unexpected

Tales of the Unexpected debuted in 1956. Its first issue features a story in which an orchestra plays weird and unusual music because the musicians are from other planets, and a tale about a grizzled old-timer who claims that his "dream-lamp" sends him on amazing adventures while he's asleep. In another story, a cartoonist discovers that the alien creatures he depicts in his strip are coming to life. In the most interesting story, "The Secret of Cell Sixteen," a prisoner is told he will be given a pardon and safe passage if he discovers the secret exit to his cell. After he makes several attempts that end in failure, he learns that his cell door has always been unlocked. Unfortunately, even if one could believe that he wouldn't just give the door a try out of desperation, the main problem with the story is that its genre is suspense and not sci-fi or fantasy.

As in *House of Mystery*, many of the stories are hoaxes, elaborate plots to catch a suspected murderer or intimations of sorcery where nothing supernatural has really occurred. A woman who runs a boarding house for ladies is suspected of benign witchcraft because every girl who lives there becomes famous and successful, but she's really very wealthy and uses her money to manipulate things for her tenants. A painter who murders a love rival and accidentally kills the woman he adores thinks the woman has come back to life, but she was never dead, and it's all a plot to get him to confess. In one especially bizarre story, "The Girl in the Bottle" in *Tales* 6, people are found floating in giant bottles in the ocean, and claim they have no idea how they got there. It turns out to be a very complex ploy for a few foreigners to enter the country illegally!

The comic eventually begins running tales of sci-fi adventure with heroic individuals encountering alien criminals and overcoming them through ingenuity. There are many stories which present a menace that has to be defeated—a giant magnet employed by aliens to stop the Earth from revolving—or sometimes turn out to be benign. For instance, a man returns to his hometown to find it occupied by Martians, but learns that they are all just actors in a movie—aside from two people who really *are* Martians. But they have no sinister intent; they are merely filming a movie of their own for Martian viewers.

A genuinely clever story, "The 3-D Camera That Could Rob," drawn by Leonard Starr, appears in *Tales* 8. A scientist is working on a new 3-D camera when it is struck by lightning. He finds that now he can reach into any photograph he's taken with the camera and remove any object, which instantly becomes three-dimensional. Observing this, criminal Adam Hale kills its inventor in a scuffle and steals the camera. At the opera, Hale photographs a wealthy woman's necklace, and then plucks it right out of the picture as the real necklace disappears from around the woman's neck! Hale continues to use the camera to steal a variety of items. The authorities come up with a plan to trap the perpetrator, substituting a radioactive material for gold bars. Knowing the police are on his trail via Geiger counter, Hale figures out a way of putting living things inside pictures and then retrieving them, and tries this approach to avoid capture, giving instructions to the janitor's son before putting *himself* on film. Unfortunately, before Hale can be rescued, the dead scientist's cat breaks the camera.

In "The Two-Dimensional Man" (Jack Kirby) in *Tales* 24, Devers, a railroad executive, receives a summons from biologist Dr. Moore, who has invented something that will greatly reduce freight costs. His special powder, given to cattle, makes them nearly as flat and thin as ribbons after 90 minutes. An antidote must be administered within six hours or they will die of dehydration. When Devers accidentally ingests some of this powder, he turns into a "two-dimensional" person. There follows a desperate race against time as Devers and his butler learn that Moore is out of the country, and they must fly to St. Anthony Island where he is visiting. A strong wind nearly blows Devers away, and there are similar, harrowing incidents which would almost be comical were it not for the horrifying situation the man finds himself in. He is eventually given the antidote.

Tales 40 begins the adventures of businessman Rick Starr, aka Space Ranger, "Guardian of the Solar System." (Jim Mooney was the series' primary artist; Bob Brown also worked on the strip.) Before this, the character had appeared in issues of *Showcase*. Starr's companion on his various cases is a shape-shifting alien named Cryll, who actually seems to do most of the heavy lifting, literally and figuratively. Accidentally teleported from his own universe into ours, Cryll is a small fellow with a rounded body, potbelly, spindly legs and two antennae growing out of his head. Starr's pretty blonde secretary, Myra Mason, also participates in many adventures.

Beginning with *Tales* 43, Space Ranger is featured on every cover until 82, the point at which he disappeared from the series. (He reappeared in *Mystery in Space*.) Although Space Ranger did not have the appeal or staying power of Adam Strange, who virtually became a superhero, his series ran for quite some time.

Space Ranger and his pals battle all manner of aliens, bad guys, criminal gangs and bug-eyed monsters. In *Tales* 54, he is up against dinosaurs that are being controlled by aliens, and nearly becomes a meal for a voracious T. Rex. In another story, Myra inadvertently inhales a gas that temporarily gives her superpowers; in yet another, Space Ranger is wrongly presumed dead and a sophisticated robot takes his place. Cryll occasionally becomes a menace when he metamorphoses into some monstrous creature and loses his memory; on one occasion, he has to battle an evil member of his own race. Cryll and Rick nearly become stone statues in "The Man Who Petrified Heroes" in *Tales* 74. A bizarre-looking enemy called Dr. Elektro creates an army of Space Ranger duplicates in *Tales* 78.

The only really memorable Space Ranger story is "The Alien Brat from Planet Byna" in *Tales* 65. In this rather charming tale, a cute alien boy named Morvi claims that his father is president of Byna and that both of his parents have been kidnapped. As Rick and Cryll try to find the parents, Morvi keeps getting into mischief, firing a ray gun as if it were a toy, and trying to ride on the back of a dangerous bucking beast. He eventually admits that his father isn't the president, and it later develops that his parents were never kidnapped. They have been frantically searching for him while he has been off on a treasure hunt. Even though he inadvertently led Rick and Cryll to several fugitives from justice, his father still gives him a spanking, which Rick and his buddy thoroughly enjoy. The story was written by Arnold Drake and drawn by Bob Brown.

Even pre–Space Ranger, the *Tales of the Unexpected* stories were becoming more and more juvenile. There are a surplus of alien law enforcement officers chasing after extraterrestrial criminals, and Earthlings who assume the aliens they encounter are unfriendly or dangerous because of their appearance. Still, an occasional story is a little different. For instance, "The Planet with Three Faces" in *Tales* 45, drawn by Nick Cardy, deals with a world that can summon up lifelike three-dimensional images, including entire cities and races, from the subconscious imaginations of astronauts. The concept was later used on such TV series as *Star Trek*.

Tales 65 features "The Man Who Hunted His Own Body." Drawn by Howard Purcell, it utilizes the interesting concept of temporarily putting people's consciousnesses into robot bodies so that they can travel to worlds where the atmosphere would not sustain humans. After reporter Kevin Dorn has his mind transferred into a robot, he spots a Martian criminal named Kezor, who has his own mind transferred into Dorn's body! Now in his robot form, Dorn tracks Kezor, hamstrung because he doesn't dare do anything that might injure or destroy his own body which Kezor is wearing.

"I Was Half-Man/Half-Machine," drawn by Bernard Bailey in *Tales* 98, is a truly fantastic tale about a heart transplant written just about the same time that Dr.

Christiaan Barnard performed the first such operation. Jason Baird wakes up after heart surgery to discover that his heart stopped dead and was replaced by an experimental new metal-and-plastic mechanical heart. Jason recovers and seems to be stronger than ever, but discovers an alarming side effect to the operation: He begins turning into metal! First his legs are affected, with his feet turning into wheels and then into tank-like treads. Then his hands become metallic claws. When Jason learns that two astronauts have landed in an impenetrable mountain area and can't be spotted from the air, he realizes that he alone might have the strength to reach them on foot. Using his unique metal parts, he's able to make his way to the men, but has to wade through water that is full of acid to rescue them. Knowing the acid will undoubtedly dissolve the lower, metallic half of his body, he goes to them anyway, turning on flares that signal their location. Hospitalized again, Jason discovers that the acid has provided the antidote to his "metabolic affliction."

Tales 83 presents the first in a series of stories about the "green glob," a force of energy that has made its way to Earth, where its presence causes strange things to happen to the people it encounters. Not only are these stories mediocre in quality, they are poorly drawn by George Roussos. Jerry Siegel, co-creator of Superman, wrote the glob story "Judy Blonde, Secret Agent!", in which a mousy secretary is transformed into a glamorous spy after she wins a prize. It is worse than the usual glob story, most of which were written by Dave Wood.

Automan, a nominal superhero, makes his debut in *Tales* 91 in 1965 in the story "Robot for Hire." Prof. Sterling creates robots—one of which is Automan, short for Automatic Man—to be hired for various services. Automan can hold a conversation, has great strength, and has a camera and a type of laser beam in his head. On his first assignment, he winds up working for some smugglers who think he's just a machine who will carry out all of their commands. But Prof. Sterling has built anti-crime attitudes into his robots, and Automan brings about the smugglers' capture. In *Tales* 94, he is bodyguard for an actress whose bag was accidentally switched with one being used by spies to transfer stolen secrets. In *Tales* 97, Automan battles Mutant-Man, a hulking monster humanoid stalking a scientist's island. It turns out that Mutant-Man and the scientist are the same person, and that he wanted to pit his mutated prowess against the incredible robot. And then Automan was gone for good, an okay concept but not as good as the Metal Men or Robotman from *Doom Patrol*. The Automan art is unimpressive, which is true of many of the *Tales of the Unexpected* stories, although on rare occasions there is work by such artists as Gil Kane and Lee Elias.

In its final issues, the series ran reprints from *House of Secrets* and *My Greatest Adventure* along with new material. *Tales* 104 (October 1967) was the last issue. It was rebooted as *The Unexpected*, primarily a horror title, the very next month.

Other notable *Tales of the Unexpected* stories:

- "The Earth Gladiator" (20): An unarmed man is forced to fight an alien for the sake of the whole Earth, and uses his wits to defeat him.

- "I Was Marooned on Planet Earth" (20): A reporter on Saturn accidentally winds up in a rocket and lands on Earth, where he has trouble convincing people he's an alien and getting the radium he needs for the return trip.
- "The Giants from Outer Space" (23): Gargantuan aliens cause havoc by scooping up samples of the Earth's water and sand.
- "The Man Who Saved the Solar System" (25): A humble doctor is given an award for his life-saving services on various planets, even when his own life is in danger.
- "The Tiny Spaceship" (26): A boy finds a rocketship filled with tiny beings. His father helps them find a replacement for the fuel that will help them get back to their sub-atomic world.
- "The Giant with My Face" (38): On an asteroid, a space prospector discovers a gigantic version of himself with the same name, memories and outfit.
- "Death of a Robot" (86): A sentient robot with a soul races to save his own life but sacrifices himself to save others when he spots a plane about to crash.
- "Earth's Second Sun" (86): A new sun appears in the sky and affects young children, turning them into giants with astonishing intellects. This story was obviously influenced by H.G. Wells' *The Food of the Gods*.

Cave Carson

"Cave Carson Adventures Inside Earth" first appears in *The Brave and the Bold* 31. Cave Carson is known as "The King of the Underground Cave Explorers" and his team consists of geologist Christie Madison and former sandhog and tunnel expert Bulldozer Smith. His machine, the Mighty Mole, can "climb, swim or dive" and in its nose is a thermo-ray that can burn through solid rock. This comes in handy when the team discovers a "magnetic monster" that resembles a robot, a hulking creature that took millions of years to form. Before destroying this menace, they also encounter a voracious plant that entangles the mole in an underground lake, a huge lizard-like sea beast, and a cavern full of colorful and unusual flora. Ed Herron filled his script with plenty of excitement and harrowing adventure, and the serviceable art was by Bruno Premiani.

In *Brave and the Bold* 32 Cave and his associates discover a magnificent city peopled by intelligent green beings in a cavern 100 miles below the surface. This city is lit up by a gigantic golden globe hanging in the "sky." A civil war is ongoing because some of the inhabitants want to make their way to the surface, a situation that would be disastrous for humans as well as the underground dwellers. Cave and his group side with those who wish to remain below, who also employ a variety of bizarre creatures for their army. It all ends with the explosion of the artificial sun, destroying both sides and obliterating the city. Bernard Bailey's art is rather crude, but it does boast a very striking three-quarter-page panel depicting the underground city and its source of light and energy. Ed Herron did the script. *Brave and the Bold* 33 has a script by Dave Wood and art by Bailey. In this story, Cave and his companions battle aliens who, from their underground base, send out giant, destructive robots until Cave turns one of the automatons against the others. The story could have made use of virtually any heroic figure and the below-the-Earth location is of secondary importance.

Cave & Co. returned for two more *Brave and the Bold* issues, and then a three-issue run in *Showcase*. In *BATB* 40, a nasty character named Zenod wants to gain ultimate power by grabbing three crystals that were buried deep in the Earth by a long-deceased wizard. Using the crystals, Zenod gives life to rocks that chase after the men. Meanwhile, Christie has her hands full with a giant earthworm. There is also an egg that hatches to reveal a dinosaur-like reptile that grows to huge size within moments and nearly makes a snack of our heroes. Written by Ed Herron, the story is enlivened by a very good art job by Joe Kubert, one of the best of DC's Silver Age artists.

Writer Jack Miller and artist Mort Meskin are the creative team for *BATB* 41. A group of desperadoes from another dimension hop into our world, where they use their own boring machine to steal gold, gems and other loot. This they plan to sell back in their own dimension, a foolproof way to commit robbery and get away with it. Cave and his group outwit the thieves. Meskin's clean, attractive art helps put over a mediocre if somewhat exciting script.

The powers-that-be at DC felt it would be a shrewd move to try out Cave Carson in *Showcase* rather than give him his own magazine. The creative team for *Showcase* 48 is Bob Haney on scripts and Lee Elias on art. Cave, Christie and Bulldozer had been fairly colorless and one-dimensional in their earlier appearances, but Haney makes some improvements. Bulldozer proves to be an ex-con who has made "one mistake" and paid for it, while Christie carries a torch for a man named Johnny Blake, putting the kibosh on Cave's romantic plans for her. In Paris, Christie designs new uniforms for the trio, while Bulldozer acquires a pet in Lena, the lemur.

The team enters a cave in search of a prehistoric bison that has been launching attacks in the vicinity. Along the way, the group finds freshly done paintings depicting them in various difficulties. Eventually they encounter a gigantic beetle that carries off Cave, while Christie and Bulldozer nearly become a meal for an outsized arachnid. Christie becomes convinced that old boyfriend Johnny, an obnoxious, conceited spelunker who was a rival of Cave's and who disappeared underground years ago, may still be alive, but their opponent turns out to be Emile Basto. Basto wants revenge on Cave for exposing him as a saboteur of his competitors' supplies during a cave-exploring contest. Basto befriended a race of gruesome mole men, thawed out the frozen bison and a saber-tooth tiger, and made giants out of underground insects. Cave and the others escape from a maze by blowing the ceiling off of a cavern beneath the sea and reaching the surface via the ocean.

Showcase 49 is a convoluted but engaging story of the group's attempts to stop the destruction of a modern South American city by native Indians and their Fire God. The Fire God's "essence" takes over the minds of Christie and Johnny (he *did* turn out to be alive, and as disagreeable as ever), putting them into suspended animation. In one excellent sequence, Cave, Bulldozer and a man named Jose descend by balloon into a huge cavern to rescue Christie. One of the fiery cavern creatures sets fire to the balloon. Cave and Bulldozer are wearing parachutes (Jose is not), so they cut the lines to the gondola—where Jose remains—clasping on to those lines while they bail out and open their chutes. This way they are able to safely lower the gondola while they descend on their parachutes. Haney and Elias remained the creative team, as they did for *Showcase* 52, Cave Carson's final Silver Age appearance.

Cave's Mighty Mole machine had not been seen since his appearances in *The Brave and the Bold*. He has a new vehicle in *Showcase* 52, a saucer that smoothly flies on compressed air. With Cave, Christie, Bulldozer and Johnny aboard, the saucer is hit by a red ray that pulls it down under the earth to a lost civilization called Xanadu. One of its leaders, Dr. Dorian, claims to be nearly 200 years old. Decades ago, he was a passenger on a riverboat that was pulled into an underground tributary. Somehow Dorian knows of Cave's existence and hopes that Cave will become the leader of this lost society, which has grown crops without sun, built beautiful edifices out of clay, and maintains a loving and peaceful existence. (Xanadu is typical of "peaceful" lost societies, such as that of *Lost Horizon*, who think kidnapping is acceptable.)

Johnny wants no part of this and tries to escape in the saucer, but winds up being turned to stone. A monstrous once-human energy being attacks and destroys Xanadu, and Cave and his companions do their best to save the lives of the underground dwellers. They obliterate the monster after several attempts. Cave opts to return to the surface with Christie, but Bulldozer likes the peacefulness of Xanadu and stays to help them rebuild. It looked as if Bob Haney had decided to put a period on the series by leaving Johnny as a block of stone and ditching Bulldozer, but at the very end of the story, Johnny returns to normal—Cave thinks that Christie will have to make up her mind as to which man she really wants—and Bulldozer decides to rejoin his companions.

Cave Carson appeared in the 1990 series *Time Masters* and starred in the 2016 maxi-series *Cave Carson Has a Cybernetic Eye*.

Suicide Squad/Task Force X

The Brave and the Bold 25 in 1959 is the first of six issues detailing the adventures of Task Force X, popularly known as the Suicide Squad, a group from Military Intelligence that was "created to combat perils that defy conventional methods of defense." The team's commanding officer is Colonel Rick Flag and his colleagues include physicist Jess Bright, astronomer Dr. Evans and nurse Karin. Flag was the only survivor when his squadron engaged with a flat top and Karin was the only survivor when her plane went down. They consider it a sacred duty to carry on for their colleagues who died. Karin and Rick are in love but the latter feels that duty comes before their personal lives. Bright and Evans are also in love with Karin. These two were the sole survivors when a nuclear bomb went off prematurely.

A group of "polar bear" swimmers are startled to see a reddish, hot wave of foam heading towards the beach. This red mass, which seems to have something vague in its center, sets fire to everything nearby, including an amusement park. Firefighters find their hoses melting, foam bombs dropped on the mass have no effect, and a fiery tongue lashes upward to destroy the plane overhead. In their "flying laboratory," the Task Force drops a stream of absolute zero cold on the mass and freezes it. But from this frozen block comes a humongous reptilian monster that can pick up ships and subs in its claws and instantly freeze-dry them. Dropping an A-bomb on the creature doesn't work when it grabs the bomb and freezes *it*, destroying its controls. It is decided to drop sodium on the monster, but all this does is turn the beast green in color, as well as giving it the ability to leech the chlorophyll out of all plant life, turning the landscape completely white. The Suicide Squad gets the monster to chase their moon rocket; the monster attaches itself to the rocket and is pulled into outer space, where it eventually loses its grip on the spaceship and goes into endless orbit around the sun. The story ends with Flag determined to get everyone back to Earth. Written by Robert Kanigher and drawn by Ross Andru and Mike Esposito, this intro to the group was guaranteed to excite the senses of the juvenile reader.

The Suicide Squad returns for *Brave and the Bold* 26 with the same creative team. The first third of the story details the group's attempts to return to Earth, where they learn that due to its slower speed their rocket will bypass their planet and send them back out into space. Rick comes up with the daring idea of using meteorites to give the ship one bump after another, increasing its speed. This works, but solar radiation has the effect of reducing the passengers in size. Landing in a lake in an unfriendly foreign country, the group takes refuge in a matchbox, and realize they are near a base from which the enemy plans to launch a missile attack. Despite their tiny size, they prevent the attack and eventually regain their normal stature.

While on a furlough in Paris, our heroes encounter "The Serpent in the Subway." The gargantuan serpent, a relic of the dinosaur age (origin unknown), appears in the Paris Metro, then emerges in the Seine to attack a tourist boat. The group finally defeat it by dropping a huge plastic bag over its head and cutting off its air supply. (A final note warns children not to play with plastic bags.)

BATB 27 presents "The Creature of Ghost Lake." A professor has experimented with a growth formula, inadvertently creating a huge moth that attacks the group's plane and a giant caterpillar that nearly kills Rick. It is intimated that the professor himself has mutated into a gigantic creature with bumpy red skin and a hideous countenance. This creature picks up a powerful bomb in one hand and Christie in the other, and Rick comes to the conclusion that to save everyone in the city—which the monster is fast approaching—he may have to destroy Christie along with the creature. Fortunately he is able to disarm the bomb and tow the unconscious creature out to sea.

BATB 37 begins a new three-issue run for the Suicide Squad with Kanigher-Andru and Esposito remaining the creative team. In the first BATB 37 story, the group is up

A striking cover for a Suicide Squad appearance in *The Brave and the Bold* #39. Art by Andru and Esposito.

against a horde of intelligent dinosaurs from another dimension. These creatures seem to be controlled by one central brain, and when it is destroyed they turn on each other. In one sequence, the foursome is trapped on a dock which is being tipped over by the huge and hungry mouth of a carnivorous sea creature. Our heroes are slowly sliding down toward its jaws, but some depth charges keep them from becoming its supper. In the second story, the cyclops Polyphemes, still alive in the 20th century, snatches a plane carrying important weapons. The Suicide Squad has a lively battle with this towering creature. In the meantime, Christie has become a painter of note.

The Suicide Squad has two opponents in *BATB* 38: The first is a giant alien who keeps his ship hidden in a cloud. He sends out pterodactyls to snatch up items as if he were an extraterrestrial falconer and they his pets. The Squad's second opponent is the Mirage Master, a nasty man from another dimension who uses optical illusions to bedevil the team and attempts to pit one against the other. In one *BATB* 39 story, the team discovers a vast subterranean lake. Setting sail on it, they are swallowed alive by a dinosaur, a scene depicted on the issue's striking cover (Andru and Esposito). Inside the dinosaur, they are baffled to find a whole world of prehistoric animals and vegetation instead of internal organs. It turns out to be a spaceship shaped like a dinosaur, and containing an interplanetary zoo. In the second *BATB* 39 story, the team runs afoul of a sinister sculptor who creates realistic statues by encasing real people in gold. Rick and the others, encased, can think but are unable to move. The only thing that can free them is extreme heat, which happens when a spurt of lava hits Rick dead on.

Task Force X and the original members of the Suicide Squad were not seen again for many years. When they re-emerged, the Squad consisted of super-villains wanting a chance at a pardon. They are kept in line by Rick Flag, with Karin at his side. In *The Brave and the Bold*, Rick is continually telling Karin that they have to hide their love for one another because their other team members also love her and the disclosure of their feelings would hurt them and affect their working relationships. Karin undoubtedly got sick of hearing this.

The Suicide Squad, possibly unrelated to the original group, also appeared in several issues of *Star Spangled War Stories* as part of "The War That Time Forgot," battling dinosaurs and each other.

G.I. Robot

The G.I. Robot first appeared in *Star Spangled War Stories* 101, published at a time when the comic was exclusively running lead stories in which soldiers mix it up with dinosaurs, with many of the tales taking place on Dinosaur Island in "The War That Time Forgot." In this excellent story, written by Robert Kanigher and drawn by Ross Andru and Mike Esposito, Prof. Zurin introduces a corporal named Mac to a robot G.I. called Joe, the "soldier's Buddy." Mac is going to team with Joe out in the field and see if the robot will respond to orders. After jumping out of a plane towards an island where they will undergo the testing, the odd couple are blown off course by a tremendous wind. They wind up, of course, in a lost world of pterodactyls and dinosaurs. Mac has to keep reminding himself that he must give Joe direct orders or the robot will not act. Despite some hairy moments, they work well as a team as they dodge huge creatures out of time. Mac is baffled when he falls into quicksand and, his mouth full of wet sand, cannot give Joe orders—but Joe saves him anyway.

Joe gets an overhaul in *Star Spangled War Stories* 102, in which they are again flying to a faraway island for more testing. An enormous saurian in the waters below grabs the wing of the plane, and soon Mac and Joe are once again being beset by hungry monsters in a land that time forgot. In addition to dinosaurs, they must contend with a robot, about 50 feet tall, left behind by Nazi soldiers. In the sequel in the following issue, Mac is afraid that the gigantic robot and Joe will bond, both being artificial creatures of nuts and bolts, but Joe fires up at the metal Nazi and destroys him. The term "Dinosaur Island" is first used in this story.

The G.I. Robot reappears in *Star Spangled War Stories* 125 in a story written by Robert Kanigher and expertly drawn by Joe Kubert. Even though Kanigher wrote the earlier stories, the *robot's* name is now Mac, and the corporal with that name has disappeared. Then it is revealed that this robot is actually "Mac the Second," so the first G.I. robot (and presumably the corporal) are "missing in action." Reed, a soldier (and Suicide Squad member), meets Mac on a secret island base and the two are flown to another island to test the robot under combat conditions. Naturally the plane is attacked by pterodactyls (which for some reason the soldiers and pilots are never warned about) and crashes with a tank and its crew inside. The survivors are Reed, Mac and the tank commander, Sgt. Trask, who is so grief-stricken at the deaths of his men that he practically has a nervous breakdown. Furious that the robot is "alive" but his crew is dead, Trask tries to kill Mac and even Reed. Mac is destroyed when he uses a grenade to kill a hungry Tyrannosaurus. Reed realizes that there was much more than anyone realized to the robot, who is able to take action even without being given orders, and who sacrificed his life for his buddies.

The G.I. Robot returned in new stories in the Bronze Age.

12

Dell; Fago

Dell

Men Into Space

Men Into Space (aka *Four-Color* 1083) came out in 1960 and is based on the CBS television show of the same name. Written by Gaylord DuBois and drawn by Murphy Anderson, the comic is one of Dell's best TV adaptations. Some of the material in the comic comes from a few of the teleplays. In "Space Probe," Colonel Edward McCauley and his men take a trip to the moon, and McCauley is accidentally set adrift while outside the ship making repairs. The crew members are able to go after and rescue him, but there's a question if they have enough fuel for re-entry. Their ship lands at the North Pole, where McCauley and the others are nearly crushed by an advancing iceberg.

In "Moon Landing," another voyage makes it to the lunar surface with four men aboard, including McCauley. As they investigate, they spot a "crater" and wonder if it would be a good location for a base. While they are in the crater, there's a moonquake that causes a boulder to land on one of the men, Pat. With the lesser gravity, the other three men lift the boulder, but Pat has no feelings in his legs. He is climbing with the others' help, when another quake hits, and he deliberately sacrifices himself, cutting the rope so that the others can survive. It is believed that Pat is dead, buried in the dust below, so no attempt is made to retrieve him.

In "The Dust and the Depths," McCauley and the others, exploring lunar caves, discover there is a slight residue of oxygen deep below the moon's surface. After their rocketship is badly damaged by meteorites, only one of the men, McCauley (who draws the shortest piece of chalk), can return to Earth in an escape pod or "lifeboat." McCauley makes it back to Earth despite some harrowing moments; his superiors will immediately send a rescue ship. The two men on the moon may find plenty of breathable atmosphere if they get deep enough below the lunar surface.

Voyage to the Deep

Dell came out with the short-lived series *Voyage to the Deep* in 1962. The comic is undoubtedly inspired by the previous year's hit film *Voyage to the Bottom of the Sea*,

Inspired by the 1961 film *Voyage to the Bottom of the Sea*, Dell's *Voyage to the Deep* did not last long.

which featured a large souped-up submarine. The *Proteus* in the comic is not only the world's largest atomic sub, but also it has the ability to change its shape due to a special outer skin; it can expand from 60 to 400 feet. The main characters are Admiral Jonathan Leigh, who designed the ship, and Captain Duke Peters, the husband of Leigh's secretary Judy. In each issue, the *Proteus* is all that stands between the destruction of the world and the evil machinations of an unspecified group or nation known only as "the Enemy."

In the first issue, the Enemy pumps helium into the Earth's core and tilts it out of orbit, creating tidal waves. In subsequent issues, they try to create a new Ice Age, vaporize the world with anti-matter energy, and cause tremendous devastation with volcanoes created by sonic bombardment. The stories always feature at least one gigantic monster—a lamprey, a manta ray, a lobster—who make for some striking apparitions on the series' painted covers (the best thing about the comic). *Voyage to the Deep* should have been much more fun than it was but both the art and writing are uneven, a mix of striking panels with rushed, mediocre work and interesting plots hampered by some awkward scripting. The art is by Sam Glanzman and the cover paintings by John McDermott. Paul S. Newman was responsible for some of the scripts.

Space Man

Space Man debuted in 1962. The series details the adventures of astronaut Ian Stannard, 14-year-old Space Academy cadet Johnny Mack (whose father Hugh died in space) and Mary Lansing, Ian's fiancée. Ian and Johnny take off on a flight and discover to their surprise that the Earth has already established a base on the moon headed by Colonel Hooper, who went missing some time before. Thanks to contact with alien races, the moon base has speedy flying saucers that make most Earth craft seem snail-like in comparison. Hooper tells Johnny and Ian what only the president knows: A malevolent, ancient being called Garrack-Axos is out to conquer the galaxy.

Axos has already used subterfuge to remove the giant race of Atlanteans, called Titans, from the Earth and turn them into slaves. He lords it over a thousand of his kind, an ape-like race, each with one eye and the ability to absorb knowledge instantly. They have all been alive for thousands of years; if kept too long from their rejuvenating machines, they will literally fall apart into bones. Disguised as small Titan children, Ian, Johnny and Mary fly to Axos' home planet and, with the aid of many Titan slaves, destroy all of the rejuvenating machines and Axos himself in the exciting fourth issue.

Although in the early issues the comic's main characters had thought mankind was merely on the verge of space exploration, in short order everyone seemed to know of other races on planets near and far. In *Space Man* 5, Ian and his pals help quell a revolution on Pluto engineered by elderly scientists who built themselves amazing—and amazingly ugly—robot bodies. *Space Man* 6 has some interesting concepts as the group battles General Royhep, a despot from dimension X with formidable mind-control powers. This strange dimension has realistic images of everything from dinosaurs to the Battle of Bunker Hill but they are only historical mirages. Royhep's own power of illusion is so strong that throughout the story, he is accompanying Ian and the others but they think he's their giant Atlantean friend

Jo-Kap. Royhep continues to cause trouble in the following issue, in which Mary Lansing is given a larger role than usual. She rescues Earth people who had been waylaid by Royhep's forces, and discusses future plans with Ian, with both agreeing to sacrifice marriage plans in favor of duty.

In *Space Man* 8, an analyzer built on a planetoid to record data from millions of

Dell's *Space Man* presents the adventures of astronaut Ian Stannard.

miles around becomes sentient and turns into a menace. Royhep, who has hypnotized everyone into thinking he is Colonel Hooper, tries to use his power on the machine and gets fried for his temerity. This is the final original issue of the series; the first two issues were reprinted as *Space Man* 9 and 10 in 1972. *Space Man* was discontinued just as it was developing into a fairly decent series with some interesting concepts and characters, although Jack Sparling's artwork is never more than serviceable. John Schoenherr's dramatic covers are more on the mark. Ken Fitch and Joe Gill did most of the scripts.

Drift Marlo

With a 1962 debut, *Drift Marlo* concerns the exploits of a detective assigned to keep watch over the space program. An anti-missile missile known as the Peace-Maker is about to be launched in a craft called the Atlas but the scientist who built it, Dr. Fowler, seems to be having a nervous breakdown. Fowler is convinced that the Peace-Maker, meant to destroy attacking missiles, can too easily be turned against mankind. The head of the project is Dr. Hugo Barcus, whose secretary Claire, Drift's girlfriend, repeatedly asks him if he will take her to a masquerade ball that evening. The launch is successful, but now Fowler tries to stop a test missile from firing. Noticing an odd taste in a cup of coffee given to him by Fowler, the not-so-swift Drift drinks it anyway, and the drugged "space detective" barely manages to stop Fowler's sabotage. The test missile is fired and the Peace-Maker destroys it as intended. Apparently Fowler is off his rocker, which is made clear when he starts talking about inventing television!

Combining a private eye with the space program doesn't make much sense as surely military intelligence would have been responsible for security on such a project and not Drift. Claire is a stereotypical comics female of the period, ignoring everything important that is going on and waxing about her red-headed boyfriend's good looks and persistently whining about the masquerade ball. It's frightening to think that a man with such obvious mental problems as Fowler wouldn't be committed or at least turned over for therapy and ridiculous that he would be allowed to wander around unaccompanied.

Drift Marlo 2 presents an entertaining story in which Drift, accompanied by a jealous Claire, goes to the airport to greet a pilot named Maybelle. Maybelle turns out to be a cute chimpanzee who develops a crush on Drift, but Claire is satisfied that the ape is no competition. Maybelle is to be sent up in a rocket to gather more data, but enemy agents are determined to go up in their own ship and snatch the chimp so they can use her info for their own space program. Although Drift is not an astronaut, he has received some training, and insists on going on an American rocket to rescue Maybelle. After nearly being smashed by the foreign spaceship, he gets the chimp out of the capsule and into his own ship. Claire comes over the next day and makes breakfast for Drift and Maybelle.

Drift Marlo was based on a syndicated comic strip that lasted from 1961 to 1971. Philip Evans wrote the strip and the two comic books, and Tom Cooke did the art for both. Cooke's work in the comic features large panels with detailed drawings of rockets and missiles that have a certain veracity and eye appeal.

The Outer Limits

Dell came out with a series based on *The Outer Limits* in 1964. The TV series had been compelled to insert monsters into the stories due to network demands, and the comic follows the series' lead. The stories, often apocalyptic, are on the silly side, and often feature juvenile protagonists. The first issue deals with aliens that have been taking people and things from Earth for decades. They finally realize what terror they have been causing when three of them are forcibly teleported to Earth. *OL* 3 presents a suspenseful if unsatisfying tale of an astrophysicist who is convinced his rockets are being sabotaged by gremlins that only he can see. The creative team for these and future issues was Paul S. Newman on scripts and Jack Sparling on art.

OL 8 is a variation on *The Blob* when scientists decode a message from outer space, concoct a formula from this code, and find out that aliens have used this method to send a nearly unkillable, constantly growing lifeform to exterminate everyone on Earth. At the end, the world's nations work together, disarm all missiles and use them to blanket the Earth with a cloud that cuts off all sunlight and destroys the blob. This superior issue is like a good "B" movie. *OL* 11 presents a harrowing if improbable tale in which a formula that is meant to turn back the evolutionary clock on certain animals only reveals that aliens took the animals' forms centuries ago and said formula turns them back into their monstrous and dangerous original selves.

All of the *Outer Limits* stories were full-length until issue 12, which contains three tales: A bullied boy gets his revenge when he turns into a giant gill-man; an amazing Olympic champion turns out to be a robot; a vine unleashes green and scaly plant-men. The comic no longer has any resemblance to the TV show but instead runs whimsical stuff you might find in Charlton's fantasy comics. The Japanese monster movie *Rodan* inspired two separate stories! In the amusing "Multi-man" in *OL* 13, a crazy professor and a washed-up wrestler team up as the scientist uses the athlete's body to create dozens of duplicates in order to storm the White House and take over the world. But all of the duplicates are linked to the original, and when the wrestler drops dead of a heart attack, *they* also bite the dust—along with the professor's plans of conquest. The wonderful "Martian Stimulators Inc." in *OL* 14 stars a hen-pecked man who accidentally drinks a cure for baldness that increases his stature both in his physique and in the office. This elicits jealousy in his nasty wife, whose fate is not so marvelous. *OL* 16 features a variation of Hodgson's "The Voice in the Night" set on a space station beset by a fungus-like creature.

Dell Movie Comics

Dell and Gold Key were especially prolific when it came to movie adaptations, with Dell taking the lead in sheer quantity. Dell's comic adaptation of Walt Disney's 1954 *20,000 Leagues Under the Sea,* released at the start of the Silver Age, is almost as entertaining as the film version. Paul S. Newman's script follows the movie closely. Frank Thorne's art is reasonably effective, if undistinguished, but it does pull the reader along at a fast pace. None of the characters resemble the actors in the film.

In 1957, Dell came out with a poor adaptation of *The 7th Voyage of Sinbad* which lacks the excitement and wonder of the excellent movie. Gaylord Du Bois' script eliminates the climactic fight with the skeleton. Future Marvel superstar John Buscema's art job is not one of his better ones. In 1975, there was another adaptation of the movie in *Marvel Spotlight* 25, written by John Warner and drawn by Sonny Trinidad. It was not appreciably better than the Dell version.

Dell's *The Land Unknown* (1957), about an expedition to the South Pole that searches for a patch of warm weather and discovers a lost land of prehistoric monsters, is almost as exciting as the movie. Beautifully rendered by gifted artist Alex Toth, the comic boasts a couple of spectacular half-page panels, one depicting a T. Rex advancing on a helicopter as it takes to the air. In another, a monster rises from a lake and capsizes a raft. Aside from some real-life lizards, the film's monsters are mechanical beasties with limited movement, but Toth, while maintaining the basic look of the creatures, gives them a more fluid and attractive appearance. The characters in the comic approximate the look of the actors without closely resembling them; the male characters all tend to look alike. The comic adds a couple of extra touches such as the heroine nearly being popped into the mouth of a lizard. Robert Ryder's script compresses some scenes and dialogue in an intelligent fashion. In the comic, the character of Dr. Hunter, who tries to assault the one lady in the group, apologizes for his actions, which he never does in the film.

Hercules (1958), an Italian mythological epic starring Steve Reeves, was dubbed and heavily promoted in the American market. Hercules tries to clear his old teacher of the murder of a king and help his teacher's son Jason take his rightful place as ruler. Jason, Hercules, Ulysses and others travel to Colchis to regain the golden fleece, which was stolen years before. *Hercules* is an entertaining if minor adventure flick and the Dell comic is about on the same level, although the only resemblance between Steve Reeves and Hercules in the comic is that they both have a beard. The Paul S. Newman script actually fills in some of the gaps in the movie's continuity and makes the relationships between certain characters much clearer. The art is by John Buscema and it was clear that he was destined for greater things. Unfortunately, Buscema depicts the dragon guarding the fleece almost exactly as it looks in the film, and as the movie's dragon is a rather pitiful specimen, that's not a good thing.

Dell came out with the comics version of the sequel, *Hercules Unchained,* in

1960. *Unchained* is somewhat better than *Hercules*, with a more interesting story, as the demi-god becomes involved in a war between two brothers, sons of Oedipus; both of them want to rule Thebes. Much of the film takes place on the island of Lidia, where a kidnapped Hercules—who has lost his memory due to inadvertently drinking the "waters of forgetfulness"—has been taken to become the latest plaything of Queen Omphale, who memorializes all her murdered lovers by preserving their bodies. Hercules gets away with the aid of Ulysses, but his disappearance blitzes a truce between the aforementioned brothers. A full-scale war breaks out in an exciting climax that features the brothers fighting a literal duel to the death.

Paul S. Newman again crafted an excellent script for the comic version, clearing up some plot points and establishing relationships that were a little fuzzy in the film. Newman adroitly compressed events so that the comic is actually better-paced than the movie. The art is by no less than Reed Crandall, and it is generally attractive work, if not necessarily his best. Crandall and George Evans inked over Crandall's pencils. Hercules looks like Steve Reeves, and the other actors are also well-delineated.

Dell released an adaptation of the film *Journey to the Center of the Earth* in 1959. Written by Robert Schaefer, it eliminates some unnecessary scenes such as the kidnapping of Alec (Pat Boone) but also jettisons such scenes as the giant boulder that nearly crushes the adventurers, the caverns of crystal and, worst of all, the sequences with the dimetrodons on the beach and the giant red lizard that attacks at the climax. This is strange, because Verne's novel did include the monsters (as well as a giant humanoid shepherd). The script incorporates much of the film's dialogue and pulls the reader along in an entertaining fashion, but the art by John Ushler is pedestrian.

Dell's *The Lost World* (1960) is a fair-to-middling adaptation of the second film version—produced and directed by Irwin Allen—of Sir Arthur Conan Doyle's classic novel of modern-day man finding dinosaurs atop a South American plateau. Paul S. Newman's script follows the movie closely and makes few changes. The penciling is done by comics legend Gil Kane, but it is not the artist's best work; one might have trouble even recognizing it as Kane. The problem may have been the inking reportedly done by Mike Peppe. The comic book makes two improvements on the film: The giant arachnid that menaces a native girl is a trapdoor spider with big eyes, emerging from the ground instead of dangling unconvincingly from an overhead web; and the disembodied tentacles barring the cave entrance (they look pitiful in the movie) are shown as long, sinuous and very dangerous appendages. The poodle that accompanies Jill St. John everywhere on the plateau is eliminated. Some of the characters in the comic resemble the actors. The name of big game hunter Lord John Roxton is changed to Ruxton.

In another 1960 Dell movie adaptation, *Dinosaurus!*, the frozen bodies of a brontosaurus, a T. rex and a caveman thaw out and cause havoc on an island. Construction overseers Ward and Chuck do their best to save pretty Betty, a little boy and the other residents from danger. The Eric Freiwald-Robert Schaefer script follows the film closely, but eliminates the character of Chuck, aside from a mention in one word balloon. Also excised is a scene when the Tyrannosaur crushes several people inside a bus. With its mediocre artwork by Jesse Marsh, the comic is roughly equivalent to the motion picture with its poor models and crude stop-motion effects.

Dell also adapted *The 3 Worlds of Gulliver* in 1960. The film details our hero's adventures in Lilliput with its tiny citizenry and then Brobdingnag with its colossal inhabitants, and has more-than-decent Ray Harryhausen effects. Paul S. Newman adapted the script and employs a great deal of the movie's dialogue. The pencils are by Mike Sekowsky of *Justice League of America* fame but it looks like a rush job and it hardly displays his mastery of composition. Mike Peppe's inks do as little for Sekowsky as they did for Gil Kane in the *Lost World* adaptation. The comic does not compare favorably to the motion picture, although the sequence when Gulliver wakes up in the giants' doll house with his fiancée is handled more dramatically than in the movie.

The Sword and the Dragon is a 1960 dubbed American release of a creditable 1956 Russian fantasy film, *Ilya Muromets*. Ilya is a farmer who is given a special sword and sets off to aid his king by fighting an evil despot and his minions, which include a three-headed, fire-breathing dragon. Dell's adaptation is an excellent and faithful rendering of the movie with some very nice art. It's attributed to Jack Sparling in some sources, but it looks a lot more like John Buscema. Leo Dorfman did the script, which eliminates such moments as when four warriors are impaled on one spear. The scene when the despot orders all of his constituents to climb on top of one another and form a living mountain *is* depicted.

Dell's final 1960 movie adaptation, *The Time Machine*, depicts the hero's adventures in 800,000 AD where the human race has divided into the sheep-like Eloi above ground and the cannibalistic Morlocks underground. The uncredited script for the comic follows the film version closely, and there is respectable art by Alex Toth; it might have been better if Toth had let someone else ink over his pencils. The comic book is unable to capture what is the highlight of the film, the time-lapse photographic effects that create the illusion of time travel for the viewer.

Dell's adaptation of Jules Verne's *Mysterious Island* (1961) is a near-perfect encapsulation of the film, in which some Civil War soldiers are trapped on an island inhabited by gigantic animals. All the monsters—a giant crab, a big testy bird, plus-sized bees and a mean-tempered squid—are depicted, albeit briefly, and the uncredited script incorporates much of the film's literate dialogue. Tom Gill's artwork is clean and efficient. (Herb Trimpe inked the backgrounds while Gill embellished the main figures.) In the comic, the exchanges between Captain Harding and reporter Spilitt over the morality of Captain Nemo's actions, such as destroying warships and all hands aboard, are eliminated, with Nemo simply presented as a man who seeks peace. The characters do not much resemble the actors in the movie. In 1964, Dell came out with another adaptation of Verne's novel—*Jules Verne's Mysterious Isle*—that is more faithful to the novel, which *has* no monsters.

Atlantis the Lost Continent was a 1961 George Pal production in which a fisherman named Demetrius takes a shipwrecked princess back to her native land of Atlantis and discovers that the evil powers behind the throne are building a destructive, laser-like weapon with which they hope to conquer the world. Dell's comic book version in no way measures up to Pal's very entertaining movie. Although penciler-inker Dan Spiegle later emerged as a significant talent in the comics industry, his art here is disappointing. That said, there are a couple of effective half-page panels depicting a volcano blowing its top and the giant laser running amok. The comic eliminates the scene when the mutated beast men turn against their creator. And although we see evil Zaran and the sanctimonious priest being blasted by the super-weapon, they are not instantly skeletonized as in the movie—a nifty touch and a shock for kid viewers. There is no attempt to make the comic book characters look anything like the actors. A sympathetic character played by Jay Novello only appears briefly in the comic. The serviceable script is by Eric Freiwald and Robert Schaefer.

Dell's version of *Voyage to the Bottom of the Sea* came out in 1961. The movie was Irwin Allen's attempt to duplicate the box office of both *20,000 Leagues Under the Sea* and *Journey to the Center of the Earth*. This story of a fantastic nuclear sub, the *Seaview*, going on a mission to save the world when the Van Allen radiation belt catches fire, is one of Allen's best and most entertaining pictures, but the comic adaptation just doesn't compare. Sam Glanzman's standard penciling is not well-served by his own inks. There are numerous small changes in the (uncredited) script and one major change: Instead of a gigantic octopus attacking the sub just before the climax, the comic has a sea serpent—"ten thousand times the size of a boa constrictor" and with a maw big enough to swallow the *Seaview*—wrap itself around the sub and start to drag it into its lair just as another serpent comes along to try to get it for its own supper. I can only imagine that kids who read the comic book first were sorely disappointed when they saw that this action doesn't occur in the movie. Stars Walter Pidgeon and Peter Lorre are well-depicted in the comic.

Another 1961 Dell movie adaptation is *Master of the World*, loosely based on two novels by Jules Verne. Vincent Price plays a variation on Captain Nemo, in a heavier-than-air flying machine instead of a submarine. Gaylord Du Bois' script follows the basic plot of the film but uses little of the screenplay's dialogue, and even makes some changes along the way; for instance, the two men who are rivals for the heroine come to an understanding in the comic, something that never quite occurs in the movie. Jack Sparling's art is functional and no more.

Released in 1963, *Jason and the Argonauts* depicted a search for the golden fleece amidst a variety of deadly perils. It emerged as one of the finest fantasy films ever made and is perhaps special effects master Ray Harryhausen's greatest achievement. In addition to the wonderful effects work, the movie is classy on every level: Bernard Herrmann's musical score, production values, costuming and art direction. Alas, the Dell comic is vastly inferior to the motion picture. Paul S. Newman's script is mostly faithful to the screenplay aside from a couple of relatively minor deviations: Jason is forced to go on his voyage because of threats to his sister; Hermes takes Jason to Olympus in a chariot. But penciller John Tartaglione seems little inspired by the wealth of mythological material at hand. Dick Giordano and Vince Colletta's inks can only help so much. Scenes that crackle with excitement in the movie are comparatively pallid in the comic. The scene with the many-headed hydra is a little better than the others.

Dell released a tie-in comic for the Boris Karloff film *Die, Monster, Die* in 1965, and it is as mediocre as the movie. A loose and inferior adaptation of H.P. Lovecraft's masterful novella *The Colour Out of Space*, the film focuses on the effects of a glowing meteor on people, animals and plant life. The hero does his best to get his girlfriend, a member of an affected family, to safety before disaster strikes. Joe Gill's comic script follows the film faithfully and Gill, who did much work for Charlton, does the best he can with the material. Despite a bit of help from Vince Colletta's inking, John Tartaglione's pencils are uninspired. A scene when the heroine is attacked by a killer plant is as ludicrous in the comic as it is in the movie.

In 1968, producer Ivan Tors came out with an imitation of *Voyage to the Bottom of the Sea*: In *Around the World Under the Sea*, a submarine transverses the globe underwater putting seaquake warning sensors on the ocean bottom. There are a variety of minor dangers, including an alleged "attack" by a giant moray eel. The Dell comic, written by Paul S. Newman, follows the story almost exactly but eliminates the unconvincing romance between two of the characters. It is actually a bit more enjoyable than the rather bland movie. Jack Sparling turns in a better-than-usual art job. The characters all look exactly like the actors (Lloyd Bridges, David McCallum and Brian Kelly) in the movie.

The Valley of Gwangi (1969) is a major dinosaur flick with superb stop-motion effects by Ray Harryhausen. A circus hopes to attract new business with a little prehistoric horse that escaped from a hidden valley. But the circus gets more than it bargained for when it captures a full-grown T. Rex that escapes from its cage *à la* King Kong and rampages in the nearby village. The uncredited script of the Dell comic follows the movie fairly closely but it nearly eliminates the climax, the very best thing in the movie, when "the T. Rex pads around inside a gigantic cathedral as the hero tries to evade and/or destroy it. Artist Jack Sparling does not offer up an especially notable art job, although there is a fairly impressive full-size panel of the first dramatic appearance of Gwangi (the T. Rex), and some of the dino-action is reasonably well-done. The hero in the comic resembles *Gwangi* star James Franciscus. The front cover boasts the beautiful painting for the movie's poster, which was drawn by Frank McCarthy.

Fago

Tense Suspense

Fago Publications had a very limited amount of sci-fi–fantasy material in the Silver Age. *Atom Age Combat* suggests alien invasions in a couple of stories but most are simply ordinary war tales. *Tense Suspense,* like *AAC*, lasted only two

Fago's *Tense Suspense* #2 has a great cover, but the contents are pure schlock.

issues. *TS* 1 contains several stories, the first of which is "The Curse of Smallness": A man, desperate to find a legendary jungle city, has run out of money. He steals a rare statuette that promises "the curse of smallness" to the person who takes it. He is convinced that he is shrinking by degrees and nearly goes mad with terror. Then he encounters other people and realizes he is still his normal size. Apparently he found the lost city and it belonged to a race of *giants*, explaining why everything there was out of proportion.

Another story concerns a self-described "runt" who invents a shrinking formula so he can reduce everyone else to microscopic size and rule the world. He winds up being taken down to a sub-atomic world where his antisocial tendencies can be cured. "He Must Be Stopped" concerns a scientist who tries to go back in time to stop the inventor of a device that will result in the deaths of millions. This is not the atomic bomb, but *the wheel*, which has led to the deaths of so many on the highways. But the story doesn't take into account all of the advantages society has had due to the wheel. In "Those Eyes Are Evil," a man's girlfriend comes back from Haiti possessed by an evil practitioner of voodoo who not only wants to get back to America but also envies the woman's beauty.

TS 2 has a great cover depicting the members of an expedition who are unaware that their camp is in the middle of a gargantuan footprint, and that giants are watching them just out of sight. But the story inside, "They Come to the Canyon," isn't much better than the rest of the issue's schlocky contents. The story turns out to be a dream of one of the giants, who is terrified that little people will discover his race and turn them into circus attractions. This is unlikely as the giants are *so* colossal that they would never fit in any tent. All of the stories in both issues are drawn (some quite well) by Dick Ayers. Some of the uncredited scripts may have been written by Paul S. Newman.

13

Gold Key; Harvey

Gold Key

Space Family Robinson

Space Family Robinson debuted in 1962. The Robinson family—Craig and June and their children Tim and Tam—are the first family to live on a space station for research purposes. They are accompanied by a dog, Clancy, and a parrot, Yakker. In the first issue, the Robinsons get a distress signal from an alien race menaced by a despot with a weather control machine. Craig feels that the family's primary mission must be research and not rescue. Young Tim and Tam request permission to go off on their own and the children manage to help the aliens and defeat the despot in a dull but not badly drawn adventure.

In the second issue, there is already a new direction for the series as the explosion of an asteroid sends the space station drifting out into unknown space, getting the Robinsons "lost in space." While the parents repair the station, the children are off on another bizarre adventure involving lizard women, a mad doctor who wants to dissect the children (Tim and Tam), a race of little people, and a gigantic space insect, all somewhat silly and reminiscent of *Flash Gordon* and the like. The station is once again in working order but the Robinsons have no idea how to get back to Earth. The really odd thing is that we have to assume that Earth is in the early days of space exploration, yet none of the Robinsons show the slightest surprise at the sight of the aliens and creatures they encounter. The clean, attractive, perfectly composed art is by Dan Spiegle, who gets better with each issue. George Wilson contributes some striking cover paintings. Series editor Del Connell, Don R. Christensen and Gaylord Du Bois did the scripts.

A five-page continuing back-up series starring Captain Venture and his associate and buddy Scotty MacKay begins in *SFR* 6. The two space explorers have their adventures on a watery planet with many caverns, hostile alien tribes and hungry creatures. Like the Robinsons, Venture and MacKay just want to get home, but everything seems to conspire against them. The best installment, with especially noteworthy Dan Spiegle art, has the two men caught inside the belly of a sea creature

(*SFR* 23). Venture was awarded his own comic after many requests but it only lasted two issues. The first consisted of reprint material from *SFR* and the second a new story wherein the guys cross swords with a scientist who experiments on humans.

There was a gradual improvement in the adventures of the space-lost Robinsons. Their searching for a gyro takes them to a prehistoric planet full of bellicose beasties (*SFR* 4). They land on a world which seems to be Earth but isn't and are nearly defeated by energy-absorbing aliens before they team up with another captive of huge proportions (5). In the seventh issue, they come upon a race of people frozen stiff as statues, as well as a fire-breathing lizard with three huge rectangular mouths. In *SFR* 8, they are pursued by walking carnivorous plants with eyeballs on stalks. In one of their most exciting early adventures, the family helps destroy man-eating, giant, flying manta rays that bedevil gentle alien farmers (*SFR* 17).

In the letters column of *SFR* 14, a fan asks if the comic would ever be adapted for TV. The series had been published for three years when producer Irwin Allen's new TV series *Lost in Space* debuted with much publicity. At first, *Lost in Space* was not an official adaptation of the comic but the similarities are obvious. On the show, a family named Robinson takes off on a spaceship but due to sabotage is lost somewhere in the galaxy, unable to get home. They constantly encounter strange creatures on alien planets—sound familiar? The program changed the first names of the characters, made the girl child several years older, and added a handsome astronaut, a nasty doctor and a benevolent robot, but it was clear to everyone that it was basically *Space Family Robinson*.

Gold Key told Allen that he could avoid a lawsuit if he allowed them to make *Space Family Robinson* the official comic of the show, with the name being changed to *Space Family Robinson Lost in Space* with the 15th issue. (It would have been adding insult to injury for Allen to allow another comic book firm to do a licensed adaptation of the TV series.) Ironically, the comic book improved, becoming less childish after the change, while the TV show degenerated into nearly unwatchable silliness.

An interesting phase began for the comic with the eighteenth issue when the Robinsons land on a planet decimated by nuclear war and full of mutated beasts (*à la Mighty Samson*). More importantly, the Robinsons find several figures in suspended animation: eight-foot-tall humanoids and some 12th-century knights, ladies and squires kidnapped centuries ago from Earth. The alien ship had to land on this planet and it was decided to put everyone to sleep until such a time as the radioactivity was no longer a danger. The sleeping people are revived (whatever shock or dismay they might have felt at being thousands of years in the future far from Earth is not dwelled upon), and the leader of the alien race gives the Robinsons a phase-drive machine that manipulates the space-time continuum and will help them get back to their own galaxy. They briefly wind up in 12th-century England, but most of the knights decide to stay on another planet that reminds them of home.

Now for the first time, stories continued from issue to issue. The next story arc has them accidentally traveling back in time to when Mars had a civilization, and from there visiting prehistoric Earth, and then ancient Atlantis just before the cataclysm that destroys the continent (*SRM* 22–25). Other memorable issues involve giant flesh-eating amoeba (29), walking plant monsters that attack a friendly alien ship (30) and an archway that leads into a world of aggressive and hungry giant insects (33).

The series' first volume ended with the 36th issue in 1969. By now the TV series had gone off the air and this undoubtedly affected sales. In 1973, Gold Key continued the series, which was now known as *Space Family Robinson LOST IN SPACE on Space Station One*. A prologue in the 37th issue recaps what had gone before. The Captain Venture back-up series was discontinued with the boys presumably still lost on the watery planet. Dan Spiegle continued to do an exemplary job on the art while Gaylord Du Bois handled the scripting. "Web of Doom" presents giant intelligent man-spiders that menace the Robinsons (38), while "Planet of Monsters" with its weird creatures and thrilling episodes has non-stop action and danger (45).

In the 50th issue, the Robinsons encounter a ship from Earth that is searching for an antidote to a plague. Some of the Robinsons are infected with the plague. After some harrowing moments with dangerous alien animals that carry certain necessary fluids, a serum is finally created. The hopeful Robinsons prepare to follow the other ship back to Earth. But a solar flare-up knocks them off course and the poor family is once more "lost in space." In *SFR* 53, they finally return to Earth, only it turns out to be an illusion created by a massive alien brain that mind-controls an entire planet. The series lasted one more issue, with the four Robinsons still hopeful of finding their way back to Mother Earth. The next five issues were reprints.

While the emphasis in *Space Family Robinson* was almost always on action and weird aliens, sometimes the focus was on family values, as a particular story would illustrate the depth of affection and love felt by each member of the Robinson family for the others. A good example is *SFR* 14, when they land on a planet whose sun begins aging the Robinsons beyond their years as they struggle to gather enough fuel to get away. A harrowing tale in *SFR* 40 shows the ingenuity of the family, especially the children: Tim and Tam shrink in size and still manage to help aliens caught in a tidal wave.

Although there are many monsters and very strange and hostile alien species, the comic does not deal with super-powered characters. The forty-first issue introduces an alien king with startling mind powers who can create objects out of nothing and teleport himself vast distances, but generally there are no standard super-heroes in the series.

The suspenseful scripts are highly effective because they pile one danger on top of another—for instance, as an attempt is made to rescue someone from quicksand, a ravenous monster comes along and threatens the rescuers; or a space armada will attack right in the midst of Mr. and Mrs. Robinson's frantic search for missing Tim and Tam. Originally conceived strictly for children with Tim and Tam taking center stage, the series eventually expanded its readership and gave the adult characters more to do. It is ultimately one of the Silver Age's more memorable sci-fi series.

Mighty Samson

Gold Key's *Mighty Samson* debuted in 1964. It takes place mostly in New York City after the world has been decimated by an atomic war. Radiation has turned plants and both land and sea animals into grotesque monsters. Some humans have also been affected, including a young man who gains such great strength that he becomes known as Samson. He lives with a peaceful tribe called the N'Yarks in the city of the same name. A battle with a huge, mutated "liobear" leaves him with an eye patch and a cloak of yellow fur. Samson has a girlfriend named Sharmaine; her father Mindor is the equivalent of a scientist. Also in the cast are the bestial Kull the Killer, savage leader of a tribe of brutes, and would-be queen Terra of Jerz (New Jersey), whose ancestors built a fortress in the Palisades to withstand the fallout and destruction. The fortress is filled with scientific marvels.

Terra has a hankering for Samson and can't see what he sees in "that wretched peasant girl," even though it is Sharmaine who saves the day when the power-mad Terra inadvertently unleashes a gargantuan suction monster that vacuums up everything in front of it: Sharmaine lures a whale into the monster's path so that it will be pulled into the beast's mouth, suffocating it. Terra tries various schemes to become Queen of N'Yark, including riding around Manhattan in a Coast Guard cutter and lobbing shells at residents (*Mighty Samson* 12).

Mighty Samson's monstrous mutations include the three-headed gator and many-headed shark, Titano-turtle, a tentacled gorilla, a horned rhinophant, the Gulping Blob, a kangorilla, a spidersaurus (a giant spider with the head of a dinosaur and many teeth), a jetbird (a serpentine bird with "exhaust" coming from below membranous wings), a clawed squid and a flame fish that creates underwater fire and cooks its victims alive. And on occasion there are some mighty terrible plants as well.

In "Seeds of Disaster" (*MS* 17), Terra joins forces with a group of "roofians" who grow plants on top of roofs in a forbidden forest (where the Lower East Side of Manhattan used to be). The roofians want nothing to do with "groundians." Terra helps them in exchange for their giving her seeds for experimental plants. First Terra unleashes swordgrass—"grass with blades as sharp and hard as little steel words"— that nearly cut Samson and his pals to ribbons. She follows this with a particularly nasty species of Venus flytrap, and then large strangling vines. Even though Samson saves Terra's life when the roofians turn against her, she's angry because he did it only to get a fungus to kill the vines—not because he loves her.

After a lot of silliness, a genuinely compelling story appears in *MS* 19. Torrential rains create floods that turn the streets of N'Yark into canals. Samson desperately searches for the missing Sharmaine and Mindor while he beats off assorted monsters and comes to the rescue of dozens of the city's inhabitants. He builds an ark by lashing several boats together, and tries to dissuade the passengers from seeking shelter in the Palisades because they would have to deal with Terra and her forces. In response, the passengers toss him overboard. He is reunited with Sharmaine and Mindor when they save him from a lobster-shark. He then prevents Terra from harming one of the ingrates who threw him into the river. The story boasts a very striking panel showing Samson's raft heading toward the ruins of Manhattan, wild, weird birds flying

The premise of Gold Key's *Mighty Samson* was borrowed from Stephen Vincent Benét.

overhead. This story, written by Otto Binder and drawn by Jack Sparling, almost captures the wonder and odd poetry of the basic notion of the series.

Despite its interesting premise—derived from Stephen Vincent Benét's 1937 short story "By the Waters of Babylon," in which a man explores the ruins of a post-apocalyptic New York—*Mighty Samson* never really amounted to much. It suffered from too many poor stories (mostly by Otto Binder) and uneven artwork. Sometimes the pencil work was good, even striking, but the inking left something to be desired. This is certainly true of the work of Jack Sparling, who inked his own pencils. Frank Thorne also did work for the series, and George Wilson contributed the beautiful cover paintings. After 20 issues, *Mighty Samson* began running reprints in late 1969. Nine new stories were published in 1974.

M.A.R.S. Patrol

In 1965, Gold Key came out with the unusual series *Total War*. It details the adventures of the Marine Attack Rescue Service (M.A.R.S.), which has its hands full in the first issue when the shores of America and most other major countries are besieged by murderous bald soldiers (with guns and tanks) of unknown origin. They nearly manage to take over Manhattan before M.A.R.S. routs them, at a terrific cost of lives and property. The invaders blow themselves up rather than risk capture. The battlefield switches to Niagara Falls and Canada for *TW* 2. With the third issue, the comic title is changed to *M.A.R.S. Patrol Total War.*

The hairless invaders come from another planet and use teleportation beams to move themselves and their weaponry around. They are referred to as "skinheads" and "baldies." They attack Washington D.C. with vibration weapons, and use weather control machines to level New Orleans with a hurricane and a 40-foot tidal wave. The aliens use other weapons to bring down the World Trade Center and other skyscrapers. In the eighth issue, an alien named Victor is captured. His father, a commander, ordered his death because he (the father) was afraid Victor would talk. Victor reveals that his world has gone through its natural resources due to warfare, and they now want the assets of Earth.

The four lead characters are members of the Advanced Training Squad: Lt. Cy Adams, expert in aerial combat; Sgt. Joe Striker, electronics (later communications) expert; Sgt. Ken Hiro, expert in seagoing warfare; and Corporal Russ Stacey, weapons specialist. In virtually every issue, someone makes a "Nip" or "chopstick" joke to Japanese-American Hiro, who responds with a "proverb" about big mouths getting their teeth knocked in. In *MPTW* 5, where the battleground is San Francisco, Hiro reunites with his lady love Pat, but just after she makes a commitment to him, she is killed when a building collapses in an alien attack. In *MPTW* 6, Stacey falls for a Pentagon secretary who turns out to be an alien spy with a wig covering her bald head. Striker, a black man, has better luck with a woman named Lisa, who has been taken in by his family. In *MPTW* 9, an injured Russ is temporarily replaced by the gung ho Jace Crane, who is brave but stupid. Crane learns to be a team player just before his death.

The series lasted only ten issues, ending in 1969. The first couple of issues have splendid art by Wally Wood and Dan Adkins; the art by Mike Roy and Mike Peppe in the rest of the run is only adequate. George Wilson did the dynamic cover paintings. While one could not say the characterizations were three-dimensional, there is some attempt at humanizing the squad members, and the tone of the series is more grim and serious than the usual Gold Key comic. Leo Dorfman did all the scripts. Years later, Marvel had a big hit with a similar series about a military squadron fighting fantastic foes, *G.I. Joe*.

UFO Flying Saucers

In 1968, Gold Key's *UFO Flying Saucers* appeared as a 65-page one-shot with short features examining tales of sightings of unidentified flying objects, some of which may have been extraterrestrial flying saucers. Appearing two years later, the second issue was more of the same (but shorter). Another two years went by before the third issue, which contains the speculative non-fiction story "Who Is Killing Our Astronauts?" The story posits the theory that the real-life accidental deaths of many astronauts (both in space vehicles and elsewhere) are actually attempts by unknown forces to delay man's entry into space. A year later, the fourth issue introduced a section called "Hoaxmaster," which covers attempts to fool people into thinking aliens have landed or that people have seen flying saucers. The twelfth issue finally gets around to a feature on the "Men in Black" who are supposed to pay calls on anyone who has seen a UFO.

The series was published quarterly beginning in 1975. The covers began to depict more monstrous aliens than UFOs in some striking paintings. With the fourteenth issue, the title was changed to *UFO and Outer Space*, but the content remained the same. The next three issues were filled with reprint material. The comic begins presenting new material with *UFO* 17, including a dopey comic strip about the aliens "U" and "Fo." There were also many more reports from readers claiming to have seen UFOs. The nineteenth issue reports that in 1938, Chinese scientists discovered skeletal remains along with hundreds of discs—recording or writing devices that told how these people came from a spaceship that crash-landed—in remote caverns in an area called Bayan-Kara-Ula. Details of this story can now be found on Internet websites, but nowhere else, which suggests that the whole thing originated with this issue of *UFO* comics! Some of the stories are labeled "what if" and are clearly fictional. The comic was canceled with its twenty-fifth issue.

Voyage to the Bottom of the Sea

Gold Key turned the popular TV series *Voyage to the Bottom of the Sea* into a comic in 1964. Like the motion picture it was based on, the series was set on an amazing submarine in the near-future. The first compelling issue has Admiral Nelson and his wondrous sub the *Seaview* taking on the evil Dr. Gamma, who plans to use his tidal wave machine to blackmail the world. The fourth issue features the bizarre "Robinson Crusoe of the Depths," in which the *Seaview* comes across a centuries-old giant living beneath the Sargasso Sea. It was the kind of story that might have appeared in *Sea Devils*, but it's handled with a great deal more intelligence. In "The Great Undersea Safari" in issue 5, a mentally disturbed hunter who has lost his nerve tries to redeem himself by hunting the *Seaview* as if it were a huge, deadly beast. It is as much a psychological study as an adventure tale.

Voyage 12 presents an alarming tale of what might happen if an intelligent dolphin gained control of the sea's denizens and turned the whole undersea kingdom against mankind, cutting off a major food supply, tying up shipping lanes, etc. The wildest story is in *Voyage* 14: Found in fissures beneath the Earth, a fluid so affects the *Seaview* itself that the submarine grows gills and scales and becomes a *living* creature, even dripping acid in order to digest the crew inside it. The two subsequent issues feature reprints of earlier stories.

The *Voyage* art was contributed by Mike Sekowsky, Don Heck, Alberto Giolitti, George Tuska, et al., with striking cover paintings primarily by George Wilson. Their art is of a high order: clean, well-composed and attractive with some large, spectacular panels of the *Seaview* being tossed about by waves or sailing through gigantic caverns. There are also shots of thrashing blue whales, undersea earthquakes and mutant behemoths. Since there were no budgetary limitations as on the TV show, the imagination of the writers (including Dick Wood) and artists could run wild. The stories can be fantastic, but never as silly as anything on the TV series. *Voyage to the Bottom of the Sea* is one of the very best television-to-comic adaptations.

Star Trek

The original *Star Trek* series, which lasted three seasons (1966-69), was turned into a comic by at least three different companies, Gold Key, Marvel and DC. Gold Key's *Star Trek* series debuted in 1967 and lasted a lot longer than the TV series. The first issue has an energetic if somewhat absurd tale called "Planet of No Return" with the *Enterprise* crew battling a variety of intelligent and often carnivorous fauna. The second issue is more down-to-earth but also has a good idea: The *Enterprise* investigates the asteroid home of prisoners who are condemned to die when the asteroid blows up.

"The Haunted Asteroid" in *Star Trek* 19 is an intriguing tale of a planetoid that has been made into a shrine for a dead princess. (The three-quarter page panel by Alberto Giolitti and Sal Trapani depicting this shrine is quite striking.) Now the shrine is said to be haunted by the ghosts of those who tried to steal the treasures inside. *ST 22*'s "Siege in Superspace" (1974) introduces a bio-mechanical menace—"botanical-mechanical" might be a better term for it as the creature is composed of both vegetable and metallic parts—three years before *Alien*.

With the thirtieth issue, the once-attractive art underwent a change and the series lost its visual gloss, although there were still some marvelous painted covers, some issues had solid inside art jobs, and there were still some solid scripts. *ST* 33 has the *Enterprise* heading toward the section of space where the "Big Bang" that created the universe is said to have taken place. There they encounter another James Kirk who claims to come from the universe that existed before ours. The two men wind up fighting a "duel to the death." When our Kirk does not kill the earlier one, he is told that he has made the right choice. Al Moniz's story has a lot of intriguing elements even if it doesn't quite go anywhere, and even Captain Kirk wonders if the whole thing even happened.

ST 41 is a superior issue with an excellent story by Arnold "Doom Patrol" Drake and first-rate art by Al McWilliams, who makes the people resemble recognizable human beings and not cartoon characters. In "The Evictors," the *Enterprise* crew members celebrate the 10,000th year of recorded history of the planet Nraka with its rulers. These people have always worshiped a legendary being called Zotar. To their surprise, a huge spaceship arrives containing a race of beings, the Soonora, whose appearance is similar to Zotar's. An emissary from the ship says that they were the original inhabitants of Nraka, who had to flee due to a natural disaster. Now, half a million years later, they want their planet back. If the current Nrakians do not leave, they will be destroyed. Dvor, ruler of Nraka, thinks that the Soonora are mere space pirates. Kirk is inclined to agree but tries to remain neutral. Finally he admits that if it were Earth, he wouldn't give up without a fight. The Nrakians (most of whom have declared that their "god [Zotar] is dead" and are rioting against all foreigners) and the Soonora engage in bloody warfare, until the latter are routed. Then a shocked Kirk discovers that their story was actually true. The tragedy is that if the Soonora had suggested a compromise, the conflict might have been avoided and they might have regained at least a portion of their home planet.

The last few years of the *Star Trek* comic were all drawn by Al McWilliams, who seemed to get better and better at it, turning in some highly satisfactory art jobs. Most of the scripting was handled by George Kashdan. *ST* 56 features a creepy Kashdan tale in with Kirk and Spock try to reverse the negative effects that a mad dictator's trip back to the days of Hannibal has made on the present universe. The series ended in 1979 with issue 61, in which Harry Mudd tries pulling a con on some Klingons.

There were other notable stories during the Gold Key series' lengthy run:

- Robotic machine-builders keep building cities where none are needed and threaten an entire planet (*ST* 3).
- Kirk and Spock must come up with a way to keep two inhabited planets from colliding (6).
- Inhabitants of a planet are shrinking to microscopic size (25).
- After centuries, a benevolent scientist is released from a cryonic tube. But Kirk and the others wonder if he's really who he says he is (39).

- The *Enterprise* crew discovers a world where radiation is making everyone get younger and younger until they disappear into nothingness (42).

Other stories are less effective: "The Voodoo Planet" in *ST* 7 has an interesting concept: Whatever happens to a facsimile of a famous Earth structure (such as the Eiffel Tower), also happens to the real one on Earth. But the explanation for it is ludicrous. *ST* 10 has a striking cover of a huge genie holding onto the *Enterprise*, but the story itself is a forgettable mix of the TV episode "Catspaw" and Sinbad movies. *ST* 18 has another interesting concept—the 300 million inhabitants of a planet are put on tape for easier transport—except a similar idea had already been used on the TV series *The Outer Limits*. Occasionally a story will be a rip-off of a TV episode, such as *ST* 23's tale of a world without adults, where children are doomed to die of a plague. There are also variations of "Who Mourns for Adonais?" and a sequel to an episode about "the companion," "Metamorphosis."

The Invaders

Gold Key brought out *The Invaders*, based on the excellent if short-lived 1966 science fiction series in which David Vincent (Roy Thinnes) tries to warn the world about an outer space invasion, waging a lonely battle against murderous aliens. In the first issue, Vincent tells scientists at a radar base about the aliens' sinister interest in them but as usual he is rebuffed. Vincent then discovers that an alien saucer is hidden behind the illusion of a mountain in the nearby desert. In the second issue, Vincent intervenes when an Air Force major is mind-controlled by the aliens, going so far as to try to commit sabotage and even murder his own little boy, who's seen too much. "The Moon Tilters" in *Invaders* 3 has the aliens plotting to wipe out the world's inhabitants with massive flooding. Vincent and some allies race to open a dam and destroy the device causing the rising waters.

The Invaders 4 has two excellent stories. In "The Doomsday Window," Vincent and his colleague Edgar Scoville grab a device, a circular hoop, from the aliens. The hoop turns out to be a dimension warp that upon being enlarged can bring the aliens' ships across the galaxies with even greater speed and in greater numbers than before. In "Rendezvous at Grizzly Mesa," an alien named Primus reveals that he and others like him want to remain on Earth and live free, and are willing to fight off the invasion along with Vincent and Scoville.

The Invaders lasted for four issues, failing to survive past the cancellation of the series. The stories are as good as the ones on the TV show, and Dan Spiegle's art is, as usual, adept and attractive.

Gold Key Movie Comics

Gold Key's *Captain Sindbad* (1963), based on the feature film starring Guy Williams, features attractive art by Russ Manning. But writers Eric Freiwald and Robert

Schaefer make quite a few changes from the movie. Sindbad comes back from a long voyage hoping to be reunited with a beautiful princess, but discovers that the land has been taken over by the tyrannical El Kerim. This dictator is impervious to death because his heart is protected in a great tower in the middle of a deadly swamp. The first half of the comic follows the movie faithfully, but the second half adds new sequences. Perhaps they were in the original screenplay but were never filmed (or filmed and then left on the cutting room floor). In the comic, the hydra is replaced by a minotaur and a chimera. In the comic, Sindbad and his men are beset by giant ants that at the end are magically transformed back into 8000 missing men. None of this occurs in the finished film. Sindbad and El Kerim do not have a battle on the top of the tower as in the film, and the comic's ending is a bit abrupt. Overall, it does not compare that favorably to the very colorful and exciting motion picture.

A film adaptation of H.G. Wells' *The First Men in the Moon* premiered in 1964 and that same year Gold Key came out with a comics version. Unlike Wells' novel, much of the film is very silly and it takes nearly an hour for three voyagers—scientist Cavor, playwright Bedford and Bedford's fiancée Kate—to make it to the moon in their gravity-defying sphere. The adventurers discover a society of busy, insect-like creatures inside the moon along with gigantic moon cows that resemble outsized caterpillars. Paul S. Newman's script for the comic is well-done, although it eliminates the subtext of Bedford introducing the "Selenites" (the moon people) to violence. The rest follows the movie very closely, and this includes the prologue and epilogue that take place in modern times (astronauts discover a Union Jack on the moon!). Fred Fredericks' art is only slightly better than serviceable. The moon men and moon cows look pretty much as they do in the movie, and the characters are at least the same type as the actors although they only resemble them superficially.

In 1966, Gold Key issued an adaptation of the wonderfully absurd *Fantastic Voyage*, in which a team in a sub is shrunk to microscopic size and injected into the artery of an important scientist who needs a brain operation performed *within* his body! Paul S. Newman's script omits the sub's voyage through the inner ear and the subsequent attack of antibodies on the curvaceous Raquel Welch, and gives the sub's inner journey the name Operation Lilliput. The film is a wonder to behold, with its incredible sets, art direction and special effects that still hold up. The look of the comic is not on the same level, although Dan Adkins' pencils are reasonably adept and they are inked by the combo of Tony Coleman and Wally Wood. Whatever its flaws, the comic adaptation is still quite entertaining.

In 1968, 35 years after its initial release, Gold Key came out a giant 64-page adaptation of the 1933 classic *King Kong*. Beautifully done, the comic, scripted by Gary Poole, is almost as exciting, suspenseful and entertaining as the movie. There are some minor changes made from the film. The characters, especially Ann Darrow and Carl Denham, look nothing like the actors who portrayed them. The comic eliminates the more gruesome scenes of the movie (which were excised after the film's initial release) depicting Kong chewing on people, stomping on natives, etc.

The scene with Kong attacking and bashing the elevated train is also not depicted. The comic adds a scene when Kong battles two horned triceratops, and expands on the sequence when Ann and Jack Driscoll escape from the big ape by fleeing down the river. In one scary panel, Kong's giant hand reaches into the water and nearly grabs the couple as they swim away. Another change has the ape battling the big snake not in Kong's lair as in the movie but at the foot of the mountain.

The art by Giovanni Ticci and Alberto Giolitti is generally first-rate, especially in the scenes depicting a reptile rising from a river to overturn a raft carrying Denham, Driscoll and their fellow crew members. Other knock-out panels show Kong bursting through the wall built by the natives, escaping his chains in the Broadway theater, and trying to swat away the planes as they fly at him atop the Empire State Building. Oddly, the characters are depicted with 1960s-style haircuts and clothing, but the climax still uses the old-fashioned biplanes of the movie. The first appearance of Kong in the comic is not nearly as dramatic as in the picture. Otherwise, this is arguably the best of the fantastic movie adaptations. George Wilson's cover painting is outstanding.

Gold Key issued a comic book tie-in with *Beneath the Planet of the Apes* in 1970. This terrible sequel to the extremely popular *Planet of the Apes* has Earth astronauts from the past involved with unpleasant talking apes and mutated humans who worship a hydrogen bomb. In both movie and comic, the Earth is blown apart at the end. The uncredited comic book script follows the movie very closely, and the art by Alberto Giolitti and Sergio Costa is more than acceptable. The lead characters greatly resemble the actors Charlton Heston and James Franciscus but only in a couple of panels. Marvel Comics also did an adaptation of the movie, as well as of *Planet of the Apes* (see Chapter 16).

Harvey

Race for the Moon

Race for the Moon appeared in 1958 and lasted three issues. In the first story in *Race* 1, crime has virtually been eliminated and wrongdoers are sentenced to life in an asylum, which—in an ending that solicits groans—turns out to be planet Earth. In "Supreme Penalty," lawbreakers are also shot into space, unable to return because of some kind of mysterious barrier. A scientist develops the technology to pierce the barrier—meaning space exploration can finally begin—and commits a crime so that he, too, will be sent into space. He gets a life sentence on Earth instead. "Disc Jockey" is a comical story about a radio host so awful that aliens come down to snatch him away and permanently remove him from the airwaves. "The Invasion" rips off Orson

Welles' *War of the Worlds* radio broadcast when a couple, hearing a fictional story of an invasion from outer space, pack up in a hurry and head for the hills. The only story that has anything to do with the moon is "The First Man on the Moon," a two-pager in which an astronaut lands on the lunar surface, explores everywhere he can but finds no signs of life until he gets back into his spaceship and hears something knocking on the door. All of the stories are drawn by Bob Powell.

There was a six-month gap between *Race for the Moon* 1 and 2 and what a difference it made. For one thing, the *Race* 2 stories were penciled by Jack Kirby—aside from a one-page story penciled by Paul Reinman—with inking assists from Al Williamson and Marvin Stein. Kirby may also have done the scripts for these stories but that is highly debatable. Even in later decades, Kirby's scripting could be quite stilted and amateurish, and the *Race* scripts seem much too polished. (However, it's possible that the editor, Leon Harvey, fixed up the scripts.) Kirby's pencils are excellent throughout the issue.

In "The Thing on Sputnik 4," a spaceship crew discovers a tiny creature of unknown origin inside a metallic cube. This creature is somehow related to a monstrous organism that is clinging to the Russian sputnik satellite and reunites with it before they both shoot off into far-flung space. In "Lunar Trap," a female Soviet colonel on the moon accuses an American geologist of destroying Russian equipment on the lunar surface, but the true culprit is a barely seen monstrosity that is large and strong enough to fling boulders at the soldiers. As the colonel and the geologist hide in a cavern, they see the enormous eyes of the creature staring in at them, and drive it away with laser-type weapons. In "Island in the Sky," astronaut Bill Fenner dies in an accident and his body is placed in a tube so it can float free forever in space. But it is drawn into the giant "red eye" of Jupiter, a place Fenner always hated. Shortly afterward, the tube with Fenner inside—alive!—comes shooting out to be retrieved by the spaceship. Fenner has no memory of what happened to him before his "death" or inside the eye, but scientists confirm that he has picked up an alien presence inside his brain, a black dot that revived him. It is not only keeping him alive but also will probably make him near-immortal.

In "The Face on Mars," members of an expedition discover a huge face built into a mountain on Mars. They climb the face and enter one of the eyes. One of the crew members finds himself in a fantastic world full of beautiful giant people and technological wonders, then learns that these people were attacked by a planet that no longer exists, once located between Mars and Jupiter, and they were forced to destroy it to save themselves. Unfortunately, it is too late for the Martians, whose atmosphere was destroyed by the invaders. The crew member experienced all of this in a kind of hallucination inside the giant face. All of the stories in *Race for the Moon* 2 are intriguing although it could be argued that they end just when they start to get really interesting.

Race for the Moon 3 features the adventures of the Three Rocketeers: Captain Kip McCoy, Sgt. Beefy Brown and "Figures" Faraday. In the first story, McCoy and Brown are taking the criminal "Big Shot" to a prison on the moon when he uses knock-out gas to escape. McCoy blames Brown for not searching their prisoner more thoroughly. The two fly off to recapture Big Shot when they discover a stowaway, Figures, a worker in the science section; Figures has always been aching for action. When Big Shot escapes in yet another ship, McCoy assumes they will all be court-martialed, but Figures points out that Big Shot's vehicle is on a fifteen-year non-stop round trip, the exact length of his sentence. This was the first and last appearance of Harvey's Three Rocketeers.

In the second story, the Moon Scouts encounter a hulking red robotic alien whom they mistakenly believe is issuing poison in an attempt to kill them. They finally realize that this alien actually breathes this toxic atmosphere and it is accidentally escaping from his casement. The Moon Scouts bring his plight to the attention of his fellow aliens, who come and rescue him. In "Space Garbage," a family of prospectors rescue an infamous crook from an outer space death trap and manage to capture him. They discover a deposit of a rare chemical that can affect the optic nerve and cure blindness.

"Garden of Eden" is of interest because it may be the first of many comic book stories about living sentient planets. Astronauts landing on another planet are greeted by a beautiful woman, Anizaar, who leads them to sumptuous quarters and a delicious repast. The men are delighted with this situation and are in no hurry to leave, but the captain is suspicious—everything is just *too* perfect—and he steers his men back to the ship. Anizaar disappears along with the beautiful landscape, and there is a violent upheaval because the real Anizaar—the entire planet—doesn't want them to leave. (Years later, the superhero Green Lantern encountered a living world, as did the Marvel hero, Thor.) The art for these stories was done by Jack Kirby and Al Williamson.

Alarming Tales

Alarming Tales debuted in 1957 and lasted six issues. The first issue presents a variety of weird stories, all of them penciled, inked and apparently scripted by Jack Kirby. The stories "The Cadmus Seed" and "The Last Enemy" anticipate material that Kirby presented many years later. The first story deals with a mad scientist who has come up with microscopic cells that resemble fetuses, as well as human-type men who grow from plants. This story is reminiscent of the strange experiments going on in the so-called Evil Factory during issues of Kirby's run on *Jimmy Olsen*. The second story has the protagonist travelling centuries into the future where humanity has been wiped out in a holocaust and "dumb" animals of all kinds have developed intelligence and become the dominant species. There is now a war between canines and other creatures vs. nasty human-sized rats. Kirby worked on a series entitled *Kamandi* that also took place in a future world where animals are intelligent and wage war on one another.

"The Fourth Dimension is a Many-Splattered Thing" has a man pursuing a thief into a dimensional barrier and entering a landscape of peculiar shapes (he himself is continually transformed into equally weird formations). The "thief" turns out to be a pretty alien who was hunting for souvenirs. "Donnegan Daffy's Chair" has a janitor testing out a chair that has been dropped off at the patent office. Touching the wrong button, he flies off into space, past the moon and beyond, and comes back years later, landing in the middle of city traffic, speaking a strange language no one can understand. It's a fairly flat ending to an otherwise whimsical story.

Jack Kirby did most of the work for *Alarming Tales* 2. "The Hole in the Wall" concerns an elderly man, fired from his job and forced to move into a miserable basement room in a boarding house. He discovers a hole in the wall from which comes enough warmth to keep him from freezing, as well as some odd objects. Finally he enters the hole and finds the lovely world with friendly inhabitants that he has always been dreaming of, a poignant metaphor for a compassionate afterlife. "I Want to Be a Man!" concerns a gigantic computer, Fabiac, who tells his inventor, David, that he is desperate to be a man, a task that seems impossible. Fabiac is eventually given the form of a hulking and somewhat grotesque-looking robot; David does his best to keep Fabiac out of sight. Alas, when Fabiac sees himself in a mirror, he commits suicide by blowing his top. "I cannot bear the truth" is written on ticker tape.

"The Fireballs" posits the theory that UFOs are a form of energy species that live in Earth's upper atmosphere. This comes to light when they communicate with energy beings that hail from within the sun. "The Big Hunt" takes place in an alternate dimension where a boastful hunter uses a friend's machine to cross into a world with unique animals. He is offered $200,000 to bring back one of these creatures and prove that everything he claims is the truth, but the animal is too big to fit into his machine.

Kirby did the art for only one story in *Alarming Tales* 3 and the scripts were all written by Jack Oleck. The other stories are drawn by Doug Wildey and Ernie Schroeder. In the Kirby tale, two sinister men wake up after centuries in a cave and try to use their mind-control powers on modern man, an idea that backfires. The other stories concern a little boy who can temporarily walk on water but loses this ability when he is taken from his mysterious guardian; a man who fears that his child is abnormally intelligent and perhaps dangerous but learns the real mutant is the boy's dog; an elderly man who uses a spell to get rid of his nephew, but regrets it in more ways than one; and a wealthy man who incurs the wrath of a hag with supernatural powers and discovers that no one, including his friends and servants, remember him. Wildey and Schroeder contribute some very atmospheric and effective artwork.

Kirby wrote and drew one story in *Alarming Tales* 4 with the rest of the art done by Wildey and Bob Powell. The other scripts were written by Oleck and Carl Wessler. In the Kirby tale, a Martian boy who dreams of the stars runs away to the space port but crashes in the desert where his father rescues him from a snake-like cat creature. The father tells his son to wait until he's an adult to journey into space. Other stories deal with a timid man bedeviled by a stranger who turns out to be his subconscious, and a college student trying to convince his brother that his collection of rag dolls can't talk to him. Or can they?

The issue's best story is "The Monster from 1977 A.D." by Wessler and Powell, in which a poor old man, who has no money to buy his little grandson a present for his birthday, gives him the best present of all—the gift of life. Twenty years in the future, the boy, now a grown man, is menaced by a 40-foot Gila monster created by atomic testing. Somehow a telepathic connection between the two men reaches through time and the grandfather, "hearing" the boy's terrified voice, shoots every Gila monster he can find until he kills the one that would have become irradiated in the near-future and endangered his grandson.

The stories in the last two issues of *Alarming Tales* were scripted by Dick Wood and Carl Wessler, with the art chores assigned to Bob Powell, Fred Kida, Paul Reinman, Bernard Bailey, Bob Brown, Norman Nodel and the Al Williamson-Angelo Torres team. Matt Baker drew "Half Man-Half What?" in which a scientist conducting experiments in petrifying objects becomes half-human and half-metal. In "My Robot Plants," a scientist invents robot plants that don't need to be watered. But he accidentally unleashes a monster plant created by nuclear energy leaking from the robots. Similar to the Carl Stephenson story "Leiningen versus the Ants," "12,000 to 1" details one man's struggle against a horde of driver ants attacking his missile observation center in South America. These lively critters seem more intelligent and resourceful than usual but, in the end, the conflict of nature versus man ends in a draw.

In "King of the Ants" (Wood-Williamson and Torres) in *Alarming Tales* 6, Jack Flaherty is fascinated by the ants on his friend's plantation. Anticipating the Marvel superhero Ant-Man, who debuted a few years later, a combination of chemicals reduces Flaherty in size and he encounters a group of ants that are about to be attacked by a beetle. Flaherty uses a thorn to kill the beetle, and the grateful ants make him their king. Flaherty is impressed when a horde of deadly driver ants approach and his group of ants leave morsels of food in their path. As the driver ants battle each other for the morsels, Flaherty's ants attack their distracted opponents and overcome them. Back at normal size, Flaherty learns that a group of human raiders are about to attack the plantation. He instructs his friend to leave all items of value in their path and, like the driver ants, the raiders fight over the loot. This gives the plantation workers time to acquire smoke bombs to rout the raiders.

Set in Paris, *Alarming Tales* 6's "The Emotion Maker" (Wood-Kida) deals with a nasty man, David Dubois, who is able to steal emotions from people and imbue those emotions in others. He sucks emotions from an actor portraying a coward on the stage and installs them in a bullfighter just as he comes into the ring. The man is now terrified of the bull, completely destroying his career and probably his life. Some people benefit from his irresponsible actions while others, such as a bank president who runs off with the bank's money, are ruined. A man who knows what Dubois has done uses his stolen essences to get him to repent and feel shame over his actions. But he really deserved a much darker and more violent fate.

14

Marvel

Strange Worlds

At the start of the Silver Age, Marvel Comics was still calling itself Atlas. Marvel came out with several sci-fi–fantasy mags in the late '50s, including *Strange Worlds*, which ran for five issues in 1958–59. *Strange Worlds* 1 has an interesting mix of stories about robots, flying saucers, the Abominable Snowman, and even Adam and Eve. "I Discovered the Secret of Flying Saucers!" reveals that UFOs seen all around the world do not contain aliens, but actually *are* rather large aliens who resemble spaceships. Artist Jack Kirby contributed a striking panel (two-thirds of a page) depicting the aliens' amazing city, with towering machine-like buildings and a variety of speeding airborne rockets.

"I Am the Last Man on Earth," drawn by Don Heck, tells the story of a couple who watch as the last Earthlings leave to go to another world where everyone will live 500 years. The couple, members of the anti-exodus society, think it's a sacrilege of sorts for everyone to simply abandon Earth after all that human society has gone through on this tired but still vital world—but longevity is obviously not to be sneered at. That the couple turns out to be Adam and Eve, starting a new society, is what nearly ruins an otherwise interesting concept. In "I Am Robot," an intelligent robot is tested on its ability to care for and protect a scientist's young son. Due to a misadventure with nasty aliens, the experiment is deemed a failure when the robot actually did a fine job. "I Captured the Abominable Snowman!," a story told more than once in Marvel's fantasy mags, has a man pursuing the Yeti (spelled Yetti in the story) and discovering that the Snowman was once human and that he (the hunter) will have to take his place as a shaggy beast. Steve Ditko did the art. Stan Lee edited the series and is generally credited as scripter of most stories, along with his brother Larry Lieber, although this cannot be confirmed.

Strange Worlds 2 features a story about an egotistical genius, the smartest man on Earth, who seeks new challenges. He rockets into space where he intends to conquer an alien race, only to learn that by their standards he's a moron, eventually becoming an exhibit in a zoo. In another *SW* 2 tale, an assault team rises from the depths of domed Atlantis to wage war on the surface world. But they must retreat when they encounter a gargantuan baby boy on a beach: The Atlanteans are just a fraction of the size of ordinary humans. In *SW* 3, a young man, worried that his claustrophobia will get him booted out of the space service, foils a bunch of space pirates; a lady reporter does a story on a monster that escaped from its glass cage; and a gypsy boy screws up his life by refusing to work or educate himself. In a swamp, he reverts to a baby by inhaling fumes from the Fountain of Youth; will he apply himself this time or just make the same mistakes? "I Fly to the Stars!" (Kirby–Christopher Rule) is another story on a popular theme: Time passes more slowly on Earth than it does for astronauts, meaning they can never marry because when they return to Earth, they are still young but their women are old enough to be their grandmothers.

In *SW* 4, "I Was the Changing Man," drawn by Al Williamson, presents the story of the highly unpleasant Duncan Sloane, who has invented a way to dematerialize himself so that his mind can take over wealthy and powerful individuals. He admits that he doesn't care about the men whose lives he takes over. But something always goes wrong after Duncan occupies someone: a rich man goes bankrupt; a handsome actor is shot by a jealous woman; a dictator has to flee for his life. At the end, Duncan decides to stay as himself. This selfish person deserved a horrible fate. "Manhunt on Mars," drawn by John Buscema, follows the exploits of Anton Volchek, a dissident in a Communist nation—obviously Russia—who makes the mistake of openly espousing the cause of freedom. Comic books of this period, especially Marvel, frequently used the Reds as bad guys in everything from superhero tales to science fiction stories, although no particular country is ever named (as if it needed to be).

Fleeing from the authorities, Volchek climbs into an unmanned rocketship headed for Mars, figuring he'd rather be free on another planet than imprisoned in the country where he was born. On Mars, he barely survives an encounter with aliens who want to shoot him on sight. Back on Earth, he is hailed as a hero by his countrymen but manages to escape to America as soon as the opportunity arrives. He warns the U.S. of the Martians' warlike ways, but neglects to do the same for his own former government, which sends a delegation to Mars thinking the inhabitants are friendly. Volchek is clearly overstating when he says, "At least my people will be free of those power-mad tyrants."

"We Are the 3 Who Vanished" in *Strange Worlds* 5, the final issue, starts out as a locked room mystery and turns into an outré time travel tale. Mad inventor Hastings forces two colleagues to help him finish his latest invention, even threatening to shoot them if they don't comply. Three days go by and the police, advised that the two scientists are missing, break down the door to Hastings' laboratory and find it deserted. Reading one scientist's diary, they learn that Hastings and the others planned to use the completed machine to go back to the 17th century. The police theorize that they were simply disintegrated. In the final panel of the story, we see the three men dressed in the fashions of the 1600s, enjoying tankards of ale in an tavern! Hastings and the others initially think that the time machine didn't work, but they truly did travel to the past, although they are unaware of it. "Even if a man didst travel in time, he'd never know it," Hastings tells the others in the tavern. "When he arrived at a different year, he'd think he had always lived in that year." This is a unique notion as regards time travel, but it opens up a hornet's nest of unanswerable questions regarding the men's lives and identities in that distant past.

World of Fantasy

World of Fantasy, under the Atlas banner, debuted in 1956. The first issue has several unmemorable stories: a Martian invasion that goes awry; a weird plant threatening to dominate the garden of an elderly couple; a boy's encounter with the sun god, Apollo; a mysterious mountain peak that no one ever returns from; and a cave full of gold and an old sorcerer. "One Night" (Oleck-Forgione-Abel) in *WOF* 2 is a slight improvement. Cooper, a bitter old man, has worked on space freighters for 30 years. On the planet Antares, everyone seems to live like a king, but outlanders are not allowed to live there. Not looking forward to returning to a poverty-stricken life on Earth, Cooper gets into a fistfight with an Antarean and is sentenced to death—but he's told that he will have one fabulous night of absolute luxury before his execution. Cooper's supervisor manages to get him free so he can return to Earth, but then tells him that on Antares one night lasts the equivalent of *93 years*!

Many of the *WOF* stories have similarly ironic endings (a thief with a guilty conscience thinks he's shrinking but has actually entered a hothouse full of gigantic vegetables; natives think a parachutist is a bird-god and treat him like a king but then expect him to jump off a high cliff)—but that's *all* they have going for them. But even when they aren't great, many of the stories have compelling premises:

- In a Communist country, a man uses sorcery to save the life of his rebel son and destroy his oppressor.
- A man suspects that his father is responsible for kidnapping scientists who vanish within a thick black cloud.
- A selfish man jumps into a lifeboat on a sinking liner and thinks only a couple of years have passed when he is rescued, but it's really been *decades* and he is aged, his whole life wasted.
- A window washer falls 35 stories as people below and in the building watch with horror, but he completely disappears before he hits the ground.

In "Whose Face Have I?" (*WOF* 8), drawn by Paul Reinman, a man wakes up wearing the face of a friend who saved his life during the war. He goes to the friend's house and meets his mother, who is dying, and who is overjoyed to see a man she thinks is her son. After she dies, he learns that she was notified of her son's death in a plane crash. In this way, the hero is able to repay a debt to his late friend, who wanted his mother to see him one last time before dying and come to the conclusion that the story of his death was untrue.

Around this time, Marvel's *Astonishing*, *Mystery Tales* and *Marvel Tales* series were cancelled, so some of the inventory wound up in *World of Fantasy*. *WOF* 9 features "Quarantine" (Wessler–Robert Q. Sale), in which Ted, a clerk with a nagging wife named Muriel, supports his brother, Horace, an alleged genius who is working on a time machine that he is sure will bring him millions. Horace finishes the machine, disappears, and comes back saying he spent an hour in the year 2000. Everyone is excited by the possibilities, but when the news gets out—thanks to chattering Muriel—the government comes by and decides Horace needs to be put in quarantine for six months because he might have brought some disease back from the future. When Muriel and Ted use the time machine to go to 2000 to get an affidavit stating that there is no disease, they discover the machine only goes so far and then stops—Horace never actually got to 2000. While Ted wants to do something to help his brother, Muriel tells him that all Horace has to do is tell the authorities the truth.

"When Marty Moves" is a sad tale of an old woman named Mary, who is delighted when her doll of a little boy comes to life after an electrical accident. She calls the boy Marty and he brings new joy to the lonely woman's life. Rocco, a neighbor, takes advantage of the boy's size by getting him to squeeze through the window bars of a bank and steal money. Mary learns of this and tries to keep Rocco from taking the child with him to rob again. Rocco inadvertently starts a fire. Rocco runs out of the building but Marty uses what was left of his energy to drag Mary out onto the sidewalk. The police find her clutching a plastic doll and crying.

With its final issue, *WOF* 19, the series went out on a high note with two above-average stories. In "Deluge," drawn by Steve Ditko, the world is endangered when a scientist focuses a magnetic beam on the moon. His plan is to create a lunar atmosphere so that people will be able to live there. Instead, the beam raises the level of Earth's oceans, causes mass flooding and torrential downpours. The scientist is unable to turn the machine off or reverse its effects. A military man, discovering the source of the magnetic disruption, flies through the torrent to the scientist's lab and destroys the machine, saving the Earth.

In "I Was Stranded in Space," drawn by Joe Sinnott, criminal Joe Burke is being returned to Earth by spaceship to serve an eight-year sentence for armed robbery. Escaping, he hides out on a seemingly deserted planet as the ship continues its journey. He then realizes that he would have been better off staying on the ship, as there isn't a soul around, and the world is full of dangerous beasts, man-eating plants and deadly meteorite showers. He cannot signal any ships that go by and fears he will be alone on this lonely outpost for the rest of his life. When an earthquake hits, he crosses the mountains he had never scaled before and finds a welcoming civilization. Exactly eight years have gone by. Burke is determined to turn his life around now that he has been saved, and he doesn't yet know that the people on the planet knew he was there all the time; he had to serve his sentence first.

The *WOF* series' artists included Richard Doxsee, Gene Colan, Joe Sinnott, Kurt

Schaffenberger, Steve Ditko, Carl Burgos, Al Williamson, Jack Kirby, John Forte and Don Heck.

Other notable stories include:

- "Three Dead Flies" (14): A chemist's son gets revenge on the man who cheated him out of his company years before by offering him a phony youth formula. Or is it phony?
- "It Hides in the Forest" (17): Alien invaders plant a scout on Earth and tell the world they will conquer the planet if the Earthlings can't ferret out the scout in a month. On the last day, a boy and his dog figure out that the alien is a tree.
- "The Man from Tomorrow" (17): A penny-ante crook comes up with an idea to make money by pretending to be a man from the future out of a phony time machine, but real time travelers believe him and send him "back to the future."
- "The Creatures Who Captured Earth" (18): A man suspects that generous aliens are making life easier for Earthlings only to make the whole world ripe for conquest.
- "Xom, the Menace from Outer Space!" (18): Aliens beg a group of Earth astronauts to help them destroy a huge, hairy, fierce-looking monster that they say will kill them all. But they really want the poor harmless beast slaughtered for his ivory teeth.

Strange Tales of the Unusual

Strange Tales of the Unusual debuted at the very end of the Golden Age. The first issue presents a batch of unmemorable stories, although "Who Walks in the Dark?," drawn by John Romita, deals with a familiar theme: An "element X" in the ground of unexplored African territory causes strange size changes in the animals. A group of explorers leave this territory after encountering gigantic chimps and lizards. The critters apparently return to normal size the next day, but the explorers are unaware that they themselves have grown to enormous stature.

STOTU 2 has one memorable tale in "He Waits in the Dark Alley," a sympathetic study of homelessness and hopelessness drawn by Bill Everett. The unnamed protagonist—it is fitting that he is not named—remembers that, when he was a boy, his father told him, "If you dream hard enough and long enough, your dreams are bound to come true." From his spot in the filthy alley where he is resting, he thinks: "How wrong can you be? Dreams are nothing but caves that a man crawls into to forget. They never come true." In another alley, he finds a newspaper that has tomorrow's date and he reads about a financier who was shot at. He decides to go the next day to the scene of the upcoming crime, and knocks the man to the sidewalk just before the bullet is fired. But instead of the gratitude and reward he was hoping for, he is arrested for assault—no one noticed the gunman in the car. This turns out to be a dream, but the next day he finds a newspaper in the same spot as before but burns it to warm himself, not knowing if it was just an old paper or the one he saw in his dream.

In *STOTU* 6's "City in the Sky," pilot Jeb Ogden is astonished to see a city floating several miles above the Earth. He lands his plane and discovers a town named Blyston and learns that decades earlier, a scientist had used an anti-gravity device to lift the city up into the air, where it has been ever since. Jeb is attracted to Jane Rawles, granddaughter of the scientist. Time has bypassed Blyston and everyone remains ignorant of such modern developments as planes and skyscrapers. Learning that every inhabitant of Blyston wants to return to Earth and rejoin society, Jeb carefully reverses the effects of the machine so that the town safely lands where it used to be. Everyone is happy and the place becomes a tourist attraction. But Jed gradually notices that the people of Blyston seem to be changing, and not for the better. Although he and Jane are engaged, he catches her going out with an oily suitor who tells him he's "boring." Waiting until all visitors have left Blyston, Jeb surreptitiously reactivates the anti-gravity machine. Blyston—and Jane—are never seen again.

The story is more interesting for what it *doesn't* say. It is possible that the uncredited scripter doesn't realize how utterly selfish and irresponsible Jeb's actions are, and that they are more motivated by his jealousy than anything else. It doesn't occur to him that everyone in the town *wanted* to rejoin modern society, or that it was only his opinion that their losing their old-fashioned, quaint attitudes was necessarily a bad thing. He doesn't think of the possibility that bonds of love and friendship might have been formed between the Blyton inhabitants and the many tourists. It's impossible for the reader to feel any sympathy for Jeb.

"Mass Murder" (*STOTU* 10) presents a thought-provoking situation: Dr. Farnum thinks there are two likely methods of protecting the U.S. from atomic attack. Since time seems to be of the essence, the scientist creates exact *duplicates* of several scientists and sends the original men to the Arctic to work on one method, while he works with the duplicates on a second method on a Pacific atoll. He and the doubles come up with a kind of dust blanket that will neutralize any atomic-type warhead. Farnum then disintegrates the duplicates as they are no longer needed. While it's obvious that keeping these doubles around will cause major complications, especially for the original scientists, they are still seen as heroes and Farnum is arrested for "mass murder." Farnum argues that these duplicates were not men, but mere images; what he did was no different than tearing up a photograph. The story ends with the jury filing out to deliberate, with a caption asking the reader how he or she would decide. Robert Q. Sale did the art; the inventive script is uncredited.

Strange Tales of the Unusual only lasted 11 issues. Other notable stories include:

- "The Man Who Feared Mirrors" (7): A guilty conscience over how he betrayed a group of subterranean dwellers convinces a man that he has become hideous like them and can only work in a circus sideshow.

Marvel's long-running *Strange Tales* kept reinventing itself: first horror, then sci-fi-fantasy, then superheroes and spies.

- "The Five Sinister Statues" (11): A man's inheritance is five portly Oriental statues which talk to him and give him whatever he wants. It all backfires when his ill-gotten gain comes to the attention of the authorities.

Strange Tales

Strange Tales began life in the Golden Age as a sci-fi–horror title, eventually became primarily a horror book; in the Silver Age, it opted for sci-fi and fantasy stories with many giant monster tales before turning into a superhero title. This was also true of sister publications *Tales of Suspense* and *Tales to Astonish*. "The Eyes of Mr. Moody" (Carl Wessler-Jack Keller) in *ST* 45 is a discouraging tale of an unsuccessful hypnotist who is tired of reading about other people's triumphs. He fears that he doesn't have the strength or charisma to amount to anything. Staring into a mirror, he hypnotizes himself to be confident and powerful for a full year. He is sure that by the time the spell wears off, he will be a new man. During the year, he gets a great job, takes over a company, becomes a giant in industry with many friends and a beautiful mansion. Then … the spell fades and he realizes it was all just a dream and he never left his miserable apartment. This is a *literal* fantasy story.

Strange Tales 67 presents "I Was the Invisible Man" (Kirby-Rule): Scientist Adam Clayton develops the ability to become invisible and to run at the speed of light. His first act is to snatch away a payroll from some bank robbers and return it to the police. He realizes that with his incredible abilities, he could easily become rich and famous, not by robbing banks, but by doing many amazing deeds before revealing his true identity. He saves a man from a falling safe, knocks out a boxer with an invisible fist in front of the astonished opponent, builds an entire house while the workers are on their lunch break, etc. After a few weeks of this, Adam feels abnormally tired and is shocked when he looks in the mirror and sees an elderly man looking back at him. He has aged about a year per day. Instead of the glory he was hoping for, he is now a tired old man who is nearly run over by a truck driver for moving too slow. Adam's fate seems exceptionally cruel as he *could* have used his power to get rich by committing robberies, but chose not to.

In a more positive story, *ST* 69's "Rocket Ship X-200," drawn by Don Heck, Charlie Brewster is an old war horse who ekes out a living flying his slow, old-fashioned spaceship and taking on cargo and passengers. More modern spaceships can do in a few hours what it takes Charlie days to do, so he does little business. Charlie has become an object of pity and contempt. But one day, out in space, he sees an armada of warships approaching the Earth. Modern-day spacecraft go too fast to see these ships, but they are very clear to Charlie, who immediately contacts the Earth and warns the authorities. Charlie returns to Earth to learn that he is now a hero who saved the world from conquest, and he will be the head of a new fleet of slower ships that will ensure that the Earth is never unprepared again.

In *ST* 84's "The Wonder of the Ages! Magneto!" (Kirby-Ayers), an eight-foot misfit named Hunk is taken into the city by a would-be promoter who thinks they can both make a killing in the world of sports. Despite his size and strength, Hunk proves inept at basketball, baseball, boxing and just about everything else. Left on his own, he gets a job in a freak show, but is fired when he nearly kills a man who taunts him.

He volunteers for a space mission, but radiation turns him into a human magnet, able to both draw and repel whatever he wants. Angered over his former mistreatment, he turns to crime and destruction. His former promoter and the authorities lure him into another rocketship complete with enough food for months, in the hopes he will come to a world that will accept him. Hunk cries tears of joy, but in reality this would probably only make him feel like his entire world had abandoned him!

Marvel Comics had a completely different style from DC, which at least appeared to be much more polished in its presentation. Marvel also had a hyperbolic approach and one sensed a tongue-in-cheek inclination in its narration. "Could you prove that this didn't happen?" or words to that effect, appear at the end of several stories. All of their monster stories have some kind of extra element that makes them a little different. Rising up from the Earth in *ST* 95, "The Two-Headed Thing" can take on the shape of any flora or fauna. It inadvertently frees a Death Row convict and temporarily takes over *his* form. In *ST* 82 "It," created by a scientist wanting revenge, may look monstrous but actually has a conscience and compassion that his creator completely lacks.

By this time, Marvel had started publishing their soon-to-be-famous superhero titles such as *Fantastic Four* and *Spider-Man*, so some of the credits, especially for "Stan Lee and Steve Ditko," are prominently displayed on the cover and inside pages. Beginning with issue 101, *Strange Tales* became a superhero title featuring the adventures of the fiery, high-flying Human Torch of the Fantastic Four.

Other notable stories include:

- "Next Stop—Mars" (68): A man whose life is saved by a very short friend repays a debt by designing a spaceship that only the diminutive fellow can fly.
- "I Was in the Clutches of the Living Shadow" (79): Aliens bent on conquest turn into dark elastic beings that can literally hide in the shadows of Earthlings.
- "Orrgo, the Unconquerable" (90): An alien hypnotizes the entire human race to make them easy for conquest, but he is defeated by an angry gorilla whose trainer has neglected to feed him.
- "Somewhere Sits a Lama" (92): A man enters a lamasery in order to learn the secret of eternal life—and does learn it, to his eternal regret.
- "Earth Will Be Lost Tonight" (93): A highly successful pop singer is really an alien whose latest record will send out waves to hypnotize and enslave the populace.
- "The Imitation Man" (100): A dictator orders a scientist to use his machine to make a perfect duplicate of him as a decoy for assassins. But the duplicate is *too* perfect and wants to take over.

Tales to Astonish

Tales to Astonish debuted in 1959. In "I Was Captured by the Creature from Krogarr" (Kirby-Ayers) in *Astonish* 25, lazy and scatterbrained Joe Hanson discovers as he watches TV that a grotesque alien being is watching *him* from inside the TV screen. The alien tells Joe how to fix the TV so that he (the alien) can journey from his planet, Krogarr, to Earth and do things that will benefit mankind. Unfortunately, after the alien emerges from the TV set, he grabs Joe and takes him back to Krogarr as part of a plan to conquer the Earth. This unnamed alien wants to show his superiors that his teleportation device works by presenting them with a human. Joe is horrified to learn that if the plan is approved, thousands of aliens will emerge from TV sets to attack the residents of Earth. But just as the alien's superiors are about to arrive, Joe suddenly vanishes from the otherwordly chamber. His superiors think the alien was lying to them, and they blast him out of existence. Back in his living room, Joe realizes that he was swept back to Earth instantly because he forgot to pay the electric bill, thereby saving the Earth when the power suddenly cut off!

"The Man Who Blew Up the Earth" (Kirby-Ayers) in *Tales to Astonish* 29 presents the sad case of Elias Cragston, a genius who happens to be quite ugly and has been made fun of all of his life. When he tells a pretty co-worker that he's in love with her, she haughtily compares him to Quasimodo. (Tactfulness is not her strong suit.) This drives Elias over the edge and he takes off into outer space tugging a devasting bomb with which he intends to blow up the entire planet. One might stop feeling sorry for Elias at this point—surely not everyone was cruel to him, and there are other ugly and disfigured people in the world, not to mention children—but you still pity him a bit when he realizes that he is too far out in space for gravity to pull the bomb towards Earth, and the only one who is blown to bits is Elias. The uncredited scripter tries to put a positive slant on the story by suggesting that the explosion out in space and the resulting light show is a thing of beauty.

As noted, Marvel comics during this period frequently made Russians, Communists and "Commie sympathizers" the villains. The ultimate anti–Red story is probably "The Pretender" in *Tales to Astonish* 31: A man discovers that an extraterrestrial bent on conquest has landed on Earth and disguised himself as a human being. Finding a picture of what the alien now looks like, he thinks, "It is too late to save mankind. Alas it is *much* too late"—as he looks at a photo of Nikita Khrushchev!

Like *Strange Tales* and every other Marvel mag, *Tales to Astonish* is given to hyperbole, boasting on the cover of *Astonish* 34 that the lead story, "Monster at My Window," would become a certified classic. It is just a typical Marvel fantasy story with an unconvincing twist at the end: A science fiction writer is pursued by an alien who insists that he present only *friendly* extraterrestrials in his stories so that humankind will be lulled into a false sense of security before his people invade. The writer turns out to be an equally hideous alien, whose planet is also bent on conquest, and the two creatures battle it out on the roof, the winner undisclosed at the end.

With the very next issue, *Tales to Astonish* began presenting the adventures of the diminutive Ant-Man (later Giant-Man).

Tales of Suspense

Tales of Suspense first appeared in 1959. It presents stories in several genres, sci-fi–fantasy, mild horror, ghost stories and more or less straight suspense stories with climactic twists. In "I Dared Explore the Unknown Emptiness," drawn by Don Heck, in *Suspense* 1, Colonel Frank Stevens of the U.S. Air Force leads a group of men into outer space to seek a planet for the Earth's expanding population. On one world, they find dinosaur-like monsters; on another, hostile men of metal; then a world completely devoid of oxygen; then another world that is *alive* and whose surface would completely absorb anything that landed on it. They finally locate the perfect planet only to find that *its* inhabitants are also facing a population crisis. Returning to Earth, Stevens does not deem their mission a failure: "The Earth is meant for us," he says; it is "a garden of Eden," and Mankind will have to stop using up all of its resources so quickly. An early message of conservation.

"Beware of the Robots" in *Tales of Suspense* 4, drawn by Al Williamson, looks at both sides of the debate over robots. When Joe Hughes loses his job on an assembly line because robots have taken over, he decides to fight back by writing an article that explores the negative affect this has had on so many now-unemployed workers. His article is only the first of many, leading to a career as a journalist, author and lecturer. After preaching against robots for months, he does a complete about-face: He realizes that if he hadn't been fired, he would still be on the assembly line and would never have developed his writing ability and had his new career and all of its rewards, including a World Literature Award. He argues that robots will free Mankind from drudgery.

Joe's argument is ludicrous. There's no reason why working on an assembly line or any other mundane job would have prevented him from desiring a career as a writer; in fact, the dull job might have inspired him to write and get *off* the assembly line. An even greater argument is that Joe is fortunate enough to have talent, something which is not true of all the other fired factory workers.

Considering the controversy that surrounded the comic book industry in the early '50s due to the graphic nature of horror and crime comics, it is surprising to see "Sazzik the Sorcerer," drawn by Kirby and Ayers, in *Tales of Suspense* 32. The protagonist is Boris Grumm, a television producer whose programs are protested due to their violent and disturbing content. (TV's *The Untouchables* was coming under fire for just that reason around this time.) The narration describes Grumm as "unscrupulous," and he is depicted as being concerned only with dollars and to hell with the complaining members of civic groups. These groups blame Grumm's programs for the crime on the streets just as authorities unfairly blamed comic books for juvenile delinquency. (That it might be considered unjust and unreasonable to blame a TV show for a rising crime rate is never brought up.) The story introduces a fantastic element after Grumm is told by the network that his shows have been canceled, and he decides to go out with one last, profitable burst of glory. Looking for the most disturbing program he can find, he focuses on the supernatural and makes the stories on the show as gruesome as possible, even disturbing his cameramen. (Nothing graphic is ever shown in the story, however.) Then Grumm runs afoul of an ancient sorcerer whom he inadvertently summons, and Grumm is never seen again. "No one will ever miss him," says a crew member.

Gigantism was always a popular theme in sci-fi comics—along with people shrinking to microscopic size—and "The Coming of the Giants," drawn by Don Heck, in *TOS* 34 is one of the best stories with this premise. A humongous spaceship lands on Earth and out from it emerge extraterrestrials who are so huge that all of Manhattan seems like a matchbox city in comparison. A rocket fired at one of the aliens proves to be no more annoying than a mosquito. These beings completely overlook the human race and can find no signs of intelligent life on the planet. Eventually they leave after deciding that Earth is completely beneath their notice. This is humbling to those Earthmen who thought they would undoubtedly be superior to everyone else in the universe.

Tales of Suspense was taken over by the adventures of superhero Iron Man, who made his debut in issue 39.

Stan Lee did many but not all of the scripts for the series, with art by Steve Ditko, Paul Reinman, and others. Other notable tales:

- "I Fought the Tyrannosaurus" (5): A man brings a dinosaur egg back to a native village and unleashes a terror that he feels he alone must destroy.
- "Nothing Can Save Us" (29): Members of a space expedition want to destroy a fire-breathing dragon on an alien planet. But the creature saves *them* from an oncoming meteor with his fiery breath.
- "Meet Mr. Meek, the Most Dangerous Man in the World" (36): A man develops the Midas Touch but it backfires when everything he touches, including food and people, turn to solid gold, and anyone who simply touches these objects also turns to gold, creating a city-wide panic.
- "Haag, Hunter of Helpless Humans" (37): An extraterrestrial hunter uses a teleportation beam to snatch people right off the streets until an Earth hunter comes up with a scheme to trap the over-confident alien.

Amazing Adventures

Amazing Adventures debuted in 1961. It underwent a metamorphosis to *Amazing Adult Fantasy* with the seventh issue and billed itself as the "magazine that respects your intelligence." Supposedly this meant that the fantasy–sci-fi comic would stay away from the typical giant-rampaging-monster stories that ran in it and other Atlas-Marvel magazines. But then the cover story for *AAF* 9 is entitled "The Terror of Tim Boo Ba." Tim Boo Ba does not turn out to be an Asian dragon or alien monstrosity but is rather the malevolent ruler of a microscopic kingdom located on a kid's scale model planet—a tiny Attila the Hun wiped out along with everyone else in his kingdom by a drop of water. The trouble with this and most of the *AAF* stories is that they are terribly trite, with predictable—or just childish and over-familiar—wind-ups. Stan Lee did most of the scripts while Steve Ditko handled the art chores. Simplicity in both scripting and penciling are the rule of the day, as the *AAF* stories won't tax anyone's brain. In one tale, space invaders decide to transform into what they think is Earth's dominant creature, the better to conquer us, only they turn into flies and in the final panel are swatted. A couple of issues later, other space invaders plan to dominate mankind by turning into television sets (so they can influence our thinking). It's hard to believe that even kid readers didn't moan when they came to the endings of such stories.

Occasionally one of these *Twilight Zone* rejects would have some resonance, however, such as "Where Walks the Ghost" in *AAF* 11. In this Civil War story, a mother and father, fearing their son is dead, wait for him to come home after the fighting ends. When he does return and can't see them, it turns out that the *parents* are the ones who are dead, killed by artillery shelling. The story taps into the poignant connection between parent and child. Many years later, this twist ending—somebody unexpectedly turns out to be dead—is still being used in one form or another in major motion pictures. "The Man in the Sky" in *AAF* 14 prefigures the entire X-Men phenomenon in the story of a young man with special powers, including the ability to fly. He is warned telekinetically that he is a mutant and the world isn't ready for him.

AAF 15 introduced Spider-Man to the world and the rest is history.

PART THREE

The Bronze Age

15

Charlton; DC

Charlton

Doomsday + 1

Doomsday + 1 debuted in 1975. Besieged on all sides, General Rykos of a banana republic decides to fire two ICBMs, one at Moscow and one at New York. Blaming each other, the American and Russian leaders quickly retaliate and soon every major city in the world is utterly decimated. In space, Captain Boyd Ellis of the U.S. Air Force is on a mission with his girlfriend, NASA scientist Jill Malden, and Japanese lady physicist Ikei Yashida, who is also attracted to Boyd. Aware of what has happened, they decide to stay in orbit until their food supply runs out. Electing to come down in Greenland because there is less radioactivity there, they find a thawed-out woolly mammoth and a caveman named Kuno, who joins the group. They make their way to a village of Eskimos where everyone is dead, then set sail. They are shocked that a fighter jet starts firing upon them.

At a Canadian air base, they are attacked by hordes of robotic troops. Captured, Boyd is taken to a stronghold where he faces a giant computer. He also meets a scientist and cyborg named Dr. Vladislav Yomorov who suffered "severe atomic burns." Yomorov welcomed the destruction and is planning to take over what little is left of the world with his robots. Boyd's three companions fly after him to Northern Russia, where Kuno throws Yomorov off a balcony (he survives). When Boyd mentions marriage to Jill, she suggests that things have changed and they should wait—and gives Kuno a significant look.

In *Doomsday* 3, our heroes contend with a group of cyborg-like aliens who call themselves the Peacekeepers. They have decided that Earth is a dangerous, war-like world that needs to be destroyed. Ironically, it is the bestial but rather kind-hearted Kuno who convinces them otherwise and they vow not to return for 100 years. In *Doomsday* 4, the group encounter two warring factions of an undersea society: the amphibians, who used to live in the Hidden Empire, and the gill-men, egg-laying creatures created by the amphibians but who have reproduced quickly and taken over their city. In *Doomsday* 5, the group discovers two more survivors at an Air

Charlton's *Doomsday + 1* is an interesting series that wasn't given enough time to build a readership.

Force base, but these men are military renegades who shot their commanding officers. The rogues try to make time with the ladies and attempt to kill Boyd and Kuno. When our heroes escape, one of these Neanderthals tries to send a missile after them but he only succeeds in blowing up the whole base and destroying himself and his creepy buddy.

In the sixth and last all-new issue of *Doomsday + 1*, the group encounters an assemblage of beings from a parallel Earth, a world that seems like a paradise full of beautiful people. But then Boyd and the others realize that these "beautiful people" have enslaved a race from yet another dimension. The group pretends to want to stay in this dimension, but plot to escape in one of their ships and make their way back to the real Earth.

Doomsday + 1 writer Joe Gill came up with some interesting scripts, but he also boxed himself into a corner. Since almost everyone on Earth is dead, he is forced to come up with menaces from under the ocean or on alternate Earths; eventually this gimmick might have worn thin. Although judging from the first couple of issues, no one would have imagined that John Byrne would eventually emerge as a super-star artist (and writer); his work gets better with each issue, although it doesn't compare to what he would do later.

Boyd Ellis and his companions later appeared in two black-and-white issues of *Charlton Bullseye*, written and drawn by Byrne. In this, the group interacts with new characters and a horde of dinosaurs, and it seems as if an attempt is being made to turn them into costumed heroes. In 1986, the original series was reprinted by Fantagraphics as *The Doomsday Squad*, probably due to Byrne's fame.

Space: 1999

Charlton's adaptation of the TV show *Space: 1999* debuted in 1975. In the first issue, as in the TV series, the residents of Alpha, a scientific base on the moon, find themselves cut off from Earth when a magnetic explosion of atomic wastes sends the moon spiraling out of the solar system. Searching for a suitable home, the crew—led by Commander John Koenig and chief science officer Helena Carter—land on a world called Pearl. The jabbering residents seem afraid of them, but much more formidable are gigantic, tentacled slugs, one of which carries off Helena. Descending into caverns below the planet's surface, they discover a sleek, modern city—and also the fact that the slugs are actually friendly. Unfortunately, conditions on the surface make it a poor prospect for a new home for Alpha's 311 crew members.

Space: 1999 2 has an excellent tale wherein Koenig and a hulking alien who may or may not be friendly, are temporarily stranded on a planet full of dangerous and hungry creatures. The two eventually work together to stay alive until they can be rescued. Equally good is *Space* 3, in which Koenig, Carter and Prof. Bergman are imprisoned in a spaceship that is an interplanetary zoo. As the ship heads towards the home planet of their captors, the other "specimens"—a wide variety of creatures, mostly non-humanoid—try to figure out how to escape and who their keepers really are.

In *Space* 4, the Alpha crew discovers a "Jekyll and Hyde" planet where the differing influences of dual suns cause severe psychological changes in the people, who are completely unaware that this generally peaceful race periodically converts into vicious barbarians. The fifth issue employs the notion (previously used in *Star Trek* and elsewhere) that the legendary Gods of Mount Olympus are actually aliens who settled on Earth for a spell and then went back into space. The Alpha crew encounters a race, modeled on Greek culture, who have to deal with another race of giants, including cyclopes and ancient "gods" such as Zeus. These giant gods turn out to be like children, and the Alpha crew make friends with them before departing.

Space: 1999 6 features Commander Koenig in an intense and harrowing survival story: After his ship is smashed by an explosive bolt from an ancient weapon, he has to stay alive in airless space without a helmet. He manages to get a helmet and make his way back to the remains of his ship, where he is eventually rescued. *Space* 7, the final issue, has two stories, the first of which has to do with Maya, a woman who can morph into any animal. After her villainous father dies, she goes off with the Alpha crew to begin a new life. In the second story, Maya is of great assistance in rescuing Koenig and Carter after they are captured by savage aliens who hold them hostage.

Nicola Cuti did all the scripts for the first five issues, with John Byrne scripting for *Space: 1999* 6. Joe Staton did the art for the first two issues, and it is effective in its cartoonish way. Byrne drew issues 3 to 6 and some of his work is quite good, if uneven; he did an especially notable job with the lay-out and pencils for *Space* 6, possibly because his own tense script inspired him. The seventh issue is written by Michael Pellowski and drawn by Pat Boyette. Boyette also did the cover painting for *Space* 7. Generally, the actors who play the characters on the TV series—Martin Landau, Barbara Bain, and Barry Morse—are realistically depicted in the comic. Charlton also did a magazine version of *Space: 1999* which contains articles as well as stories. It lasted slightly longer than the comic book.

The Six Million Dollar Man

Charlton got the rights to the popular TV series *The Six Million Dollar Man* in 1976. The premise of the show has test pilot Colonel Steve Austin crack up his plane and sustain such devastating injuries that the only way to keep him alive is to make him part-cyborg. His artificial legs can run extremely fast, his one artificial eye can see vast distances, and he is incredibly strong. This makes him a useful agent for the Office of Strategic Information (O.S.I.). In *The Six Million Dollar Man* issue 1, Austin's adversaries are Red Chinese who have a big robot as well as missiles aimed at the U.S. In the second issue, a miniature replica of Austin almost functions as a voodoo doll, enabling him to see whatever the "doll" sees but also making him vulnerable to its manipulation. An excellent story in *SMDM* 4 has Austin traveling through the time barrier to about a day before his accident. He gets across the country to his base on time, but is stopped by his liaison from telling his "past" self about what is going to happen: There is a danger that preventing the accident might play havoc with the time stream (not to mention that the Air Force wants to protect its six-million-dollar investment). Future-Austin is sent back to his own time period.

In *SMDM* 5, a man can steal things by entering a parallel dimension, which makes him merely a ghostly image in ours (somewhat similar to the Shadow-Thief in *Hawkman*). Austin gets his very own Eurasian "Dragon Lady" in the person of Simone Lee, who from her private island runs Group IV, a spy outfit that first tries to sabotage a U.S. surveillance satellite, and then use it for its own purposes (*SMDM* 6). In one of the best stories in the series, Austin has to test two jet fighters from competing companies and say which one he thinks is superior. In the process, he gets caught up in a whirlwind of industrial espionage, attempted murder and international skullduggery (8). In the ninth and final issue, Austin faces two deadly wanted criminals—one male, one female—who have been outfitted with bionic arms and legs.

The Six Million Dollar Man is arguably much more entertaining than the TV series, the comic medium able to take advantage of the premise in a way that television at the time could not. The early issues have some effective art by Joe Staton; Pat Boyette did the final issues. Scripts are mostly by Joe Gill, with Nicola Cuti also contributing a couple of stories. Austin is shown running at super-speed—very briefly—in only one issue, perhaps because superhero The Flash already had that particular power sewn up in the comics.

DC

Hercules Unbound

Hercules Unbound debuted in 1975. It is set in the weeks immediately following World War III, which was started, it is inferred, by Ares, the God of War. Young Kevin is in Rome as bombs explode, but manages to make his way to a bomb shelter; his brother and father aren't as lucky. Two weeks later, Kevin and other survivors emerge to discover a world in ruins and crazed, irradiated humans running about like maniacs in search of food. Kevin sets sail with his Siberian husky Basil, and they come across an island where Hercules has been imprisoned by his half-brother Ares for a thousand years (Ares hates Hercules because the latter has always been Zeus' favorite). The demigod is now free of his chains, and he and Kevin—who turns out to be blind—fight off monsters that surround the island. Back in Paris, they come across a pack of normal humans, including model Jennifer Monroe, David Rigg and a middle-aged British gent named Simon St. Charles, all of whom seem strangely unaffected by the disaster. Hercules is a bit suspicious of Kevin, who seems pretty spry for someone who's blind.

In *Hercules Unbound* 2 and 3, Ares unleashes Lord Cerebus, a bald Nubian, and his two-headed Hell Hounds. After a vivid battle between Hercules and Lord Cerebus, Lord Cerebus runs off with Jennifer. Herc and Kevin are forced to descend into Hades—which they do with incredible if not ludicrous ease—to rescue her. Next the group encounters Hunter Blood, a nutty super-villain mutant type with death-beam eyes. Most of the humans in London have been vaporized and the city is occupied by intelligent animals created by a chemical unleashed during the nuclear blast. The best thing in the story is when Hunter Blood uses his eye beams to shatter Big Ben and Hercules catches half the building in his hands. But the brave dog Basil is killed by falling debris. However, the animal is resurrected by, of all people, Ares, after his half-brother Hercules defeats him in battle (*HU* 6).

With a chastened Ares more or less out of the picture after six issues, new antagonists had to be created for Hercules. (In truth, all Ares had really done was strut around hoping for Total Blackness.) The Loch Ness Monster turns out to be the gigantic Titan Oceanus in *HU* 7. The next two issues have Hercules and his friends caught in a war fought by robots and simulacrums conjured by an elderly paralyzed woman who, it turns out, inadvertently started World War III in the first place.

Hercules is given a stylish uniform in *HU* 11, but he doesn't get to wear it for long, as the next issue is the last one—the series was selling poorly. As the editors had had some warning of this, a few loose ends are cleared up in the final two issues. Hercules learns that, years before, Zeus had forced the evil side of the gods' natures out of their bodies, but this evil took on a life of its own and formed the Anti-Gods. Zeus managed to imprison them, but needed Hercules' strength to keep them from escaping. Hence it was Zeus who had directed Ares to bind his brother on the island beneath which the Anti-Gods were kept captive. Hercules' constant struggle with his chains had eventually effected his release, and hence the escape of the Anti-Gods. Naturally Hercules feels betrayed by this, as he feels he could have helped against the Anti-Gods if he'd known the truth.

The Anti-Ares, a giant, attacks Hercules and kills Jennifer in *HU* 11. Hercules learns that young Kevin had actually been destroyed by the Anti-Ares in the *first* issue; Kevin was only a shell inside which the Anti-Ares was resting, gathering his strength for the inevitable confrontation. When he and the other Anti-Gods attack Mount Olympus, Hercules saves the day, but in the end decides he wants to be among humans, not gods. Zeus brings Jennifer back to life. At the end of *HU* 12, the two are together, frolicking with Basil, and poor Kevin is just sort of forgotten. True, the boy was never *really* Kevin, just his personality and memories, used by the Anti-Ares, but as the blind boy was plucky and likable, his "death" was still a bit of a shock.

Gerry Conway wrote the first six issues of the series, with David Michelinie providing scripts for issues 7, 8 and 9. Cary Bates took over with *HU* 10, and while that was a forgettable issue, Bates introduced some good ideas with the final two issues and provided a fairly neat wind-up for the series. The excellent art for the first six issues was contributed by José L. García-López and Wally Wood. Walt Simonson was the penciler for the remainder of the series, first inked by Wood—which provides some visual continuity—then by Bob Layton, which is less felicitous. He then did his own inks, achieving the more recognizable style—half-crude, half-dynamic—that we associate with the artist. The comic's covers were uniformly poor, and couldn't have helped sales. While the mixture of apocalyptic future with Old World mythology did not always jell, *Hercules Unbound* had a lot of potential, which it didn't quite realize until the very end of its run.

Star Hunters

The Star Hunters, created by David Michelinie, first appeared in *DC Super-Stars* 16 in 1977. This story introduces Irish soldier of fortune Donovan Flint, who is in the solid tradition of devil-may-care swashbuckling heroes. Flint is a loner, but he is forced to join a group by a man named Farrell who works for the dominant Corporation that rules Earth in this future society. Flint doesn't like taking orders, but he's forced to do so when he learns he has been infected with a disease that will kill him in 24 hours if he remains on Earth. Away from Earth, he will be all right, and when he completes his mission—to find where a certain artifact comes from—he will be cured and can return to Earth. The others on the team have also been infected: leader Darcy Vale; mountainous Jake Hammersmith; Bruce Sellers, a surgeon and medical doctor; Minday Yano, a computer and electronics specialist, and the African American Dr. McGavin. Farrell reports to a Chairman, who is also known as Charlie Bane, a shy man whom Darcy dates for career reasons but doesn't like. The team traveling in their special spaceship is unaware of the real reason for their journey, as are the comic book's readers. The art for this issue is by Don Newton and Bob Layton, with a script by Michelinie.

The story continues in *Star Hunters* 1, which has the same creative team. Michelinie did all the scripts for the short-lived series; Larry Hama and Mike Nasser did the pencils for *SH* 2 and 3 and Rich Buckler the art for the later issues, although neither Bob Layton nor Tom Sutton are the best inkers for him. Buckler played around with panel shapes as if he were making a jigsaw puzzle, a style that really did nothing for the art.

In their ship, the *Sunrider*, the motley group goes to the asteroid Merdd, where the Earth and other planets dump all of their waste. They find the artifact they seek and also encounter unpleasant "junkmen," their squirmy, slug-like "watchdogs" and some bizarre mutations. An energy drain on their ship prompts the crew to land on the planet Darkever to investigate in *SH* 2 and 3; there they discover a group of "Annihilators" who have a weapon with which they plan to decimate the Earth. After this group is dispatched, the *Sunrider* explodes and Donovan Flint dies—or at least his body does, for a time.

A cosmic entity called … the Entity … has saved and healed Flint and sends him on a new mission, which means he must go back to Earth. Darcy Vale is overruled and the whole group starts back to their home planet in the Annihilators' ship, rechristened *Sunrider II*, which happens to have a talking computer named Ozzie. Darcy comes over to Flint's side when she discovers that the Corporation's Charlie Bane was using her instead of the other way around. Before reaching Earth, they take out the asteroid of Sonora, which helps the Corporation communicate with its far-flung outposts. Charlie Bane has an unpleasant encounter with his true master, the creepy Vilislith, Prince of Bones, of the Blood Legion, who are uneasy allies of the Corporation (*SH* 4–5).

SH 6 is a rousing issue in which Flint and Dr. Sellers are captured by the Corporation and taken to a prison asteroid called Avernus. A prisoner named Sturm seems to have influence over everyone else, including the prison officials. Flint tries to team up with Sturm so that there can be a mass break-out while *Sunrider II* bombards the asteroid as a diversion. Sturm initially agrees, but then betrays Flint. Flint and his allies still manage to take over Avernus in *SH* 7, where Flint tells the assemblage that the Entity that saved him has made him an agent for gods who are engaging in a cosmic war of good vs. evil. If the Corporation and Blood Legion aren't defeated, it will result in a dismal fate for all mankind.

The Star Hunters and the prison escapees arrive on Earth only to discover that the Corporation is prepared for them and has amassed a huge force of ships. Although Flint tells Dr. McGavin to stay out of the conflict because he is not a trained fighter, the latter is so anxious to see his family again that he flies off in a ship and is almost immediately destroyed. Flint winds up crash-landing on Earth, where the infection he was given will kill him within a number of hours. This final issue leaves Flint vowing to get back out into space while a blurb announces that the next issue—which never materialized—will detail the final battle between the Corporation and the Star Hunters.

Star Hunters was an interesting series even if it traded on over-familiar elements: the Errol Flynn–like hero, the Marvel Comics–like Cosmic Entity and so on. The characters are a bit underdeveloped as well, and the art is very uneven. In any case, the series was a victim of what became known as the "DC Implosion": DC unleashed a great number of new titles and had to cancel most of them due to disappointing sales.

Time Warp

Time Warp, edited by Jack C. Harris, made its debut in 1979. From the first issue it was clear that the comic would have a darker approach than DC's previous science fiction series. In "If the World Had to End Twice" (O'Neill-Buckler), Commander Jake Saturn, an artist, uses devastating laser beams to wipe out billions of Earth inhabitants, along with a race of invaders, just to keep humans from becoming slaves. Sarah, the woman who loves him, thinks he's insane, even evil, but "you're all I have." They live on a satellite along with young Billy, whose parents were killed by

Jake when he took over the satellite so he could embark on his monstrous scheme—Billy was too young at the time to know what happened. A fourth resident is a baby girl born to Sarah and Jake, who was not pleased by the pregnancy. After the laser beams wiped out civilization, the Earth became a frozen wasteland. Fifteen years go by and Jake realizes that the satellite has fallen out of orbit and is going to crash. He sends Billy and his daughter to Earth after using those same lasers to clear a designated area of ice. Sarah and Jake die when the satellite explodes. On Earth, Billy notices that the lasers have inadvertently carved a "self-portrait" of Jake into the rock. Denny O'Neil's story certainly has provocative elements, but it doesn't do that much with them.

"Mating Game" (Fleischer-Ditko) is a sci-fi–horror story in which a woman meets a handsome and chivalrous fellow who takes her and her friends back to his home planet, where he reveals that he and *his* friends are actually giant shape-shifting spiders, "black widowers" who bear the young on their planet after mating with and killing the females. In "The Monsters" (Fleischer-Grandenetti), Michael Denton travels to a distant planet with his wife Gloria and their friend Les Harding to search for Michael's brother Steven, who never came back from an expedition. Michael doesn't know that Gloria and Les are in love and plotting to murder him during the trip. Michael encounters and kills a monstrous creature that he later realizes is his brother, transformed by foodstuffs that Michael himself has also eaten, causing his own hideous transformation. Les is killed. Gloria, who has also transformed, waits with her husband for rescue, although it is clear they will be instantly destroyed by whoever finds them.

The grimness continues in *Time Warp* 2. In "Return to the Stars" (Martin Pasko-Howard Chaykin), Captain Waters presides over the crew in the first manned faster-then-light starship. Waters and his crew encounter hideous and malevolent aliens who take them captive and try to wrest the location of Earth from their brains, resulting in the deaths of each crew member. They are a bit more careful probing Waters, with the result that he survives but feigns amnesia. He manages to get to his ship, planning to stay far away from Earth so the aliens can't follow, but discovers the ship is automatically heading back to his home planet. Once he is back on Earth, he is desperate to warn everyone about the aliens. He races to his base where people seem to think he's an imposter. He discovers to his horror that he skipped backwards in time, and that "he" is even now about to take off in his spaceship. No wonder no one believes his story! This is a very successful piece with somewhat crude but effective artwork by Chaykin.

In "The Saviors" (DeMatteis-Kane), a male and a female astronaut, their bodies ravaged by radiation, are rescued by aliens who promise they can save them by transferring their minds into "forms grown in our body banks." At first the two humans are thrilled by the prospect, but they wind up not in the bodies of the beautiful humanoids they *think* have been speaking to them, but in those of the true masters, tentacled blob-like horrors with reddish mottled skin. In the vaguely homoerotic "Metal" by Jack C. Harris, drawn by Joe Orlando, a man on a lonely outpost builds a robot to keep him company, and continuously talks about how wonderful women are, but the "male" robot obliterates an approaching ship that might have rescued the protagonist out of apparent jealousy. "I-want-you-to-stay-here-and-make-me-into-woman," says the robot as it dies.

In *Time Warp* 3, Denny O'Neil's "Rites of Spring" concerns a post-apocalyptic world where there are supposedly no men, and women congregate in underground shelters where they learn to fire weapons against the giant slug-like monsters that thrive above ground. One young woman goes to the surface where she saves a fellow who has been snared by one of the slugs—then kills *him,* as she has been told all her life that men are the enemy. The very minor tale is enlivened by attractive art by Dick Giordano.

"Pen Pal" (Bob Haney-Fred Carrillo) in *TW* 4 is the story of Susan Hoskins, a technician at a satellite control station on Earth in the near-future. She has become friends with Jon, a man who works on a botanical satellite up on orbit around the planet. Like old-fashioned pen pals who have never met, the two exchange radio greetings and photographs. Although everyone considers Susan to be plain, herself included, Jon is quite handsome and claims to like her looks. When Susan is plagued by terrible dreams, her psychiatrist tells her she *must* do everything she can to meet Jon face to face. Susan schemes to get up to the satellite to meet her beloved, and discovers that Jon is actually a weird-looking alien creature—a beaked green face with a head covered with circular ridges, a body with slithering tendrils—who has cloned Susan through a lock of her hair. Utterly disgusted by both the alien and the clone, Jon's "lover," she shoots the clone. Jon then tells her that she has two options: go to jail for murder (killing a clone is a capital crime) or stay forever on the satellite with him. Bob Haney's story has little sympathy for Susan, who has poor judgment but isn't necessarily evil. Although Susan is supposed to be unattractive (part of the reason for her desperation), Fred Carrillo draws her as a rather pretty woman.

After five issues, *Time Warp* was replaced by the revival of *Mystery in Space*, with DC hoping that using the name of a long-running comic might attract more readers. While *Time Warp* was not an especially notable series, it featured a few other decent stories:

- "Rescue" (1): An astronaut who always complains about the figurative "bugs" in his ship comes afoul of aliens who see him and his companions as literal bugs.
- "I, The Creature" (4): Rivals search for the futuristic equivalent of the Abominable Snowman but one of them winds up having *too* close an encounter with a Yeti.
- "Asteroid Treachery" (4): Former lovers turned rivals encounter chameleon-like aliens who can look like anyone or anything. The ex-lovers are undone by their mistrust of one another.

- "Until I Find a Way in Time" (5): A scheming man travels back to the 19th century with a plan to get rich quick, using industrial diamonds from Mars, but doesn't reckon with the Martian flu.

Mystery in Space

DC Comics came out with a revival of *Mystery in Space* in 1980, edited by Len Wein. The numbering continued where it left off at 111. In issue 112's "Howl" (DeMatteis-Weiss-Austin), a spaceship's crew wonders if they will get any action in the latest interplanetary war. They come across an escape pod from another ship that was obliterated by the enemy; inside is a beautiful woman who fascinates the males on the ship. She turns out to be a vampire seeking blood. The story seems influenced by the 1966 sci-fi film *Queen of Blood*.

"Trouble in Paradise" (Kashdan-Golden-Wiacek) has three computer specialists traveling to a distant planet widely known as a utopia. They find that they only have to do one hour's work a day, and the rest is fun time. But when they want to return home to see friends and family, they are refused—why would they want to leave this paradise? It develops that organic brains in the humanoids on this planet have all been replaced with computerized circuits, and the initial horror felt by the newcomers is changed to joy once the surgery is completed. This is an interesting premise but it doesn't really go anywhere. "Ark" (*MIS* 117) is a credible action tale in which a ship transporting a variety of animals is hit by a meteor. The sole human occupant discovers that, due to a throat injury, the computer no longer recognizes him and sees him as an intruder. What happens afterward is a desperate fight for survival. This has a good script by Mike W. Barr, but the art by George Tuska and Bob Wiacek is mediocre.

Some of the *Mysteries in Space* stories are reminiscent of the brief, poorly developed tales that filled Atlas comics in the Golden Age and Charlton comics in the Silver Age. *MIS* 117 contains stories that seem like bad jokes. Aliens seek out a representative of Earth's dominant lifeform and just happen to pick a Death Row inmate. An emissary to another world is pushed aside in favor of his secretary, because the planet is home to intelligent viruses and the secretary has a cold! Arnold Drake and Brian Bolland's "Certified Safe" is a slightly more interesting tale about a space hero and a politician who come to the same bad end, but even this is a forgettable black comedy.

"Cold Hands, Warm Hearts" (DeMatteis-Craig) in *MIS* 116 posits a future world where robots, tired of doing all the work of the world, take off for a planet of their own. Any human who sets foot on their world will be killed. When one man wants to enlist their aid against alien invaders, he arrives there posing as a robot, but eventually the inhabitants see through his disguise. When he implores the leader for help, he is told why they hate humans. Taking off her face plate, the leader reveals that she—and all the other robots—were once human beings, dissidents, undesirables, turned into mindless servants who eventually rebelled. But the man disguised as a robot has a secret as well: He is actually one of the invading aliens and he is there to destroy the entire planet, which he does.

MIS 117, the final issue, contains two notable stories. In "Dreamboat" (Jones-Veitch-Yeates), a nasty character who has fallen on hard times robs and murders an alien on a distant world and steals his spaceship. He soon finds himself in a dilemma: He can't repair the malfunctioning drive because he doesn't know the language, and if he signals for rescue, he will undoubtedly be arrested. Then he sees what he assumes is an abandoned ship nearby and gets on board. But he can't find the engine room. After falling asleep, he awakens to discover that the ship seems to be creating itself, and computers and consoles that weren't there before are now part of its design. Hoping to use this ship to go wherever he wants, he destroys the stolen spacecraft—and finds himself in airless space. He didn't realize that one of that alien ship's emergency rescue devices was the ability to create a ship literally out of thin air and imagination.

"Cyborg" (Barr-Tuska-Jensen) is the best story to appear in the series. A ship is buffeted by a meteor shower and is destroyed. The survivors—Kelsey, his wife Sherry, their little boy and Dr. Samuels—are picked up by a ship with a R.P. (Robot Pilot). This R.P. has an unpleasant attitude. The ship is struck by a flying creature and crash-lands on an alien planet. Kelsey is killed and the RP is incapacitated, a problem since he was the only one who could fly the ship and knows exactly where in the universe they are. Dr. Samuels attaches part of Kelsey's dead body to the robot, knowing the robot cannot function unless it has a whole body, a situation that understandably sickens Sherry, until the doctor reminds her they must do it to save her son. There have been many times when a human male has awoken to discover he's been turned into a cyborg—part-mechanical, part-flesh—but this time it's a robot who makes this discovery, and he isn't happy about it. Disdainful of the humans, the cyborg works on the ship. When the flying creature returns and attacks the cyborg, Sherry beats it off. The cyborg returns the favor when the flying creature tries to carry off the humans for food. Did enough of Kelsey's mind and memories remain, or was the cyborg grateful for the help? The science or logic of "Cyborg" may not endure close scrutiny, but the story works on an emotional and dramatic level.

The series employed veteran artists Johnny Craig, Carmine Infantino, George Tuska and Steve Ditko, as well as several newcomers whose work was generally not as distinguished.

G.I. Robot

Writer Robert Kanigher's "G.I. Robot" first appeared in *Star Spangled War Comics* in the Silver Age. It was re-introduced in *Weird War Tales* 101 in 1981. In most of the Silver Age stories, the robot was named Joe and was teamed with a corporal named Mac. This brief new series details the World War II exploits of J.A.K.E.

(Jungle Automatic Killer Experimental). Jake-1 is killed off during an adventure with the Creature Commandos (which was also an adventure of "The War That Time Forgot") in *WWT* 111. Two issues later, he is replaced by JAKE-2, who engages a hulking Japanese samurai robot in battle. When the samurai knocks Jake's block off, the G.I. Robot swings his own head around with the wires still attached to its neck and bashes the samurai to bits!

In *Weird War Tales* 122, JAKE-2 returns to battle another Japanese invention, this time a Sumo robot. Unfortunately, JAKE has no true personality and the series never gathers much momentum despite attempts to make him seem more human and sentient than he initially appears. This results in scenes such as the one in which his injured partner, Sgt. Coker, is taken away; instead of wiping the man from his memory banks as ordered, JAKE dives into the sea so he can follow the ship Coker is on. JAKE also seems to develop feelings for a British princess whom the Nazis try to kidnap, and Coker eventually develops real affection for the robot.

The best JAKE story is the final installment of "The War That Time Forgot" in *WWT* 120: The robot and Coker encounter a giant female ape and attempt a rescue of a platoon of Marines trapped in a cave; JAKE also gets a couple of mechanical pets. This features excellent art by Fred Carrillo.

Camelot 3000

In the year 3000, the Earth is suffering from overcrowding and hunger. Space programs have been eliminated to focus on world problems, so no one is looking to the skies when aliens come to Earth intent on conquest. They make no offers and take no prisoners. A young man named Tom Prentice tries to flee England with his parents, but they are attacked by aliens and his mother and father are killed. Tom hides out inside an archaeological dig in Glastonbury Down where he had worked. Pursued by two aliens through the tunnels under the dig, he comes upon a casket which appears to be the resting place of King Arthur Pendragon of Camelot. Arthur awakes and engages the aliens in combat, which he easily wins. The king then takes Tom to Stonehenge, where he revives the magician Merlin from *his* resting place. Merlin's first task is to retrieve Arthur's sword Excalibur. Then he uses his spells to awaken Arthur's associates, who have been reincarnated.

Thus begins DC Comics' first 12-issue maxi-series, *Camelot 3000*, which made its debut in 1982. The series was written by Mike W. Barr and drawn by Brian Bolland and Bruce D. Patterson. (Dick Giordano and Terry Austin later did the inking.) The first "reincarnate" that Arthur encounters is Queen Guinevere, who is now a military commander, Joan Acton. Jules Futrelle, the wealthiest man in the world (he even lives on his own private asteroid), turns out to be Sir Lancelot, and his asteroid is turned into New Camelot. Guinevere and Lancelot waste little time in renewing their illicit relationship, while Arthur's half-sister, the evil sorceress Morgan Le Fay, schemes—along with her alien allies—from her satellite and watches Arthur and the others with disdain.

Some of the other knights include: Sir Kay, Arthur's foster brother; Sir Percival, who has been turned into one of the hulking Neo-Men (political prisoners transformed into mindless monsters); Lancelot's son Sir Galahad, who is a Japanese warrior; Sir Tristan, who has been reincarnated as a woman and becomes aware of her true identity on her wedding day; and Sir Gawain, a black South African who has to leave his wife and son behind to join up with King Arthur. As the world celebrates the arrival of a great hero in hopes he can rout the extraterrestrial invaders, Earth's leaders, including U.N. security director Jordan Matthew, decide it would be safer for their own plans if Arthur and his "merry knights" were destroyed. However, when aliens—disguised as humans—attack New Camelot, they are easily vanquished by the knights.

Morgan Le Fay tells her ally Jordan that she used her magic to travel far from Earth in search of a power that would make her even more formidable than Merlin. Arriving at the formerly unknown tenth planet in the solar system, she was able to turn the aliens there—the lizard-like creatures attacking Earth—into her allies. Realizing that Tristan is appalled that he is now a woman, Morgan approaches her through a mirror and says she will turn her back into a man if she betrays the knights of the Round Table. Meanwhile, Arthur decides the best way to deal with Guinevere's wandering eye is to marry her again. She is shot during the wedding ceremony, but Lancelot is able to bring her back to life. The would-be assassin is McCallister, the man who almost married Tristan, now turned into a Neo-man who transforms into a horrible monstrosity in an attempt to kill his former fiancée.

Morgan uses her manipulative magic to make Jordan's new secretary a woman named Claire. Claire turns out to be a reincarnation of Tristan's great love, Isolde. They are both still attracted to each other and share a passionate kiss, but Tristan can't make love to her in "his" female body. Therefore Tristan agrees to betray the Round Table. Tom has a crush on Tristan which she rebuffs in no uncertain terms. Guinevere cannot resist Lancelot, especially when she realizes that his extreme love for her brought her back from death, so she goes to him. Arthur finds them in bed together and banishes them both from New Camelot, if only temporarily.

Arthur discovers that a talisman was destroyed, and this allowed Merlin's female nemesis, Nyreve, to reappear and recapture the sorcerer; the king sets out to find which of the knights betrayed the rest of them. It is Sir Kay, who felt sure that Merlin could fight off his attacker and hoped the whole business would snap Arthur out of his funk over his failed marriage. Despite the fact that Kay's foolish act had the best intentions, Arthur is about to put Kay to death when more aliens attack, and Kay winds up dying as he saves his brother's life. When Tom is badly injured, Arthur makes him a knight and sets out to find the Holy Grail to heal him.

While one team goes to find the grail—a sip from it cures Tom of his wounds and radiation sickness—the other goes to rescue Merlin. Another sip from the grail turns Percival back into his normal self but then he vanishes into the ether. Jordan discovers that he is actually Morgan's nephew, Modred—Arthur's son—and he snatches the grail away from Lancelot. He and his aunt destroy all of the Earth's corrupt rulers in a rapid purge and blame Arthur for the murders. Through various means, most of our crew wind up on the tenth planet, Chiron, where Merlin is being held prisoner. Guinevere learns that the aliens are ruled by a monstrous and gargantuan queen mother who hates Morgan for exploiting her children, and she forms an alliance with the Knights.

In their final battle, Arthur destroys Morgan by making the ultimate sacrifice. Modred dies when his armor, which he fashioned from the Holy Grail, comes into contact with Merlin, the son of the Devil. The aliens who allied themselves with Morgan are defeated and the Earth celebrates. Guinevere discovers she is pregnant and hopes that it is Arthur's child; after some hesitation, Lancelot agrees. Tristan rejects Tom—kindly—and goes off with Isolde, finally accepting that she is a *woman* in love with a woman.

Camelot 3000 is a highly entertaining mix of science fiction and fantasy, with a bit of sword-and-sorcery thrown in for good measure. It does become a little *too* absurd at times. While it's true that Tom's life is consistently busy, to put it mildly, once he encounters King Arthur, it's odd that he *never once* thinks of his late parents. The characterization of Jordan Matthews–Modred is odd, with him coming off at times as such a screaming fop that one wonders if he were meant to be perceived as *stereotypically* gay. The homosexual aspects of the Tristan-Isolde relationship seem celebrated on one hand, and denied on the other. They are not really queer characters; this is just a love that bypasses physicality. Still, it can be considered progressive that, at the end, Tristan goes off with Isolde and not with Tom.

Brian Bolland's work on the series is quite good and generally clean and attractive, if not always outstanding. He does get across the dramatic intensity of the story, especially the love triangle. While his compositions are sometimes not as striking as those of other artists, he occasionally hits one out of the park: a two-page spread of the Knights about to run into battle and a full page of Arthur using his sword to cleave the wing off an enemy plane in the fourth issue; a half-page panel of the knights jumping out of their aircraft to engage in war below and crashing through a door in an enemy complex in *C3* 7, as well as the startling panel of Arthur literally cleaving an alien into two messy segments; Morgan reducing the lusty African leader to a fleshless skeleton in *C3* 10; the monstrous Mother Alien with her body full of protuberances containing offspring, and Nyveve, whose mouth is stretched to encompass her entire face as her tongue slinks outward in *C3* 11; the depiction of the hideous, blob-like creature that Tristan's former fiancée turns into in *C3* 11 and 12; Morgan transformed into a gigantic she-spider as she summons her alien allies and the sky fills with warships in the final issue. Tatiana Wood's coloring helps bring it all to life in vivid fashion. Isolde's outfits are so clownish, however, that they border on camp.

Barr doesn't completely ignore the more problematic aspects of the Camelot legend, such as the "fact" that Arthur drowned a lot of babies because he feared that his son (Modred) would pose a danger to him, or the detail that Tristan was not above committing rape. These issues are mentioned in passing but never really dealt with, although on the letters page Barr insists that such behavior, while reprehensible, doesn't completely negate the knights' more glorious aspects. Perhaps…

Star Trek

After Gold Key, DC Comics was the next company to do an authorized *Star Trek* comic beginning in 1983 after the success of the film *Star Trek II: The Wrath of Khan.* The comic series follows that movie's events. Spock at this point is considered dead, and has been replaced by science officer Savaak, who is, in a sense, also a hybrid, although in this case she is a Romulan raised on Vulcan. The other well-known officers, a little grayer at the temples, are all aboard. Mike W. Barr wrote the series, with the art handled by Tom Sutton and Ricardo Villagran. The first story arc, which lasted four issues, concerns the Klingons' use of a wormhole space station, the destruction of which leads to them declaring war on the Federation. It turns out that everyone is being manipulated by one of those ubiquitous "superior" races who want ultimate knowledge of good and evil. Although the story is nothing special, the series wisely develops its supporting cast—including a "good" Klingon named Konom and a Native American named Bearclaw—and continues some stories from issue to issue, garnering more fan devotion than the previous series. *ST* 6 has an admirable, suspenseful story in which a peace ambassador is targeted for assassination by a metamorph, the only person who knows where a dying Scotty has been secreted on the *Enterprise*.

After the release of *Star Trek III: The Search for Spock*, the series again took off after the movie ended, with Spock on board and the other officers dealing with the consequences of their actions, not to mention the death of Admiral Kirk's son David. This leads directly into a story arc in which the duplicate *Enterprise* crew from the "mirror" (parallel) dimension, first introduced on the TV series, invade "our" dimension (*ST* 9–15) for the glory of their "Empire." Kirk & Co. replace the destroyed Enterprise with the one helmed by the evil Kirk, then use a more advanced ship, the *Excelsior*, to head into the parallel dimension where they masquerade as the bad guys. Kirk meets up with the parallel dimension's David, who is working with the resistance and who joins his "father" on the *Excelsior*. A mind-meld between the two Spocks results in the "real" Spock recovering from mental injuries sustained in battle and the Mirror-Spock recognizing the error of his ways and also becoming part of the resistance. The *Excelsior* joins up with the Klingons and Romulans of the mirror-dimension to put paid to the Empire. It is very entertaining stuff, although confusing at times, what with the double characters and so many warring factions to keep straight.

The series continued on for a lengthy run of 56 issues in spite of changing the format from long story arcs to single issues (with the occasional two-parter) and replacing writer Mike Barr with a dozen or so rotating authors. DC began a second *Star Trek* series in 1989 and it lasted 80 issues.

V

A comic book based on the 1980s TV series *V* (for alien *v*isitor) appeared at the tail end of the Bronze Age. The TV show presents aliens who come to Earth for supposedly peaceful reasons and who appear to be humanoid, but are really disguised reptilian creatures who desire to conquer Earthlings for food. In Los Angeles, a neutral zone has been established for visitor and human alike. Nonetheless, members of the resistance are fired upon in a club by Visitor (or Sirian) assassins. The hit was not ordered by Diana, leader of the aliens, who is just as confused as the rebels. The explanation: A man named Nathan Bates is afraid that resistance member Ham Tyler is out to get him for collaborating with the enemy. Bates has hired a trio of visitors to kill Ham (these lizards have gotten used to the good life and know it takes cash to maintain it). The first issue is full of action, but Cary Bates' script contains so much wisecracking that it makes the comic hard to take seriously. The writing quickly improved, however, and Bates wrote all but a couple of issues. Carmine Infantino did the pencils for the series, with Tony DeZungia on inks. Tod Smith filled in for the fourth and fifth issues.

As the alien trio of hit men pursue Ham, resistance leader Julie Parrish and others discover a town of mostly older people that has made a bargain with the visitors (*V* 2–3). In exchange for their pure mineral water, which they need, the visitors have cured the inhabitants of all their ailments (including giving a farmer back the arm he lost in a tractor accident), made their crops grow, and act deceptively beneficent. Julie is appalled that the townspeople seem to care only about their own well-being and not about the resistance fighters who have died, or all the people kidnapped and stored on the visitor ship to be eventually consumed as food. But when a young boy fights back against the aliens and is killed, the townspeople recover their humanity and help the resistance fight against the Visitors and destroy the springs from which the precious water comes.

The second story arc concerns an internment camp in which the Visitors subject kidnapped people to experimentation to increase their size and nutritional value as foodstuffs. At the same time, Julie's old friend Earl Meagan, feeling his space probes may have brought the Visitors to Earth, goes to the V Mother Ship to negotiate a peace settlement. Secreted in his head is a bomb that can obliterate the entire craft and every lizard aboard. But the resistance fighters realize that the ship's destruction will lead to massive and crushing retaliation so they try to spirit him off the ship. Ironically, they are helped by two aliens who are plotting against their leader Diana (*V* 4–6).

In *V* 9–10, Julie and resistance fighter Mike Donovan travel to New York to enlist aid for their cause. They are unaware that the lady mayor has been replaced by a lizard lookalike who can turn would-be Central Park muggers into dissolving blobs with her hidden weapons. However, she is also a fifth columnist and she joins with the resistance in a plan to stop a lizard attack on the great city. Meanwhile, on the mother ship, Diana is locked in a war with a military commander named Lydia; both women are out to humiliate and destroy the other. Diana seems to have won the battle when Lydia is put to death for insubordination. *V* 11–16 adds a new character, Prince Bron, ten-year-old son of the supreme lizard ruler. Learning that the boy's father has been thinking about pulling out of Earth, Diana hopes to kill the boy, his death reigniting the conflict. Bron winds up a friendly prisoner of the resistance.

The TV series had been canceled by this time and the comic editors were on tenterhooks as to whether or not the NBC network would ask for another mini-series or special to wrap up the show and its hanging plot threads. This never materialized. About 25 years later a new *V* program lasted for two seasons on ABC.

Sales for the *V* comic were flagging. It was decided to point toward a resolution in the comic with a story in *V* 16 in which the young prince, horrified at what has been done to the Earth people, sacrifices his life in hopes of bringing peace. It turns out that Lydia is still alive; she gleefully tells Diana that the boy's death will not escalate the war as she had hoped, but just the opposite. It looks like the visitors may finally be leaving. The final two issues are a fill-in scripted by Paul Kupperberg, with art by Denys Cowan and Dick Giordano, a good story in which some people who have dropped out and just want to be left alone find out that when it comes to the visitors, no one is ever really safe.

There are some very interesting ideas in the series, such as in *V* 15, in which the aliens come up with a way of dealing with the increasing number of Sirians who are questioning the invasion of Earth and becoming sympathetic to its inhabitants. The aliens in this category are sent to a facility where they are brainwashed into believing that humans came from Earth to their home world and ravaged their planet. Abducted humans are given guns and sent into a chamber that simulates the look of the Visitors' planet, whereupon the brainwashed aliens come in and use the people as living targets. It is felt that a fully indoctrinated lizard will have no problem slaughtering the humans; anyone who fails to do so is still a sympathizer and his or her death will be no loss.

16

Gold Key; Marvel

Gold Key

Tragg and the Sky Gods

Tragg and the Sky Gods debuted in 1975. Scripted by Don Glut, the series has a compelling premise mixing alien visitors with dinosaurs and savages. The series takes place after the age of the dinosaurs and during the rise of mammals, including humans. But there are isolated areas where prehistoric monsters survive and live alongside cave people (as in countless anachronistic movies). Hailing from the world of Yargon, Niken and Vonik, golden-hued scientists with long green hair and white tunics, land on Earth in a golden globe and are worshipped as "sky gods" by the savages. These scientists fear that humankind will not advance beyond their present state unless a little tinkering is done, so they mesmerize two women, take them aboard their ship, and subject them to certain processes. After the women take mates, they give birth to a boy name Tragg and a girl named Lorn, both golden-hued. They are different from the other children, more robust and intelligent.

Niken and Vonik had intended to return to Earth in 25 years to witness the results of their experimentation, but in the interim, the people of Yargon overthrow the benevolent science-based rulers and a war-like contingent takes over. A group of very unfriendly aliens come to Earth in another globe. Just before this happens, the tribe members decide that Lorn and Tragg, now fully grown, are responsible for the gods abandoning them, and try to kill them. The pair escapes into the sea (narrowly avoiding the jaws of an Elasmosaurus) and witness the landing of the second globe. Overhearing the aliens' plans to turn the "apes" into slaves, they attack these "gods" but fail to kill them. At a later point, Tragg does manage to kill one of the aliens. He and Lorn decide to go back to their tribe and tell them the truth about their "gods."

In *Tragg* 2, Tragg and Lorn go back to their people where a man named Gorth insists they be killed. The more reasonable Korr suggests that Tragg take Gorth to where the sky gods are to convince them that his story is true. Gorth betrays Tragg, attacking him, but he continues on to the globe where he winds up getting mind-controlled. Zorek, the Yargonian party commander, is betrothed to Keera, his second-in-command, but after meeting Tragg she feels that men from Yargon, who seem too dependent on their weapons, can't compare. Tragg is captured and Keera makes a blatant play for him, which enables Tragg to escape. Following Yargonian orders, Gorth arranges for a stampede of prehistoric monsters to wipe out his tribe, but Tragg saves the day by using Keera's jet pack against the horde.

An intriguing series that never attracted a large readership: Gold Key's *Tragg and the Sky Gods*.

Keera turns the tribe against Tragg and Lorn yet again, and once more they go off on their own.

As the series proceeds, Tragg's tribe comes to realize he was telling the truth about the aliens, and Keera, who has fallen hard for Tragg, begins to doubt the rightness of their mission to enslave the Earthlings. *Tragg* 3 features an attack by a huge crocodilian creature called a Phobosuchus. (It sounds like a made-up name, but such an animal actually existed.) Zorek uses alien science to combine Gorth with a saber-tooth tiger and create a hybrid monster called Sabre-Fang, which pursues Tragg and his mate. Sabre-Fang winds up caught in a tar pit. Tragg rejects Keera once again, but she can't bring herself to kill him (3–4).

Searching for other tribes who can help them against the Sky Lords, Tragg and Lorn encounter a group of man-apes, missing link–type creatures who have no love for the "no-hairs." Then they run into another human tribe, who are quite unfriendly until Tragg saves the chief's son from a hungry dinosaur. A jealous Zorek imprisons Keera but Ferenk, a Yargonian who loves her, frees her but denounces her as a traitor for helping Tragg. Predictably, she flies to Tragg's side. Keera winds up in a duel to the death with Lorn, which the latter wins (Lorn spares Keera's life, however). Tragg convinces this new tribe, who ride on three-horned triceratops, to accompany him back to the fire mountain where some of his people have been enslaved by the aliens. With members of both tribes plus the dinosaur mounts on one side, the Yargonians and their weapons on the other, there is a furious battle. It ends when the volcano explodes after some alien equipment drops into the bubbling magma (5–7).

Keera, who has become Tragg's ally after falling out with Zorek and the others, warns him of the presence of Ostellon, a sorcerer who wants to destroy Tragg and Lorn because such opponents of the Dark Gods as Dagar and Dr. Spektor (the heroes of other Gold Key comics) might be their descendants. Ostellon can reanimate old dinosaur skeletons but next to the Sky Lords he isn't very formidable (8).

Tragg 9, the final issue, did not appear for five years, and most of it was a reprint of *Tragg* 1. The rest is a back-up in which Lorn braves great danger to get healing plants for Tragg after he is bitten by a giant venomous snake. The whole gang also appear in *Gold Key Spotlight* 9, in which Zorek tries to kill Keera and Ferenk, who have declared their love for one another, along with Tragg and Lorn. Zorek sets up a new base with his troops and waits for reinforcements from Yargon. The highlight of the issue is a battle with a huge "Devil Shark" that goes after Tragg and the two women.

Jesse Santos did the inside art for the first two issues, as well as the painted covers for *every* issue. His illustrations are interesting, but although he inked over his own pencils, his drawings still seem unfinished. Dan Spiegle took over the inside art beginning with *Tragg* 3, and again the art looks unfinished. Spiegle drew in the style of Santos for consistency, because he was capable of much better work. Don Glut did all of the scripts. With all of its dinosaur action, *Tragg* is certainly fun and has an interesting premise—although it sort of locked itself into a corner. If only the art had been stronger.

Marvel

Killraven *and* The War of the Worlds

Conceived by Roy Thomas and inspired by H.G. Wells' famous science fiction novel, the series *The War of the Worlds* featured the heroic Killraven. It first appeared in *Amazing Adventures* 18 in 1973.

As in Wells' story, the Martians had been destroyed by germs against which they had no immunity. But back on Mars, the remaining aliens plan and plot and return exactly 100 years later, and this time are much more successful. Killraven was just a child named Jonathan at the time, and with the help of a black doctor named Ann Carver he and his mother Maureen Raven hid from the Martians. Unfortunately, the two women are killed by human collaborators and Jonathan—rechristened Killraven and sporting long red hair—is taught to be a warrior. He uses his skills to escape and join a colony of Freemen who secretly fight against the Martians and their human allies from a headquarters on the "island of Staten." (In the meantime, the Martians have taken over the White House and virtually all of Washington, D.C.) This was all told in the first story by writer Gerry Conway at an exciting and breathless pace, with very adept artwork by Neal Adams, Howard Chaykin and Frank Chiaramonte.

The Killraven series borrows some concepts from Gold Key's *Mighty Samson* (which in turn borrowed from other fictional sources): The post-apocalyptic world is full of slavering mutants and monsters, including a giant crab with a human head that exudes a corrosive acid; a huge parrot-octopus-plant creature; a combination of serpent and stallion. A new wrinkle is sexy female sirens who call men to their doom (Killraven is able to resist). Killraven's second-in-command is M'Shulla, a black man with whom Killraven has a friendly rivalry.

In *AA* 19, we get to see one of the Martians up close: sort of a slimy, man-sized brown potato with big, black, dull eyes, a large beak-like mouth, and many quivering tentacles. *AA* 20 introduces the Warlord, a costumed creep with super-strong prosthetics who hates Killraven for the injuries he sustained when the latter escaped from captivity when he was the Warlord's pupil in warfare. Carmilla Frost, a molecular biologist who worked with the Warlord but crosses over to Killraven's side and has a mutant pet named Grok, first appears in *AA* 21. (There is some suspense over the true identity of Grok before his transformation. He turns out to be a corrupted clone of Carmilla's scientist father.) The cast is further enlarged in *AA* 22 with the nasty giant slave trader Abraxis who has tentacles instead of arms, the suave mercenary Sabre and a green-skinned woman with the unfortunate name Mint Julep. (There was worse to come, such as Volcana Ash.)

Don McGregor took over as writer with *AA* 21, with Herb Trimpe and Frank Giacoia assuming the art chores. Other artists included Rich Buckler, Gene Colan,

Sonny Trinidad and Craig Russell, who lasted longer than the others and gave the strip a distinctive look. The series generally seemed more of a cheesy horror title than science fiction: For instance, *AA* 23 introduces the man-rat Rattack, who leads an army of ravenous rodents (reminding one of the classic rat army stories in the Golden Age *Airboy* comic). "Bigger than Ben, wilder than Willard—and they're out for blood!" shouts the cover blurb. McGregor's prose is thick with ironic captions, such as in *AA* 26 when he makes continual references to Madison Avenue in a story set in Battle Creek where a cult is guarding its treasures: old cereal boxes and the toys that came inside them. (The golden arches of McDonald's figure in another story.) McGregor was the writer for the remainder of the series' run, adding some poetical touches but failing to make the main character much more than a generic hero type. Killraven develops the ability to enter the minds of Martians, giving him more of an understanding of the asexual creatures.

Bill Mantlo wrote an especially unfortunate fill-in story for *AA* 33. Killraven comes across a group of black people who fled the cities during the invasion because they weren't interested in becoming slaves to the Martians like they were to the whites. But their idea of freedom is to sacrifice some of their number to a Martian who lives in a lake. In the space of a few pages, Killraven teaches them the error of their ways and leaves a man named Chandra in charge, even though Chandra had brutally murdered an older man who was the leader of the group. It was a very self-conscious "black rights" story that was, oddly, borderline racist.

The title of the series had been changed from *The War of the Worlds* to *Killraven*, then back to *War of the Worlds* for the thirty-sixth issue. Another terrible fill-in issue by Bill Mantlo clumsily inserts superheroes such as Iron Man, Dr. Strange and Man-Thing into the action in the form of dreams projected by an astronaut. Killraven was gone after the thirty-eighth issue. It was a good idea undone by pretentious verbiage and uneven artwork.

Marvel's Star Trek

In 1980 came the first big-screen adaptation of the '60s *Star Trek* TV show; Marvel, by then the dominant comic company, was quick to acquire rights to publish a new comic book. The first three issues are an adaptation of *Star Trek—The Motion Picture*, reprinted from a magazine "super-special." Many noted that the adaptation, with a very good script by Marv Wolfman and excellent art by Dave Cockrum and Klaus Janson, is actually an improvement over the somewhat stupid movie. Sales were good enough to continue the series, initially with the same creative team. The first *new* story (*ST* 4–5) is an entertaining if credulity-stretching two-parter in which the Klingons use new technology—and the mind of a convenient horror film archivist from Earth—to unleash materializations of monsters (everything from big bugs to Dracula) on the *Enterprise*.

Star Trek 6 has an excellent Mike W. Barr script in which an ambassador, beamed up alive from his home planet, arrives on the *Enterprise* dead. Apparently he was stabbed in the back during transport, which is impossible since at the time of his death both he and the knife that killed him would have been disembodied

The *Killraven/War of the Worlds* series in Marvel's *Amazing Adventures* never realized its full potential. (The title for the strip changed from *War of the Worlds* to *Killraven* and back again. Despite what the cover says, it was never really called *Warrior of the Worlds*.)

atoms! Spock manages to unravel the truth behind the murder, which is as clever as an Agatha Christie—or Sherlock Holmes—mystery. *ST* 12 features an exhilarating tale by Alan Brennert and Martin Pasko in which the alien crew—beings composed of energy—of a ship embarking on a centuries-long exploration of unknown space is driven mad and pose a danger to themselves, the *Enterprise* crew and the one human aboard their ship. The effective art is by Luke McDonnell and Tom Palmer. Barr and artists Ed Hannigan and Palmer are the creative team for *ST* 17's tale of a medieval planet endangered by radiation; its inhabitants make it difficult for Kirk and crew to administer an antidote. *ST* 18, the final issue, features an intriguing puzzler by J.M. DeMatteis (with art by Brozowski and Trapani) in which the friendship of Spock and Kirk teaches the concept of selflessness to an alien race inside a gigantic geometric spaceship 20 times the size of Earth.

Despite some memorable stories, Marvel's *Star Trek* did not even last 20 issues. Undoubtedly the frequent changes in writer and artist didn't help, nor did the lack of continued stories, interesting supporting characters, or subplots that could continue from issue to issue.

Adventures on the Planet of the Apes

Adventures on the Planet of the Apes, which debuted in 1975, was a comic book that reprinted black and white stories from Marvel's *Planet of the Apes* magazine in color. The stories are all written by Doug Moench and penciled by George Tuska. In the comic book, the face of Taylor is redrawn by John Romita so as not to resemble Charlton Heston, who played the character in the film version. The first six issues retell the story of the film, while the final five are based on the cinematic sequel *Beneath the Planet of the Apes*. Moench also wrote these issues, which were drawn by Alfredo Alcala.

Based on a 1963 novel by Pierre Boulle, *Planet of the Apes* begins with an Earth spaceship with four passengers crash-landing on an unknown planet. The lone female has died in transit, and Taylor, a rather obnoxious character, tells the others that they are thousands of years in the future and everyone they know is dead. They discover a race of mute, primitive humans who are lorded over by an intelligent race of apes: gorilla warriors, chimpanzee scientists and so on. Due to a throat injury, Taylor is unable to speak when he is captured, although eventually he shows Zira and Cornelius, chimps, that he is capable of both speech and thought. Chief scientist Dr. Zaius sees Taylor as a threat to ape civilization because he (Zaius) knows, as Taylor knows, that man descended from apes and not the other way around. In the Forbidden Zone they find evidence of the ancient human society that once ruled the planet. Venturing deeper into the Zone with a human female companion, Taylor discovers the ruins of the Statue of Liberty. He is horrified to realize that he has been on Earth all along. (In the original novel, he was actually on an entirely different planet, although when he returns to Earth he discovers that apes have also taken over there.) The comic is very faithful to the film with only minor changes. For instance, in the movie, Hodge is stuffed, but in the comic his head is affixed to the wall like a hunter's trophy.

In *Beneath the Planet of the Apes,* astronaut Brent winds up in the same time and place as Taylor, and manages to hook up with Zira, Cornelius and Taylor. They encounter intelligent humans whose faces have been hideously disfigured by radiation and who have telepathic powers. While *Planet of the Apes* was generally reasonable, the sequel descends into real comic book territory, using well-trod concepts such as mutant human beings living in the ruins of Manhattan and worshipping a nuclear bomb. Perhaps that's why the comic is more successful than the motion picture, because it's the kind of material that is perfect for comics. As in the movie, one of the best scenes has Brent's colleague agonizing over the fact that everyone he once knew is long dead. The comic, like the movie, ends with the aforementioned bomb going off and destroying the Earth. This didn't prevent numerous sequels to, and remakes of, the original *Planet of the Apes.*

Worlds Unknown

Worlds Unknown debuted in 1973. The cover tale, "The Day After the Day the Martians Came," was based on a story by Frederik Pohl. This bit of social satire focuses on a Florida hotel where newspapermen congregate due to the emergence of a rather hideous red Martian from a space capsule. While some watch the news stories and hear theories about the Martians, most simply make jokes—lots of jokes, substituting Martians for the usual targets, such as "Polacks." The hotel owner doesn't think the Martians' arrival will make much difference, but his black employee Ernest feels differently. "Going to make a *real* big difference to *me*," he says. This was scripted by Gerry Conway and drawn by Ralph Reese.

An adaptation of Edmond Hamilton's 1938 *Weird Tales* story "He That Hath Wings" also appears in this issue, scripted by Gil Kane and drawn by Kane and Mike Esposito. David's mother dies in childbirth and his father is already dead. Dr. Harriman thinks the baby will be a hunchback but then realizes the child is developing wings. He decides to take David with him to a private island to protect him from those who would see him as a freak, and to help him adjust to his unique physical structure. David learns how to fly, but is careful not to go too far from home. When the doctor dies, David is free to take off to see the rest of the world, and eventually falls in love with a beautiful female. She can't quite deal with his wings, so David has them surgically removed. He tries to live an earthbound life with his wife and their child, working in an office, but he constantly dreams of the skies. Eventually his wings grow back and he takes flight, flying higher and higher, flying as he was born to do, until exhausted, like Icarus, he falls dead into the sea.

Worlds Unknown 2 features adaptations of L. Sprague de Camp's "A Gun for Dinosaur" and Keith Laumer's "Doorstep." The first, scripted by Roy Thomas and drawn by Val Mayerik and Ernie Chan, deals with expeditions via time machine to bag dinosaurs in the distant past and a deadly falling-out amongst the hunters. This is a colorful and exciting story with effective artwork. "Doorstep," in which the military confront a capsule from space and argue about how to deal with whatever is inside, turns into a one-joke idea that is rather illogical. This is scripted by Gerry Conway and drawn by Gil Kane and Tom Sutton. Sutton's inks are a good fit with Kane's excellent pencils.

Worlds Unknown 3 features an adaptation of Harry Bates' "Farewell to the Master," the basis for the film *The Day the Earth Stood Still*. Scripted by Roy Thomas and drawn by Ross Andru and Wayne Howard, it is much more faithful to the short story, which suffered a great many changes in the cinematic version. For one thing, the "master" is not the man Klaatu, but the robot Gnut (Gort in the film). The whole business with Klaatu bringing a threatening warning to Earth as regards to nuclear power was invented by Hollywood. Frankly, neither the story nor the film adaptation are that memorable, and that's true of the comics version as well.

Worlds Unknown 4 presents Gerry Conway's excellent adaptation of Fredric Brown's classic story "Arena," drawn by John Buscema and Dick Giordano. In the future, space pilot Carson is sent out against an alien enemy that has attacked the Earth. Carson thinks that he and his ship have been destroyed by an enemy blast, but he wakes up in a strange world and is told by an unknown cosmic entity that the war between Earthlings and alien will be decided by combat between Carson and an alien representative. The alien is a formidable, tentacled, lizard-like horror with mottled red skin and a bad attitude, who telepathically screams out his hatred and sadistically picks the legs off a small harmless creature. Carson tries to reason with the alien, but all his opponent wants is Carson's death. A force field prevents the two combatants from approaching each other, although they *can* fling rocks at one another. As the alien creates a catapult, Carson tries a desperate (some might say foolhardy) gamble: Deducing that an unconscious person could get through the invisible barrier, he uses a rock to knock himself out, figuring he will fall *past* the barrier—and then hoping that he will regain consciousness before his adversary can pounce and kill him. This he does and, using his knife, he wins in the life-or-death battle. The adaptation is faithful to the original story, although Brown's alien is even less "humanoid" than in the comic. The attractive artwork makes the most of the exciting tale.

A E. van Vogt's "Black Destroyer" was adapted for *Worlds Unknown* 5, scripted by Roy Thomas with art by Dan Adkins and Jim Mooney. An Earth spaceship lands on a distant planet and discovers a world in ruins. Sneaking through the ruins is a coeurl: a large black panther-like animal with tentacles. This creature makes some members of the expedition nervous, while others want to study it and hope to bring it back to Earth as a specimen. It develops that this animal subsists on phosphorus and is able to somehow absorb it, mostly from people's bones, killing them. It enters the ship and is able to activate its engines; it hopes to reach Earth where it will find plenty of sustenance. Behind a closed door, the coeurl operates the ship's controls; when the crew fires at the door, the coeurl panics. It builds a small ship in which to fly back to its planet. But despite a rudimentary intelligence and deductive abilities, the alien has no real knowledge of the physical laws of space travel and overshoots its own world, and then commits suicide. The story is one of several influences on the motion pictures *It! The Terror from Beyond Space* and *Alien*.

Worlds Unknown 6 presents an effective adaptation of Theodore Sturgeon's tale "Killdozer," scripted by Gerry Conway and drawn by Dick Ayers, John Romita and Ernie Chan. On an island, a team of men have been hired to put in an air strip. When a bulldozer known as a D7 enters some ruins, all Hell breaks loose. An alien energy being that landed on Earth eons ago escapes and enters the machine, then proceeds to obliterate everyone on the island. At first the crew members believe the foreman is responsible for the deaths, but when they see the machine running amok without an operator, they realize they're up against the Unknown. As the "killdozer" tries to smash the others, the foreman comes up with a solution: electrocuting the machine, which works just in time.

An adaptation of John Wyndham's *The Day of the Triffids* was supposed to appear in *Worlds Unknown* 6, but "Killdozer" was ready earlier and was printed in that issue instead. It was then decided to present *Triffids* in two parts in the first and second issue of Marvel's new black and white magazine *Unknown Worlds of Science Fiction*. *Triffids* was adapted by Gerry Conway and drawn by Ross Andru, Ernie Chua (part one) and Rico Rival (part two).

Triffids is a fascinating and chilling tale of apocalyptic horror in the *War of the Worlds* tradition—if not quite on that level. When most of the people in the world go blind from watching a meteor shower, society falls apart. An added complication: plants called Triffids, that had appeared some time before. Triffids, which are as tall as trees, can walk, lash out with their deadly stingers, and seem determined to eradicate humankind. Now that most humans are blind, they are easy pickings for the Triffids. Hero Bill Masen and a woman named Josella—both sighted—try to survive during various misadventures. Another character is a heartless colonel who threatens to fire on a mob of blind people when they come asking for help and shelter. This very effective adaptation gets into the guts of the story and never lets go.

The last two issues of *Worlds Unknown* are devoted to an adaptation of the feature film *The Golden Voyage of Sinbad*, scripted by Len Wein and penciled by George Tuska, with Vince Colletta on inks. This is not nearly as much fun—nor does it look as good—as the film itself. Around the same time, *Marvel Spotlight* 25 presented an adaptation of the 1957 classic *The 7th Voyage of Sinbad*, scripted by John Warner and drawn by Sonny Trinidad. It is a pale imitation of a very colorful motion picture.

Bibliography

Books

Barr, Mike W. *Silver Age Sci-Fi Companion*. Raleigh: TwoMorrows, 2007.
Benton, Mike. *Science Fiction Comics*. Dallas: Taylor Publishing, 1992.
Feldstein, Al. *Incredible Science Fiction*. Milwaukie, OR: Dark Horse, 2022.
Kripal, Jeffrey J. *Mutants and Mystics: Science Fiction, Super-Hero Comics, and the Paranormal*. Chicago: University of Chicago Press, 2015.
Ro, Ronin. *Tales to Astonish: Jack Kirby, Stan Lee, and the American Comic Book Revolution*. New York: Bloomsbury, 2004.
Schelly, Bill. *Otto Binder: The Life and Work of a Comic Book and Science Fiction Visionary*. Berkeley: North Atlantic Books, 2016.
Schoell, William. *Comic Book Heroes of the Screen*. New York: Carol, 1990.
_____. *The Horror Comics: Fiends, Freaks and Fantastic Creatures*. Jefferson: McFarland, 2014.
_____. *The Silver Age of Comics*. Duncan: BearManor, 2011.
Trombetta, Jim. *The Horror! The Horror! Comic Books the Government Didn't Want You to Read*. New York: Abrams, 2010.

Websites

Atlas Tales. www.atlastales.com.
Comic Book +. www.comicbookplus.com.
The Digital Comic Museum. www.digitalcomicmuseum.com.
Grand Comics Database. www.comics.org.

Index

Numbers in ***bold italics*** indicate pages with illustrations.

Ace Publishers 7–10
Adam and Eve (trope) 49, 139, 212
Adams, Neal 248
Adkins, Dan 202, 206
Adventures into the Unknown 12–13, 109–114
Adventures on the Planet of the Apes 251–252
Ajax-Farrell 14
Alarming Tales 209–211
Alascia, Vince 145
"The Alien Brat from Planet Byna" 174
alien invasion 13, 25, 44, 60, 93, 116, 126, 219, 248–249
Allen, Irwin 197
Amazing Adult Fantasy see *Amazing Adventures* (Marvel)
Amazing Adventures (Marvel) 223–224, 248–249, ***250***
Amazing Adventures (Ziff-Davis) 96, ***97***, 98, ***99***, 100–101
Amazing Stories 1
American Comics Group (ACG) 10–13, 109–126
Anderson, Murphy 96, 155
Andru, Ross 179
Aparo, Jim 134
Around the World Under the Sea 193
Astarita, Rafael 33, 75
Astonishing 15–18
Atlantis 18, 32, 155–156, 185, 198, 211–212
Atlantis, the Lost Continent 192
Atlas Publishers 14–28
Atom Age Combat 194
Atomic Attack 95–96
Atomic Knights 155–156
Atomic War! 9–10
Attack on Planet Mars 34–35
Automan 175
Avon 29–37

Avon Fantasy 36
Ayers, Dick 195

Baker, Matt 130, 138, 139
Barr, Mike W. 237, 239, 242, 250
Bates, Cary 232, 243
Bates, Harry 253
The Beast from 20,000 Fathoms 19
Beck, Dick 112–113
Beneath the Planet of the Apes (film and comic adaptation) 207, 252
Benét, Stephen Vincent 201
Benulis, Bill 77
Binder, Otto 52, 55, 71, 72, 88, 91, 163–164, 201
Blue Bolt ***90***, 91
Bolland, Brian 239, 241
Boltinoff, Murray 161
Boyette, Pat 147
Bradbury, Ray 63–64
Brant Craig, Interplanetary Detective 94–95
Brennert, Alan 251
Broome, John 155, 156
Brown, Fredric 253
Buck Rogers 1
Buckler, Rich 233
Buscema, John 189, 253
Byrne, John 229, 230

Camelot 53, 239–242
Camelot 3000 239–242
Cameron, Lou 7, 149–150
Campbell, Stan 45
Captain Comet 48
Captain Hawkins 98, 100
Captain Science 92–95
Captain Sindbad 205–206
Captain Venture 196–197
Carrillo, Fred 236, 239
Cave Carson 176–178
Charlton 38–45, 127–148, 227–231

Charlton Premiere 147
Chris KL99 46
Clarke, Arthur C. 118
Classics Illustrated 149–150, ***151***, 152
Clipper of the Clouds (*Robur the Conqueror*) 152
Cockrum, Dave 249
Colan, Gene 131, 161
Commander Battle and the Atomic Sub 10, ***11***, 12
Conway, Gerry 232, 248, 253
Cooke, Tom 188
Crandall, Reed 190
Crom the Barbarian 30–31
Crusader from Mars 103–105
Cuti, Nicola 230
cyclopes 21, 181

Darwin Jones 48
Dave Kenton of the Star Patrol 31–32
Davis, Jack 21
The Day of the Triffids (comic adaptation) 254
The Day of the Triffids (novel) 156
DC Comics 46–56, 152–182, 231–244
de Camp, L. Sprague 253
Dell Comics 56–57, 183–193
Dell Movie Comics 189–193
Destination Moon (comic adaptation) 71
Destination Moon (film) 48, 62, 71
Die, Monster, Die! 193
dinosaurs 19, 32, 41, 44, 95, 143, 144, 174, 179, 180–181, 182, 189, 190, 191, 192, 193, 223, 229, 245–247, 253
Dinosaurus! 190–191
Ditko, Steve 128, 131, 132, 134–135, 138, 140, 148, 224
Doolan, Joe 76
Doomsday + 1 227, ***228***, 229

257

Index

Dorfman, Leo 202
Drake, Arnold 174, 204, 237
Drift Marlo 187–188
Du Bois, Gaylord 196, 198

EC Comics 2, 58–71
Eisner, Will 73
Elias, Lee 76, 177
end of the world 50, 147, 155, 201, 227, 231
Esposito, Mike 179
Evans, George 76
Everett, Bill 216

Fago Publications 194–195
Famous Funnies 1
Fantastic 95
Fantastic Voyage 206
Fantastic Worlds 87–88
Fawcett Movie Comic 72
Fawcett Publishers 71–72
Feldstein, Al 58, 71
Fiction House 1, 74–79
Finger, Bill 55
First Men in the Moon (comic adaptation) 206
The First Men in the Moon (novel) 150
Flash Gordon 1
Flint Baker 73–77
flying saucers 60, 70, 72, 121, 160, 212
Flying Saucers (Avon) 37
The Food of the Gods 152, 176
Forbidden Worlds 114, **115**, 116–119, **120**, 121
Forte, John 120
Fox, Gardner 30, 48, 164
Fox Publishers 79–80
From the Earth to the Moon 149

Gaines, Bill 58
Galaxy Knights 53
García-López, José L. 233
Gasp 126
Gernsback, Hugo 1
G.I. Robot (*Star Spangled War Stories*) 181–182, 238–239
giants 22, 23, 25, 28, 31, 49, 60–61, 128, 134, 136, 139, 140, 143, 145, 152, 159, 164, 167–168, 169, 171, 176, 197, 203, 223, 230, 232
Gibson, Walter 37
gigantism *see* giants
Gill, Joe 41, 130, 134–135, 140, 193, 229
Gill, Tom 191
Giolitti, Alberto 204, 207
Giordano, Dick 138, 236, 253
Glanzman, Sam 192
Glut, Don 245, 247
Gold Key Comics 196–207, 245–247

Gold Key Movie Comics 205–207
Green Glob 175

Hamilton, Edmond 2, 48, 54, 252
Haney, Bob 177, 178, 236
Harryhausen, Ray 192, 193
Hart, Ernie 136
Harvey Comics 207–211
Heck, Don 223
Hector Servadac (Off on a Comet) 150–152
Heinlein, Robert A. 23, 71
Herbie Popnecker 116, 124
Hercules 189
Hercules Unbound 231–233
Hercules Unchained 189–190
Herron, Ed 176
Hitler, Adolf 23, 44, 78, 113, 122
Hopper, Fran 76
House of Mystery 165–169
House of Secrets 170–172
Hughes, Richard 112–113, 115, 124, 125, 168

"I, Robot" (Otto Binder) 52, 70
"I Was Half-Man/Half-Machine" 174–175
immortality 16, 19, 54
Infantino, Carmine 51, 157, 243
Ingels, Graham 76
Interplanetary Insurance Incorporated (I. I. I.) 55
The Invaders (comic adaptation) 205
The Invisible Man 152

Janson, Klaus 249
Jason and the Argonauts 192–193
Jet Powers 83–86
Jorgensen, Christine 40
Journey into Mystery 14–15
Journey into Unknown Worlds 20–24
Journey to the Center of the Earth (comic) 190
A Journey to the Center of the Earth (novel) 150
Justice League of America 55

Kane, Gil 158, 190, 252, 253
Kanigher, Robert 53, 179, 182, 239
Kashdan, George 204
Key–Stanley Morse (Publishers) 81–83
Kida, Fred 139
Killraven 248–249
King Kong 206–207
Kirby, Jack 166, 208, 209, 212
Knights of the Round Table *see* Camelot

Kubert, Joe 30, 167, 177, 182
Kupperberg, Paul 244
Kurtzman, Harvey 58
Kurwenal, the talking dog 130

The Land Unknown 189
Lars of Mars 101, **102**
Laumer, Keith 253
Lee, Stan 212, 224
Leguizamon, Enio 146
Lieber, Larry 212
Lost in Space (TV show) 197
The Lost World 190
Lost Worlds 88–91
Lovecraft, H.P. 110, 193

Magazine Enterprises 83–86
Major Inapak 86
male-female relationships 27, 53, 61–63, 68–69, 87, 101, 105, 115–116, 119, 129, 144–145, 155, 156, 187
The Man from Planet X (comic adaptation) 72
The Man from Planet X (film) 72
Man O' Mars 78
"The Man Who Killed a World" 100
Manning, Russ 205
Mantlo, Bill 249
Mark Merlin 170
M.A.R.S. Patrol Total War 201–202
Marvel Comics 212–224, 248–254
Marvel Tales 19–20
Master of the World (comic adaptation) 192
Master of the World (novel) 152
Mastroserio, Rocco 132
Masulli, Pat 139
Matheson, Richard 167
Mayerik, Val 253
McCann, Gerard 152
McDonnell, Luke 251
McGregor, Don 248–249
McWilliams, Al 204
Memling, Carl 40–41
Men into Space 183
Meskin, Mort 166, 171, 177
Michelinie, David 233
microscopic worlds 33–34, 40, 46, 52, 58, 60, 64, 76, 77, 88, 129, 157, 159, 176, 195, 211–212, 223–224
Midnight Mystery 125
Mighty Samson 198, 199, **200**, 201, 248
miniaturization 51, 54, 56, 58, 70, 76, 83, 88, 98, 128, 134, 138, 139, 147, 158, 162, 164, 165, 167, 170, 179, 195, 198, 204, 211
Molno, Bill 7

"Monkey-Rocket to Mars" 55
Mooney, Jim 173
Morini, Phil 101
Mortellaro, Tony 82
Motion Picture Comics 71
mutants 34, 60, 67–68, 69–70, 109–110, 139, 147, 175, 224, 232
My Greatest Adventure 160–163
Mysteries of Unexplored Worlds 134, **135**, 136, **137**, 138
The Mysterious Island 191
Mystery in Space 17, 53, 163–165, 237–238

Napoli, Vince 95
Newman, Paul S. 189, 190, 191, 193, 206
Nicholas, Charles 140, 145
Nodel, Norman 150

Oleck, Jack 70, 138
O'Neil, Denny 134, 146, 147, 235
Orlando, Joe 70
Out of This World 29–30
Out of This World (Charlton) 138–139
Outer Limits (comic adaptation) 188
Outer Limits (TV show) 118, 188
Outer Space 139–141

Palais, Rudy 76
Palmer, Tom 251
parallel worlds 15
Pasko, Martin 251
"Pen Pal" 236
Planet 1, **2**, 73, **74**, 75–78
Planet of the Apes (film) 251–252
Planet of the Apes (novel) 118
Pohl, Frederik 252
Poole, Gary 206
Premiani, Bruno 176
Prize Publishers 86–87
Purcell, Howard 161

Race for the Moon 207–209
racism 69, 104
Renee, Lily 76
Robotmen of the Lost Planet 35
robots 35–36, 41, 50, 51–52, 67, 69, 70, 87, 90–91, 98, 103, 114, 119, 127, 131–132, 139, 140, 143, 146, 169, 174, 175, 176, 188, 204, 212, 222, 227, 230, 232, 237–238
Rocket Kelly 79–80
Rocket to the Moon 37
Rocketman 14
Rocky Jones, Space Ranger 41–42

"Run, Martian, Run" 87–88
Russell, Craig 249
Ryder, Robert 189

Santos, Jesse 247
Schaffenberger, Kurt 72
Schiff, Jack 157
Schoenherr, John 187
Schroeder, Ernie 210
Schwartz, Julius 157
Sekowsky, Mike 25–26, 191, 203
The 7th Voyage of Sinbad 189
sexuality 62, 69, 98, 116
The Shrinking Man (novel) 167
Siegel, Jerry 96, 98, 175
Simonson, Walt 233
The Six Million Dollar Man (comic adaptation) 230–231
Skeates, Steve 147, 148
"So Long, Fellas" 126
Space Ace 84, **85**
Space Action 7, **8**, **9**
Space Adventures (1952) 38
Space Adventures (1958) 145–147
Space Busters 105
Space Detective 29
Space Family Robinson 196–198
Space Man (Dell) 185, **186**, 187
Space Museum 156–157
Space: 1999 (comic adaptation) 229–230
Space Patrol 105–106
Space Ranger 173
Space Rangers (*Planet*) 76
Space Rangers (*Space Adventures*) 38
"Space Report" 38–39
Space Squadron 27–28
Space War 141, **142**, 143–145
Space Western 42, **43**
Space Worlds 28
Spacehawk 91
"Spaceman" 140–141
Spaceman (Atlas) 24–26
Sparling, Jack 193, 201
Spiegle, Dan 192, 196, 198, 205, 247
Stallman, Manny 21
Standard Comics 87–91
Star Publications 91
Star Hawkins 154–155, 158
Star Hunters 233–234
Star Trek (DC) 242–243
Star Trek (Gold Key series) 203–205
Star Trek (Marvel) 249–251
Staton, Joe 230
"Stay Away from Me—You Might Die!" 162
Strange Adventures 46, **47**, 48–53, 152–160

Strange Suspense Stories 131, 132, **133**
Strange Tales **218**, 219–220
Strange Tales of the Unusual 216–218
Strange Worlds (Avon) 31, 32, **33**, 34–36
Strange Worlds (Marvel) 212–214
Sturgeon, Theodore 40, 60, 98, 254
sub-atomic worlds *see* microscopic worlds
Suicide Squad (*The Brave and the Bold*) 178, 179, **180**, 181
Super-powers 17, 34, 138, 147, 154, 168, 174, 224
Sutton, Tom 253
The Sword and the Dragon 191

Tales of Suspense 221–222
Tales of the Unexpected 172–176
Tales to Astonish 220–221
"Taps for a Trumpeteer" 117
"Target Planet Dead Ahead–Open Fire!" 117–118
telekinesis 131
telepathy 24, 36, 66, 138, 147, 157, 198
teleportation 17, 36, 147, 164, 221, 223
Tense Suspense **194**, 195
Thomas, Roy 248
The 3 Worlds of Gulliver 191
Ticci, Giovanni 207
The Time Machine (comic adaptation) 191
The Time Machine (novel) 150
time travel 13, 16, 32, 38, 66, 69, 70, 84, 88, 93–94, 103, 123, 124, 126, 134, 139, 144, 146, 148, 159, 160, 197, 209, 213–214, 215, 216, 230–231, 235, 253
Time Warp 234, 237
Tom Corbett, Space Cadet (Dell) 56–57
Tom Corbett, Space Cadet (Prize) 86–87
Total War see M.A.R.S. Patrol Total War
Toth, Alex 89, 189
Tragg and the Sky Gods 245, **246**
"Transformation" 39–40
transsexualism 39–40, 64
Trapani, Sal 204
Trimpe, Herb 191
Trombetta, Jim 7
TruVision 10
Tuska, George 26, 27
20,000 Leagues Under the Sea (comic adaptation) 189

Index

20,000 Leagues Under the Sea (novel) 149
The Twilight Zone (TV show) 131

UFO Flying Saucers 202
UFOs *see* flying saucers
Unknown World (film) 114
Unknown Worlds 121, **122**, 123–125
Unknown Worlds of Science Fiction 254
Unusual Tales 127–131

V (comic adaptation) 243–244
Valley of Gwangi 193
van Vogt, A.E. 253–254
Verne, Jules 1, 149–152
Vic Torry 72
Voyage to the Bottom of the Sea (Dell) 192
Voyage to the Bottom of the Sea (Gold Key comic adaptation) 202–203
Voyage to the Deep 183, **184**, 185

The War of the Worlds (comic adaptation) 248
The War of the Worlds (novel) 149–150
Weird Adventures 101, 103
Weird Fantasy 64, **65**, 66
Weird Science 58, **59**, 60–64
Weird Tales of the Future 81
Weird Thrillers 103
Weird War Tales 238
Wellman, Manly Wade 49, 54
Wells, H.G. 149–152
Wessler, Carl 18
When Worlds Collide (comic adaptation) 71–72
When Worlds Collide (film) 71–72
When Worlds Collide (novel) 50–51
Whitney, Ogden 116
Wildey, Doug 210
Williamson, Al 18, 86
Wilson, George 150, 201, 202, 203, 207
Wolfman, Marv 249
Wolverton, Basil 21, 82, 83, 91
Wood, Dick 203
Wood, Wally 29, 36, 67, 202, 233
World of Fantasy 214–216
World War III 10
Worlds Unknown 252–254

Youthful Publishers 92–96

Ziff-Davis Publishing 96

www.ingramcontent.com/pod-product-compliance
Lightning Source LLC
Chambersburg PA
CBHW060338010526
44117CB00017B/2876